Americans 55 & Older

A CHANGING MARKET

Americans 55 & Older

A CHANGING MARKET

2nd edition

edited by Sharon Yntema

New Strategist Publications, Inc.

Ithaca, New York

New Strategist Publications, Inc.
P.O. Box 242, Ithaca, New York 14851
607/273-0913
www.newstrategist.com

ISBN 1-885070-23-3

Printed in the United States of America

Table of Contents

Chapter 4. Income

Chapter 5. Labor Force

Chapter 6. Living Arrangements

Chapter 7. Population

Chapter 8. Spending

Chapter 9. Wealth

Tables

Chapter 1. Attitudes & Behavior

Chapter 2. Education

Chapter 3. Health

Chapter 4. Income

Chapter 5. Labor Force

Chapter 6. Living Arrangements

Chapter 7. Population

Chapter 8. Spending

Chapter 9. Wealth

Illustrations

Chapter 7. Population

Chapter 8. Spending

Chapter 9. Wealth

Introduction

A revolution is in the making. The 55-or-older population is in the process of being transformed—radically—by the aging of the baby-boom generation. No segment of the population will change as much as older Americans during the next two decades. For many businesses, the older market offers great opportunities for growth and profit. For others—the ones not paying attention—the market poses a threat to their bottom line. Those who are unprepared for the new older market are destined to be trampled by the ones who have positioned themselves to serve increasingly powerful older consumers.

Unfortunately, many businesses aren't listening to the drumbeat of revolution. They are too busy chasing young adults under the mistaken impression that the young are their best customers. But those who examine this second edition of

Population aged 55 and older

(percent of people aged 55 or older in the population, 1920 to 2020)

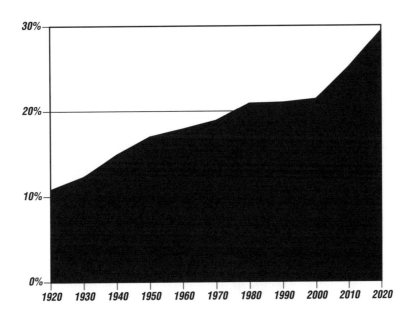

Americans 55 & Older: A Changing Market may discover, to their surprise, that older Americans are their best customers after all.

This year, there are 58 million people aged 55 or older. By 2005, the number will have expanded to 66 million as the enormous baby-boom generation (born between 1946 and 1964) enters the age group. Even more important, older consumers are a growing share of the population. Today, a record 21 percent of Americans are aged 55 or older. Records are made to be broken: during the next two decades, the proportion will soar to 29 percent.

Not only are their numbers growing, but the characteristics of older Americans are changing. The educational level of people aged 55 or older, which has been rising steadily for decades, will surge. A larger share of older men and women will work. The affluent among them will expand by the millions. Already, older Americans are the biggest consumers of many products and services. As the sophistication of the older population grows with the aging of boomers, Americans aged 55 or older will become the prime market for many businesses.

Perhaps the biggest story told by *Americans 55 & Older: A Changing Market* is that the stereotypes of aging—poverty, ill health, and an unwillingness to do or spend—must be put to rest. Older Americans are busy, healthy, and happy. A small minority are poor or sick. We no longer need to wring our hands about the aged, because most of the aged are doing quite well.

Whether businesses pay attention to older Americans or not, invariably they will find consumers aged 55 or older making up a larger share of their customers in the years ahead. Those who understand the changing wants and needs of older consumers will prosper. Those who ignore older consumers turn their backs on opportunity.

How to Use This Book

Americans 55 & Older: A Changing Market is designed for easy use. It is divided into nine chapters, organized alphabetically: Attitudes and Behavior, Education, Health, Income, Labor Force, Living Arrangements, Population, Spending, and Wealth.

Most of the tables in the book are based on data collected by the federal government, in particular the Bureau of the Census, the Bureau of Labor Statistics, the National Center for Education Statistics, and the National Center for Health Statistics. The federal government continues to be the best source of up-to-date, reliable information on the changing characteristics of Americans. To explore the opinions of people aged 55 or older, most of the tables in the Attitudes and Behavior chapter are based on data from the nationally representative General Social Survey of the University of Chicago's National Opinion Research Center (NORC). Attitudinal data for all age groups are shown for comparative purposes. NORC is the oldest nonprofit, university-affiliated national survey research facility in the nation. It conducted the General Social Survey annually from 1972 through 1994, except for the years 1979, 1981, and 1992. It now conducts the survey every two years, with 1996 being the latest year for which data are available.

While most of the data in this book are produced by the federal government, the tables in *Americans 55 & Older* are not simply reprints of the government's tabulations—as is the case in many reference books. Instead, each table is individually compiled and created by New Strategist's editors, with calculations designed to reveal the trends. Each chapter of *Americans 55 & Older* includes the demographic and lifestyle data most important to researchers. Each table tells a story about older Americans, a story explained by the accompanying text, which analyzes the data and highlights future trends. If readers need more information than the tables and text provide, they can plumb the original source listed at the bottom of each table.

The book contains a lengthy table list to help researchers locate the information they need. For a more detailed search, there is an index at the back of the book. Also there is the glossary, which defines many of the terms commonly used in the tables and text. A list of telephone and web site contacts also appears at the end of the book, allowing researchers to access government specialists and web sites.

With *Americans 55 & Older: A Changing Market* in hand, researchers can gain an understanding of the changing 55-or-older population. With this knowledge, they will be able to position their business to profit from the coming revolution.

1

Attitudes & Behavior

♦ Older Americans are the happiest, with 39 percent of people aged 65 to 74 saying they are "very happy"—a larger share than in any other age group.

♦ People aged 55 or older are not as cynical as boomers and younger adults. The majority think most people try to be helpful and fair.

♦ People aged 65 to 74 are more likely to have experienced a traumatic event in the past five years than those in any other age group. The majority have experienced the death of one or more relatives.

♦ Most older Americans think preschoolers suffer if their mother works. This attitude may be due to their lack of experience with working mothers—fewer than one-half of people aged 65 or older had mothers who worked.

♦ Thirty-one percent of workers aged 53 or older have saved at least $100,000 for retirement. One in five has saved less than $10,000.

♦ Older Americans are more likely than younger adults to believe in God without any doubts. They are also most likely to attend church at least weekly.

♦ Party loyalties still run strong among people aged 55 or older. The largest share identify themselves as Democrats, but few older Americans regard themselves as liberal.

Older Americans Are Happiest

They are least likely to feel rushed.

The percentage of people who say they are "very happy" peaks in the 65-to-74 age group at 39 percent. Those aged 55 to 64 are close behind, with 37 percent saying they are very happy. Happiness peaks among people aged 55 or older because some of their most serious responsibilities are behind them. Careers are winding down and children are grown.

People aged 55 or older are less likely to say they always feel rushed than younger adults. Only 20 percent of people aged 55 to 64 always feel rushed, a figure that falls to just 9 percent among people aged 75 or older. The 57 percent majority of people aged 75 or older say they almost never feel rushed.

A slower pace of life has its drawbacks. A 43 percent minority of people aged 65 or older think life is exciting. Fourteen percent of people aged 75 or older say life is downright dull. But people aged 55 to 64 are more likely than those in any other age group to say life is exciting. Many are filling their expanding leisure time with travel, hobbies, and social activities.

◆ The proportion of Americans in their fifties who think life is exciting has grown over the past few decades as a more educated and affluent generation has entered the age group.

Happiness peaks in older age groups

(percent of people aged 18 or older who say they are very happy, by age, 1996)

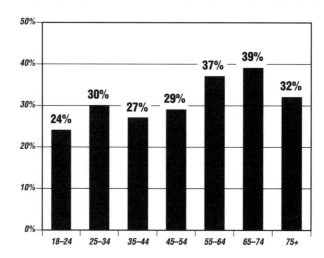

Personal Happiness, 1996

"Taken all together, how would you say things are these days—would you say that you are very happy, pretty happy, or not too happy?"

(percent of people aged 18 or older responding by age, 1996)

	very happy	pretty happy	not too happy
Total people	30%	57%	12%
Aged 18 to 24	24	62	13
Aged 25 to 34	30	59	10
Aged 35 to 44	27	59	13
Aged 45 to 54	29	58	13
Aged 55 to 64	37	50	11
Aged 65 to 74	39	51	10
Aged 75 or older	32	53	16

Note: Numbers may not add to 100 because "don't know" and no answer are not shown.
Source: 1996 General Social Survey, National Opinion Research Center, University of Chicago; calculations by New Strategist

Feeling Rushed, 1996

"In general, how do you feel about your time—would you say you feel rushed even to do things you have to do, only sometimes feel rushed, or almost never feel rushed?"

(percent of people aged 18 or older responding by age, 1996)

	always	sometimes	almost never
Total people	30%	52%	18%
Aged 18 to 24	24	63	13
Aged 25 to 34	34	56	9
Aged 35 to 44	37	53	9
Aged 45 to 54	39	48	11
Aged 55 to 64	20	49	30
Aged 65 to 74	13	48	39
Aged 75 or older	9	34	57

Note: Numbers may not add to 100 because "don't know" and no answer are not shown.
Source: 1996 General Social Survey, National Opinion Research Center, University of Chicago; calculations by New Strategist

Is Life Exciting? 1996

"In general, do you find life exciting, pretty routine, or dull?"

(percent of people aged 18 or older responding by age, 1996)

	exciting	pretty routine	dull
Total people	**49%**	**45%**	**4%**
Aged 18 to 24	47	46	6
Aged 25 to 34	52	45	2
Aged 35 to 44	50	45	4
Aged 45 to 54	50	45	4
Aged 55 to 64	53	42	5
Aged 65 to 74	43	54	1
Aged 75 or older	43	43	14

Note: Numbers may not add to 100 because "no opinion" and no answer are not shown.
Source: 1996 General Social Survey, National Opinion Research Center, University of Chicago; calculations by New Strategist

People Aged 55 or Older Are Less Cynical

Younger Americans are the most jaded.

Although older Americans are the most experienced, they are the least cynical. In contrast to younger adults, they believe other people try to be fair rather than take advantage, and they think others try to be helpful rather than just look out for themselves. Most older Americans do agree, however, that you can't be too careful in dealing with others.

While only 29 percent of 18-to-24-year-olds think other people try to be fair, the proportion rises to a peak of 62 percent among 55-to-64-year-olds and remains above 50 percent in the older age groups. Similarly, while only 28 percent of the youngest adults say others try to be helpful, the figure again peaks among 55-to-64-year-olds at 60 percent. Many people aged 55 to 64 also think most people can be trusted, with 46 percent saying so. Nevertheless, 50 percent believe you can't be too careful when dealing with others, as do an even higher share of people aged 65 or older.

♦ Older Americans were raised to have faith in authority, while younger generations were told not to trust strangers. The contrasting messages society sent to the young of different eras are evident in these generational differences of opinion.

Opinion of Others, 1996

"Would you say most people can be trusted or you can't be too careful in dealing with people? Would you say most of the time people try to be helpful, or they are mostly just looking out for themselves? Would you say most people would try to take advantage of you if they got a chance, or would they try to be fair?"

(percent of people aged 18 or older responding by age, 1996)

	trust		helpfulness		fairness	
	most people can be trusted	you can't be too careful	try to be helpful	just look out for themselves	would try to be fair	would take advantage
Total people	**34%**	**61%**	**43%**	**49%**	**50%**	**42%**
Aged 18 to 24	18	77	28	67	29	66
Aged 25 to 34	25	70	35	56	45	46
Aged 35 to 44	35	59	39	53	48	41
Aged 45 to 54	47	48	47	45	54	37
Aged 55 to 64	46	50	60	33	62	32
Aged 65 to 74	29	62	54	40	57	35
Aged 75 or older	33	59	56	32	59	31

Note: Numbers may not add to 100 because "depends," "don't know," and no answer are not shown. "Depends" was not included because it was a volunteered response.
Source: 1996 General Social Survey, National Opinion Research Center, University of Chicago; calculations by New Strategist

Small Towns Most Popular among People Aged 55 or Older

The largest share of people aged 55 or older live in small towns and cities.

Careers often dictate where people live. People aged 55 to 64, most of whom still work, are more likely than the average adult to live in a big city. Those aged 65 or older—most of whom are retired—are less likely to be city dwellers.

When asked where they would prefer to live, many Americans choose small towns. That's exactly where the largest share of people aged 65 or older live—42 to 44 percent. In contrast, the 55-to-64 age group is less likely than older people to live in a small city or town (34 percent) and more likely to live in the suburbs surrounding a big city (23 percent).

The majority of older Americans live in a single-family detached home. The figure peaks at 72 percent among people aged 55 to 74, then falls to 56 percent among those aged 75 or older. A large share of the oldest Americans live in apartment houses with five or more units (27 percent). Many of these apartment dwellers may have moved to smaller quarters when they could no longer maintain a home by themselves.

♦ A large share of baby boomers say they are going to move after they retire. If boomers do as they say, the proportion of older Americans who live in small towns or the countryside could grow.

Community Type, 1994

"Would you describe the place where you live as . . . "

(percent of people aged 18 or older responding by age, 1994)

	a big city	suburbs or outskirts of a big city	small city or town	country village	farm or home in the country
Total people	**19%**	**24%**	**40%**	**4%**	**10%**
Aged 18 to 24	26	23	39	5	6
Aged 25 to 34	21	23	43	3	8
Aged 35 to 44	20	27	36	6	9
Aged 45 to 54	13	28	41	2	15
Aged 55 to 64	23	23	34	6	11
Aged 65 to 74	18	17	44	7	11
Aged 75 or older	17	19	42	4	13

Note: Numbers may not add to 100 because "don't know" and no answer are not shown.
Source: 1994 General Social Survey, National Opinion Research Center, University of Chicago; calculations by New Strategist

Type of Dwelling, 1996

"How would you describe the place in which you dwell?"

(percent of people aged 18 or older responding by age, 1996)

	detached single-family home	apartment house (5+ units)	two-to-four-family house	mobile home	rowhouse	other
Total people	**59%**	**18%**	**8%**	**8%**	**5%**	**2%**
Aged 18 to 24	40	26	10	11	8	2
Aged 25 to 34	43	25	13	9	6	1
Aged 35 to 44	63	15	8	7	5	1
Aged 45 to 54	68	13	6	5	4	2
Aged 55 to 64	72	9	5	7	5	1
Aged 65 to 74	72	13	4	7	3	0
Aged 75 or older	56	27	4	5	5	3

Note: Numbers may not add to 100 because "don't know" and no answer are not shown.
Source: 1996 General Social Survey, National Opinion Research Center, University of Chicago; calculations by New Strategist

Trauma Most Likely in 65-to-74 Age Group

The majority have experienced at least one traumatic event in the past five years.

Fifty-two percent of people aged 65 to 74 have experienced at least one traumatic event in the past five years, a much higher share than the 35 percent of all adults who have had such an experience. A traumatic event, according to the General Social Survey, is defined as death, divorce, unemployment, hospitalization, or disability. Only 15 percent of people aged 65 to 74 have experienced no traumatic event in the past five years versus a much larger 33 percent of people aged 75 or older.

In many cases, the traumatic event experienced by people in the 65-to-74 age group is the death of the spouse. More than half the people aged 55 to 74 have experienced the death of a relative in the past five years versus 32 percent of all adults. Among people aged 75 or older, a 42 percent minority have experienced the death of a relative in the past five years.

♦ Living through trauma, such as the death of a loved one, is a common experience for older Americans. As people attempt to cope with emotional upheavals, they create a market for spiritual products and services.

Many older Americans have experienced the death of a relative

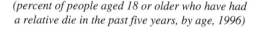

(percent of people aged 18 or older who have had a relative die in the past five years, by age, 1996)

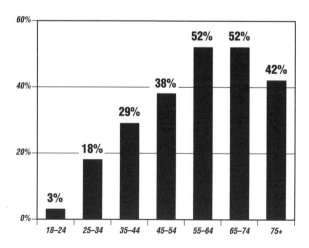

Traumatic Events during Past Five Years, 1994

"Have you experienced a death, divorce, unemployment, or other traumatic event during the past five years?"

(percent of people aged 18 or older responding by age, 1994)

	none	one	two or more
Total people	32%	35%	28%
Aged 18 to 24	45	26	26
Aged 25 to 34	40	32	26
Aged 35 to 44	34	33	26
Aged 45 to 54	28	36	26
Aged 55 to 64	23	36	38
Aged 65 to 74	15	52	27
Aged 75 or older	33	35	28

Note: Traumatic events are death, divorce, unemployment, and hospitalization/disability. Numbers may not add to 100 because no answer is not shown.
Source: 1994 General Social Survey, National Opinion Research Center, University of Chicago; calculations by New Strategist

Deaths of Relatives in Past Five Years, 1994

"Have you experienced the death of a relative in the past five years?"

(percent of people aged 18 or older responding by age, 1994)

	none	one or more
Total people	**67%**	**32%**
Aged 18 to 24	97	3
Aged 25 to 34	81	18
Aged 35 to 44	70	29
Aged 45 to 54	59	38
Aged 55 to 64	48	52
Aged 65 to 74	46	52
Aged 75 or older	53	42

Note: Numbers may not add to 100 because no answer is not shown.
Source: 1994 General Social Survey, National Opinion Research Center, University of Chicago; calculations by New Strategist

Big Differences in Attitudes toward Working Mothers

Most older Americans were not raised by working mothers, and they don't approve of them when children are young.

The majority of people aged 55 or older think preschoolers suffer if their mother works. This is in stark contrast to the opinion of those under age 55, the majority of whom disagree with the notion that working mothers harm preschoolers.

Older Americans may think working mothers are harmful because most were raised by stay-at-home moms. While 50 percent of people aged 55 to 64 had a mother who worked for pay for at least one year while they were growing up, the figure drops to 44 percent among 65-to-74-year-olds and to just 27 percent among those aged 75 or older.

♦ As younger generations replace older ones, working mothers become increasingly accepted. This trend is likely to continue as the number of Americans raised by stay-at-home moms shrinks.

Older Americans wary about working mothers

(percent of people aged 18 or older who think preschoolers suffer if their mother works, by age, 1996)

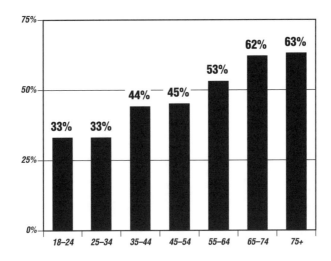

Do Young Children Suffer If Mother Works? 1996

"A preschool child is likely to suffer if his or her mother works—do you agree or disagree?"

(percent of people aged 18 or older responding by age, 1996)

	strongly agree	agree	disagree	strongly disagree	agree, total	disagree, total
Total people	8%	36%	41%	11%	45%	52%
Aged 18 to 24	2	31	52	12	33	64
Aged 25 to 34	7	27	52	12	34	64
Aged 35 to 44	10	34	39	14	44	53
Aged 45 to 54	7	38	40	11	45	51
Aged 55 to 64	10	43	37	6	53	43
Aged 65 to 74	12	50	27	5	62	32
Aged 75 or older	13	50	26	3	63	29

Note: Numbers may not add to 100 because "don't know" and no answer are not shown.
Source: 1996 General Social Survey, National Opinion Research Center, University of Chicago; calculations by New Strategist

Did Your Mother Work? 1996

"Did your mother ever work for pay for as long as a year while you were growing up?"

(percent of people aged 18 or older responding by age, 1996)

	yes	no
Total people	**63%**	**35%**
Aged 18 to 24	82	18
Aged 25 to 34	78	21
Aged 35 to 44	67	32
Aged 45 to 54	62	37
Aged 55 to 64	50	48
Aged 65 to 74	44	54
Aged 75 or older	27	71

Note: Numbers may not add to 100 because "don't know" and no answer are not shown.
Source: 1996 General Social Survey, National Opinion Research Center, University of Chicago; calculations by New Strategist

Marital Happiness Peaks among Older Americans

Many older people support modern sex roles, but many also think a husband's career comes first.

Regardless of age, the majority of Americans think a modern relationship is best—one where both husband and wife share responsibility for earning money and taking care of home and family. But this majority is smallest among those aged 55 or older, with 52 to 61 percent supporting a modern relationship while 37 to 47 percent prefer a more traditional arrangement.

Many older Americans believe a wife should put her husband's career first. When asked whether they agree with the statement that it is more important for a wife to help her husband's career than to have one herself, only 39 percent of people aged 75 or older disagree. The figure is a higher 51 percent among those aged 65 to 74, and a still higher 69 percent among those aged 55 to 64. Among younger adults, more than 80 percent disagree that a husband's career should come first.

Despite dramatic change in the roles of husbands and wives over the past few decades, older Americans are the ones most happily married. Fully 72 percent of couples aged 65 to 74 say their marriage is "very happy," versus only 61 percent of all couples.

♦ Many older Americans would say their traditional attitude toward marriage has contributed to their marital happiness. Younger generations would disagree. Only time will tell whether the marriages of boomers and younger adults improve with age.

Traditional or Modern Relationship? 1996

**"Which type of relationship with a spouse or partner would you prefer?
One in which the man has the main responsibility for providing the household
income and the woman has the main responsibility for taking care of home and family
or one in which the man and woman equally share responsibilities?"**

(percent of people aged 18 or older responding by age, 1996)

	man provides income, woman cares for home and family	responsibilities are shared
Total people	**30%**	**70%**
Aged 18 to 24	17	83
Aged 25 to 34	23	76
Aged 35 to 44	31	68
Aged 45 to 54	26	74
Aged 55 to 64	40	60
Aged 65 to 74	37	61
Aged 75 or older	47	52

Note: Numbers may not add to 100 because "don't know" and no answer are not shown.
Source: 1996 General Social Survey, National Opinion Research, University of Chicago; calculations by New Strategist

Husband's Career More Important? 1996

"It is more important for a wife to help her husband's career than to have one herself—do you agree or disagree?"

(percent of people aged 18 or older responding by age, 1996)

	strongly agree	agree	disagree	strongly disagree	agree, total	disagree, total
Total people	**3%**	**17%**	**53%**	**24%**	**20%**	**77%**
Aged 18 to 24	2	12	54	30	14	84
Aged 25 to 34	2	10	56	30	12	86
Aged 35 to 44	3	11	54	29	14	83
Aged 45 to 54	2	12	58	24	14	82
Aged 55 to 64	3	24	51	18	27	69
Aged 65 to 74	6	38	44	7	44	51
Aged 75 or older	7	45	34	5	52	39

Note: Numbers may not add to 100 because "don't know" and no answer are not shown.
Source: 1996 General Social Survey, National Opinion Research Center, University of Chicago; calculations by New Strategist

Marital and Relationship Happiness, 1996

"Taking all things together, how would you describe your marriage/romantic relationship? Would you say it is very happy, pretty happy, or not too happy?"

(percent of people aged 18 or older responding by age, 1996)

	marriage			romantic relationship		
	very happy	pretty happy	not too happy	very happy	pretty happy	not too happy
Total people	**61%**	**36%**	**2%**	**42%**	**44%**	**5%**
Aged 18 to 24	60	35	3	49	46	3
Aged 25 to 34	69	28	2	46	43	3
Aged 35 to 44	53	44	3	38	52	6
Aged 45 to 54	58	39	2	40	38	5
Aged 55 to 64	67	32	1	33	33	13
Aged 65 to 74	72	26	2	33	22	11
Aged 75 or older	62	34	2	11	44	11

Note: Asked of people who were married or involved in a romantic relationship at the time of the survey.
Numbers may not add to 100 because "don't know" is not shown.
Source: 1996 General Social Survey, National Opinion Research, University of Chicago; calculations by New Strategist

Many Older Wives Control Purse Strings

Few husbands are the family financial manager.

Who makes the financial decisions among older couples, husband or wife? Usually, both husband and wife, or the wife alone. Rarely do husbands control family finances. This is even more true for the oldest Americans than it is among younger adults.

Among the oldest married couples, the most common method of financial management is to have the wife manage the money while the husband has some personal spending money (41 percent). The husband is the money manager for only 11 percent of the oldest couples. Among couples aged 55 to 74, the most common system of financial management is to pool money, and each spouse takes out what he or she needs (32 to 37 percent).

Americans aged 65 or older are the ones most satisfied with the amount of money they are managing. Forty-five percent say they are "pretty well satisfied" with their financial situation, a much higher share than the 28 percent of all adults who are that satisfied.

◆ Today's older Americans have benefited financially from a confluence of events—the generous pension and Social Security benefits offered their generation and a rapid rise in housing values over the past few decades. The next generation of older Americans may not be as financially satisfied.

Who Controls Family Finances? 1996

"Which of the following comes closest to describing the system that you and your husband/wife use to organize your finances?"

(percent of people aged 18 or older responding by age, 1996)

	all money pooled, each takes out what he/ she needs	wife manages money, except husband's personal spending money	some money pooled, each partner has some separate	husband manages money, except wife's personal spending money	wife has housekeeping allowance, husband manages rest of money	keep finances completely separate
Total people	37%	28%	13%	9%	8%	5%
Aged 18 to 24	53	22	11	11	0	3
Aged 25 to 34	36	29	12	11	9	4
Aged 35 to 44	40	31	11	7	9	4
Aged 45 to 54	34	25	18	8	8	5
Aged 55 to 64	32	30	14	11	10	2
Aged 65 to 74	37	24	11	4	11	11
Aged 75 or older	30	41	7	7	4	11

Note: Asked of people who were married at the time of the survey. Numbers may not add to 100 because no answer is not shown.
Source: 1996 General Social Survey, National Opinion Research, University of Chicago; calculations by New Strategist

Satisfaction with Financial Situation, 1996

"So far as you and your family are concerned, would you say that you are pretty well satisfied with your present financial situation, more or less satisfied, or not satisfied at all?"

(percent of people aged 18 or older responding by age, 1996)

	pretty well satisfied	more or less satisfied	not at all satisfied
Total people	**28%**	**44%**	**28%**
Aged 18 to 24	23	42	35
Aged 25 to 34	20	50	29
Aged 35 to 44	22	47	31
Aged 45 to 54	28	42	30
Aged 55 to 64	34	42	23
Aged 65 to 74	45	33	21
Aged 75 or older	45	41	13

Note: Numbers may not add to 100 because "don't know" and no answer are not shown.
Source: 1996 General Social Survey, National Opinion Research Center, University of Chicago; calculations by New Strategist

177327

Most Are Confident in Retirement Plans

But one in three are not confident about their financial preparations for retirement.

Sixty-seven percent of workers aged 53 or older are confident in having enough money for a comfortable retirement, with 31 percent saying they are very confident. This may be the same 31 percent who have already saved at least $100,000 for retirement.

More than 1 in 10 workers aged 53 or older has saved nothing for retirement. The majority have saved less than $50,000, an amount that won't last long once people withdraw from the workforce. The lack of savings may be why most older Americans do not plan on dropping out of the labor force entirely, with 67 percent saying they will work part-time in retirement.

The largest share of older workers expect personal savings to be their most important source of income in retirement. Only 21 percent will depend primarily on Social Security.

◆ Many older workers have already accumulated significant retirement savings, while others haven't even begun to save. These differences in financial preparedness will lead to differences in retirement lifestyles. Some older Americans will be comfortably well off, while others will struggle to make ends meet.

Attitudes of Older Workers toward Retirement, 1997

(percent of working people aged 53 or older responding, 1997)

Amount saved for retirement

None	11%
Under $10,000	8
$10,000–$49,999	32
$50,000–$99,999	18
$100,000 or more	31

Confidence in having enough money for a comfortable retirement

Very confident	31
Somewhat confident	36
Not too confident	19
Not at all confident	13

Expected most important source of retirement income

Personal savings	42
Employer-provided money	26
Social Security	21

Expect to retire at age 55 or younger	**7**
Want to retire at age 55 or younger	**17**
Expect to work part-time in retirement	**67**

Source: 1997 Retirement Confidence Survey, *Employee Benefit Research Institute, Mathew Greenwald & Associates, Inc., and American Savings Education Council*

Older Americans Are the Biggest Consumers of Media

They are more likely to read newspapers and watch TV than younger adults.

In this era of media proliferation, newspapers have a difficult time attracting young adults. Their best customers are older Americans. Daily newspaper readership rises with age. Only 17 percent of 18-to-24-year-olds read the newspaper every day. Readers do not become the majority until the 45-to-54 age group, and readership peaks at 71 percent among people aged 65 to 74.

Older Americans are also the best customers of television. They are least likely to watch only one hour or less of television a day—just 11 percent of those aged 65 or older fall into this category. They are most likely to watch five or more hours of television each day, with one-fourth of those aged 65 to 74 and one-third of those aged 75 or older do so.

♦ Businesses marketing to older Americans need look no further than the traditional media. Advertising placed in daily newspapers or on television is likely to be seen by the majority of older consumers.

Newspaper Readership, 1996

"How often do you read the newspaper?"

(percent of people aged 18 or older responding by age, 1996)

	every day	a few times a week	once a week	less than once a week	never
Total people	**42%**	**24%**	**16%**	**11%**	**6%**
Aged 18 to 24	17	33	21	21	7
Aged 25 to 34	22	33	23	17	6
Aged 35 to 44	39	30	15	11	6
Aged 45 to 54	51	19	15	10	4
Aged 55 to 64	58	17	9	9	6
Aged 65 to 74	71	9	11	3	5
Aged 75 or older	66	10	8	3	12

Note: Numbers may not add to 100 because no answer is not shown.
Source: 1996 General Social Survey, National Opinion Research Center, University of Chicago; calculations by New Strategist

Television Viewing, 1996

"On the average day, about how many hours do you personally watch television?"

(percent of people aged 18 or older responding by age, 1996)

	one hour or less	two to four hours	five or more hours
Total people	**24%**	**60%**	**16%**
Aged 18 to 24	23	60	17
Aged 25 to 34	26	62	13
Aged 35 to 44	28	58	13
Aged 45 to 54	30	57	13
Aged 55 to 64	22	64	15
Aged 65 to 74	11	64	25
Aged 75 or older	11	57	33

Note: Numbers may not add to 100 due to rounding.
Source: 1996 General Social Survey, National Opinion Research Center, University of Chicago; calculations by New Strategist

Older Americans Are Deeply Religious

Most are Protestant and attend church weekly.

The majority of Americans believe in God without any doubts, but people aged 55 to 64 are the most devout. Fully 72 percent say they believe in God without a doubt, as do between 64 and 66 percent of those aged 65 or older. In contrast, a 47 percent minority of the youngest adults are so certain of God's existence.

People aged 55 or older are far more likely to be Protestant than younger adults. Between 69 and 71 percent are Protestant versus a 41 percent minority of people aged 18 to 24. Only 4 to 6 percent of older Americans have no religious affiliation, a far smaller share than the 22 percent of the youngest adults who have none.

During the past few decades, many religious congregations have been aging, and with good reason. Those most likely to attend religious services regularly are people aged 55 or older. From 36 to 45 percent of them attend services at least weekly, compared with only 18 to 21 percent of people under age 35. People aged 75 or older are the ones most likely never to attend religious services, but this may be due to greater prevalence of disability in the age group, which makes it difficult for many to attend.

◆ The differences in the religious preferences and practices of Americans by age guarantee that change is in store for religious institutions over the next few decades.

More Protestants among older Americans

(percent of people aged 18 or older who are Protestant, by age, 1996)

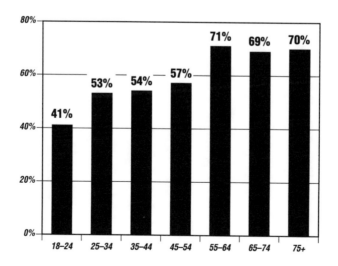

Belief in God, 1994

"Which statement comes closest to expressing what you believe about God?
1) I don't believe in God; 2) I don't know whether there is a God and I don't
believe there is any way to find out; 3) I don't believe in a personal
God, but I do believe in a higher power of some kind; 4) I find myself
believing in God some of the time, but not at others;
5) While I have doubts, I feel that I do believe in God;
6) I know God really exists and I have no doubts about it."

(percent of people aged 18 or older responding by age, 1994)

	no doubts	believe, but have doubts	believe sometimes	higher power	don't know, no way to find out	don't believe
Total people	**62%**	**15%**	**4%**	**9%**	**3%**	**2%**
Aged 18 to 24	47	25	4	8	5	5
Aged 25 to 34	58	21	4	7	4	2
Aged 35 to 44	62	14	3	12	3	2
Aged 45 to 54	64	13	4	11	3	3
Aged 55 to 64	72	12	2	10	1	1
Aged 65 to 74	66	9	6	6	1	4
Aged 75 or older	64	13	3	8	0	2

Note: Numbers may not add to 100 because "don't know" and no answer are not shown.
Source: 1994 General Social Survey, National Opinion Research Center, University of Chicago; calculations by New Strategist

Religious Preference, 1996

"What is your religious preference? Is it Protestant, Catholic, Jewish, some other religion, or no religion?"

(percent of people aged 18 or older responding by age, 1996)

	Protestant	Catholic	Jewish	other	none
Total people	**57%**	**24%**	**2%**	**5%**	**12%**
Aged 18 to 24	41	29	1	7	22
Aged 25 to 34	53	23	1	7	15
Aged 35 to 44	54	25	3	6	12
Aged 45 to 54	57	24	3	5	11
Aged 55 to 64	71	20	1	2	6
Aged 65 to 74	69	24	2	1	4
Aged 75 or older	70	17	6	2	5

Note: Numbers may not add to 100 because "don't know" and no answer is not shown.
Source: 1996 General Social Survey, National Opinion Research Center, University of Chicago; calculations by New Strategist

Attendance at Religious Services, 1996

"How often do you attend religious services?"

(percent of people aged 18 or older responding by age, 1996)

	weekly or more	one to three times a month	up to several times a year	never
Total people	**29%**	**16%**	**37%**	**15%**
Aged 18 to 24	18	17	43	18
Aged 25 to 34	21	18	42	16
Aged 35 to 44	30	15	38	14
Aged 45 to 54	29	17	37	15
Aged 55 to 64	36	15	34	12
Aged 65 to 74	45	14	27	11
Aged 75 or older	41	11	26	19

Note: Numbers may not add to 100 because no answer is not shown.
Source: 1996 General Social Survey, National Opinion Research Center, University of Chicago; calculations by New Strategist

Americans Aged 55 or Older Are Most Concerned about Privacy

Nearly half regard computerized information as a very serious threat.

The generations least familiar with computers are the ones most fearful of their impact. From 45 to 46 percent of Americans aged 55 or older believe the federal government's computerized information about people is a "very serious threat" to individual privacy. Another 25 to 31 percent regard it as "a fairly serious threat." Overall, more than 70 percent of people aged 55 or older believe individual privacy is threatened by the government's computerized information.

Only 24 percent of people aged 18 to 24 regard computerized information held by the federal government as a very serious threat. From 27 to 28 percent of adults under age 45 say it is either not a serious threat or not a threat at all. Only 15 to 19 percent of people aged 45 or older agree.

♦ Because younger generations are not as threatened by computer information as older Americans, the privacy issue may become less volatile as computer-literate generations replace those less familiar with the technology.

Privacy and Personal Information, 1996

"The federal government has a lot of different pieces of information about people, which computers can bring together very quickly. Is this a very serious threat to individual privacy, a fairly serious threat, not a serious threat, or not a threat at all to individual privacy?"

(percent of people aged 18 or older responding by age, 1996)

	very serious threat	fairly serious threat	not a serious threat	not a threat at all	can't choose
Total people	**36%**	**32%**	**19%**	**4%**	**7%**
Aged 18 to 24	24	35	26	1	11
Aged 25 to 34	30	34	25	3	7
Aged 35 to 44	33	32	23	5	6
Aged 45 to 54	41	33	14	4	6
Aged 55 to 64	45	31	11	4	7
Aged 65 to 74	45	25	9	7	11
Aged 75 or older	46	25	10	9	6

Note: Numbers may not add to 100 because no answer is not shown.
Source: 1996 General Social Survey, National Opinion Research Center, University of Chicago; calculations by New Strategist

Few Think Average Citizen Has Much Political Influence

But most older Americans identify with a political party.

Older Americans are just as jaded about politics as younger Americans. People aged 55 or older are as likely as younger adults to believe the average citizen has little influence on politics. While 31 to 37 percent believe the average citizen has considerable influence, a larger share of 39 to 48 percent believe the average person does not have much influence. Despite this cynicism, the voting rate is highest among older Americans. More than 70 percent of people aged 55 to 74 voted in the November 1996 election.

Older Americans are much more likely to align themselves with a political party than younger adults. The Democratic party is the one with which most of them identify. Forty-eight percent of people aged 75 or older say they are Democrats. Despite their identification with the Democratic party, people aged 55 or older are less likely to say they are liberal than younger adults. Conservatives outnumber both liberals and moderates among 55-to-74-year-olds, while moderates are most common among people aged 75 or older.

♦ Older Americans are the last of the party loyalists. As younger generations of political independents replace party loyalists in the older age groups, the Democratic and Republican parties may find themselves increasingly irrelevant.

Political Influence of Average Citizen, 1996

**"The average citizen has considerable influence
on politics—do you agree or disagree?"**

(percent of people aged 18 or older responding by age, 1996)

	strongly agree	agree	neither	disagree	strongly disagree	agree, total	disagree, total
Total people	**4%**	**27%**	**19%**	**36%**	**10%**	**31%**	**46%**
Aged 18 to 24	3	23	21	36	9	26	45
Aged 25 to 34	3	22	18	39	13	25	52
Aged 35 to 44	5		22	35	10	5	45
Aged 45 to 54	5	30	20	31	10	35	41
Aged 55 to 64	4	27	15	41	7	31	48
Aged 65 to 74	2	35	14	32	9	37	41
Aged 75 or older	6	30	10	33	6	36	39

Note: Numbers may not add to 100 because "don't know" and no answer are not shown.
Source: 1996 General Social Survey, National Opinion Research Center, University of Chicago; calculations by New Strategist

Political Leanings, 1996

"We hear a lot of talk these days about liberals and conservatives. On a seven-point scale from extremely liberal to extremely conservative, where would you place yourself?"

(percent of people aged 18 or older responding by age, 1996)

	slightly to extremely liberal	moderate, middle of the road	slightly to extremely conservative
Total people	**24%**	**36%**	**35%**
Aged 18 to 24	25	36	31
Aged 25 to 34	26	35	34
Aged 35 to 44	28	34	34
Aged 45 to 54	26	36	34
Aged 55 to 64	19	38	39
Aged 65 to 74	16	38	40
Aged 75 or older	18	41	31

Note: Numbers may not add to 100 because "don't know" and no answer are not shown.
Source: 1996 General Social Survey, National Opinion Research Center, University of Chicago; calculations by New Strategist

Political Party Identification, 1996

"Generally speaking, do you usually think of yourself as a Republican, Democrat, Independent, or what?"

(percent of people aged 18 or older responding by age, 1996)

	Democrat	independent	Republican
Total people	34%	37%	28%
Aged 18 to 24	27	51	20
Aged 25 to 34	28	41	29
Aged 35 to 44	31	38	30
Aged 45 to 54	37	36	25
Aged 55 to 64	36	32	31
Aged 65 to 74	42	25	31
Aged 75 or older	48	24	26

Note: Numbers may not add to 100 because "other" and no answer are not shown.
Source: 1996 General Social Survey, National Opinion Research Center, University of Chicago; calculations by New Strategist

Voting Rate by Age, 1996

(total number of U.S. citizens aged 18 or older, and percent who reported being registered and having voted in the election of November, by age, 1996; numbers in thousands)

	total	registered	voted
Total citizens	**179,936**	**70.9%**	**58.4%**
Aged 18 to 19	6,788	46.7	32.4
Aged 20 to 24	15,686	56.4	36.9
Aged 25 to 29	17,050	61.3	44.9
Aged 30 to 34	18,801	65.5	51.1
Aged 35 to 44	39,935	72.2	59.6
Aged 45 to 54	30,828	76.4	66.0
Aged 55 to 64	19,959	79.8	71.4
Aged 65 to 74	17,559	81.0	72.6
Aged 75 to 84	10,533	79.5	67.9
Aged 85 or older	2,797	70.1	52.2

Source: Bureau of the Census, Voting and Registration in the Election of November 1996, *Current Population Reports P20-504, 1998*

Volunteering Is below Average in Older Age Groups

Religious organizations are the only ones to get a substantial proportion of older Americans to volunteer.

Religious organizations receive the most volunteer support. Among all Americans, 24 percent volunteered for a religious organization during the past year. This is the only volunteer area in which some older Americans have an above-average participation rate. Twenty-nine percent of people aged 55 to 64 volunteered for a religious organization in the past year, as did 24 percent of those aged 65 to 74. Older people are also the ones most likely to attend religious services regularly.

Few older Americans volunteer for education or youth development organizations. Most of the volunteers in these areas are middle-aged people whose children are involved in these activities.

Older Americans are about as likely as the average person to volunteer for environmental, arts and culture, and political organizations.

♦ Community organizations dependent on volunteers should look toward the 55-or-older population as a potential resource. Older Americans have more free time than middle-aged adults. Many may contribute some of those hours to a worthy cause if encouraged to do so.

Volunteer Work, 1996

"In which, if any, of these areas have you done some volunteer work in the past 12 months?"

(percent of people aged 18 or older responding by age, 1996)

	religious organizations	education	youth development	health	environment	arts, culture, humanities	political organizations or campaigns
Total people	**24%**	**17%**	**15%**	**10%**	**7%**	**7%**	**5%**
18 to 24	16	16	18	8	11	7	4
25 to 34	21	17	16	13	6	5	3
35 to 44	28	24	20	12	7	6	6
45 to 54	30	22	17	13	9	12	6
55 to 64	29	10	11	5	6	9	5
65 to 74	24	6	3	6	4	4	5
75 or older	9	6	3	7	4	2	3

Note: Numbers may not add to 100 because no answer is not shown.
Source: 1996 General Social Survey, National Opinion Research Center, University of Chicago; calculations by New Strategist

Participation in the Arts by Older Americans Is Below Average

People aged 55 or older are less likely to attend art events or participate in art activities than is the average person—but that's about to change.

Older Americans are not as involved in the arts as younger adults. They are less likely to attend nearly every type of art event than is the average person. Classical music concerts are the only exception. People aged 55 to 74 are more likely than average to go to a classical music concert.

People aged 55 or older are also less likely than the average person to participate in art activities, with few exceptions. Weaving is one art in which older Americans are more likely to participate than the average person. In fact, people aged 65 to 74 are more likely than those in any other age group to participate in weaving.

Participation by older Americans in most leisure activities is also well below average. Home repair and gardening are exceptions, however. Those aged 55 to 64 are more involved than the average person in home repair, while those aged 55 to 74 are avid gardeners. People aged 65 to 74 are more likely to garden than those in any other age group.

◆ Behind the below-average arts participation of people aged 55 or older is their relatively low educational level. As the well-educated baby-boom generation enters the 55-plus age group, arts participation by older Americans will soar.

Attendance at Arts Events, 1997

(percent of people aged 18 or older and people aged 55 or older attending art event or reading literature at least once in the past 12 months, 1997)

	total	55 to 64	65 to 74	75 or older
Read literature*	63.1%	57.6%	58.9%	61.2%
Visited art/craft fair	47.5	44.3	40.0	23.6
Visited historic park	46.9	44.5	37.1	25.1
Visited art museum	34.9	29.7	28.0	19.7
Musical play	24.5	23.0	24.0	15.4
Non-musical play	15.8	14.4	14.6	12.5
Classical music	15.6	16.3	17.9	13.8
Dance, except ballet	12.4	11.5	12.3	6.3
Jazz performance	11.9	8.8	8.2	3.7
Ballet	5.8	4.8	5.3	3.8
Opera	4.7	4.9	4.1	3.3

* Literature is defined as plays, poetry, novels, or short stories.
Source: National Endowment for the Arts, 1997 Survey of Public Participation in the Arts, Summary Report, Internet web site <http://arts.endow.gov/pub/Survey/SurveyPDF.html>

Participation in the Arts, 1997

(percent of people aged 18 or older and people aged 55 or older participating in art activity at least once in the past 12 months, 1997)

	total	55 to 64	65 to 74	75 or older
Buying art	35.1%	31.1%	23.0%	7.6%
Weaving	27.6	29.2	32.4	28.1
Photography	16.9	10.0	9.6	5.4
Drawing	15.9	9.4	7.3	3.7
Pottery	15.1	9.7	9.7	3.4
Dance, except ballet	12.6	7.5	14.1	9.2
Writing	12.1	5.4	4.8	5.7
Classical music	11.0	8.8	6.3	6.2
Singing in groups	10.4	11.1	9.9	6.5
Musical play	7.7	5.0	8.2	5.8
Non-musical play	2.7	1.4	0.7	0.3
Jazz	2.2	0.9	3.5	0.1
Opera	1.8	2.1	1.1	2.3
Ballet	0.5	0.3	0.0	0.0

Source: National Endowment for the Arts, 1997 Survey of Public Participation in the Arts, Summary Report, Internet web site <http://arts.endow.gov/pub/Survey/SurveyPDF.html>

Participation in Leisure Activities, 1997

(percent of people aged 18 or older and people aged 55 or older participating in leisure activities at least once in the past 12 months, 1997)

	total	aged 55 to 64	aged 65 to 74	aged 75 or older
Exercise program	75.7%	69.4%	64.9%	55.7%
Home improvement/repair	65.9	70.6	55.2	44.3
Went out to the movies	65.5	46.0	38.4	28.2
Gardening	65.4	68.8	75.0	65.2
Went to an amusement park	57.0	40.2	28.8	18.4
Played a sport	44.9	19.1	22.5	12.9
Outdoor activities	44.3	33.0	23.8	13.8
Volunteer or charity work	43.2	43.5	39.9	39.8
Went to a sporting event	41.2	32.9	20.8	16.3
Used a computer for entertainment	40.4	22.7	10.6	7.3

Source: National Endowment for the Arts, 1997 Survey of Public Participation in the Arts, Summary Report, Internet web site <http://arts.endow.gov/pub/Survey/SurveyPDF.html>

CHAPTER

2

Education

◆ The educational level of older Americans has increased enormously since 1940, with the proportion of those who are high school graduates rising from 16 to 73 percent among men and from 18 to 71 percent among women.

◆ Older Americans are educationally diverse. Twenty-eight percent of men aged 55 to 59 are college graduates compared with just 16 percent of men aged 75 or older.

◆ Twenty-one percent of women aged 55 to 59 have graduated from college, versus just 11 percent of women aged 75 or older.

◆ Educational attainment varies sharply by race among older Americans. While 24 percent of white men aged 55 or older are college graduates, the proportion is only 9 percent among both black and Hispanic men.

◆ Fourteen percent of white and 11 percent of black women aged 55 or older are college graduates. Among Hispanic women in the age group, only 6 percent have a college degree.

Big Gain in Education of Older Americans

A high school diploma did not become the norm for people aged 55 or older until the 1980s.

In 1998, 73 percent of men and 71 percent of women aged 55 or older had a high school education, up from only 16 percent of men and 18 percent of women in 1940. In the latter year, only 4 percent of men and 2 percent of women aged 55 or older had a college diploma, but now the proportions are 23 and 14 percent, respectively. Despite the dramatic rise in the educational attainment of older Americans, a substantial 27 percent still lack a high school diploma. Among all Americans aged 25 or older, only 18 percent are not high school graduates.

◆ The educational attainment of older Americans is rising because better-educated generations are replacing those with less education. As the baby-boom generation enters the 55-plus age group, the educational level of the older population will continue its rapid rise.

◆ Marketing strategies that have worked because of the lack of sophistication among older Americans will have to be abandoned as the educational level of the market soars.

Educational attainment on the rise

(percent of men and women aged 55 or older who are high school graduates or more, 1940 and 1998)

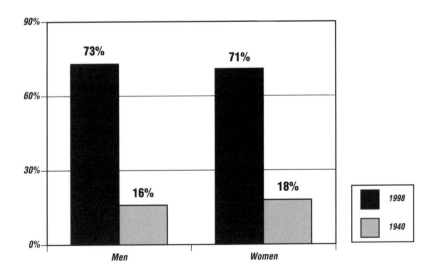

Educational Attainment of Persons Aged 55 or Older, 1940 to 1998

(percent distribution of people aged 55 or older by sex and educational attainment, 1940 to 1998)

	total	not a high high school graduate	high school graduate or more	some college or more	college, four or more years
Men					
1998	100.0%	26.8%	73.2%	41.1%	22.7%
1990	100.0	38.5	61.5	30.2	18.1
1980	100.0	50.4	49.6	22.5	12.6
1970	100.0	65.9	34.1	15.8	8.9
1960	100.0	79.2	20.8	11.1	5.3
1950	100.0	78.4	21.6	8.7	4.6
1940	100.0	84.2	15.8	6.9	3.7
Women					
1998	100.0	28.7	71.3	32.2	13.8
1990	100.0	38.2	61.8	22.9	10.6
1980	100.0	49.4	50.6	17.7	7.9
1970	100.0	62.8	37.2	14.0	6.3
1960	100.0	75.4	24.6	11.1	4.0
1950	100.0	76.4	23.6	8.4	3.3
1940	100.0	82.2	17.8	6.0	2.2

Source: Bureau of the Census, Educational Attainment in the United States: March 1998, *detailed tables from Current Population Reports P20-513, 1998; calculations by New Strategist*

Oldest Men Are the Least Educated

High school and college graduates are much more prevalent among men aged 55 to 59 than among men aged 75 or older.

Men aged 55 to 59 are much better educated than older men. Fully 82 percent are high school graduates compared with only 63 percent of men aged 75 or older. The gap between the proportions of older men with a college diploma is also large. Among men aged 55 to 59, 28 percent are college graduates, but only 16 percent of men aged 75 or older are.

The proportion of men aged 55 to 59 with a master's degree is more than double the proportion among their counterparts aged 75 or older, 8 versus 3 percent. But the share of older men with professional or doctoral degrees shows little variation by age.

◆ Older men cannot be targeted as a single market. Not only are they segmented by health and lifestyle, but also by education.

More than 80 percent of men aged 55 to 59 are high school graduates

(percent of men aged 55 or older who are high school graduates, by age, 1998)

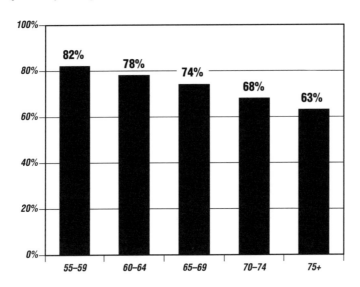

Educational Attainment of Men Aged 55 or Older, 1998

(number and percent distribution of total men aged 25 or older and men aged 55 or older by highest level of education, 1998; numbers in thousands)

	total	aged 55 or older total	55–59	60–64	aged 65 or older total	65–69	70–74	75+
Total men	**82,376**	**24,197**	**5,869**	**4,804**	**13,524**	**4,286**	**3,706**	**5,532**
Not a high school graduate	14,175	6,495	1,037	1,072	4,386	1,124	1,201	2,061
High school graduate	26,575	7,745	2,022	1,639	4,084	1,286	1,112	1,687
Some college, no degree	14,122	3,575	919	670	1,986	678	538	771
Associate's degree	5,670	886	275	218	393	147	97	148
Bachelor's degree	14,090	3,099	883	667	1,549	577	458	514
Master's degree	4,640	1,304	445	299	560	253	165	142
Professional degree	1,749	583	143	123	317	128	66	124
Doctoral degree	1,353	510	142	118	250	94	70	85
High school graduate or more	68,199	17,703	4,829	3,734	9,140	3,163	2,506	3,471
Some college or more	41,624	9,957	2,807	2,095	5,055	1,877	1,394	1,784
Bachelor's degree or more	21,832	5,496	1,613	1,207	2,676	1,052	759	865
Total men	**100.0%**	**100.0%**	**100.0%**	**100.0%**	**100.0%**	**100.0%**	**100.0%**	**100.0%**
Not a high school graduate	17.2	26.8	17.7	22.3	32.4	26.2	32.4	37.3
High school graduate	32.3	32.0	34.5	34.1	30.2	30.0	30.0	30.5
Some college, no degree	17.1	14.8	15.7	13.9	14.7	15.8	14.5	13.9
Associate's degree	6.9	3.7	4.7	4.5	2.9	3.4	2.6	2.7
Bachelor's degree	17.1	12.8	15.0	13.9	11.5	13.5	12.4	9.3
Master's degree	5.6	5.4	7.6	6.2	4.1	5.9	4.5	2.6
Professional degree	2.1	2.4	2.4	2.6	2.3	3.0	1.8	2.2
Doctoral degree	1.6	2.1	2.4	2.5	1.8	2.2	1.9	1.5
High school graduate or more	82.8	73.2	82.3	77.7	67.6	73.8	67.6	62.7
Some college or more	50.5	41.1	47.8	43.6	37.4	43.8	37.6	32.2
Bachelor's degree or more	26.5	22.7	27.5	25.1	19.8	24.5	20.5	15.6

Source: Bureau of the Census, Educational Attainment in the United States: March 1998, *detailed tables from Current Population Report P20-513, 1998; calculations by New Strategist*

Educated Women Will Redefine Older Market

College graduates are twice as prevalent among women aged 55 to 59 as among women aged 75 or older.

Women aged 55 to 59 are much better educated than those aged 60 or older, representing the leading edge of a sweeping change now overtaking the older market. Fully 82 percent of women aged 55 to 59 are high school graduates compared with a much smaller 62 percent of women aged 75 or older. The gap between proportions of older women with college diplomas is also large. Among women aged 55 to 59, 20.5 percent are college graduates; among women aged 75 or older, only 10.5 percent are.

Overall, 4 million women aged 55 or older have a college degree, accounting for one-fifth of the nation's college educated women in 1998. Nearly 10 million women aged 55 or older (or 32 percent) have been to college for at least one year.

◆ Because women comprise the great majority of older Americans, their growing educational level has far-reaching implications for marketers. Most important, older consumers will become increasingly sophisticated, making many traditional marketing strategies obsolete.

More than 80 percent of women aged 55 to 59 have a high school diploma

(percent of women aged 55 or older who are high school graduates, by age, 1998)

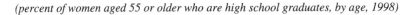

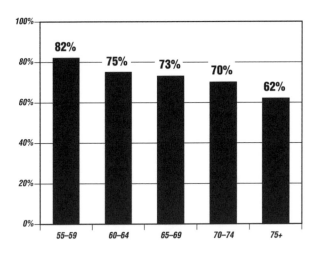

Educational Attainment of Women Aged 55 or Older, 1998

(number and percent distribution of total women aged 25 or older and women aged 55 or older by highest level of education, 1998; numbers in thousands)

| | | aged 55 or older | | | | | | |
| | | | | | aged 65 or older | | | |
	total	*total*	*55–59*	*60–64*	*total*	*65–69*	*70–74*	*75+*
Total women	**89,835**	**30,140**	**6,321**	**5,261**	**18,558**	**5,075**	**4,807**	**8,677**
Not a high school graduate	15,381	8,640	1,142	1,307	6,191	1,386	1,462	3,342
High school graduate	31,599	11,780	2,462	2,187	7,131	2,174	1,926	3,030
Some college, no degree	15,516	4,065	989	748	2,328	606	643	1,079
Associate's degree	7,198	1,495	431	239	825	270	245	311
Bachelor's degree	14,215	2,736	844	496	1,396	406	352	638
Master's degree	4,592	1,145	381	220	544	176	150	218
Professional degree	820	174	40	38	96	34	22	40
Doctoral degree	515	105	32	26	47	24	6	17
High school graduate or more	74,455	21,500	5,179	3,954	12,367	3,690	3,344	5,333
Some college or more	42,856	9,720	2,717	1,767	5,236	1,516	1,418	2,303
Bachelor's degree or more	20,142	4,160	1,297	780	2,083	640	530	913
Total women	**100.0%**	**100.0%**	**100.0%**	**100.0%**	**100.0%**	**100.0%**	**100.0%**	**100.0%**
Not a high school graduate	17.1	28.7	18.1	24.8	33.4	27.3	30.4	38.5
High school graduate	35.2	39.1	38.9	41.6	38.4	42.8	40.1	34.9
Some college, no degree	17.3	13.5	15.6	14.2	12.5	11.9	13.4	12.4
Associate's degree	8.0	5.0	6.8	4.5	4.4	5.3	5.1	3.6
Bachelor's degree	15.8	9.1	13.4	9.4	7.5	8.0	7.3	7.4
Master's degree	5.1	3.8	6.0	4.2	2.9	3.5	3.1	2.5
Professional degree	0.9	0.6	0.6	0.7	0.5	0.7	0.5	0.5
Doctoral degree	0.6	0.3	0.5	0.5	0.3	0.5	0.1	0.2
High school graduate or more	82.9	71.3	81.9	75.2	66.6	72.7	69.6	61.5
Some college or more	47.7	32.2	43.0	33.6	28.2	29.9	29.5	26.5
Bachelor's degree or more	22.4	13.8	20.5	14.8	11.2	12.6	11.0	10.5

Source: Bureau of the Census, Educational Attainment in the United States: March 1998, *detailed tables from Current Population Report P20-513, 1998; calculations by New Strategist*

Most Older Hispanics Lack a High School Diploma

But a majority of whites and blacks are high school graduates.

While 75 percent of white men aged 55 or older are high school graduates, the proportion is much smaller among blacks and Hispanics. Only 52 percent of black men aged 55 or older have a high school diploma. Among Hispanics, the proportion is an even-smaller 41 percent. Similarly, older white women are much better educated than their black and Hispanic counterparts. While 74 percent of white women aged 55 or older are high school graduates, only 53 percent of black and 37 percent of Hispanic women in the age group have a high school diploma.

Among older men, whites are more than twice as likely as blacks or Hispanics to have a college degree. Twenty-four percent of white men aged 55 or older are college graduates versus only 9 percent of black and Hispanic men in the age group. The gap is much smaller between white and black women. Fourteen percent of white and 11 percent of black women aged 55 or older are college graduates. Among Hispanic women of the age group, only 6 percent have a college degree.

◆ As the better-educated blacks of the baby-boom generation enter the 55-plus age group, the proportion of older blacks with a high school diploma will rise sharply.

◆ Because many younger Hispanics are immigrants with little formal schooling, the educational attainment of the older Hispanic population will not rise much in the years ahead.

Educational Attainment of Men Aged 55 or Older by Race and Hispanic Origin, 1998

(number and percent distribution of men aged 55 or older by educational attainment, race, and Hispanic origin, 1998; numbers in thousands)

	white	black	Hispanic
Total men aged 55 or older	**21,321**	**2,036**	**1,450**
Not a high school graduate	5,319	980	850
High school graduate	6,962	554	286
Some college, no degree	3,240	244	131
Associate's degree	784	74	43
Bachelor's degree	2,805	94	81
Master's degree	1,200	62	23
Professional degree	538	14	11
Doctoral degree	472	14	19
High school graduate or more	16,001	1,056	594
Some college or more	9,039	502	308
Bachelor's degree or more	5,015	184	134
Total men aged 55 or older	**100.0%**	**100.0%**	**100.0%**
Not a high school graduate	24.9	48.1	58.6
High school graduate	32.7	27.2	19.7
Some college, no degree	15.2	12.0	9.0
Associate's degree	3.7	3.6	3.0
Bachelor's degree	13.2	4.6	5.6
Master's degree	5.6	3.0	1.6
Professional degree	2.5	0.7	0.8
Doctoral degree	2.2	0.7	1.3
High school graduate or more	75.0	51.9	41.0
Some college or more	42.4	24.7	21.2
Bachelor's degree or more	23.5	9.0	9.2

Source: Bureau of the Census, Educational Attainment in the United States: March 1998, *detailed tables from Current Population Report P20-513, 1998; calculations by New Strategist*

Educational Attainment of Women Aged 55 or Older by Race and Hispanic Origin, 1998

(number and percent distribution of women aged 55 or older by educational attainment, race, and Hispanic origin, 1998; numbers in thousands)

	white	black	Hispanic
Total women aged 55 or older	**26,372**	**2,878**	**1,802**
Not a high school graduate	6,983	1,344	1,140
High school graduate	10,646	876	390
Some college, no degree	3,732	262	109
Associate's degree	1,373	77	47
Bachelor's degree	2,428	159	80
Master's degree	975	137	21
Professional degree	153	5	6
Doctoral degree	85	18	6
High school graduate or more	19,392	1,534	659
Some college or more	8,746	658	269
Bachelor's degree or more	3,641	319	113
Total women aged 55 or older	**100.0%**	**100.0%**	**100.0%**
Not a high school graduate	26.5	46.7	63.3
High school graduate	40.4	30.4	21.6
Some college, no degree	14.2	9.1	6.0
Associate's degree	5.2	2.7	2.6
Bachelor's degree	9.2	5.5	4.4
Master's degree	3.7	4.8	1.2
Professional degree	0.6	0.2	0.3
Doctoral degree	0.3	0.6	0.3
High school graduate or more	73.5	53.3	36.6
Some college or more	33.2	22.9	14.9
Bachelor's degree or more	13.8	11.1	6.3

Source: Bureau of the Census, Educational Attainment in the United States: March 1998, *detailed tables from Current Population Report P20-513, 1998; calculations by New Strategist*

Few Older Americans Are Going to School

Of the nation's 70 million students, only 250,000 are aged 55 or older.

Just one-half of 1 percent of people aged 55 or older are currently enrolled in school. This figure is much smaller than the proportion of middle-aged Americans in school, but it is likely to grow in the future as the well-educated baby-boom generation enters the age group. The more educated a person, the more likely he or she is to return to school to get even more education.

Among older students, women far outnumber men—184,000 to 70,000. Women aged 55 to 59 are the ones most likely to be students, with 1.3 percent enrolled in school. This compares with just 0.5 percent of men in the age group.

◆ As well-educated boomers age into their fifties and sixties, expect to see school enrollment rise among older Americans.

Women are more likely than men to be in school

(number of people aged 55 or older enrolled in school, by sex, 1998)

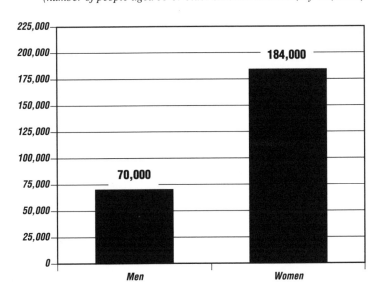

School Enrollment of People Aged 55 or Older, 1996

(number of people aged 3 or older and aged 55 or older, and number and percent enrolled in school by sex, fall 1996; numbers in thousands)

	total	enrolled number	enrolled percent
Total people	**253,175**	**70,297**	**27.8%**
Total aged 55 or older	52,894	254	0.5
Aged 55 to 59	11,233	107	1.0
Aged 60 to 64	9,781	75	0.8
Aged 65 or older	31,880	72	0.2
Total males	**123,103**	**35,092**	**28.5**
Total aged 55 or older	23,421	70	0.3
Aged 55 to 59	5,412	29	0.5
Aged 60 to 64	4,613	26	0.6
Aged 65 or older	13,396	15	0.1
Total females	**130,073**	**35,205**	**27.1**
Total aged 55 or older	29,473	184	0.6
Aged 55 to 59	5,821	78	1.3
Aged 60 to 64	5,168	49	0.9
Aged 65 or older	18,484	57	0.3

Source: Bureau of the Census, School Enrollment—Social and Economic Characteristics of Students: October 1996, *detailed tables from Current Population Report P20-500, 1998; calculations by New Strategist*

Most Older Students Attend College Part-Time

Nine out of 10 older college students are part-timers.

As the number of older college students has grown over the past few decades, so has the number of students attending college part-time. Many older Americans enrolled in college work during the day and take classes at night. Others are actively pursuing a college degree while also enjoying retirement.

Overall, 225,000 people aged 55 or older are in college, accounting for just 1.5 percent of total college enrollment. While this age group represents just 0.3 percent of full-time students, its members are a more significant 3.7 percent of part-time students.

◆ Look for college enrollment among people aged 55-plus to surge as the well-educated baby-boom generation enters the age group.

Older students are part-timers

(percent of total college students and college students aged 55 or older who attend school part-time, 1996)

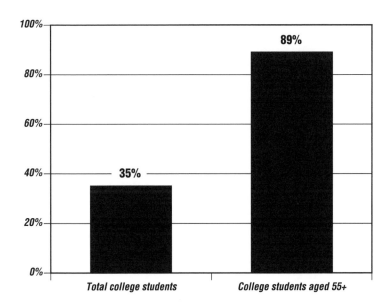

College Students Aged 55 or Older by Attendance Status, 1996

(number and percent distribution of people aged 15 or older and aged 55 or older enrolled in institutions of higher education, by full- or part-time attendance status, 1996; numbers in thousands)

	total	full-time	part-time
Total people enrolled	**15,226**	**9,839**	**5,388**
Total aged 55 or older	225	25	200
Aged 55 to 59	92	12	80
Aged 60 to 64	68	5	62
Aged 65 or older	65	8	58
Percent distribution by attendance status			
Total people enrolled	**100.0%**	**64.6%**	**35.4%**
Total aged 55 or older	100.0	11.1	88.9
Aged 55 to 59	100.0	13.0	87.0
Aged 60 to 64	100.0	7.4	91.2
Aged 65 or older	100.0	12.3	89.2
Percent distribution by age			
Total people enrolled	**100.0%**	**100.0%**	**100.0%**
Total aged 55 or older	1.5	0.3	3.7
Aged 55 to 59	0.6	0.1	1.5
Aged 60 to 64	0.4	0.1	1.2
Aged 65 or older	0.4	0.1	1.1

Source: Bureau of the Census, School Enrollment—Social and Economic Characteristics of Students: October 1996, *detailed tables from Current Population Report P20-500, 1998; calculations by New Strategist*

Adult Education Is Popular among Older Americans

Most participate for personal reasons.

Fully 40 percent of people aged 17 or older took some type of adult education course in 1995. Among older Americans, 28 percent of those aged 55 to 64 and 15 percent of those aged 65 or older participated in adult education during the year. These activities range from bachelor's degree programs to money management seminars. Overall, 11 million people aged 55 or older took part in adult education during the past year, accounting for 14 percent of total participants.

Among people aged 55 to 64 who take adult education courses, 52 percent cite personal or social reasons, while 54 percent participate for professional advancement (more than one reason could be cited). Among those aged 65 or older, 86 percent do so for personal or social reasons.

◆ As well-educated younger generations age into their fifties and sixties, the proportion of older Americans participating in adult education will rise.

Adult Education by Age, 1995

(number and percent of people aged 17 or older not attending elementary or secondary school full-time who have been enrolled in any educational activity in the past 12 months, and percent distribution by reason for taking course, by age, 1995; numbers in thousands)

| | | participants in adult education | | | | | |
| | | total | | reason for taking course | | | |
	total	number	percent	personal/ social	advance on the job	train for a new job	complete degree or diploma
Total people	**189,543**	**76,261**	**40%**	**44%**	**54%**	**11%**	**10%**
Aged 17 to 24	22,407	10,539	47	39	33	21	19
Aged 25 to 34	40,326	19,508	48	41	56	14	8
Aged 35 to 44	42,304	20,814	49	40	64	10	9
Aged 45 to 54	31,807	14,592	46	39	65	7	10
Aged 55 to 64	21,824	6,117	28	52	54	4	6
Aged 65 or older	30,876	4,691	15	86	14	1	3

Note: Percent distribution by reason will not add to 100 because some participants took more than one course or had more than one reason for participating.
Source: Bureau of the Census, Statistical Abstract of the United States: 1998

CHAPTER

3

Health

♦ The proportion of people aged 50 to 59 who rate their health as excellent rose from 23 to 30 percent between 1976 and 1996.

♦ Over half of people aged 71 or older would give up their favorite foods to eat a healthy diet, compared with only 39 percent of all adults.

♦ Only 15 percent of men aged 65 or older smoke cigarettes today, down from 29 percent in 1965.

♦ Just 1 percent of people aged 65 or older are without health insurance, versus 14 percent of those aged 55 to 64 and 16 percent of all Americans.

♦ People aged 45 or older accounted for only 21 percent of those who suffer from colds, flu, or other acute conditions in 1995.

♦ People aged 45 or older accounted for fully 84 percent of those who suffer from arthritis in 1995.

♦ While most Americans aged 80 or older are severely disabled, only a minority need help in managing their daily lives.

♦ The number of older Americans using home health care services surpasses the number in nursing homes.

♦ Eighty-four percent of all deaths in the U.S. occur among people aged 55 or older, and over half occur among those aged 75 or older.

Older Americans Feel Better Than Ever

A growing share of older Americans rate their health as excellent.

The proportion of older Americans who rate their health as "excellent" has grown substantially since 1976. The share of people aged 50 to 59 who are in excellent health has grown from 23 to 30 percent. Among those aged 60 to 69, the rise has been from 18 to 23 percent. Only among people aged 70 or older has the share reporting excellent health not grown.

The share of people in their sixties and seventies who report "good" health has also grown significantly. Consequently, the proportion of people aged 60 to 69 who say their health is good or excellent stood at a lofty 71 percent in 1996, up from just 50 percent in 1976. Among those aged 70 or older, the figure rose from 54 percent in 1976 to 63 percent in 1996.

While poor health is more common among older than younger adults, only 8 percent of the oldest Americans say their health is poor, down from 15 percent who reported poor health in 1976.

◆ The health of older Americans has been improving as better-educated and more affluent generations enter the 50-plus age group. As boomers age, the health of older Americans should continue to improve.

The physical well-being of sixtysomethings has soared

(percent of people aged 60 to 69 who say their health is good or excellent, 1976 and 1996)

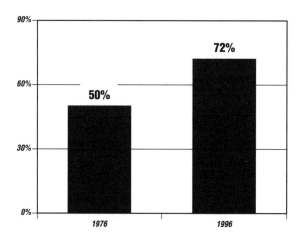

Health Status, 1976 and 1996

"Would you say your own health, in general, is excellent, good, fair, or poor?"

(percent of people aged 18 or older responding by age, 1976–96)

	excellent		good		fair		poor	
	1996	*1976*	*1996*	*1976*	*1996*	*1976*	*1996*	*1976*
Total people	**31%**	**31%**	**49%**	**42%**	**16%**	**20%**	**4%**	**7%**
Aged 18 to 29	36	44	49	44	14	10	1	2
Aged 30 to 39	35	41	52	44	10	11	2	3
Aged 40 to 49	32	27	50	47	15	19	3	7
Aged 50 to 59	30	23	44	44	19	23	7	9
Aged 60 to 69	23	18	49	32	18	37	9	12
Aged 70 or older	17	17	46	37	29	31	8	15

Note: Numbers may not add to 100 because no answer is not included.
Source: General Social Surveys, National Opinion Research Center, University of Chicago; calculations by New Strategist

Older Americans Are Coffee Drinkers

They are almost twice as likely as the average person to drink coffee daily.

Coffee is the most popular beverage among Americans aged 50 or older. Soft drinks are consumed by no more than half of people in the 50-plus age groups on an average day, while alcoholic beverages are consumed by fewer than one-quarter. Eighty percent of men aged 60 to 69 drink coffee on an average day, as do 69 percent of women in the age group. At least 70 percent of people in their fifties are daily coffee drinkers, as are the same proportion of people aged 70 or older.

Americans aged 50 or older are just as likely to eat junk food as the average person. About four in ten consume cakes, cookies, pastries, or pie on an average day. At least 24 percent eat crackers, popcorn, pretzels, or corn chips. But people aged 50 or older are less likely than the average person to eat French fries.

◆ The food preferences of older Americans will change as younger generations enter the 50-plus age groups. Expect coffee consumption to decline and French fries to grow in popularity.

Food Consumption of People Aged 50 or Older by Sex, 1994–95

(percent of total people and people aged 50 or older consuming selected types of foods on an average day, by sex, 1994–95)

	total people	aged 50–59		aged 60–69		aged 70+	
		men	women	men	women	men	women
Grain products	**97.1%**	**96.8%**	**97.7%**	**97.2%**	**98.4%**	**99.1%**	**99.0%**
Yeast breads and rolls	66.5	68.7	73.1	77.2	73.3	74.8	74.9
Cereals and pastas	47.0	43.6	42.3	48.9	49.2	61.5	57.6
Ready-to-eat cereals	28.8	23.4	23.5	27.6	28.4	38.2	37.2
Rice	11.3	12.3	9.6	11.3	9.1	8.8	7.4
Pasta	7.0	6.0	6.3	7.8	6.2	5.2	5.4
Quick breads, pancakes, French toast	22.6	26.2	22.5	25.1	22.2	22.4	19.6
Cakes, cookies, pastries, pies	40.8	40.9	38.4	43.8	42.0	45.6	44.3
Crackers, popcorn, pretzels, corn chips	28.0	26.0	27.3	25.4	30.3	23.8	23.8
Mixtures, mainly grain	35.9	24.6	27.6	19.5	21.6	19.6	20.6
Vegetables	**82.9**	**84.8**	**86.4**	**88.0**	**87.6**	**84.7**	**86.3**
White potatoes, total	43.7	44.5	39.4	44.6	40.2	43.1	36.9
Fried	26.3	21.1	15.2	20.2	12.5	14.2	6.7
Dark-green vegetables	9.7	13.1	15.4	12.0	14.0	12.1	17.9
Deep-yellow vegetables	12.9	13.3	18.0	16.6	16.8	18.5	17.3
Tomatoes	38.3	36.2	37.4	41.2	39.2	37.8	35.1
Lettuce, lettuce-based salads	24.6	29.0	8.1	29.3	34.1	24.4	23.9
Green beans	8.1	8.4	7.4	11.1	11.9	12.7	13.3
Corn, green peas, lima beans	11.7	13.5	12.0	11.9	12.1	15.8	15.9
Other vegetables	42.8	50.4	53.2	53.4	57.7	53.0	51.5
Fruits	**54.2**	**57.2**	**58.0**	**61.1**	**67.5**	**70.6**	**71.5**
Citrus fruits and juices, total	26.7	28.8	31.8	29.8	37.3	38.8	41.9
Juices	20.5	22.5	23.2	21.8	26.6	26.5	31.8
Other fruits, mixtures, and juices	39.5	42.9	43.3	46.2	52.3	56.2	52.8
Apples	12.2	12.4	12.2	13.3	17.9	14.4	15.1
Bananas	13.1	15.0	17.4	24.0	18.7	29.2	26.9
Melons and berries	7.9	11.5	13.5	11.0	14.9	11.7	10.1
Other fruits and mixtures, mainly fruit	13.9	14.4	16.2	16.8	18.6	18.5	21.7
Noncitrus juices and nectars	8.7	5.0	2.4	4.0	5.5	7.8	6.3
Milk and milk products	**79.1**	**72.6**	**76.7**	**79.9**	**80.4**	**86.0**	**82.7**
Milk, milk drinks, yogurt	60.8	50.4	56.6	61.6	63.1	71.8	66.0

(continued)

(continued from previous page)

	total people	aged 50–59		aged 60–69		aged 70+	
		men	women	men	women	men	women
Fluid milk	56.0%	48.1%	51.1%	58.5%	59.5%	68.6%	63.5%
Whole	19.3	12.2	12.6	14.0	14.2	16.1	16.5
Low fat	26.7	24.8	21.3	28.0	27.6	38.7	30.6
Skim	10.7	11.4	16.7	13.9	17.8	13.4	17.2
Yogurt	3.9	3.0	8.4	–	5.0	2.6	2.3
Milk desserts	18.1	17.5	17.9	21.0	21.8	24.5	22.5
Cheese	32.5	27.8	32.0	27.1	29.3	28.3	25.7
Meat, poultry, and fish	**86.5**	**93.3**	**86.7**	**92.8**	**89.9**	**92.4**	**88.1**
Beef	21.6	23.1	19.4	24.9	19.9	19.3	14.3
Pork	15.9	22.7	18.9	23.1	21.8	23.6	18.1
Frankfurters, sausages, luncheon meats	28.6	30.1	22.6	31.6	26.5	31.4	24.3
Poultry	23.1	24.8	27.2	23.7	22.2	20.2	23.4
Chicken	19.4	19.2	21.0	18.2	18.8	16.8	19.8
Fish and shellfish	7.7	12.4	10.5	11.1	9.8	10.9	9.6
Mixtures, mainly meat, poultry, fish	35.8	40.5	29.6	39.6	33.8	36.6	36.3
Eggs	19.2	22.3	18.6	26.9	22.0	27.4	18.6
Legumes	13.2	11.8	13.4	13.8	14.9	14.6	12.0
Nuts and seeds	9.9	10.0	8.3	10.1	8.6	10.4	11.1
Fats and oils	54.7	64.5	65.9	70.0	69.1	66.9	66.0
Table fats	30.8	35.0	41.9	47.1	43.2	46.0	45.3
Salad dressings	29.1	32.2	36.1	33.5	34.8	29.4	26.9
Sugars and sweets	53.6	59.0	57.8	61.3	56.0	65.8	63.2
Sugars	28.2	40.3	39.2	45.9	38.1	46.2	42.2
Candy	15.4	14.0	13.6	11.6	8.8	7.2	7.4
Beverages	**87.2**	**95.2**	**95.2**	**94.4**	**91.3**	**91.7**	**88.8**
Alcoholic	12.6	23.4	14.1	19.3	14.0	14.9	4.6
Wine	3.6	6.5	7.8	5.5	8.4	4.6	2.1
Beer and ale	7.8	14.1	3.9	10.5	–	6.9	–
Nonalcoholic	86.1	93.2	94.5	93.8	91.0	90.9	88.1
Coffee	39.7	71.7	71.1	79.5	69.3	74.4	70.5
Tea	23.3	23.1	31.3	24.2	33.3	26.3	33.5
Fruit drinks and ades	19.3	15.5	11.8	10.7	10.3	10.0	11.0
Carbonated soft drinks	50.4	50.8	45.8	36.8	35.0	27.2	21.9
Regular	39.0	32.8	25.2	22.0	20.6	17.9	12.7
Low calorie	13.0	19.4	21.8	16.1	15.7	9.5	9.6

Note: (–) means sample is too small to make a reliable estimate.
Source: USDA, ARS Food Surveys Research Group, 1994 and 1995 Continuing Survey of Food Intakes by Individuals, Internet web site <http://www.barc.usda.gov/bhnrc>

On an Average Day, Most Fiftysomethings Eat Out

But a minority of people aged 60-plus eat away from home on an average day.

Fifty-seven percent of Americans eat out on an average day. The proportion is a slightly higher 60 percent among men aged 50 to 59 and a slightly lower 54 percent among women in their fifties. Only 49 percent of men and 39 percent of women in their sixties eat out on an average day. The figures are even lower for people in their seventies—29 percent of men and 28 percent of women eat away from home on an average day.

Eating out does not necessarily mean going to a restaurant. Many people eat away from home at stores or other people's homes, for example. On an average day, at least one-third of men and women aged 50 or older eat at sit-down restaurants. A smaller share eat at fast-food restaurants. Among older women, eating at someone else's home is more common than eating at a fast-food restaurant. At least one-quarter of women aged 50 or older eat at someone else's home or consume a gift of food on an average day.

♦ Older Americans are loyal patrons of sit-down restaurants because they have the time to enjoy being waited upon. As boomers age and gain more free time, sit-down restaurants could surge in popularity.

People Aged 50 or Older Consuming Food Away from Home by Location, 1994–95

(percent of total people and people aged 50 or older eating away from home on an average day, and percent distribution of those eating away from home by location, by sex, 1994–95)

	total people	men				women			
		total	50 to 59	60 to 69	70 or older	total	50 to 59	60 to 69	70 or older
Percent eating away from home	**57.1%**	**61.2%**	**59.6%**	**49.0%**	**28.7%**	**51.3%**	**53.8%**	**38.6%**	**28.4%**
Total eating away from home	**100.0**	**100.0**	**100.0**	**100.0**	**100.0**	**100.0**	**100.0**	**100.0**	**100.0**
Fast-food restaurant	32.4	37.2	32.5	29.9	21.8	29.5	20.2	19.5	17.1
Sit-down restaurant	26.8	31.7	36.5	41.4	42.9	33.7	34.5	39.7	33.6
Store	24.1	28.1	24.0	11.2	12.6	22.0	20.4	15.5	11.8
Someone else/gift	22.6	16.9	13.5	19.4	17.1	22.9	24.3	29.3	25.7
School cafeteria	11.4	1.6	1.0	1.0	0.0	2.0	3.4	1.5	0.0
Cafeteria	7.0	8.5	9.4	7.3	8.5	10.2	11.8	8.1	7.7
Day care	2.3	0.2	0.0	0.9	0.4	1.0	0.5	0.5	2.5
Other	23.3	29.5	29.6	22.5	22.2	25.3	21.6	17.5	21.9

Note: Numbers will not add to 100 because food may be eaten at more than one location during the day.
Source: USDA, ARS Food Surveys Research Group, 1994 and 1995 Diet and Health Knowledge Survey, 1997; Internet web site <http://www.barc.usda.gov/bhnrc>

The Healthiest Eaters Are Older Americans

People aged 50 or older are most likely to watch their diets.

Older Americans are more likely than younger ones to practice healthy eating— probably because they are under doctor's orders to do so. While 79 percent of all Americans say they eat healthy foods, the figure ranges from 83 percent among people aged 50 to 64 to over 90 percent of those aged 71 or older. Older Americans are also more likely than the average person to maintain a low-fat, low-cholesterol diet.

When chronic conditions become a factor in people's food choices, they are more likely to forgo their favorite foods in order to eat healthier. People aged 71 or older are much more likely than the average person to avoid favorite foods in order to eat a healthier diet—39 percent of all adults do so versus 52 percent of people aged 71 or older. Older Americans are also more likely than the average person to give up convenience and taste for health benefits.

♦ The rising health consciousness of older Americans is one factor behind their improved physical well-being.

♦ As the population ages, healthy foods are likely to become even more important to food shoppers—particularly as scientific research reveals more about the link between diet and long-term health.

Eating Habits of People Aged 50 or Older, 1996

(percent of people aged 18 or older and aged 50 or older who always or usually follow selected practices, by age, August/September 1996)

	total	50 to 64	65 to 70	71 or older
Eat healthy foods	79%	83%	86%	91%
Read food package labels	66	68	67	68
Choose low-fat dairy foods	53	59	62	68
Maintain a low-cholesterol diet	51	57	65	75
Maintain a low-fat diet	50	53	55	69
Choose products made with whole grains	49	50	53	60
Balance healthy foods with less healthy foods I enjoy more	43	41	42	41
Avoid some favorite foods in order to eat healthier	39	41	43	52
Try new food products	34	31	33	23
Avoid some favorite foods to lose weight	32	31	26	36
Give up convenience for health benefits	28	31	37	43
Maintain a low-calorie diet	26	29	31	45
Avoid foods that contain red meat	22	20	22	23
Give up good taste for health benefits	15	17	21	29
Choose foods/beverages to improve mental performance	14	14	11	23
Maintain a vegetarian diet	9	11	11	11
Choose foods/beverages to improve athletic performance	9	7	4	4

Source: 1997 HealthFocus Trend Report, *HealthFocus, Des Moines, Iowa, 1997*

People Aged 45 to 64 Had Lots of Children

The parents of baby boomers had three or four children, on average.

Family size in the United States had been declining for decades until post–World War II young adults married and had children. Family size rose in the 1950s and 1960s, resulting in the baby-boom generation.

Fifty-one percent of women aged 45 to 64 have had at least three children, according to a 1992 survey. Among women aged 65 or older, a smaller 45 percent have had that many children.

Not only did people aged 45 to 64 have more children than younger or older Americans, they also are less likely to be childless than those in any other age group. Only 11 percent of women aged 45 to 64 have had no children compared with 16 percent of women aged 40 to 44 and 65 or older.

♦ Because today's older Americans had so many children, they are likely to be well cared for in old age since families provide most care to the frail elderly. The situation will be different for boomers in old age because many of them have only one child or no children at all.

Women by Age and Number of Children Ever Born, 1992

(percent distribution of women aged 18 or older by age and number of children ever born, 1992)

	total	*none*	*one or more*	*one*	*two*	*three*	*four or more*
			number of children ever born				
Total women	**100.0%**	**26.0%**	**74.1%**	**16.3%**	**26.5%**	**15.5%**	**15.8%**
Aged 18 to 19	100.0	84.9	15.1	12.6	1.9	0.5	0.1
Aged 20 to 24	100.0	65.6	34.7	20.7	10.2	2.4	1.1
Aged 25 to 29	100.0	42.4	57.6	23.1	22.0	9.1	3.4
Aged 30 to 34	100.0	24.1	75.8	21.1	32.8	14.8	7.1
Aged 35 to 39	100.0	18.9	81.0	17.0	36.1	17.6	10.3
Aged 40 to 44	100.0	16.4	83.5	17.3	37.3	18.6	10.3
Aged 45 to 64	100.0	10.8	89.3	10.9	27.4	22.2	28.8
Aged 65 or older	100.0	15.5	84.5	14.3	25.5	17.5	27.2

Source: Bureau of the Census, Fertility of American Men, *Population Division Working Paper No. 14, 1996*

Many Older Americans Exercise Weekly

One in four men aged 60 to 69 exercises vigorously every day.

People aged 60 to 69 are more likely to exercise vigorously on a daily basis than the average adult. Among men in this age group, 27 percent exercise every day. Among women, the figure is 16 percent. Even among men and women aged 70 or older, the share of those who exercise vigorously every day is close to the national average.

Not surprisingly, the oldest men and women are more likely than the average adult to exercise rarely or never. While only 37 percent of all men say they exercise rarely or never, the figure is 57 percent among men aged 70 or older. Of women aged 70 or older, 72 percent exercise rarely or never, a much higher percentage than the 44 percent of all women who admit being couch potatoes.

Men in their fifties and sixties are no more likely to be sedentary than the average man. Among women in their fifties, the proportion of those who exercise rarely or never matches that for all women. But among women in their sixties, the figure is well above average, with the 55 percent majority saying they exercise rarely or never.

♦ Some older Americans want to stay fit, while others never got into the fitness habit. As today's elderly are replaced by better-educated and more health-conscious generations, the proportion of those who exercise rarely or never is likely to shrink.

People Aged 50 or Older by Frequency
of Vigorous Exercise, 1994–95

(percent distribution of people aged 20 or older and aged 50 or older by frequency of vigorous exercise, 1994–95)

	total	daily	5–6 times per week	2–4 times per week	once a week	1–3 times per month	rarely or never
Total people	**100.0%**	**18.5%**	**6.8%**	**23.9%**	**8.2%**	**5.8%**	**36.5%**
Total men	**100.0**	**24.6**	**7.9**	**25.7**	**8.3**	**4.9**	**28.2**
Aged 50 to 59	100.0	20.2	7.5	23.3	9.0	4.8	34.7
Aged 60 to 69	100.0	26.9	6.0	19.6	4.8	3.6	38.5
Aged 70 or older	100.0	18.9	2.5	14.9	3.9	1.9	57.1
Total women	**100.0**	**12.9**	**5.8**	**22.3**	**8.0**	**6.5**	**44.2**
Aged 50 to 59	100.0	15.1	8.3	20.0	6.4	5.5	44.5
Aged 60 to 69	100.0	15.5	3.5	16.6	5.2	4.5	54.5
Aged 70 or older	100.0	11.2	2.6	9.3	2.2	1.9	71.9

Source: USDA, ARS Food Surveys Research Group, 1994 and 1995 Diet and Health Knowledge Survey, 1997; Internet web site <http://www.barc.usda.gov/bhnrc>

Most Older Americans Walk for Exercise

Two in three people aged 50 to 59 have walked for exercise at least once in the past year.

Walking is the nation's most popular recreational activity. Even among the oldest Americans, those aged 60 or older, most have walked for exercise at least once in the past year. Many are regular exercise walkers. Walking is the only recreational activity with a participation level above 50 percent among older Americans.

Other popular recreational activities among people aged 50 or older include picnicking, swimming, birdwatching, bicycling, motor boating, and fishing. Golf makes it into the top ten among people aged 60 or older, with 10 percent having golfed at least once in the past year. Although a larger share of people in their fifties have played golf (12 percent), it ranks only 12th in popularity for this age group.

Several strenuous activities are popular among older Americans. Eighteen percent of people in their fifties have been hiking in the past year, as have 10 percent of those in their sixties. Seventeen percent of people aged 50 to 59 have been jogging in the past year, as have 8 percent of people aged 60 or older.

♦ As people age, they often choose less strenuous recreational activities. But with the fitness-conscious baby-boom generation now entering its fifties, look for growing participation among fiftysomethings in a variety of more active recreational pursuits.

Participation in Outdoor Recreational Activities by People Aged 50 or Older, 1994–95

(percent of people aged 50 or older participating in selected recreational activities at least once in the past 12 months, 1994–95; ranked by percent participating)

aged 50 to 59		aged 60 or older	
Walking	65.5%	Walking	51.8%
Picnicking	47.7	Picnicking	35.1
Swimming (pool)	34.8	Birdwatching	28.9
Birdwatching	32.8	Swimming (pool)	21.8
Swimming (nonpool)	30.5	Swimming (nonpool)	16.7
Bicycling	22.0	Fishing (freshwater)	13.9
Motor boating	21.1	Motor boating	13.3
Fishing (freshwater)	20.2	Bicycling	10.7
Hiking	18.1	Golf	10.3
Running, jogging	17.2	Hiking	9.6
Camping (developed area)	15.6	Camping (developed area)	9.0
Golf	12.0	Running, jogging	8.0
Camping (primitive area)	9.2	Fishing (saltwater)	5.4
Fishing (saltwater)	8.3	Camping (primitive area)	4.3
Volleyball	6.9	Tennis	3.1
Hunting (big game)	6.6	Sailing	2.8
Hunting (small game)	6.4	Rowing	2.7
Softball	6.3	Hunting (big game)	2.6
Tennis	6.1	Hunting (small game)	2.3
Canoeing	4.9	Softball	1.9
Basketball	4.7	Canoeing	1.9
Snorkeling	4.7	Sledding	1.8
Backpacking	4.5	Mountain climbing	1.7
Sledding	4.4	Volleyball	1.6
Horseback riding	4.3	Caving	1.6
Rowing	4.0	Backpacking	1.5
Skiing (cross-country)	4.0	Snorkeling	1.4
Skiing (downhill)	3.9	Floating, rafting	1.4
Baseball	3.8	Horseback riding	1.2
Sailing	3.7	Skiing (cross-country)	1.2
Water skiing	3.6	Basketball	1.1
Floating, rafting	3.3	Baseball	1.1
Caving	2.9	Hunting (migratory bird)	1.0

(continued)

(continued from previous page)

aged 50 to 59		aged 60 or older	
Ice skating	2.5%	Skiing (downhill)	1.0%
Mountain climbing	2.3	Orienteering	0.9
Snowmobiling	2.1	Water skiing	0.8
Hunting (migratory bird)	2.0	Snowmobiling	0.8
Personal watercraft riding	1.8	Ice skating	0.8
Rock climbing	1.8	Rock climbing	0.7
Soccer	1.5	Windsurfing	0.4
Orienteering	1.5	Personal watercraft riding	0.4
Football	1.1	Football	0.3
Kayaking	0.9	Surfing	0.3
Windsurfing	0.6	Kayaking	0.2
Snowboarding	0.6	Soccer	0.1
Surfing	0.5	Snowboarding	0.1

Source: USDA Forest Service, 1994–95 National Survey on Recreation and the Environment

Smoking and Drinking Are Less Common among Older Americans

People aged 65 or older are less likely to drink or smoke than the average American.

While 69 percent of Americans aged 18 or older drink alcoholic beverages at least occasionally, the proportion is slightly lower among people aged 50 to 69 and sharply lower among those aged 70 or older. Over half the people in the 70-plus age group do not drink alcohol at all.

Older Americans are much less likely to smoke cigarettes today than they were several decades ago. In 1965, over half the men aged 45 to 64 were smokers. This proportion had fallen to 27 percent by 1995. Among men aged 65 or older, the proportion of those who smoke fell from 29 to 15 percent during those 30 years. Women aged 45 to 64 are also less likely to smoke than they once were, the share falling from 32 to 24 percent. But women aged 65 or older are slightly more likely to smoke because older nonsmokers are being replaced by women with higher rates of smoking.

◆ The decline in cigarette smoking among older Americans has greatly contributed to their improved physical well-being.

Among men, smoking has declined in all age groups

(percent of men aged 18 or older who currently smoke cigarettes by age, 1965 and 1995)

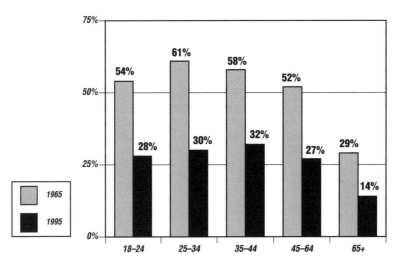

Alcohol Consumption by Age, 1994

"Do you ever have occasion to use any alcoholic beverages such as liquor, wine, or beer, or are you a total abstainer?"

(percent of people aged 18 or older who currently drink alcohol or abstain, by age, 1994)

	currently use	abstain
Total people	**69.1%**	**30.9%**
Aged 18 to 29	80.6	19.4
Aged 30 to 39	79.6	20.4
Aged 40 to 49	67.4	32.6
Aged 50 to 59	63.5	36.5
Aged 60 to 69	67.3	32.7
Aged 70 to 79	43.1	56.9
Aged 80 or more	40.0	60.0

Source: 1994 General Social Survey, National Opinion Research Center, University of Chicago; calculations by New Strategist

Cigarette Smoking by Sex and Age, 1965 and 1995

(percent of people aged 18 or older who currently smoke cigarettes by sex and age, 1965 and 1995; percentage point change, 1965–95)

	1995	1965	percentage point change, 1965–1995
Total people	**24.7%**	**42.4%**	**–17.7%**
Total men	**27.0**	**51.9**	**–24.9**
Aged 18 to 24	27.8	54.1	–26.3
Aged 25 to 34	29.5	60.7	–31.2
Aged 35 to 44	31.5	58.2	–26.7
Aged 45 to 64	27.1	51.9	–24.8
Aged 65 or older	14.9	28.5	–13.6
Total women	**22.6**	**33.9**	**–11.3**
Aged 18 to 24	21.8	38.1	–16.3
Aged 25 to 34	26.4	43.7	–17.3
Aged 35 to 44	27.1	43.7	–16.6
Aged 45 to 64	24.0	32.0	–8.0
Aged 65 or older	11.5	9.6	1.9

Source: National Center for Health Statistics, Health United States 1998; *calculations by New Strategist*

Nearly 100 Percent of Americans Aged 65 or Older Have Health Insurance

But a substantial proportion of those aged 55 to 64 do not.

Overall, 16 percent of Americans do not have health insurance. But among people aged 65 or older, just 1 percent are without insurance coverage. Ninety-six percent of the elderly are covered by Medicare, the federal government's health insurance program for older people.

Among people aged 55 to 64, a substantial 14 percent do not have health insurance—over 3 million people in 1997. Two in three 55-to-64-year-olds with health insurance have private group coverage—most of them through their own or their spouse's employer. Only 4 percent of people aged 55 or older have health insurance provided by the military, while a larger 8 percent are covered by Medicaid, the federal government's health insurance program for the poor.

♦ Americans aged 55 to 64 face a window of vulnerability. They are reaching the age when chronic conditions become increasingly common, yet millions lack health insurance.

Health Insurance Coverage of People Aged 55 or Older, 1997

(number and percent distribution of total people and people aged 55 or older by health insurance coverage status, 1997; numbers in thousands)

| | | *covered by private or government health insurance* | | | | | | | |
| | | *private health insurance* | | | *government health insurance* | | | | |
	total	*total*	*total*	*employment based*	*total*	*Medicaid*	*Medicare*	*military*	*not covered*
Total	**269,094**	**225,646**	**188,532**	**165,091**	**66,685**	**28,956**	**35,590**	**8,527**	**43,448**
55 or older	54,337	50,814	37,435	25,429	34,713	4,410	32,664	2,220	3,523
55 to 64	22,255	19,065	16,748	14,466	3,771	1,509	1,794	1,095	3,190
65+	32,082	31,749	20,687	10,963	30,942	2,901	30,870	1,125	333

Percent distribution by type of coverage

Total	**100.0%**	**83.9%**	**70.1%**	**61.4%**	**24.8%**	**10.8%**	**13.2%**	**3.2%**	**16.1%**
55 or older	100.0	93.5	68.9	46.8	63.9	8.1	60.1	4.1	6.5
55 to 64	100.0	85.7	75.3	65.0	16.9	6.8	8.1	4.9	14.3
65+	100.0	99.0	64.5	34.2	96.4	9.0	96.2	3.5	1.0

Percent distribution by age

Total	**100.0%**	**100.0%**	**100.0%**	**100.0%**	**100.0%**	**100.0%**	**100.0%**	**100.0%**	**100.0%**
55 or older	20.2	22.5	19.9	15.4	52.1	15.2	91.8	26.0	8.1
55 to 64	8.3	8.4	8.9	8.8	5.7	5.2	5.0	12.8	7.3
65+	11.9	14.1	11.0	6.6	46.4	10.0	86.7	13.2	0.8

Note: Numbers may not add to total because some people have more than one type of health insurance coverage.
Source: Bureau of the Census, unpublished tables from the 1998 Current Population Survey; calculations by New Strategist

Older Americans Less Confident in Medicine

Sixtysomethings have less confidence in the leaders of medicine than any other age group.

Only 37 percent of people aged 60 to 69 say they have a great deal of confidence in the people running medicine compared with 47 percent 20 years earlier. Among people aged 70 or older, the proportion having a great deal of confidence in the people running medicine fell from 49 to 44 percent between 1976 and 1996.

The proportion of Americans who say they have hardly any confidence in the leaders of medicine also dropped during the past two decades. In contrast, the percentage citing "only some confidence" has climbed as the extremes have shrunk. Among people in their sixties, the proportion of those who have only some confidence in medicine is now larger than the proportion of those who have a great deal of confidence. Twenty years earlier, the opposite was the case. Among people aged 70 or older, the proportion of those with a great deal of confidence still surpasses the proportion with only some confidence.

♦ The rising cost of health care, as well as the introduction of managed care, has soured many Americans on the health care system. The loss of confidence has been particularly acute among people in their sixties, many of whom are facing their first serious health problems.

Confidence in Medicine, 1976 to 1996

"As far as the people running medicine are concerned, would you say you have a great deal of confidence, only some confidence, or hardly any confidence at all in them?"

(percent of people aged 18 or older responding by age, 1976–96)

	a great deal		only some		hardly any	
	1996	*1976*	*1996*	*1976*	*1996*	*1976*
Total people	**44%**	**54%**	**45%**	**35%**	**9%**	**9%**
Aged 18 to 29	55	60	37	32	7	7
Aged 30 to 39	44	58	50	36	6	5
Aged 40 to 49	40	55	48	34	11	11
Aged 50 to 59	42	48	45	45	12	5
Aged 60 to 69	37	47	52	36	9	16
Aged 70 or older	44	49	41	29	11	16

Note: Numbers may not add to 100 because "don't know" and no answer are not included.
Source: General Social Surveys, National Opinion Research Center, University of Chicago; calculations by New Strategist°≠

Weight Is a Big Concern for 55-to-64-Year-Olds

Forty percent of people aged 55 to 64 report weight problems.

While feeling overweight is the number one health problem for people aged 55 to 64, among those aged 65 or older, weight problems rank only fourth in importance. Arthritis is the biggest health problem for the oldest Americans, reported by 38 percent. The second-biggest problem for both age groups is muscle aches and pains, mentioned by 37 percent of 55-to-64-year-olds and 32 percent of people aged 65 or older.

Sleep difficulties are the third-biggest health problem among people aged 65 or older, mentioned by 29 percent. Arthritis is the third-ranking health problem among those aged 55 to 64.

Although people aged 55 to 64 claim to be troubled by their weight, only 10 percent say they have overindulged in food in the past two weeks. And while people aged 65 or older say they have sleeping problems, only 11 percent report feeling fatigued recently. Other health problems that are relatively uncommon among older Americans are acne, diarrhea, anxiety, and hay fever.

♦ As the population ages, a growing number of people will be looking for ways to lose weight, manage their arthritis pain, and get a good night's sleep.

Top Health Problems for People Aged 55 or Older

(percent of people aged 55 or older reporting health problems during the two weeks prior to the survey, by type of problem, 1992; ranked by percent reporting problem)

	percent of people aged 55 to 64 reporting problem		percent of people aged 65 or older reporting problem
Overweight problems	40%	Arthritis/rheumatism	38%
Muscle aches/pains	37	Muscle aches/pains	32
Arthritis/rheumatism	34	Sleep problems	29
Upset stomach	30	Overweight problems	26
Sleep problems	30	Upset stomach	22
Eye problems	26	Eye problems	21
Common cold	24	Bunions/corns/calluses	20
Lip problems	24	Common cold	19
Sinus problems	21	Headache	17
Headache	20	Lip problems	17
Back problems	18	Constipation	17
Teeth problems	17	Sinus problems	15
Minor cuts/scratches	16	Back problems	14
Bunions/corns/calluses	16	Painful dry skin	14
Painful dry skin	15	Teeth problems	13
Anxiety	14	Fatigue	11
Fatigue	13	Anxiety	10
Constipation	13	Bruises	8
Bruises	10	Minor cuts/scratches	6
Overindulgence in food	10	Overindulgence in food	6
Sore throat without cold	9	Hay fever	6
Diarrhea	7	Diarrhea	5
Hay fever	7	Acne/pimples	3
Acne/pimples	6	Sore throat without cold	3

Source: Consumer Healthercare Products Association, Self-Medication in the '90s: Practices and Perceptions, *1992*

Acute Conditions Less Likely in Old Age

Older Americans account for a small share of people suffering from acute health conditions such as colds and flu.

People aged 45 or older accounted for only 21 percent of all acute conditions experienced by Americans in 1995, according to the National Center for Health Statistics. Among the 61 million people suffering from colds severe enough to send them to a doctor or keep them in bed for at least half a day, only 12 million (or 20 percent) occurred among people aged 45 or older. Similarly, of the 108 million flu sufferers who sought medical attention or stayed in bed, only 19 million (or 21 percent) were older Americans.

Some acute conditions are common among older Americans, however. People aged 45 or older account for fully 41 percent of acute musculoskeletal conditions, 40 percent of acute urinary conditions, 37 percent of pneumonia, and 36 percent of acute eye conditions.

♦ Older Americans are less likely to experience acute conditions in part because they have developed immunities through years of exposure to many viruses.

Acute Health Conditions Experienced
by People Aged 45 or Older, 1995

(total number of acute conditions, number and rate per 100 people aged 45 or older, and share of total acute conditions accounted for by age group, 1995; numbers in thousands)

	total	45 to 64 number	45 to 64 rate	45 to 64 share of total	65 or older number	65 or older rate	65 or older share of total
Total acute conditions	**456,874**	**61,540**	**119.0**	**13.5%**	**32,397**	**103.0**	**7.1%**
Infective and parasitic diseases	**52,605**	**4,490**	**8.7**	**8.5**	**1,866**	**5.9**	**3.5**
Common childhood diseases	3,105	–	–	–	–	–	–
Intestinal viruses	12,447	1,015	2.0	8.2	269	0.9	2.2
Viral infections	16,875	1,782	3.4	10.6	770	2.4	4.6
Respiratory conditions	**223,037**	**29,785**	**57.6**	**13.4**	**12,262**	**39.0**	**5.5**
Common cold	60,564	8,349	16.1	13.8	3,832	12.2	6.3
Influenza	108,009	14,477	28.0	13.4	4,401	14.0	4.1
Acute bronchitis	13,250	1,651	3.2	12.5	1,667	5.3	12.6
Pneumonia	5,113	1,207	2.3	23.6	684	2.2	13.4
Digestive system conditions	**15,828**	**2,311**	**4.5**	**14.6**	**1,706**	**5.4**	**10.8**
Dental conditions	3,503	440	0.9	12.6	81	0.3	2.3
Indigestion, nausea, and vomiting	7,323	1,002	1.9	13.7	487	1.5	6.7
Injuries	**64,619**	**12,024**	**23.3**	**18.6**	**6,201**	**19.7**	**9.6**
Fractures and dislocations	8,200	1,433	2.8	17.5	776	2.5	9.5
Sprains and strains	12,961	2,871	5.6	22.2	844	2.7	6.5
Open wounds and lacerations	12,417	1,785	3.5	14.4	737	2.3	5.9
Contusions and superficial injuries	12,295	2,048	4.0	16.7	1,352	4.3	11.0
Selected other acute conditions							
Eye conditions	2,431	309	0.6	12.7	567	1.8	23.3
Acute ear infections	23,568	949	1.8	4.0	112	0.4	0.5
Acute urinary conditions	7,089	1,383	2.7	19.5	1,417	4.5	20.0
Skin conditions	5,474	609	1.2	11.1	748	2.4	13.7
Acute musculoskeletal conditions	7,866	1,945	3.8	24.7	1,257	4.0	16.0
Headache, excluding migraine	4,128	392	0.8	9.5	280	0.9	6.8
Fever, unspecified	6,282	75	0.1	1.2	201	0.6	3.2

Note: The acute conditions shown here are those that caused people to seek medical attention or to restrict their activity for at least half a day. (–) means not applicable or sample is too small to make a reliable estimate.
Source: National Center for Health Statistics, Current Estimates from the National Health Interview Survey, 1995, *Series 10, No. 199, 1998; calculations by New Strategist*

Chronic Conditions Emerge in Middle-Age

Rates of chronic conditions are highest among the oldest Americans.

Although the incidence of acute conditions diminishes as people enter the 45-plus age groups, chronic illnesses begin to emerge. People aged 45 or older account for the majority of victims of most chronic condition. Some of the exceptions are acne, migraines, asthma, and hay fever.

The prevalence of chronic conditions rises sharply in the older age groups. The most prevalent chronic condition among 45-to-64-year-olds is arthritis (experienced by 232.9 per 1,000 persons in the age group, or 23 percent), followed by high blood pressure (22 percent). Arthritis is also the most prevalent chronic condition among people aged 65 or older, affecting 45 percent of 65-to-74-year-olds and 55 percent of people aged 75 or older. High blood pressure is also common, experienced by 39 percent of people aged 65 to 74 and by 42 percent of those aged 75 or older. Thirty-five percent of people aged 75 or older have hearing impairments.

◆ As the large baby-boom generation ages into its fifties and sixties, expect rapid growth in the number of people with arthritis, high blood pressure, heart disease, and hearing problems.

Chronic Health Conditions Experienced by People Aged 45 or Older, 1995

(total number of people with chronic conditions, number and rate per 1,000 persons aged 45 or older, and share of total chronic conditions accounted for by age group, 1995; numbers in thousands)

	total	45 to 64			65 to 74			75 or older		
		number	rate	share of total	number	rate	share of total	number	rate	share of total
Skin and musculoskeletal conditions										
Arthritis	32,663	12,047	232.9	36.9%	8,269	447.9	25.3%	7,133	548.5	21.8%
Gout, including gouty arthritis	2,478	1,182	22.9	47.7	563	30.5	22.7	312	24.0	12.6
Intervertebral disc disorders	5,927	2,399	46.4	40.5	557	30.2	9.4	452	34.8	7.6
Bone spur or tendinitis, unspecified	2,750	1,326	25.6	48.2	234	12.7	8.5	214	16.5	7.8
Disorders of bone or cartilage	1,793	572	11.1	31.9	392	21.2	21.9	331	25.5	18.5
Bunions	3,262	1,234	23.9	37.8	523	28.3	16.0	445	34.2	13.6
Bursitis, unclassified	5,372	2,013	38.9	37.5	996	54.0	18.5	509	39.1	9.5
Sebaceous skin cyst	1,288	372	7.2	28.9	43	2.3	3.3	75	5.8	5.8
Acne	5,339	323	6.2	6.0	16	0.9	0.3	–	–	–
Psoriasis	2,489	863	16.7	34.7	295	16.0	11.9	175	13.5	7.0
Dermatitis	9,333	1,852	35.8	19.8	544	29.5	5.8	349	26.8	3.7
Dry, itching skin, unclassified	6,440	1,561	30.2	24.2	815	44.1	12.7	681	52.4	10.6
Ingrown nails	5,371	1,496	28.9	27.9	579	31.4	10.8	566	43.5	10.5
Corns and calluses	4,347	1,482	28.7	34.1	613	33.2	14.1	765	58.8	17.6
Impairments										
Visual impairment	8,511	2,496	48.3	29.3	1,006	54.5	11.8	1,384	106.4	16.3
Color blindness	2,966	947	18.3	31.9	143	7.7	4.8	233	17.9	7.9

(continued)

(continued from previous page)

	total	45 to 64			65 to 74			75 or older		
		number	rate	share of total	number	rate	share of total	number	rate	share of total
Cataracts	6,256	996	19.3	15.9%	1,945	105.4	31.1%	3,050	234.5	48.8%
Glaucoma	2,478	636	12.3	25.7	756	41.0	30.5	891	68.5	36.0
Hearing impairment	22,465	7,484	144.7	33.3	4,366	236.5	19.4	4,567	351.2	20.3
Tinnitus	6,805	2,834	54.8	41.6	1,341	72.6	19.7	797	61.3	11.7
Speech impairment	2,747	470	9.1	17.1	147	8.0	5.4	97	7.5	3.5
Absence of extremities	1,195	453	8.8	37.9	204	11.1	17.1	36	2.8	3.0
Paralysis of extremities	1,509	374	7.2	24.8	340	18.4	22.5	194	14.9	12.9
Deformity or orthopedic impairment	31,784	9,079	175.6	28.6	3,094	167.6	9.7	2,509	192.9	7.9
Digestive conditions										
Ulcer	4,297	1,486	28.7	34.6	561	30.4	13.1	247	19.0	5.7
Hernia of abdominal cavity	4,664	1,676	32.4	35.9	1,007	54.5	21.6	718	55.2	15.4
Gastritis or duodenitis	3,663	1,164	22.5	31.8	543	29.4	14.8	518	39.8	14.1
Frequent indigestion	7,196	2,129	41.2	29.6	785	42.5	10.9	575	44.2	8.0
Enteritis or colitis	2,409	841	16.3	34.9	279	15.1	11.6	205	15.8	8.5
Spastic colon	2,437	789	15.3	32.4	275	14.9	11.3	153	11.8	6.3
Diverticula of intestines	2,121	597	11.5	28.1	806	43.7	38.0	489	37.6	23.1
Frequent constipation	3,644	886	17.1	24.3	415	22.5	11.4	799	61.4	21.9
Genitourinary, nervous, endocrine, metabolic, and blood conditions										
Goiter or other thyroid disorders	4,521	1,557	30.1	34.4	882	47.8	19.5	602	46.3	13.3
Diabetes	8,693	2,399	63.8	27.6	2,455	133.0	28.2	1,523	117.1	17.5
Anemias	4,177	973	18.8	23.3	225	12.2	5.4	417	32.1	10.0
Epilepsy	1,443	331	6.4	22.9	150	8.1	10.4	53	4.1	3.7

(continued)

(continued from previous page)

	total	45 to 64			65 to 74			75 or older		
		number	rate	share of total	number	rate	share of total	number	rate	share of total
Migraine headache	11,897	3,001	58.0	25.2%	485	26.3	4.1%	150	11.5	1.3%
Neuralgia or neuritis, unspecified	373	83	1.6	22.3	122	6.6	32.7	76	5.8	20.4
Kidney trouble	3,022	796	15.4	26.3	455	24.6	15.1	211	16.2	7.0
Bladder disorders	4,135	1,022	19.8	24.7	692	37.5	16.7	828	63.7	20.0
Diseases of prostate	2,591	871	16.8	33.6	1,029	55.7	39.7	521	40.1	20.1
Diseases of female genital organs	5,362	1,458	28.2	27.2	265	14.4	4.9	98	7.5	1.8
Circulatory conditions										
Rheumatic fever	2,166	821	15.9	37.9	315	17.1	14.5	202	15.5	9.3
Heart disease	21,114	6,247	120.8	29.6	4,949	268.1	23.4	4,732	363.9	22.4
High blood pressure	29,954	11,516	222.7	38.4	7,234	391.9	24.2	5,458	419.7	18.2
Cerebrovascular disease	3,314	773	14.9	23.3	958	51.9	28.9	1,285	98.8	38.8
Hardening of the arteries	1,845	482	9.3	26.1	531	28.8	28.8	763	58.7	41.4
Varicose veins of lower extremities	7,396	2,390	46.2	32.3	1,426	77.2	19.3	1,132	87.0	15.3
Hemorrhoids	9,077	3,290	63.6	36.2	1,001	54.2	11.0	753	57.9	8.3
Respiratory conditions										
Chronic bronchitis	14,533	3,305	63.9	22.7	1,219	66.0	8.4	798	61.4	5.5
Asthma	14,878	2,754	53.3	18.5	845	45.8	5.7	407	31.3	2.7
Hay fever or allergic rhinitis	25,730	5,964	115.3	23.2	1,494	80.9	5.8	799	61.4	3.1
Chronic sinusitis	37,003	9,258	179.0	25.0	2,893	156.7	7.8	1,935	148.8	5.2
Deviated nasal septum	1,705	529	10.2	31.0	156	8.5	9.1	72	5.5	4.2
Chronic disease of tonsils and adenoids	2,706	246	4.8	9.1	57	3.1	2.1	–	–	–
Emphysema	1,870	671	13.0	35.9	662	35.9	35.4	410	31.5	21.9

Note: Chronic conditions are those that last at least three months or belong to a group of conditions that are considered to be chronic regardless of when they begin. (–) means sample is too small to make a reliable estimate.
Source: National Center for Health Statistics, Current Estimates from the National Health Interview Survey, 1995, Series 10, No. 199, 1998; calculations by New Strategist

Many Older Americans Have Disabilities

But even among the oldest, few need help managing their lives.

The majority of people aged 80 or older are severely disabled, but only 34 percent need personal assistance to manage their daily lives. The most common disabilities in this age group are difficulty lifting 10 pounds, climbing stairs, or walking three city blocks. At least one in four people aged 80 or older has trouble seeing or hearing, going outside alone, or doing light housework. Nineteen percent have a mental disability. While these disability rates are much higher than those for younger adults, they leave the majority of the oldest Americans capable of functioning independently.

Among people aged 55 to 64, 22 percent are severely disabled, as are 28 percent of those aged 65 to 79. The most common disabilities in these age groups are the same as in the oldest age group—limitations in lifting, carrying, or walking. The prevalence of hearing problems doubles between the 55-to-64 and 65-to-79 age groups, then doubles again among people aged 80 or older.

◆ Most people associate age with disability, but this stereotype should be abandoned. Even among the oldest old—people aged 80 or older—a minority have difficulty taking care of themselves.

People Aged 55 or Older with Disabilities, 1994–1995

(total number of people aged 15 or older and aged 55 or older, and percent with a disability, by type of disability, 1994–95; numbers in thousands)

	total	55 to 64	65 to 79	80 or older
Total people	**202,367**	**20,647**	**24,471**	**6,785**
With any disability	**24.0%**	**36.3%**	**47.3%**	**71.5%**
Severe	12.5	21.9	27.8	53.5
Not severe	11.5	14.4	19.5	18.1
With a mental disability	4.8	4.5	5.7	18.8
Uses wheelchair	0.9	1.3	2.1	6.9
Used cane/crutch/walker for six or more months	2.6	3.3	7.8	24.3
Difficulty with or unable to perform				
one or more functional activities	16.4	26.2	41.2	67.8
Seeing words and letters	5.8	6.0	10.0	25.2
Hearing normal conversation	6.2	6.5	12.5	28.2
Having speech understood	1.0	1.3	2.0	4.5
Lifting, carrying 10 pounds	7.9	12.9	20.9	39.6
Climbing stairs without resting	8.9	15.3	25.2	45.3
Walking three city blocks	9.1	15.5	25.2	48.5
Difficulty with or unable to perform				
one or more ADLs	4.0	6.0	10.5	27.5
Getting around inside the home	1.7	2.3	4.6	14.7
Getting in and out of bed or chair	2.7	4.1	6.9	18.0
Bathing	2.2	3.0	5.8	19.4
Dressing	1.6	2.4	3.8	12.2
Eating	0.5	0.8	1.4	3.4
Getting to/using toilet	0.9	1.3	2.5	8.9
Difficulty with or unable to perform				
one or more IADLs	6.1	8.1	15.3	40.4
Going outside alone	4.0	5.5	10.8	31.4
Keeping track of money and bills	1.9	1.7	3.8	15.8
Preparing meals	2.1	2.2	5.0	17.8
Doing light housework	3.4	4.7	8.6	23.7
Taking prescribed medicines	1.5	1.3	3.4	12.8
Using the telephone	1.3	1.3	3.6	13.3
Needs personal assistance				
with an ADL or an IADL	4.7	6.1	11.5	34.1

Note: An ADL is an activity of daily living; an IADL is an instrumental activity of daily living.
Source: Bureau of the Census, Internet web site <http://www.census.gov>

Older Americans Will Soon Dominate Health Care Visits

People aged 45 or older visit health care providers more often than the average person.

People aged 45 or older visited physician offices, outpatient departments, and emergency rooms 402 million times in 1996, accounting for 45 percent of the 892 million ambulatory health care visits that year. While older Americans were only 30 percent of emergency room patients and 37 percent of visitors to hospital outpatient departments, they accounted for 48 percent of all visits to physician offices.

People aged 75 or older visit health care providers an average of 7.2 times a year (or 718.7 times per 100 people). This compares with a rate of 3.4 times a year for the average person. The health care visit rate by people aged 45 to 64 is only slightly above average, at 3.7 per year, while the 5.8 visits per year by people aged 65 to 74 are well above average.

♦ As the large baby-boom generation ages into its fifties and sixties, the 45-and-older age group will become the majority of ambulatory health care patients. Doctors who understand the aging process and cater to the wants and needs of older Americans will be in great demand.

Health Care Visits by People Aged 45 or Older, 1996

(number, percent distribution, and annual rate of ambulatory care visits by total people and people aged 45 or older, by place of care, 1996; numbers in thousands)

	total	physician offices	outpatient departments	emergency departments
NUMBER OF VISITS				
Total visits	**892,025**	**734,493**	**67,186**	**90,347**
Aged 45 or older	402,312	350,107	25,132	27,072
Aged 45 to 64	198,885	170,229	14,911	13,745
Aged 65 to 74	105,624	93,879	5,799	5,945
Aged 75 or older	97,803	85,999	4,422	7,382
PERCENT DISTRIBUTION BY PLACE				
Total visits	**100.0%**	**82.3%**	**7.5%**	**10.1%**
Aged 45 or older	100.0	87.0	6.2	6.7
Aged 45 to 64	100.0	85.6	7.5	6.9
Aged 65 to 74	100.0	88.9	5.5	5.6
Aged 75 or older	100.0	87.9	4.5	7.5
PERCENT DISTRIBUTION BY AGE				
Total visits	**100.0%**	**100.0%**	**100.0%**	**100.0%**
Aged 45 or older	45.1	47.7	37.4	30.0
Aged 45 to 64	22.3	23.2	22.2	15.2
Aged 65 to 74	11.8	12.8	8.6	6.6
Aged 75 or older	11.0	11.7	6.6	8.2
VISITS PER 100 PERSONS				
Total visits	**337.3**	**277.8**	**25.4**	**34.2**
Aged 45 to 64	373.7	319.9	28.0	25.8
Aged 65 to 74	579.3	514.9	31.8	32.6
Aged 75 or older	718.7	632.0	32.5	54.2

Note: Ambulatory care visits are defined as individuals seeking personal health services who are not currently admitted to any health care institution on the premises.
Source: National Center for Health Statistics, Ambulatory Care Visits to Physician Offices, Hospital Outpatient Departments, and Emergency Departments: United States, 1996, *Vital and Health Statistics, Series 13, No. 135, 1998; calculations by New Strategist*

Hospital Care Less Likely for Older Americans

Hospital stays have shortened for people aged 65 or older.

In 1980, the average hospital stay for people aged 65 or older was 11 days. Today, it is just seven days. With more medical procedures being performed on an outpatient basis, and with insurance companies forcing hospitals to release patients sooner, hospital care has been sharply curtailed.

The number of hospital discharges per 1,000 persons fell 30 percent nationally between 1980 and 1995. The decline was less for older people—a 10 percent drop for those aged 65 or older, and an even smaller 7 percent drop for those aged 75 or older.

Americans aged 65 or older still spend many more days in the hospital than younger people, but the number of days of hospital care per 1,000 persons in this age group is well below what it was in 1980. People aged 65 or older experienced 2,352 days of hospital care per 1,000 persons (or 2.4 days per person) in 1995, down from 4,098 days of care per 1,000 persons in 1980. Among Americans of all ages, the rate of hospital care was 544 days per 1,000 persons in 1995, just half the rate of 1980.

♦ The curtailment of hospital care, often at the insistence of health insurance providers, has angered many health care consumers. It is one of the reasons for Americans' declining confidence in medicine.

Hospital Discharges, Days of Care, and Length of Stay for People Aged 45 or Older, 1980 and 1995

(hospital discharges and days of care per 1,000 persons by age, and average length of stay in days, for nonfederal short-stay hospitals, 1980 and 1995; percent change in rate and change in length of stay, 1980–95)

	1995	1980	percent change 1980–95
TOTAL DISCHARGES (PER 1,000 PERSONS)			
Total people	**104.7**	**158.5**	**–33.9%**
Aged 45 to 64	118.2	194.8	–39.3
Aged 65 or older	344.6	383.7	–10.2
Aged 65 to 74	257.6	315.8	–18.4
Aged 75 or older	455.2	489.3	–7.0
TOTAL DAYS OF CARE (PER 1,000 PERSONS)			
Total people	**544.3**	**1,129.0**	**–51.8%**
Aged 45 to 64	655.6	1,596.9	–58.9
Aged 65 or older	2,352.4	4,098.4	–42.6
Aged 65 to 74	1,669.0	3,147.0	–47.0
Aged 75 or older	3,220.1	5,578.7	–42.3

	1995	1980	change 1980–95
AVERAGE LENGTH OF STAY (IN DAYS)			
Total people	**5.2**	**7.1**	**–1.9**
Aged 45 to 64	5.5	8.2	–2.7
Aged 65 or older	6.8	10.7	–3.9
Aged 65 to 74	6.5	10.0	–3.5
Aged 75 or older	7.1	11.4	–4.3

Source: National Center for Health Statistics, Health, United States, 1996–97; *calculations by New Strategist*

Home Health Care Is Popular

Home health care services allow many older Americans to live at home rather than move into a nursing home.

The number of older Americans using home health care services now surpasses the number of nursing home residents. Home health care has grown rapidly during the past few years because of its inclusion in Medicare coverage and because the elderly prefer to remain at home rather than move to an institution for care.

Seventy-two percent of the recipients of home health care are aged 65 or older, and half are aged 75 or older. More than two in three are women. The majority of home health care patients have never married or are widowed, which explains why they need home health care services—no one is at home to help them after an illness.

The growing popularity of home health care has helped reduce the rate at which the elderly are institutionalized. While the number of nursing home residents aged 65 or older rose 48 percent between 1973–74 and 1995, the rate at which older Americans were institutionalized fell 5 percent during those years. The drop was steepest for the oldest, aged 85 or older.

♦ While home health care benefits are likely to be curtailed in the future, the preferences of older Americans are clear. Look for slowing growth in the nursing home population and continued expansion of home health care.

Home Health Care Patients by Age, Sex, and Marital Status, 1996

(number and percent distribution of current home health care patients by age at admission, sex, and marital status, 1996)

	number	percent distribution
Total patients	**2,427,500**	**100.0%**
Age		
Under age 45	347,400	14.3
Aged 45 to 54	130,200	5.4
Aged 55 to 64	187,600	7.7
Aged 65 or older	1,753,400	72.2
Aged 65 to 69	213,600	8.8
Aged 70 to 74	314,300	12.9
Aged 75 to 70	416,200	17.1
Aged 80 to 84	404,300	16.7
Aged 85 or older	404,900	16.7
Sex		
Male	798,700	32.9
Female	1,628,500	67.1
Marital status		
Never married	455,100	18.7
Married	703,000	29.0
Divorced or separated	100,100	4.1
Widowed	857,600	35.3
Unknown	311,600	12.8

Source: National Center for Health Statistics, An Overview of Home Health and Hospice Care Patients: 1996 National Home and Hospice Care Survey, *Advance Data, No. 297, 1998*

Nursing Home Residents Aged 65 or Older by Sex, 1973–74 and 1995

(number of nursing home and personal care home residents aged 65 or older, and number of residents per 1,000 persons in age group, by sex, 1973–74 and 1995; percent change in number and rate, 1973–74 to 1995)

	1995	1973–74	percent change 1973–74 to 1995
NUMBER			
Total residents aged 65 or older	1,422,600	961,500	**48.0%**
Aged 65 to 74	190,200	163,100	16.6
Aged 75 to 84	511,900	387,900	32.0
Aged 85 or older	720,400	413,600	74.2
Male residents aged 65 or older	356,800	265,700	**34.3**
Aged 65 to 74	79,300	65,100	21.8
Aged 75 to 84	144,300	102,300	41.1
Aged 85 or older	133,100	98,300	35.4
Female residents aged 65 or older	1,065,800	695,800	**53.2**
Aged 65 to 74	100,900	98,000	3.0
Aged 75 to 84	367,600	282,600	30.1
Aged 85 or older	587,300	315,300	86.3
RATE (per 1,000 persons)			
Total people aged 65 or older	**42.4**	**44.7**	**–5.1%**
Aged 65 to 74	10.1	12.3	–17.9
Aged 75 to 84	45.9	57.7	–20.5
Aged 85 or older	198.6	257.3	–22.8
Total men aged 65 or older	**26.1**	**30.0**	**–13.0**
Aged 65 to 74	9.5	11.3	–15.9
Aged 75 to 84	33.3	39.9	–16.5
Aged 85 or older	130.8	182.7	–28.4
Total women aged 65 or older	**53.7**	**54.9**	**–2.2**
Aged 65 to 74	10.6	13.1	–19.1
Aged 75 to 84	53.9	68.9	–21.8
Aged 85 or older	224.9	294.9	–23.7

Source: National Center for Health Statistics, Health, United States, 1996–97; *calculations by New Strategist*

Over 22 Million Americans Care for Older People

Most caregivers are women, with an average age of 46.

Most care recipients are also women, with an average age of 77, according to a report by the National Alliance for Caregiving and the American Association of Retired Persons. The survey revealed a tripling in the number of American households caring for a relative or friend aged 50 or older, rising from just 7 million in 1988 to more than 22 million in 1996.

The largest share of caregivers (39 percent) are aged 35 to 49. Another 26 percent are aged 50 to 64, while 22 percent are under age 35. Just 12 percent of caregivers are aged 65 or older. Most caregivers are married, do not have children under age 18 at home, and are employed full-time.

◆ The number of caregiving households has surged because baby boomers are aging into the prime caregiving age groups.

◆ Because the parents of the baby-boom generation had so many children, boomers with ailing parents can share their caregiving responsibilities with their many siblings, lightening the load.

Profile of Caregivers, 1996

(total number of people providing unpaid care to a relative or friend who is aged 50 or older, and distribution of caregivers by selected characteristics, 1996; numbers in thousands)

Total number	**22,411**
Total percent	**100.0%**
Sex	
Women	72.5
Men	27.5
Age	
Under age 35	22.3
Aged 35 to 49	39.4
Aged 50 to 64	26.0
Aged 65 or older	12.4
Marital status	
Married	65.7
Single, never married	12.6
Divorced or separated	13.0
Widowed	8.0
Children under age 18 in household	**41.3**
Employment status	
Employed full-time	51.8
Employed part-time	12.3
Retired	15.9
Not employed	19.7
Household income	
Under $15,000	14.0
$15,000 to $24,999	18.0
$25,000 to $49,999	33.6
$50,000 to $74,999	14.0
$75,000 or more	10.9
Median income	$35,000

Source: The National Alliance for Caregiving and The American Association of Retired Persons, Family Caregiving in the U.S.—Findings from a National Survey, *Final Report, 1997*

Most Older Americans Support Physician-Assisted Suicide

Even among people aged 70 or older, most support euthanasia.

Support for allowing the incurably ill to hasten their deaths has grown over the past few decades. The majority of Americans (68 percent) favor giving the terminally ill the option of having a doctor end their lives. This is a larger majority than the 59 percent who favored it in 1977.

While older Americans are not as willing as younger Americans to allow doctors to end the life of the terminally ill, they are much more supportive than they once were. Among people aged 60 to 69, support has grown from 55 to 61 percent between 1977 and 1996. Among Americans aged 70 or older, a 45 percent minority favored it in 1977. By 1996 the proportion had grown to the 57 percent majority.

♦ As younger generations of Americans replace today's elderly, support for euthanasia is likely to continue to grow.

Support for euthanasia has grown

(percent of people aged 50 or older who favor physician-assisted suicide for the terminally ill, 1977 and 1996)

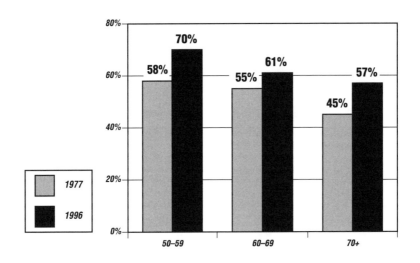

Attitudes toward Physician-Assisted Suicide, 1977 to 1996

"When a person has a disease that cannot be cured, do you think doctors should be allowed by law to end the patient's life by some painless means if the patient and his family request it?"

(percent of people aged 18 or older responding by age, 1977–96)

	yes		no	
	1996	*1977*	*1996*	*1977*
Total people	**68%**	**59%**	**28%**	**36%**
Aged 18 to 29	75	70	23	26
Aged 30 to 39	68	60	28	37
Aged 40 to 49	68	57	28	40
Aged 50 to 59	70	58	26	37
Aged 60 to 69	61	55	35	40
Aged 70 or older	57	45	35	43

Note: Numbers may not add to 100 because "don't know" and no answer are not included.
Source: General Social Surveys, National Opinion Research Center, University of Chicago; calculations by New Strategist

Heart Disease and Cancer
Kill Most Older Americans

More than one-third of deaths among Americans aged 55 or older are due to heart disease.

Among the 2.3 million Americans who died in 1996, 84 percent were aged 55 or older. More than half (54 percent) were aged 75 or older. People aged 55 or older account for 93 percent of all deaths due to heart disease, 94 percent of deaths due to pneumonia, and 99 percent of deaths due to Alzheimer's disease. But this age group accounts for only 8 percent of deaths due to HIV infection, 28 percent of suicides, and 40 percent of accident victims.

Cancer is the leading cause of death for people aged 55 to 74. Only among people aged 75 or older does heart disease rise to the number one spot. It accounts for 35 percent of deaths to 75-to-84-year-olds and for 41 percent of deaths among people aged 85 or older.

♦ With most Americans now living to old age, growing numbers of Americans must cope with the disabilities of aging. The expanding market of consumers with special needs provides opportunities for businesses ranging from medical equipment manufacturers to health care service providers.

Causes of Death for People Aged 55 or Older, 1996: Number of Deaths

(number of deaths among total people and people aged 55 or older, for the 10 leading causes of death among the total population and the population aged 65 or older, 1996

	total	total	55 to 64	65 to 74	75 to 84	85+
			aged 55 or older			
Total deaths	**2,314,690**	**1,947,450**	**233,725**	**473,894**	**663,290**	**576,541**
Diseases of heart*	733,361	679,534	67,335	144,915	229,762	237,522
Malignant neoplasms*	539,533	469,816	86,828	160,864	154,480	67,644
Cerebrovascular diseases*	159,942	150,164	9,676	25,306	54,520	60,662
Chronic obstructive pulmonary diseases*	106,027	101,516	10,046	30,171	40,952	20,347
Accidents*	94,948	37,701	6,871	8,780	11,662	10,388
Pneumonia and influenza*	83,727	78,592	3,613	10,597	26,355	38,027
Diabetes mellitus*	61,767	54,805	8,429	16,553	18,989	10,834
Human immunodeficiency virus	31,130	2,402	1,794	503	87	18
Suicide	30,903	8,780	2,925	2,806	2,290	759
Chronic liver disease and cirrhosis	25,047	15,349	5,312	5,725	3,507	805
Nephritis, nephrotic syndrome, nephrosis*	24,304	22,548	1,679	4,633	8,353	7,883
Septicemia*	21,423	19,096	1,759	4,058	6,781	6,498
Alzheimer's disease*	21,397	21,363	286	2,049	8,319	10,709
All other causes	381,181	285,786	27,172	56,934	97,233	104,447

* One of the 10 leading causes of death among people aged 65 or older.
Source: National Center for Health Statistics, Deaths: Final Data for 1996, National Vital Statistics Report, vol. 47, no. 9, 1998; calculations by New Strategist

Causes of Death for People Aged 55 or Older, 1996: Percent Distribution by Cause

(percent distribution of deaths by cause for total people and people aged 55 or older, for the 10 leading causes of death among the total population and the population aged 65 or older, 1996)

| | | aged 55 or older | | | | |
	total	total	55 to 64	65 to 74	75 to 84	85+
Total deaths	100.0%	100.0%	100.0%	100.0%	100.0%	100.0%
Diseases of heart*	31.7	34.9	28.8	30.6	34.6	41.2
Malignant neoplasms*	23.3	24.1	37.1	33.9	23.3	11.7
Cerebrovascular diseases*	6.9	7.7	4.1	5.3	8.2	10.5
Chronic obstructive pulmonary diseases*	4.6	5.2	4.3	6.4	6.2	3.5
Accidents*	4.1	1.9	2.9	1.9	1.8	1.8
Pneumonia and influenza*	3.6	4.0	1.5	2.2	4.0	6.6
Diabetes mellitus*	2.7	2.8	3.6	3.5	2.9	1.9
Human immunodeficiency virus	1.3	0.1	0.8	0.1	0.0	0.0
Suicide	1.3	0.5	1.3	0.6	0.3	0.1
Chronic liver disease and cirrhosis	1.1	0.8	2.3	1.2	0.5	0.1
Nephritis, nephrotic syndrome, nephrosis*	1.0	1.2	0.7	1.0	1.3	1.4
Septicemia*	0.9	1.0	0.8	0.9	1.0	1.1
Alzheimer's disease*	0.9	1.1	0.1	0.4	1.3	1.9
All other causes	16.5	14.7	11.6	12.0	14.7	18.1

* One of the 10 leading causes of death among people aged 65 or older.
Source: National Center for Health Statistics, Deaths: Final Data for 1996, National Vital Statistics Report, vol. 47, no. 9, 1998; calculations by New Strategist

Causes of Death for People Aged 55 or Older, 1996:
Percent Distribution by Age

(percent distribution of deaths by age for people aged 55 or older, for the 10 leading causes of death among the total population and the population aged 65 or older, 1996)

	total	aged 55 or older				
		total	55 to 64	65 to 74	75 to 84	85+
Total deaths	**100.0%**	**84.1%**	**10.1%**	**20.5%**	**28.7%**	**24.9%**
Diseases of heart*	100.0	92.7	9.2	19.8	31.3	32.4
Malignant neoplasms*	100.0	87.1	16.1	29.8	28.6	12.5
Cerebrovascular diseases*	100.0	93.9	6.0	15.8	34.1	37.9
Chronic obstructive pulmonary diseases*	100.0	95.7	9.5	28.5	38.6	19.2
Accidents*	100.0	39.7	7.2	9.2	12.3	10.9
Pneumonia and influenza*	100.0	93.9	4.3	12.7	31.5	45.4
Diabetes mellitus*	100.0	88.7	13.6	26.8	30.7	17.5
Human immunodeficiency virus	100.0	7.7	5.8	1.6	0.3	0.1
Suicide	100.0	28.4	9.5	9.1	7.4	2.5
Chronic liver disease and cirrhosis	100.0	61.3	21.2	22.9	14.0	3.2
Nephritis, nephrotic syndrome, nephrosis*	100.0	92.8	6.9	19.1	34.4	32.4
Septicemia*	100.0	89.1	8.2	18.9	31.7	30.3
Alzheimer's disease*	100.0	99.8	1.3	9.6	38.9	50.0
All other causes	100.0	75.0	7.1	14.9	25.5	27.4

* One of the 10 leading causes of death among people aged 65 or older.
Source: National Center for Health Statistics, Deaths: Final Data for 1996, National Vital Statistics Report, vol. 47, no. 9, 1998; calculations by New Strategist

Leading Causes of Death for People Aged 55 to 64, 1996

(number and percent distribution of deaths for the 10 leading causes of death for people aged 55 to 64, 1996)

		number	*percent*
	All causes	**233,725**	**100.0%**
1.	Malignant neoplasms	86,828	37.1
2.	Diseases of heart	67,335	28.8
3.	Chronic obstructive pulmonary disease	10,046	4.3
4.	Cerebrovascular diseases	9,676	4.1
5.	Diabetes mellitus	8,429	3.6
6.	Accidents	6,871	2.9
7.	Chronic liver disease and cirrhosis	5,312	2.3
8.	Pneumonia and influenza	3,613	1.5
9.	Suicide	2,925	1.3
10.	Human immunodeficiency syndrome	1,794	0.8
	All other causes	30,896	13.2

Source: National Center for Health Statistics, Deaths: Final Data for 1996, *National Vital Statistics Report, vol. 47, no. 9, 1998; calculations by New Strategist*

Leading Causes of Death for People Aged 65 to 74, 1996

(number and percent distribution of deaths for the 10 leading causes of death for people aged 65 to 74, 1996)

		number	*percent*
	All causes	**473,894**	**100.0%**
1.	Malignant neoplasms	160,864	33.9
2.	Diseases of heart	144,915	30.6
3.	Chronic obstructive pulmonary diseases and allied conditions	30,171	6.4
4.	Cerebrovascular diseases	25,306	5.3
5.	Diabetes mellitus	16,553	3.5
6.	Pneumonia and influenza	10,597	2.2
7.	Accidents and adverse effects	8,780	1.9
8.	Chronic liver disease and cirrhosis	5,725	1.2
9.	Nephritis, nephrotic syndrome, and nephrosis	4,633	1.0
10.	Septicemia	4,058	0.9
	All other causes	62,292	13.1

Source: National Center for Health Statistics, Deaths: Final Data for 1996, *National Vital Statistics Report, vol. 47, no. 9, 1998; calculations by New Strategist*

Leading Causes of Death for People Aged 75 to 84, 1996

(number and percent distribution of deaths for the 10 leading causes of death for people aged 75 to 84, 1996)

		number	*percent*
	All causes	**663,290**	**100.0%**
1.	Diseases of heart	229,762	34.6
2.	Malignant neoplasms	154,480	23.3
3.	Cerebrovascular diseases	54,520	8.2
4.	Chronic obstructive pulmonary diseases and allied conditions	40,952	6.2
5.	Pneumonia and influenza	26,355	4.0
6.	Diabetes mellitus	18,989	2.9
7.	Accidents and adverse effects	11,662	1.8
8.	Nephritis, nephrotic syndrome, and nephrosis	8,353	1.3
9.	Alzheimer's disease	8,319	1.3
10.	Septicemia	6,781	1.0
	All other causes	103,117	15.5

Source: National Center for Health Statistics, Deaths: Final Data for 1996, *National Vital Statistics Report, vol. 47, no. 9, 1998; calculations by New Strategist*

Leading Causes of Death for People Aged 85 or Older, 1996

(number and percent distribution of deaths for the 10 leading causes of death for people aged 85 or older, 1996)

		number	percent
	All causes	**576,541**	**100.0%**
1.	Diseases of heart	237,522	41.2
2.	Malignant neoplasms	67,644	11.7
3.	Cerebrovascular diseases	60,662	10.5
4.	Pneumonia and influenza	38,027	6.6
5.	Chronic obstructive pulmonary diseases and allied conditions	20,347	3.5
6.	Diabetes mellitus	10,834	1.9
7.	Alzheimer's disease	10,709	1.9
8.	Accidents and adverse effects	10,388	1.8
9.	Nephritis, nephrotic syndrome, and nephrosis	7,883	1.4
10.	Septicemia	6,498	1.1
	All other causes	106,027	18.4

Source: National Center for Health Statistics, Deaths: Final Data for 1996, *National Vital Statistics Report, vol. 47, no. 9, 1998; calculations by New Strategist*

Life Expectancy at Older Ages Has Grown

The biggest gains have been made since 1950.

Between 1900 and 1997, life expectancy at age 65 grew 4.3 years for men and 6.8 years for women. In 1900, the average 65-year-old could expect to live only 12 more years. In 1997, a 65-year-old man could expect to live 16 more years, while his female counterpart could anticipate 19 additional years of life. The greatest gains in life expectancy at older ages have been made since 1950 as medical science has succeeded in curtailing deaths due to heart disease, which is the biggest killer of Americans.

Life expectancy at birth stood at 76.5 years in 1997—73.6 years for men and 79.2 years for women. At all ages, the life expectancy of females is greater than that of males. Among people aged 85, men can expect to live another 5.4 years, while women can expect 6.3 more years of life.

◆ As life expectancy has increased for older Americans, more people must learn to live with the disabilities that often accompany aging. As the large baby-boom generation enters the older age groups, services that allow them to maintain their independence will become highly popular.

Years of life remaining is up

(number of years of life remaining for people aged 65 by sex, 1900 and 1997)

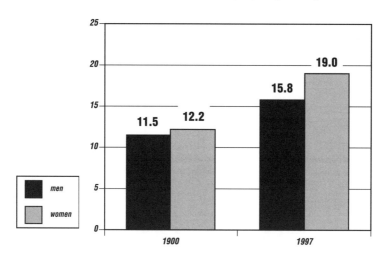

Life Expectancy at Age 65 by Sex and Race, 1900 to 1997

(years of life remaining at age 65 by sex and race; change in years of life remaining for selected years, 1900–97)

	total		white		black	
	men	*women*	*men*	*women*	*men*	*women*
1997	15.8	19.0	15.9	19.1	14.2	17.4
1990	15.1	18.9	15.2	19.1	13.2	17.2
1980	14.1	18.3	14.2	18.4	13.0	16.8
1970	13.1	17.0	13.1	17.1	12.5	15.7
1960	12.8	15.8	12.9	15.9	12.7	15.1
1950	12.8	15.0	12.8	15.1	12.9	14.9
1900	11.5	12.2	11.5	12.2	10.4	11.4
Change in years						
1990 to 1997	0.7	0.1	0.7	0.0	1.0	0.2
1950 to 1997	3.0	4.0	3.1	4.0	1.3	2.5
1900 to 1997	4.3	6.8	4.4	6.9	3.8	6.0

Source: National Center for Health Statistics, Births and Deaths: United States, 1996, *Monthly Vital Statistics Report, Vol. 46 No. 1 (S)2, 1997; and* Births and Deaths: Preliminary Data for 1997, *National Vital Statistics Reports, Vol. 47, No. 4, 1998; calculations by New Strategist*

Life Expectancy of People Aged 55 or Older by Sex and Race, 1997

(years of life remaining at birth and at selected ages between 55 and 85 by sex and race, 1997)

		men			women		
	total	total	white	black	total	white	black
At birth	76.5	73.6	74.3	67.3	79.2	79.8	74.7
Aged 55	25.3	23.2	23.5	20.3	27.1	27.3	24.7
Aged 60	21.3	19.3	19.5	17.0	22.9	23.1	20.9
Aged 65	17.6	15.8	15.9	14.2	19.0	19.1	17.4
Aged 70	14.2	12.6	12.7	11.4	15.3	15.4	14.1
Aged 75	11.1	9.8	9.8	9.2	12.0	12.0	11.3
Aged 80	8.3	7.4	7.3	7.1	8.9	8.9	8.5
Aged 85	6.0	5.4	5.3	5.4	6.3	6.3	6.2

Source: National Center for Health Statistics, Births and Deaths: Preliminary Data for 1997, *National Vital Statistics Reports, Vol. 47, No. 4, 1998*

4

Income

◆ The median income of householders aged 65 or older grew 21 percent between 1980 and 1997, after adjusting for inflation.

◆ Fifteen percent of householders aged 55 to 59 have annual incomes of $100,000 or more, as do 11 percent of those aged 60 to 64.

◆ Married couples aged 55 or older had a median household income of $42,127 in 1997, compared to an average of $28,549 for all households in the age group.

◆ The income of men aged 65 or older grew 24 percent between 1980 and 1997, while their female counterparts saw their incomes grow 22 percent.

◆ Among full-time workers aged 55 or older, non-Hispanic white men had a median income of $47,422, versus $31,111 for blacks and $28,761 for Hispanics.

◆ The median income of women aged 55 or older who work full-time ranged from a high of $31,199 for non-Hispanic whites to $18,335 for Hispanics.

◆ Social Security is the single most common source of income for Americans aged 65 or older; benefits averaged $8,690 per person in 1997.

◆ Thirteen percent of women and 7 percent of men aged 55 or older are poor.

Above-Average Income Growth for Householders Aged 55 or Older

Income of householders aged 65 or older has grown 21 percent since 1980.

The $41,356 median income of households headed by people aged 55 to 64 exceeded that of the average household by several thousand dollars in 1997. While many householders in this age group are retired, those who are still in the labor force are enjoying peak earnings. Householders aged 55 to 64 have seen their median household income climb 9 percent since 1980, after adjusting for inflation. This compares with a gain of 7 percent for households overall.

The median income of householders aged 65 or older has grown an enormous 21 percent since 1980, after adjusting for inflation—rising from $17,125 to $21,761 in 1997. Most of this growth occurred before 1990. Between 1990 and 1997, the income of elderly householders rose just 0.3 percent as interest rates (a major source of income for many elderly people) fell during the recession. This lull appears to have been temporary, however, since the incomes of people aged 65 or older grew at an above-average 4 percent between 1996 and 1997.

♦ The incomes of older households should continue to rise as the dual-earner couples of the baby-boom generation enter the 55-to-64 age group and as better-educated and more affluent cohorts fill the 65-plus age groups.

Incomes of elderly should continue to rise

(percent change in median income of total households and households headed by people aged 55 or older, 1980 to 1997; in 1997 dollars)

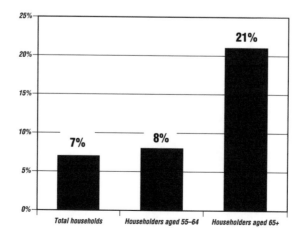

Median Income of Households Headed by People Aged 55 or Older, 1980 to 1997

(median income of total households and households headed by people aged 55 or older, 1980 to 1997; in 1997 dollars)

			aged 65 or older		
	total	*55–64*	*total*	*65–74*	*75+*
1997	$37,005	$41,356	$20,761	$25,292	$17,079
1996	36,306	40,729	19,894	23,948	16,362
1995	35,887	40,101	20,111	24,255	16,157
1994	34,942	38,156	19,597	23,200	15,954
1993	34,700	37,180	19,717	23,670	15,914
1992	35,047	38,887	19,602	23,304	15,581
1991	35,501	39,246	20,004	23,643	16,419
1990	36,770	39,744	20,698	24,919	16,148
1989	37,415	39,891	20,413	24,540	15,663
1988	36,937	39,213	20,246	23,706	16,017
1987	36,820	38,938	20,406	24,191	15,948
1986	36,460	39,211	20,275	–	–
1985	35,229	38,122	19,770	–	–
1984	34,626	37,219	19,771	–	–
1983	33,655	36,706	18,883	–	–
1982	33,864	37,061	18,536	–	–
1981	33,978	37,481	17,641	–	–
1980	34,538	38,120	17,125	–	–
Percent change					
1996–1997	1.9%	1.5%	4.4%	5.6%	4.4%
1990–1997	0.6	4.1	0.3	1.5	9.0
1980–1997	7.1	8.5	21.2	–	–

Note: (–) means data are not available.
Source: Bureau of the Census, Internet web site <http://www.census.gov>; calculations by New Strategist

Many Older Householders Are Affluent

More than 2 million householders aged 55 or older have incomes of $100,000 or more.

Household incomes fall as people age because most retire from the labor force and live on savings, pensions, and Social Security benefits. The median income of households headed by people aged 55 or older stood at $28,549 in 1997—below the median of $37,005 for all households. But incomes vary dramatically by age. The median household income of householders aged 55 to 59 was well above the national average at $45,985, while that of householders aged 75 or older was well below at $17,079.

Many older householders are affluent. Fifteen percent of householders aged 55 to 59 have annual household incomes of $100,000 or more, as do 11 percent of those aged 60 to 64. The proportion of households with such lofty incomes declines with age to fewer than 3 percent among householders aged 75 or older. Among people aged 75 or older, nearly one in four has an income below $10,000.

♦ If baby boomers stay in the labor force longer than their parents did—as seems likely—the household incomes of 55-to-64-year-olds should grow sharply as working boomers enter the age group after the turn of the century.

Income Distribution of Households Headed by People Aged 55 or Older, 1997: Total Households

(number and percent distribution of total households and households headed people aged 55 or older, by income, 1997; households in thousands as of 1998)

	total	aged 55 or older								
		total	aged 55 to 64			aged 65 or older				
			total	55–59	60–64	total	aged 65 to 74			75+
							total	65–69	70–74	
Total households	**102,528**	**34,569**	**13,072**	**6,974**	**6,098**	**21,497**	**11,272**	**5,755**	**5,517**	**10,226**
Under $10,000	11,296	5,515	1,439	638	800	4,076	1,726	859	866	2,351
$10,000 to $19,999	16,163	8,074	1,744	787	960	6,330	2,751	1,217	1,532	3,579
$20,000 to $29,999	14,319	5,460	1,593	837	756	3,867	2,063	965	1,099	1,805
$30,000 to $39,999	12,784	3,905	1,505	755	750	2,400	1,506	806	701	894
$40,000 to $49,999	10,587	2,878	1,448	745	702	1,430	916	500	416	512
$50,000 to $59,999	8,728	2,093	1,174	637	536	919	605	323	283	310
$60,000 to $69,999	7,049	1,398	794	484	309	604	404	236	168	200
$70,000 to $79,999	5,153	1,038	640	397	246	398	283	176	108	116
$80,000 to $89,999	3,953	933	561	351	211	372	257	156	100	115
$90,000 to $99,999	2,834	614	426	266	160	188	110	69	39	80
$100,000 or more	9,661	2,660	1,747	1,080	667	913	650	446	204	263
Median income	$37,005	$28,549	$41,356	$45,985	$36,763	$20,761	$25,292	$28,085	$23,003	$17,079

(continued)

(continued from previous page)

	total	aged 55 or older	aged 55 to 64			aged 65 or older	aged 65 to 74			
		total	total	55–59	60–64	total	total	65–69	70–74	75+
	100.0%	100.0%	100.0%	100.0%	100.0%	100.0%	100.0%	100.0%	100.0%	100.0%
Total households										
Under $10,000	11.0	16.0	11.0	9.1	13.1	19.0	15.3	14.9	15.7	23.0
$10,000 to $19,999	15.8	23.4	13.3	11.3	15.7	29.4	24.4	21.1	27.8	35.0
$20,000 to $29,999	14.0	15.8	12.2	12.0	12.4	18.0	18.3	16.8	19.9	17.7
$30,000 to $39,999	12.5	11.3	11.5	10.8	12.3	11.2	13.4	14.0	12.7	8.7
$40,000 to $49,999	10.3	8.3	11.1	10.7	11.5	6.7	8.1	8.7	7.5	5.0
$50,000 to $59,999	8.5	6.1	9.0	9.1	8.8	4.3	5.4	5.6	5.1	3.0
$60,000 to $69,999	6.9	4.0	6.1	6.9	5.1	2.8	3.6	4.1	3.0	2.0
$70,000 to $79,999	5.0	3.0	4.9	5.7	4.0	1.9	2.5	3.1	2.0	1.1
$80,000 to $89,999	3.9	2.7	4.3	5.0	3.5	1.7	2.3	2.7	1.8	1.1
$90,000 to $99,999	2.8	1.8	3.3	3.8	2.6	0.9	1.0	1.2	0.7	0.8
$100,000 or more	9.4	7.7	13.4	15.5	10.9	4.2	5.8	7.7	3.7	2.6

Source: Bureau of the Census, unpublished tables from the 1998 Current Population Survey, Internet web site <http://www.bls.census.gov/cps/ads/1998/sdata.htm>; calculations by New Strategist

Older Whites Have Much Higher Incomes Than Blacks or Hispanics

The greatest income disparity is in the 55-to-64 age group.

White householders aged 55 to 59 had a median household income of $48,625 in 1997, far greater than the $29,120 median for blacks and $29,174 median for Hispanics. Seventeen percent of white householders in this age group had a household income of $100,000 or more compared to 6 percent of blacks and 7 percent of Hispanics. White incomes are higher than black incomes because white households in the age group are much more likely to be headed by married couples—many of whom are dual earners. White incomes exceed those of Hispanics because many Hispanics are immigrants with little education, earning power, or pension benefits.

Hispanic householders aged 75 or older have the lowest household incomes, just $11,015 in 1997. The income of black households in the age group is not much greater, at $12,101. White householders aged 75 or older had a median household income of $17,410 in 1997.

◆ The income disparities among older householders by race and ethnicity will persist in the future because their underlying causes—the small proportion of married-couple households among blacks and the immigrant status of Hispanics—also exist in younger generations of Americans.

Income Distribution of Households Headed by People Aged 55 or Older, 1997: Black Households

(number and percent distribution of total black households and black households headed people aged 55 or older, by income, 1997; households in thousands as of 1998)

	total	aged 55 or older	aged 55 to 64			aged 65 or older	aged 65 to 74			75+
		total	total	55–59	60–64	total	total	65–69	70–74	
Total black households	12,474	3,319	1,441	763	678	1,878	1,123	572	551	755
Under $10,000	2,672	969	312	162	151	657	346	161	184	313
$10,000 to $19,999	2,491	815	290	129	160	525	309	142	168	218
$20,000 to $29,999	1,996	437	181	102	78	256	176	82	93	81
$30,000 to $39,999	1,521	353	187	88	100	166	123	67	56	43
$40,000 to $49,999	1,170	270	164	83	79	106	69	45	25	36
$50,000 to $59,999	842	131	75	54	21	56	24	12	11	33
$60,000 to $69,999	598	99	65	47	19	34	19	15	4	15
$70,000 to $79,999	337	54	40	17	23	14	11	8	3	3
$80,000 to $89,999	273	45	34	18	15	11	11	7	4	–
$90,000 to $99,999	157	32	19	13	6	13	6	6	–	6
$100,000 or more	415	111	72	48	24	39	30	27	4	8
Median income	$25,050	$19,932	$27,350	$29,120	$23,620	$14,241	$16,287	$18,551	$14,507	$12,101

(continued)

(continued from previous page)

		aged 55 or older				aged 65 or older			
			aged 55 to 64				aged 65 to 74		
Total black households	total	total	total	55–59	60–64	total	total	65–69	70–74	75+
	100.0%	100.0%	100.0%	100.0%	100.0%	100.0%	100.0%	100.0%	100.0%	100.0%
Under $10,000	21.4	29.2	21.7	21.2	22.3	35.0	30.8	28.1	33.4	41.5
$10,000 to $19,999	20.0	24.6	20.1	16.9	23.6	28.0	27.5	24.8	30.5	28.9
$20,000 to $29,999	16.0	13.2	12.6	13.4	11.5	13.6	15.7	14.3	16.9	10.7
$30,000 to $39,999	12.2	10.6	13.0	11.5	14.7	8.8	11.0	11.7	10.2	5.7
$40,000 to $49,999	9.4	8.1	11.4	10.9	11.7	5.6	6.1	7.9	4.5	4.8
$50,000 to $59,999	6.8	3.9	5.2	7.1	3.1	3.0	2.1	2.1	2.0	4.4
$60,000 to $69,999	4.8	3.0	4.5	6.2	2.8	1.8	1.7	2.6	0.7	2.0
$70,000 to $79,999	2.7	1.6	2.8	2.2	3.4	0.7	1.0	1.4	0.5	0.4
$80,000 to $89,999	2.2	1.4	2.4	2.4	2.2	0.6	1.0	1.2	0.7	–
$90,000 to $99,999	1.3	1.0	1.3	1.7	0.9	0.7	0.5	1.0	–	0.8
$100,000 or more	3.3	3.3	5.0	6.3	3.5	2.1	2.7	4.7	0.7	1.1

Note: (–) means sample is too small to make a reliable estimate.
Source: Bureau of the Census, unpublished tables from the 1998 Current Population Survey, Internet web site <http://www.bls.census.gov/cps/ads/1998/sdata.htm>; calculations by New Strategist

Income Distribution of Households Headed by People Aged 55 or Older, 1997: Hispanic Households

(number and percent distribution of total Hispanic households and Hispanic households headed people aged 55 or older, by income, 1997; households in thousands as of 1998)

	total	aged 55 or older	aged 55 to 64			aged 65 or older	aged 65 to 74			75+
		total	total	55–59	60–64	total	total	65–69	70–74	
Total Hispanic households	8,590	1,805	889	474	415	916	566	318	248	350
Under $10,000	1,441	510	174	87	86	336	173	91	81	164
$10,000 to $19,999	1,756	399	165	72	94	234	147	77	70	88
$20,000 to $29,999	1,523	261	129	82	46	132	94	52	42	39
$30,000 to $39,999	1,152	178	106	48	56	72	51	35	16	20
$40,000 to $49,999	894	142	76	49	27	66	43	28	15	23
$50,000 to $59,999	536	89	74	46	29	15	11	6	5	3
$60,000 to $69,999	368	64	48	18	29	16	11	7	4	5
$70,000 to $79,999	272	39	27	19	9	12	8	4	4	4
$80,000 to $89,999	176	35	28	19	9	7	7	6	2	–
$90,000 to $99,999	123	17	12	3	9	5	5	3	1	–
$100,000 or more	351	71	51	32	20	20	17	9	8	3
Median income	$26,628	$20,807	$27,648	$29,174	$24,316	$14,168	$15,885	$17,732	$14,044	$11,015

(continued)

(continued from previous page)

	total	aged 55 or older					aged 65 or older			
		total	aged 55 to 64			total	aged 65 to 74			75+
			total	55–59	60–64		total	65–69	70–74	
Total Hispanic households	100.0%	100.0%	100.0%	100.0%	100.0%	100.0%	100.0%	100.0%	100.0%	100.0%
Under $10,000	16.8	28.3	19.6	18.4	20.7	36.7	30.6	28.6	32.7	46.9
$10,000 to $19,999	20.4	22.1	18.6	15.2	22.7	25.5	26.0	24.2	28.2	25.1
$20,000 to $29,999	17.7	14.5	14.5	17.3	11.1	14.4	16.6	16.4	16.9	11.1
$30,000 to $39,999	13.4	9.9	11.9	10.1	13.5	7.9	9.0	11.0	6.5	5.7
$40,000 to $49,999	10.4	7.9	8.5	10.3	6.5	7.2	7.6	8.8	6.0	6.6
$50,000 to $59,999	6.2	4.9	8.3	9.7	7.0	1.6	1.9	1.9	2.0	0.9
$60,000 to $69,999	4.3	3.5	5.4	3.8	7.0	1.7	1.9	2.2	1.6	1.4
$70,000 to $79,999	3.2	2.2	3.0	4.0	2.2	1.3	1.4	1.3	1.6	1.1
$80,000 to $89,999	2.0	1.9	3.1	4.0	2.2	0.8	1.2	1.9	0.8	–
$90,000 to $99,999	1.4	0.9	1.3	0.6	2.2	0.5	0.9	0.9	0.4	–
$100,000 or more	4.1	3.9	5.7	6.8	4.8	2.2	3.0	2.8	3.2	0.9

Note: (–) means sample is too small to make a reliable estimate.
Source: Bureau of the Census, unpublished tables from the 1998 Current Population Survey, Internet web site <http://www.bls.census.gov/cps/ads/1998/sdata.htm>; calculations by New Strategist

Income Distribution of Households Headed by People Aged 55 or Older, 1997: White Households

(number and percent distribution of total white households and white households headed people aged 55 or older, by income, 1997; households in thousands as of 1998)

	total	aged 55 or older								
		total	aged 55 to 64			aged 65 or older				
			total	55–59	60–64	total	aged 65 to 74			75+
							total	65–69	70–74	
Total white households	86,106	30,359	11,163	5,946	5,217	19,196	9,917	5,019	4,898	9,279
Under $10,000	8,188	4,394	1,077	451	626	3,317	1,336	670	667	1,980
$10,000 to $19,999	13,152	7,124	1,402	632	770	5,722	2,395	1,052	1,343	3,327
$20,000 to $29,999	11,852	4,912	1,363	709	654	3,549	1,858	860	998	1,691
$30,000 to $39,999	10,778	3,459	1,270	634	635	2,189	1,355	718	638	834
$40,000 to $49,999	9,004	2,531	1,225	619	605	1,306	836	445	391	470
$50,000 to $59,999	7,590	1,898	1,063	563	499	835	559	288	271	275
$60,000 to $69,999	6,138	1,265	705	423	282	560	377	215	162	183
$70,000 to $79,999	4,612	941	578	365	215	363	260	162	97	103
$80,000 to $89,999	3,507	853	509	321	188	344	242	145	96	103
$90,000 to $99,999	2,526	555	392	248	143	163	94	55	39	68
$100,000 or more	8,762	2,428	1,580	982	598	848	605	410	195	244
Median income	$38,972	$29,345	$43,053	$48,625	$38,653	$21,374	$26,363	$29,081	$24,232	$17,410

(continued)

(continued from previous page)

	total	aged 55 or older	aged 55 to 64			aged 65 or older	aged 65 to 74			
		total	total	55–59	60–64	total	total	65–69	70–74	75+
Total white households	100.0%	100.0%	100.0%	100.0%	100.0%	100.0%	100.0%	100.0%	100.0%	100.0%
Under $10,000	9.5	14.5	9.6	7.6	12.0	17.3	13.5	13.3	13.6	21.3
$10,000 to $19,999	15.3	23.5	12.6	10.6	14.8	29.8	24.2	21.0	27.4	35.9
$20,000 to $29,999	13.8	16.2	12.2	11.9	12.5	18.5	18.7	17.1	20.4	18.2
$30,000 to $39,999	12.5	11.4	11.4	10.7	12.2	11.4	13.7	14.3	13.0	9.0
$40,000 to $49,999	10.5	8.3	11.0	10.4	11.6	6.8	8.4	8.9	8.0	5.1
$50,000 to $59,999	8.8	6.3	9.5	9.5	9.6	4.3	5.6	5.7	5.5	3.0
$60,000 to $69,999	7.1	4.2	6.3	7.1	5.4	2.9	3.8	4.3	3.3	2.0
$70,000 to $79,999	5.4	3.1	5.2	6.1	4.1	1.9	2.6	3.2	2.0	1.1
$80,000 to $89,999	4.1	2.8	4.6	5.4	3.6	1.8	2.4	2.9	2.0	1.1
$90,000 to $99,999	2.9	1.8	3.5	4.2	2.7	0.8	0.9	1.1	0.8	0.7
$100,000 or more	10.2	8.0	14.2	16.5	11.5	4.4	6.1	8.2	4.0	2.6

Source: Bureau of the Census, unpublished tables from the 1998 Current Population Survey, Internet web site <http://www.bls.census.gov/cps/ads/1998/sdata.htm>; calculations by New Strategist

Married Couples Have the Highest Incomes

Older women who live alone have the lowest incomes.

Married couples have above-average incomes regardless of age. Among all households headed by people aged 55 or older, the median income of married couples stood at $42,127 in 1997. For couples aged 55 to 59, median income was a lofty $60,830 because many are dual-earners. Fully 22 percent had incomes of $100,000 or more in 1997. For couples aged 60 to 64, median income falls to $47,931 as retirement becomes more prevalent. For households headed by people aged 65 or older, married couples had a median income of $31,239 in 1997. While this median is not as high as that for male-headed families, married couples are much more numerous.

Women who live alone have the smallest incomes in all older age groups. Among householders aged 75 or older, women who live alone had a median income of just $11,524 in 1997, well below the $17,079 median for all households in the age group.

♦ The household incomes of older Americans should rise in the years ahead as generations of working women and dual-earner couples fill the 55-plus age groups.

Income Distribution of Households by Household Type, 1997: Aged 55 or Older

(number and percent distribution of households headed by people aged 55 or older, by income and household type, 1997; households in thousands as of 1998)

		family households			nonfamily households			
					female householder		male householder	
	total	married couples	female hh, no spouse present	male hh, no spouse present	total	living alone	total	living alone
Total households	**34,569**	**17,144**	**2,775**	**738**	**10,080**	**9,725**	**3,831**	**3,498**
Under $10,000	5,514	662	321	35	3,610	3,582	887	860
$10,000 to $19,999	8,077	2,522	659	115	3,591	3,504	1,185	1,121
$20,000 to $29,999	5,460	2,919	526	129	1,290	1,239	598	533
$30,000 to $39,999	3,905	2,408	387	125	627	570	357	326
$40,000 to $49,999	2,877	1,913	322	71	311	290	260	227
$50,000 to $59,999	2,092	1,481	206	63	204	184	137	113
$60,000 to $69,999	1,397	1,002	113	58	122	112	103	82
$70,000 to $79,999	1,041	800	51	35	82	60	72	55
$80,000 to $89,999	934	756	47	35	49	31	47	33
$90,000 to $99,999	614	478	50	24	47	40	17	14
$100,000 or more	2,660	2,201	94	50	147	115	168	135
Median income	$28,549	$42,127	$27,521	$37,964	$13,568	$13,179	$19,743	$18,675
Total households	**100.0%**	**100.0%**	**100.0%**	**100.0%**	**100.0%**	**100.0%**	**100.0%**	**100.0%**
Under $10,000	16.0	3.9	11.6	4.7	35.8	36.8	23.2	24.6
$10,000 to $19,999	23.4	14.7	23.7	15.6	35.6	36.0	30.9	32.0
$20,000 to $29,999	15.8	17.0	19.0	17.5	12.8	12.7	15.6	15.2
$30,000 to $39,999	11.3	14.0	13.9	16.9	6.2	5.9	9.3	9.3
$40,000 to $49,999	8.3	11.2	11.6	9.6	3.1	3.0	6.8	6.5
$50,000 to $59,999	6.1	8.6	7.4	8.5	2.0	1.9	3.6	3.2
$60,000 to $69,999	4.0	5.8	4.1	7.9	1.2	1.2	2.7	2.3
$70,000 to $79,999	3.0	4.7	1.8	4.7	0.8	0.6	1.9	1.6
$80,000 to $89,999	2.7	4.4	1.7	4.7	0.5	0.3	1.2	0.9
$90,000 to $99,999	1.8	2.8	1.8	3.3	0.5	0.4	0.4	0.4
$100,000 or more	7.7	12.8	3.4	6.8	1.5	1.2	4.4	3.9

Source: Bureau of the Census, unpublished tables from the 1998 Current Population Survey, Internet web site <http://www.bls.census.gov/cps/ads/1998/sdata.htm>; calculations by New Strategist

Income Distribution of Households by
Household Type, 1997: Aged 55 to 59

(number and percent distribution of households headed by people aged 55 to 59, by income and household type, 1997; households in thousands as of 1998)

| | | family households | | | nonfamily households | | | |
| | | | | | female householder | | male householder | |
	total	married couples	female hh, no spouse present	male hh, no spouse present	total	living alone	total	living alone
Total households	**6,974**	**4,192**	**679**	**213**	**1,127**	**997**	**763**	**656**
Under $10,000	638	107	103	9	275	274	145	136
$10,000 to $19,999	787	251	116	24	247	221	146	136
$20,000 to $29,999	837	372	122	32	207	197	103	79
$30,000 to $39,999	755	415	85	34	133	118	86	80
$40,000 to $49,999	745	474	85	22	77	63	86	76
$50,000 to $59,999	637	448	69	26	57	43	37	27
$60,000 to $69,999	484	348	32	24	28	28	53	43
$70,000 to $79,999	397	317	12	11	25	8	32	24
$80,000 to $89,999	351	304	16	6	18	11	7	6
$90,000 to $99,999	266	218	18	9	16	11	7	5
$100,000 or more	1,080	938	21	16	45	26	60	42
Median income	$45,985	$60,830	$29,846	$44,895	$21,443	$20,172	$28,597	$26,878
Total households	**100.0%**	**100.0%**	**100.0%**	**100.0%**	**100.0%**	**100.0%**	**100.0%**	**100.0%**
Under $10,000	9.1	2.6	15.2	4.2	24.4	27.5	19.0	20.7
$10,000 to $19,999	11.3	6.0	17.1	11.3	21.9	22.2	19.1	20.7
$20,000 to $29,999	12.0	8.9	18.0	15.0	18.4	19.8	13.5	12.0
$30,000 to $39,999	10.8	9.9	12.5	16.0	11.8	11.8	11.3	12.2
$40,000 to $49,999	10.7	11.3	12.5	10.3	6.8	6.3	11.3	11.6
$50,000 to $59,999	9.1	10.7	10.2	12.2	5.1	4.3	4.8	4.1
$60,000 to $69,999	6.9	8.3	4.7	11.3	2.5	2.8	6.9	6.6
$70,000 to $79,999	5.7	7.6	1.8	5.2	2.2	0.8	4.2	3.7
$80,000 to $89,999	5.0	7.3	2.4	2.8	1.6	1.1	0.9	0.9
$90,000 to $99,999	3.8	5.2	2.7	4.2	1.4	1.1	0.9	0.8
$100,000 or more	15.5	22.4	3.1	7.5	4.0	2.6	7.9	6.4

Source: Bureau of the Census, unpublished tables from the 1998 Current Population Survey, Internet web site <http://www.bls.census.gov/cps/ads/1998/sdata.htm>; calculations by New Strategist

Income Distribution of Households by Household Type, 1997: Aged 60 to 64

(number and percent distribution of households headed by people aged 60 to 64, by income and household type, 1997; households in thousands as of 1998)

	total	family households			nonfamily households			
					female householder		male householder	
		married couples	female hh, no spouse present	male hh, no spouse present	total	living alone	total	living alone
Total households	**6,098**	**3,744**	**420**	**139**	**1,209**	**1,151**	**585**	**497**
Under $10,000	800	185	49	11	391	386	166	161
$10,000 to $19,999	960	359	99	25	342	321	134	117
$20,000 to $29,999	756	443	81	18	158	150	57	46
$30,000 to $39,999	750	452	58	22	149	142	70	57
$40,000 to $49,999	702	525	47	14	60	60	56	46
$50,000 to $59,999	536	430	21	12	44	41	31	22
$60,000 to $69,999	309	256	18	6	22	20	8	7
$70,000 to $79,999	246	199	12	6	16	12	12	5
$80,000 to $89,999	211	171	11	5	11	3	12	3
$90,000 to $99,999	160	142	6	8	2	2	3	2
$100,000 or more	667	581	19	12	16	13	39	32
Median income	$36,763	$47,931	$27,721	$38,032	$15,807	$15,269	$19,480	$17,445
Total households	**100.0%**	**100.0%**	**100.0%**	**100.0%**	**100.0%**	**100.0%**	**100.0%**	**100.0%**
Under $10,000	13.1	4.9	11.7	7.9	32.3	33.5	28.4	32.4
$10,000 to $19,999	15.7	9.6	23.6	18.0	28.3	27.9	22.9	23.5
$20,000 to $29,999	12.4	11.8	19.3	12.9	13.1	13.0	9.7	9.3
$30,000 to $39,999	12.3	12.1	13.8	15.8	12.3	12.3	12.0	11.5
$40,000 to $49,999	11.5	14.0	11.2	10.1	5.0	5.2	9.6	9.3
$50,000 to $59,999	8.8	11.5	5.0	8.6	3.6	3.6	5.3	4.4
$60,000 to $69,999	5.1	6.8	4.3	4.3	1.8	1.7	1.4	1.4
$70,000 to $79,999	4.0	5.3	2.9	4.3	1.3	1.0	2.1	1.0
$80,000 to $89,999	3.5	4.6	2.6	3.6	0.9	0.3	2.1	0.6
$90,000 to $99,999	2.6	3.8	1.4	5.8	0.2	0.2	0.5	0.4
$100,000 or more	10.9	15.5	4.5	8.6	1.3	1.1	6.7	6.4

Source: Bureau of the Census, unpublished tables from the 1998 Current Population Survey, Internet web site <http://www.bls.census.gov/cps/ads/1998/sdata.htm>; calculations by New Strategist

Income Distribution of Households by Household Type, 1997: Aged 65 or Older

(number and percent distribution of households headed by people aged 65 or older, by income and household type, 1997; households in thousands as of 1998)

| | | family households | | | nonfamily households | | | |
| | | | | | female householder | | male householder | |
	total	married couples	female hh, no spouse present	male hh, no spouse present	total	living alone	total	living alone
Total households	**21,497**	**9,208**	**1,676**	**386**	**7,744**	**7,577**	**2,483**	**2,345**
Under $10,000	4,076	370	169	15	2,944	2,922	576	563
$10,000 to $19,999	6,330	1,912	444	66	3,002	2,962	905	868
$20,000 to $29,999	3,867	2,104	323	79	925	892	438	408
$30,000 to $39,999	2,400	1,541	244	69	345	310	201	189
$40,000 to $49,999	1,430	914	190	35	174	167	118	105
$50,000 to $59,999	919	603	116	25	103	100	69	64
$60,000 to $69,999	604	398	63	28	72	64	42	32
$70,000 to $79,999	398	284	27	18	41	40	28	26
$80,000 to $89,999	372	281	20	24	20	17	28	24
$90,000 to $99,999	188	118	26	7	29	27	7	7
$100,000 or more	913	682	54	22	86	76	69	61
Median income	$20,761	$31,239	$26,528	$34,109	$12,069	$11,937	$17,086	$16,634
Total households	**100.0%**	**100.0%**	**100.0%**	**100.0%**	**100.0%**	**100.0%**	**100.0%**	**100.0%**
Under $10,000	19.0	4.0	10.1	3.9	38.0	38.6	23.2	24.0
$10,000 to $19,999	29.4	20.8	26.5	17.1	38.8	39.1	36.4	37.0
$20,000 to $29,999	18.0	22.8	19.3	20.5	11.9	11.8	17.6	17.4
$30,000 to $39,999	11.2	16.7	14.6	17.9	4.5	4.1	8.1	8.1
$40,000 to $49,999	6.7	9.9	11.3	9.1	2.2	2.2	4.8	4.5
$50,000 to $59,999	4.3	6.5	6.9	6.5	1.3	1.3	2.8	2.7
$60,000 to $69,999	2.8	4.3	3.8	7.3	0.9	0.8	1.7	1.4
$70,000 to $79,999	1.9	3.1	1.6	4.7	0.5	0.5	1.1	1.1
$80,000 to $89,999	1.7	3.1	1.2	6.2	0.3	0.2	1.1	1.0
$90,000 to $99,999	0.9	1.3	1.6	1.8	0.4	0.4	0.3	0.3
$100,000 or more	4.2	7.4	3.2	5.7	1.1	1.0	2.8	2.6

Source: Bureau of the Census, unpublished tables from the 1998 Current Population Survey, Internet web site <http://www.bls.census.gov/cps/ads/1998/sdata.htm>; calculations by New Strategist

Income Distribution of Households by Household Type, 1997: Aged 65 to 69

(number and percent distribution of households headed by people aged 65 to 69, by income and household type, 1997; households in thousands as of 1998)

| | | family households | | | nonfamily households | | | |
| | | | | | female householder | | male householder | |
	total	married couples	female hh, no spouse present	male hh, no spouse present	total	living alone	total	living alone
Total households	**5,755**	**3,125**	**498**	**114**	**1,434**	**1,377**	**584**	**528**
Under $10,000	859	159	51	3	513	512	132	131
$10,000 to $19,999	1,217	458	105	19	476	458	158	139
$20,000 to $29,999	965	546	101	18	208	194	93	86
$30,000 to $39,999	806	553	80	18	93	77	61	57
$40,000 to $49,999	500	349	68	7	45	45	31	23
$50,000 to $59,999	323	224	35	6	34	31	25	25
$60,000 to $69,999	236	163	21	8	21	21	23	17
$70,000 to $79,999	176	139	6	6	7	7	18	16
$80,000 to $89,999	156	125	5	12	9	5	7	5
$90,000 to $99,999	69	52	3	3	9	9	2	2
$100,000 or more	446	358	23	13	18	17	33	28
Median income	$28,085	$36,962	$29,287	$34,934	$13,684	$13,146	$20,125	$19,675
Total households	**100.0%**	**100.0%**	**100.0%**	**100.0%**	**100.0%**	**100.0%**	**100.0%**	**100.0%**
Under $10,000	14.9	5.1	10.2	2.6	35.8	37.2	22.6	24.8
$10,000 to $19,999	21.1	14.7	21.1	16.7	33.2	33.3	27.1	26.3
$20,000 to $29,999	16.8	17.5	20.3	15.8	14.5	14.1	15.9	16.3
$30,000 to $39,999	14.0	17.7	16.1	15.8	6.5	5.6	10.4	10.8
$40,000 to $49,999	8.7	11.2	13.7	6.1	3.1	3.3	5.3	4.4
$50,000 to $59,999	5.6	7.2	7.0	5.3	2.4	2.3	4.3	4.7
$60,000 to $69,999	4.1	5.2	4.2	7.0	1.5	1.5	3.9	3.2
$70,000 to $79,999	3.1	4.4	1.2	5.3	0.5	0.5	3.1	3.0
$80,000 to $89,999	2.7	4.0	1.0	10.5	0.6	0.4	1.2	0.9
$90,000 to $99,999	1.2	1.7	0.6	2.6	0.6	0.7	0.3	0.4
$100,000 or more	7.7	11.5	4.6	11.4	1.3	1.2	5.7	5.3

Source: Bureau of the Census, unpublished tables from the 1998 Current Population Survey, Internet web site <http://www.bls.census.gov/cps/ads/1998/sdata.htm>; calculations by New Strategist

Income Distribution of Households by Household Type, 1997: Aged 70 to 74

(number and percent distribution of households headed by people aged 70 to 74, by income and household type, 1997; households in thousands as of 1998)

| | | family households | | | nonfamily households | | | |
| | | | female hh, no spouse present | male hh, no spouse present | female householder | | male householder | |
	total	married couples			total	living alone	total	living alone
Total households	**5,517**	**2,716**	**440**	**96**	**1,646**	**1,611**	**619**	**583**
Under $10,000	866	77	46	3	594	590	147	141
$10,000 to $19,999	1,532	532	143	14	620	614	226	224
$20,000 to $29,999	1,099	669	74	20	212	209	123	109
$30,000 to $39,999	701	471	74	23	81	69	50	47
$40,000 to $49,999	416	281	42	10	58	54	26	24
$50,000 to $59,999	283	221	20	8	19	19	14	10
$60,000 to $69,999	168	106	20	9	21	17	12	8
$70,000 to $79,999	108	77	9	2	13	13	5	5
$80,000 to $89,999	100	81	3	5	5	5	6	6
$90,000 to $99,999	39	33	2	–	4	2	–	–
$100,000 or more	204	168	7	–	20	18	9	9
Median income	$23,003	$31,557	$25,107	$33,156	$12,990	$12,804	$17,656	$17,093
Total households	**100.0%**	**100.0%**	**100.0%**	**100.0%**	**100.0%**	**100.0%**	**100.0%**	**100.0%**
Under $10,000	15.7	2.8	10.5	3.1	36.1	36.6	23.7	24.2
$10,000 to $19,999	27.8	19.6	32.5	14.6	37.7	38.1	36.5	38.4
$20,000 to $29,999	19.9	24.6	16.8	20.8	12.9	13.0	19.9	18.7
$30,000 to $39,999	12.7	17.3	16.8	24.0	4.9	4.3	8.1	8.1
$40,000 to $49,999	7.5	10.3	9.5	10.4	3.5	3.4	4.2	4.1
$50,000 to $59,999	5.1	8.1	4.5	8.3	1.2	1.2	2.3	1.7
$60,000 to $69,999	3.0	3.9	4.5	9.4	1.3	1.1	1.9	1.4
$70,000 to $79,999	2.0	2.8	2.0	2.1	0.8	0.8	0.8	0.9
$80,000 to $89,999	1.8	3.0	0.7	5.2	0.3	0.3	1.0	1.0
$90,000 to $99,999	0.7	1.2	0.5	–	0.2	0.1	–	–
$100,000 or more	3.7	6.2	1.6	–	1.2	1.1	1.5	1.5

Note: (–) means sample is too small to make a reliable estimate.
Source: Bureau of the Census, unpublished tables from the 1998 Current Population Survey, Internet web site <http://www.bls.census.gov/cps/ads/1998/sdata.htm>; calculations by New Strategist

Income Distribution of Households by Household Type, 1997: Aged 75 or Older

(number and percent distribution of households headed by people aged 75 or older, by income and household type, 1997; households in thousands as of 1998)

| | total | family households | | | nonfamily households | | | |
		married couples	female hh, no spouse present	male hh, no spouse present	female householder total	living alone	male householder total	living alone
Total households	10,226	3,368	738	176	4,665	4,590	1,279	1,234
Under $10,000	2,351	135	73	8	1,837	1,820	297	292
$10,000 to $19,999	3,579	922	196	33	1,905	1,892	521	505
$20,000 to $29,999	1,805	889	148	40	506	489	221	212
$30,000 to $39,999	894	517	88	27	173	162	89	83
$40,000 to $49,999	512	284	79	18	71	67	62	59
$50,000 to $59,999	310	158	62	9	51	51	29	29
$60,000 to $69,999	200	131	23	11	29	26	7	7
$70,000 to $79,999	116	68	11	10	21	20	4	4
$80,000 to $89,999	115	75	12	7	7	7	16	14
$90,000 to $99,999	80	33	21	5	15	15	5	5
$100,000 or more	263	156	24	9	49	41	26	24
Median income	$17,079	$26,558	$25,776	$33,755	$11,584	$11,524	$15,663	$15,475
Total households	100.0%	100.0%	100.0%	100.0%	100.0%	100.0%	100.0%	100.0%
Under $10,000	23.0	4.0	9.9	4.5	39.4	39.7	23.2	23.7
$10,000 to $19,999	35.0	27.4	26.6	18.8	40.8	41.2	40.7	40.9
$20,000 to $29,999	17.7	26.4	20.1	22.7	10.8	10.7	17.3	17.2
$30,000 to $39,999	8.7	15.4	11.9	15.3	3.7	3.5	7.0	6.7
$40,000 to $49,999	5.0	8.4	10.7	10.2	1.5	1.5	4.8	4.8
$50,000 to $59,999	3.0	4.7	8.4	5.1	1.1	1.1	2.3	2.4
$60,000 to $69,999	2.0	3.9	3.1	6.3	0.6	0.6	0.5	0.6
$70,000 to $79,999	1.1	2.0	1.5	5.7	0.5	0.4	0.3	0.3
$80,000 to $89,999	1.1	2.2	1.6	4.0	0.2	0.2	1.3	1.1
$90,000 to $99,999	0.8	1.0	2.8	2.8	0.3	0.3	0.4	0.4
$100,000 or more	2.6	4.6	3.3	5.1	1.1	0.9	2.0	1.9

Source: Bureau of the Census, unpublished tables from the 1998 Current Population Survey, Internet web site <http://www.bls.census.gov/cps/ads/1998/sdata.htm>; calculations by New Strategist

Big Gains for Men and Women Aged 65+

Women aged 55 to 64 have seen their incomes grow rapidly, while their male counterparts have seen little gain.

Between 1980 and 1997, men aged 55 to 64 saw their median income rise just 0.4 percent, after adjusting for inflation. In contrast, their female counterparts experienced a 50 percent increase in median income during those years. Behind these statistics are divergent trends. A growing proportion of men aged 55 to 64 opted for early retirement between 1980 and 1997, while a growing proportion of women opted to go to work.

In contrast to 55-to-64-year-olds, income trends among people aged 65 or older have been similar for men and women. Both sexes have experienced substantial income gains since 1980, and men's increase was slightly greater than women's. As of 1997, men aged 65 or older had a median income of $17,768, up 24 percent since 1980. Women's median stood at $10,062 in 1997, up 22 percent from $8,241 in 1980. Behind the income gains in this age group is a more prosperous generation replacing less-affluent older people.

◆ The median income of women aged 55 to 64 should continue to surge as the working women of the baby-boom generation enter the age group. Men's incomes will also grow if early retirement loses its popularity.

Women aged 55 to 64 have seen the biggest gain

(percent change in median income of men and women aged 55 or older, 1980 to 1997; in 1997 dollars)

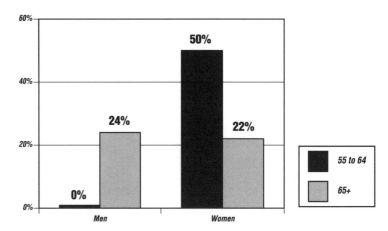

Median Income of Men Aged 55 or Older, 1980 to 1997

(median income of men aged 16 or older and aged 55 or older, 1980 to 1997; in 1997 dollars)

	total men	55–64	men aged 65 or older		
			total	*65–74*	*75+*
1997	$25,212	$31,157	$17,768	$19,651	$15,407
1996	24,381	30,203	17,067	19,032	14,827
1995	23,761	30,520	17,360	19,322	14,913
1994	23,523	29,322	16,516	17,977	14,793
1993	23,439	27,923	16,642	18,089	14,908
1992	23,400	29,303	16,699	18,086	14,741
1991	24,121	30,002	16,918	18,071	15,363
1990	24,920	30,459	17,417	19,609	14,344
1989	25,749	31,617	16,965	18,723	14,040
1988	25,653	30,726	16,920	18,914	13,877
1987	25,129	30,917	16,851	18,949	13,702
1986	25,062	30,803	16,905	–	–
1985	24,330	30,216	16,259	–	–
1984	24,098	30,164	16,143	–	–
1983	23,577	30,124	15,699	–	–
1982	23,420	29,931	15,425	–	–
1981	24,000	30,933	14,497	–	–
1980	24,436	31,035	14,312	–	–
Percent change					
1996–1997	3.4%	3.2%	4.1%	3.3%	3.9%
1990–1997	1.2	2.3	2.0	0.2	7.4
1980–1997	3.2	0.4	24.1	–	–

Note: (–) means data not available.
Source: Bureau of the Census, Internet web site <http://www.census.gov>; calculations by New Strategist

Median Income of Women Aged 55 or Older, 1980 to 1997

(median income of women aged 16 or older and aged 55 or older, 1980 to 1997; in 1997 dollars)

	total women	55–64	women aged 65 or older		
			total	*65–74*	*75+*
1997	$13,703	$14,376	$10,062	$10,141	$9,996
1996	13,109	13,622	9,847	9,878	9,818
1995	12,775	13,039	9,852	9,770	9,928
1994	12,418	11,769	9,693	9,559	9,814
1993	12,269	12,028	9,440	9,604	9,291
1992	12,257	11,592	9,361	9,398	9,325
1991	12,345	11,669	9,650	9,586	9,711
1990	12,366	11,543	9,878	10,057	9,690
1989	12,457	11,860	9,908	10,288	9,548
1988	12,053	11,365	9,637	9,844	9,421
1987	11,720	10,654	9,743	9,870	9,605
1986	11,144	10,803	9,409	–	–
1985	10,765	10,700	9,417	–	–
1984	10,609	10,561	9,299	–	–
1983	10,183	9,877	9,022	–	–
1982	9,884	9,917	9,007	–	–
1981	9,723	9,575	8,383	–	–
1980	9,595	9,607	8,241	–	–
Percent change					
1996–1997	4.5%	5.5%	2.2%	2.7%	1.8%
1990–1997	10.8	24.5	1.9	0.8	3.2
1980–1997	42.8	49.6	22.1	–	–

Note: (–) means data not available.
Source: Bureau of the Census, Internet web site <http://www.census.gov>; calculations by New Strategist

Older Men Who Work Are Paid Well

Men aged 65 or older who work full-time had a median income of $45,648 in 1997.

Among full-time workers, those with the highest incomes are the oldest men. Men aged 75 or older who work full-time had a median income of $49,672 in 1997, higher than men in any other age group. But only 4 percent of men in this age group are full-time workers. Among all men aged 55 or older, just 28 percent work full-time, including 65 percent of men aged 55 to 59, 43 percent of men aged 60 to 64, and just 7 percent of men aged 65 or older.

The pattern is the same for white, black, and Hispanic men. The oldest workers are the most highly paid. Among non-Hispanic white men aged 75 or older who work full-time, median income was $55,646 in 1997. Black men aged 70 or older who work full-time had median incomes above $37,000. Hispanics aged 75 or older who work full-time had a median income of $42,230 in 1997.

♦ Older men are likely to see their incomes rise in the future as more work full-time because of the rising age of eligibility for Social Security benefits.

Older men are highest paid

(median income of men aged 16 or older and aged 55 or older who are full-time, year-round workers, 1997)

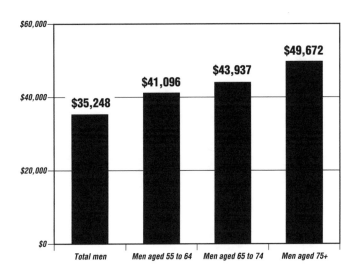

Income Distribution of Men Aged 55 or Older, 1997: Total Men

(number and percent distribution of men aged 16 or older and aged 55 or older by income, 1997; men in thousands as of 1998)

	total	aged 55 or older	aged 55 to 64			aged 65 or older	aged 65 to 74			
		total	total	55–59	60–64	total	total	65–69	70–74	75+
Total men	101,123	24,197	10,673	5,869	4,804	13,524	7,992	4,286	3,706	5,532
Without income	6,955	528	312	174	137	216	149	88	62	67
With income	94,168	23,669	10,361	5,695	4,666	13,308	7,843	4,199	3,644	5,465
Under $10,000	18,176	4,052	1,433	705	730	2,619	1,311	669	641	1,306
$10,000 to $19,999	19,561	6,788	1,869	873	997	4,919	2,688	1,285	1,402	2,229
$20,000 to $29,999	16,559	4,136	1,643	894	748	2,493	1,577	833	744	916
$30,000 to $39,999	12,944	2,720	1,498	837	662	1,222	823	486	335	401
$40,000 to $49,999	8,538	1,724	1,107	628	478	617	418	232	186	199
$50,000 to $74,999	10,938	2,173	1,391	874	516	782	552	362	190	227
$75,000 to $99,999	3,494	909	605	360	246	304	203	143	61	101
$100,000 or more	3,957	1,170	815	524	290	355	272	188	85	83
Median income of men with income	$25,212	$23,674	$31,157	$33,852	$27,598	$17,768	$19,651	$21,558	$17,947	$15,407
Median income of full-time workers	35,248	43,640	41,096	41,342	40,570	45,648	43,937	44,175	42,489	49,672
Percent working full-time	54.3%	28.3%	54.9%	64.7%	43.0%	7.4%	9.9%	13.5%	5.8%	3.6%

(continued)

(continued from previous page)

		aged 55 or older							
			aged 55 to 64			aged 65 or older		aged 65 to 74	
	total	total	55–59	60–64	total	total	65–69	70–74	75+
Total men	100.0%	100.0%	100.0%	100.0%	100.0%	100.0%	100.0%	100.0%	100.0%
Without income	6.9	2.9	3.0	2.9	1.6	1.9	2.1	1.7	1.2
With income	93.1	97.1	97.0	97.1	98.4	98.1	98.0	98.3	98.8
Under $10,000	18.0	13.4	12.0	15.2	19.4	16.4	15.6	17.3	23.6
$10,000 to $19,999	19.3	17.5	14.9	20.8	36.4	33.6	30.0	37.8	40.3
$20,000 to $29,999	16.4	15.4	15.2	15.6	18.4	19.7	19.4	20.1	16.6
$30,000 to $39,999	12.8	14.0	14.3	13.8	9.0	10.3	11.3	9.0	7.2
$40,000 to $49,999	8.4	10.4	10.7	10.0	4.6	5.2	5.4	5.0	3.6
$50,000 to $74,999	10.8	13.0	14.9	10.7	5.8	6.9	8.4	5.1	4.1
$75,000 to $99,999	3.5	5.7	6.1	5.1	2.2	2.5	3.3	1.6	1.8
$100,000 or more	3.9	7.6	8.9	6.0	2.6	3.4	4.4	2.3	1.5

Source: Bureau of the Census, unpublished data from the 1998 Current Population Survey, Internet web site <http://www.bls.census.gov/cps/ads/1998/sdata.htm>; calculations by New Strategist

Income Distribution of Men Aged 55 or Older, 1997: Black Men

(number and percent distribution of black men aged 16 or older and aged 55 or older by income, 1997; men in thousands as of 1998)

| | aged 55 or older | | | | aged 65 or older | | | | |
| | | aged 55 to 64 | | | | aged 65 to 74 | | | |
total	total	total	55–59	60–64	total	total	65–69	70–74	75+
Total black men	**2,036**	**968**	**535**	**433**	**1,068**	**657**	**379**	**279**	**411**
11,283									
Without income	101	65	49	16	36	24	20	4	12
1,613									
With income	1,935	903	486	417	1,032	633	359	274	398
9,671									
Under $10,000	614	220	106	113	394	200	102	98	194
2,860									
$10,000 to $19,999	591	216	109	108	375	255	134	121	120
2,306									
$20,000 to $29,999	319	169	97	72	150	106	69	37	46
1,840									
$30,000 to $39,999	191	124	71	53	67	53	43	10	14
1,184									
$40,000 to $49,999	98	74	39	35	24	10	7	4	13
633									
$50,000 to $74,999	76	74	46	26	2	2	2	–	–
634									
$75,000 to $99,999	29	19	12	7	10	4	–	4	6
138									
$100,000 or more	17	9	9	–	8	3	3	–	4
78									
Median income of men with income	$16,356	$20,744	$21,905	$18,306	$12,378	$13,467	$14,898	$11,679	$10,317
$18,096									
Median income of full-time workers	31,111	30,218	30,425	29,930	31,921	30,561	30,434	37,772	37,446
26,897									
Percent working full-time	25.6%	47.0%	52.7%	40.0%	6.3%	7.0%	7.7%	6.1%	5.1%
45.8%									

(continued)

(continued from previous page)

		aged 55 or older								
			aged 55 to 64			aged 65 or older				
							aged 65 to 74			
Total black men	total	total	total	55–59	60–64	total	total	65–69	70–74	75+
	100.0%	100.0%	100.0%	100.0%	100.0%	100.0%	100.0%	100.0%	100.0%	100.0%
Without income	14.3	5.0	6.7	9.2	3.7	3.4	3.7	5.3	1.4	2.9
With income	85.7	95.0	93.3	90.8	96.3	96.6	96.3	94.7	98.2	96.8
Under $10,000	25.3	30.2	22.7	19.8	26.1	36.9	30.4	26.9	35.1	47.2
$10,000 to $19,999	20.4	29.0	22.3	20.4	24.9	35.1	38.8	35.4	43.4	29.2
$20,000 to $29,999	16.3	15.7	17.5	18.1	16.6	14.0	16.1	18.2	13.3	11.2
$30,000 to $39,999	10.5	9.4	12.8	13.3	12.2	6.3	8.1	11.3	3.6	3.4
$40,000 to $49,999	5.6	4.8	7.6	7.3	8.1	2.2	1.5	1.8	1.4	3.2
$50,000 to $74,999	5.6	3.7	7.6	8.6	6.0	0.2	0.3	0.5	–	–
$75,000 to $99,999	1.2	1.4	2.0	2.2	1.6	0.9	0.6	–	1.4	1.5
$100,000 or more	0.7	0.8	0.9	1.7	–	0.7	0.5	0.8	–	1.0

Note: (–) means sample is too small to make a reliable estimate.
Source: Bureau of the Census, unpublished data from the 1998 Current Population Survey, Internet web site <http://www.bls.census.gov/cps/ads/1998/sdata.htm>; calculations by New Strategist

Income Distribution of Men Aged 55 or Older, 1997: Hispanic Men

(number and percent distribution of Hispanic men aged 16 or older and aged 55 or older by income, 1997; men in thousands as of 1998)

	aged 55 or older								
		aged 55 to 64			aged 65 or older				
						aged 65 to 74			
total	**total**	**total**	**55–59**	**60–64**	**total**	**total**	**65–69**	**70–74**	**75+**
Total Hispanic men 10,944	1,449	768	408	361	681	429	225	203	252
Without income 1,359	79	48	16	32	31	19	10	10	11
With income 9,585	1,371	721	392	329	650	409	215	194	241
Under $10,000 2,559	515	192	95	96	323	177	90	87	146
$10,000 to $19,999 3,116	396	201	100	101	195	129	65	63	67
$20,000 to $29,999 1,741	183	120	66	53	63	53	37	18	10
$30,000 to $39,999 935	96	79	50	29	17	13	5	8	4
$40,000 to $49,999 497	66	44	32	12	22	15	6	9	7
$50,000 to $74,999 486	77	54	28	24	23	18	14	4	6
$75,000 to $99,999 124	20	19	10	8	1	1	1	–	–
$100,000 or more 126	18	12	9	4	6	6	–	6	–
Median income of men with income $16,216	$13,849	$17,224	$20,051	$15,728	$10,043	$11,055	$11,632	$10,645	$7,875
Median income of full-time workers 28,761	28,761	25,795	26,939	23,596	32,105	23,896	20,889	33,312	42,230
Percent working full-time 54.6%	32.1%	51.7%	61.5%	40.7%	10.0%	12.6%	13.3%	11.8%	5.6%

(continued)

(continued from previous page)

Total Hispanic men	total	aged 55 or older total	aged 55 to 64 total	55–59	60–64	aged 55 or older total	aged 65 or older total	aged 65 to 74 65–69	70–74	75+
	100.0%	100.0%	100.0%	100.0%	100.0%	100.0%	100.0%	100.0%	100.0%	100.0%
Without income	12.4	5.5	6.3	3.9	8.9	4.6	4.4	4.4	4.9	4.4
With income	87.6	94.6	93.9	96.1	91.1	95.4	95.3	95.6	95.6	95.6
Under $10,000	23.4	35.5	25.0	23.3	26.6	47.4	41.3	40.0	42.9	57.9
$10,000 to $19,999	28.5	27.3	26.2	24.5	28.0	28.6	30.1	28.9	31.0	26.6
$20,000 to $29,999	15.9	12.6	15.6	16.2	14.7	9.3	12.4	16.4	8.9	4.0
$30,000 to $39,999	8.5	6.6	10.3	12.3	8.0	2.5	3.0	2.2	3.9	1.6
$40,000 to $49,999	4.5	4.6	5.7	7.8	3.3	3.2	3.5	2.7	4.4	2.8
$50,000 to $74,999	4.4	5.3	7.0	6.9	6.6	3.4	4.2	6.2	2.0	2.4
$75,000 to $99,999	1.1	1.4	2.5	2.5	2.2	0.1	0.2	0.4	–	–
$100,000 or more	1.2	1.2	1.6	2.2	1.1	0.9	1.4	–	3.0	–

Note: (–) means sample is too small to make a reliable estimate.
Source: Bureau of the Census, unpublished data from the 1998 Current Population Survey; Internet web site <http://www.bls.census.gov/cps/ads/1998/sdata.htm>; calculations by New Strategist

Income Distribution of Men Aged 55 or Older, 1997: White Men

(number and percent distribution of white men aged 16 or older and aged 55 or older by income, 1997; men in thousands as of 1998)

	total	aged 55 or older								
		total	aged 55 to 64			aged 65 or older				
			total	55–59	60–64	total	aged 65 to 74			75+
							total	65–69	70–74	
Total white men	**85,219**	**21,321**	**9,258**	**5,076**	**4,182**	**12,063**	**7,109**	**3,750**	**3,359**	**4,954**
Without income	4,819	360	226	112	114	134	88	51	37	46
With income	80,400	20,961	9,032	4,964	4,068	11,929	7,022	3,699	3,323	4,908
Under $10,000	14,431	3,219	1,129	556	573	2,090	1,055	525	529	1,034
$10,000 to $19,999	16,435	5,987	1,564	723	841	4,423	2,361	1,103	1,258	2,060
$20,000 to $29,999	13,987	3,717	1,409	748	659	2,308	1,458	751	706	851
$30,000 to $39,999	11,259	2,457	1,318	734	583	1,139	755	432	324	383
$40,000 to $49,999	7,540	1,585	997	565	432	588	405	224	181	182
$50,000 to $74,999	9,829	2,026	1,268	801	467	758	535	347	188	222
$75,000 to $99,999	3,195	851	566	336	230	285	192	136	57	94
$100,000 or more	3,726	1,123	783	498	284	340	261	181	80	79
Median income of men with income	$26,115	$24,483	$32,310	$35,784	$29,280	$18,476	$20,530	$22,681	$18,680	$16,074
Median income of full-time workers	36,118	45,693	42,165	42,401	41,625	48,401	46,157	46,727	45,145	52,108
Percent working full-time	55.4%	28.4%	55.7%	65.9%	43.4%	7.4%	10.1%	13.9%	5.8%	3.5%

(continued)

(continued from previous page)

			aged 55 to 64			aged 55 or older					
								aged 65 or older			
									aged 65 to 74		
Total white men	total	total	total	55–59	60–64	total	total	total	65–69	70–74	75+
	100.0%	100.0%	100.0%	100.0%	100.0%	100.0%	100.0%	100.0%	100.0%	100.0%	100.0%
Without income	5.7	2.4	2.2	2.2	2.7	1.7	1.1	1.2	1.4	1.1	0.9
With income	94.3	97.6	97.8	97.8	97.3	98.3	98.9	98.8	98.6	98.9	99.1
Under $10,000	16.9	12.2	11.0	11.0	13.7	15.1	17.3	14.8	14.0	15.7	20.9
$10,000 to $19,999	19.3	16.9	14.2	14.2	20.1	28.1	36.7	33.2	29.4	37.5	41.6
$20,000 to $29,999	16.4	15.2	14.7	14.7	15.8	17.4	19.1	20.5	20.0	21.0	17.2
$30,000 to $39,999	13.2	14.2	14.5	14.5	13.9	11.5	9.4	10.6	11.5	9.6	7.7
$40,000 to $49,999	8.8	10.8	11.1	11.1	10.3	7.4	4.9	5.7	6.0	5.4	3.7
$50,000 to $74,999	11.5	13.7	15.8	15.8	11.2	9.5	6.3	7.5	9.3	5.6	4.5
$75,000 to $99,999	3.7	6.1	6.6	6.6	5.5	4.0	2.4	2.7	3.6	1.7	1.9
$100,000 or more	4.4	8.5	9.8	9.8	6.8	5.3	2.8	3.7	4.8	2.4	1.6

Source: Bureau of the Census, unpublished data from the 1998 Current Population Survey, Internet web site <http://www.bls.census.gov/cps/ads/1998/sdata.htm>; calculations by New Strategist

Income Distribution of Men Aged 55 or Older, 1997: Non-Hispanic White Men

(number and percent distribution of non-Hispanic white men aged 16 or older and aged 55 or older by income, 1997; men in thousands as of 1998)

| | | aged 55 or older | | | | aged 65 or older | | | | |
| | | | aged 55 to 64 | | | | aged 65 to 74 | | | |
	total	total	total	55-59	60-64	total	total	65-69	70-74	75+
Total non-Hispanic white men	**74,703**	**19,922**	**8,519**	**4,692**	**3,828**	**11,403**	**6,698**	**3,530**	**3,168**	**4,705**
Without income	3,553	286	183	99	84	103	68	41	27	35
With income	71,150	19,637	8,337	4,592	3,744	11,300	6,630	3,488	3,141	4,670
Under $10,000	11,967	2,724	948	469	477	1,776	885	437	447	891
$10,000 to $19,999	13,414	5,600	1,365	625	741	4,235	2,242	1,040	1,200	1,993
$20,000 to $29,999	12,308	3,541	1,293	687	606	2,248	1,406	715	690	842
$30,000 to $39,999	10,360	2,365	1,243	687	556	1,122	743	428	315	379
$40,000 to $49,999	7,061	1,521	955	535	420	566	389	217	172	177
$50,000 to $74,999	9,366	1,950	1,216	774	443	734	519	335	184	215
$75,000 to $99,999	3,074	831	548	327	222	283	191	134	57	94
$100,000 or more	3,600	1,104	770	490	280	334	256	181	74	79
Median income of men with income	$27,559	$25,404	$34,011	$36,901	$30,706	$18,973	$21,097	$23,405	$19,178	$16,540
Median income of full-time workers	37,931	47,472	43,866	44,503	42,694	50,166	48,141	48,773	47,396	55,646
Percent working full-time	55.5%	28.1%	56.0%	66.1%	43.6%	7.2%	9.9%	14.0%	5.4%	3.4%

(continued)

(continued from previous page)

Total non-Hispanic white men

	total	aged 55 or older	aged 55 to 64			aged 65 or older	aged 65 to 74			
		total	total	55–59	60–64	total	total	65–69	70–74	75+
Total non-Hispanic white men	100.0%	100.0%	100.0%	100.0%	100.0%	100.0%	100.0%	100.0%	100.0%	100.0%
Without income	4.8	1.4	2.1	2.1	2.2	0.9	1.0	1.2	0.9	0.7
With income	95.2	98.6	97.9	97.9	97.8	99.1	99.0	98.8	99.1	99.3
Under $10,000	16.0	13.7	11.1	10.0	12.5	15.6	13.2	12.4	14.1	18.9
$10,000 to $19,999	18.0	28.1	16.0	13.3	19.4	37.1	33.5	29.5	37.9	42.4
$20,000 to $29,999	16.5	17.8	15.2	14.6	15.8	19.7	21.0	20.3	21.8	17.9
$30,000 to $39,999	13.9	11.9	14.6	14.6	14.5	9.8	11.1	12.1	9.9	8.1
$40,000 to $49,999	9.5	7.6	11.2	11.4	11.0	5.0	5.8	6.1	5.4	3.8
$50,000 to $74,999	12.5	9.8	14.3	16.5	11.6	6.4	7.7	9.5	5.8	4.6
$75,000 to $99,999	4.1	4.2	6.4	7.0	5.8	2.5	2.9	3.8	1.8	2.0
$100,000 or more	4.8	5.5	9.0	10.4	7.3	2.9	3.8	5.1	2.3	1.7

Source: Bureau of the Census, unpublished data from the 1998 Current Population Survey, Internet web site <http://www.bls.census.gov/cps/ads/1998/sdata.htm>; calculations by New Strategist

Older Women Who Work Have Far Higher Incomes Than Those Not at Work

But only 13 percent of women aged 55 or older are full-time workers.

The median income of women aged 55 or older who work full-time stood at $28,938 in 1997, more than double the $11,720 median income of all women in the age group. Few older women work full-time, however. The proportion ranges from a high of 36 percent among women aged 55 to 59 to a low of just 1 percent among women aged 75 or older. As is true for men, women's income rises with age for full-time workers. Among women aged 65 or older who work full-time, median income tops $30,000.

The majority of older women are not full-time workers, and their median income is very low. Hispanic women aged 65 or older have the lowest incomes, a median of just $6,849 in 1997. The median income of black women in this age group stood at $7,874, while that of non-Hispanic white women was $10,672.

◆ Older women will enjoy rising incomes in the years ahead as the working women of the baby-boom generation enter the 55-plus age group.

Incomes of full-time workers more than double the average

(median income of total women aged 55 or older and women aged 55 or older who work full-time, 1997)

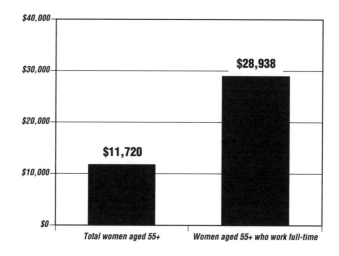

Income Distribution of Women Aged 55 or Older, 1997: Total Women

(number and percent distribution of women aged 16 or older and aged 55 or older by income, 1997; women in thousands as of 1998)

		aged 55 or older							
			aged 55 to 64			aged 65 or older			
							aged 65 to 74		
	total	total	total	55–59	60–64	total	total	65–69	70–74	75+
Total women	108,168	30,140	11,582	6,321	5,261	18,558	9,882	5,075	4,807	8,677
Without income	10,721	1,441	976	586	389	465	311	179	132	155
With income	97,447	28,700	10,607	5,735	4,872	18,093	9,571	4,896	4,675	8,522
Under $10,000	37,533	12,970	3,979	1,899	2,079	8,991	4,728	2,363	2,366	4,263
$10,000 to $19,999	24,723	8,315	2,620	1,378	1,243	5,695	2,804	1,380	1,425	2,891
$20,000 to $29,999	15,259	3,387	1,603	971	633	1,784	1,023	550	474	759
$30,000 to $39,999	9,021	1,663	1,011	594	417	652	406	247	159	246
$40,000 to $49,999	4,611	904	524	321	202	380	263	146	118	116
$50,000 to $74,999	4,350	954	592	387	207	362	213	137	75	150
$75,000 to $99,999	1,026	248	136	92	42	112	66	43	22	44
$100,000 or more	922	259	141	94	48	118	67	30	37	50
Median income of women with income	$13,703	$11,720	$14,376	$16,636	$12,069	$10,062	$10,141	$10,426	$9,900	$9,996
Median income of full-time workers	26,029	28,938	26,661	26,481	27,019	30,359	31,426	30,947	33,880	26,917
Percent working full-time	34.9%	15.3%	34.6%	41.9%	25.8%	3.3%	5.2%	8.2%	2.1%	1.2%

(continued)

(continued from previous page)

		aged 55 or older				aged 65 or older			
		aged 55 to 64					aged 65 to 74		
Total women	total	total	55–59	60–64	total	total	65–69	70–74	75+
	100.0%	100.0%	100.0%	100.0%	100.0%	100.0%	100.0%	100.0%	100.0%
Without income	9.9	8.4	9.3	7.4	2.5	3.1	3.5	2.7	1.8
With income	90.1	91.6	90.7	92.6	97.5	96.9	96.5	97.3	98.2
Under $10,000	43.0	34.4	30.0	39.5	48.4	47.8	46.6	49.2	49.1
$10,000 to $19,999	27.6	22.6	21.8	23.6	30.7	28.4	27.2	29.6	33.3
$20,000 to $29,999	11.2	13.8	15.4	12.0	9.6	10.4	10.8	9.9	8.7
$30,000 to $39,999	5.5	8.7	9.4	7.9	3.5	4.1	4.9	3.3	2.8
$40,000 to $49,999	3.0	4.5	5.1	3.8	2.0	2.7	2.9	2.5	1.3
$50,000 to $74,999	3.2	5.1	6.1	3.9	2.0	2.2	2.7	1.6	1.7
$75,000 to $99,999	0.8	1.2	1.5	0.8	0.6	0.7	0.8	0.5	0.5
$100,000 or more	0.9	1.2	1.5	0.9	0.6	0.7	0.6	0.8	0.6

Source: Bureau of the Census, unpublished data from the 1998 Current Population Survey, Internet web site <http://www.bls.census.gov/cps/ads/1998/sdata.htm>; calculations by New Strategist

Income Distribution of Women Aged 55 or Older, 1997: Black Women

(number and percent distribution of black women aged 16 or older and aged 55 or older by income, 1997; women in thousands as of 1998)

	total	aged 55 or older		aged 55 to 64			aged 65 or older	aged 65 to 74			
		total	total	55–59	60–64	total	total	65–69	70–74	75+	
Total black women	13,715	2,878	1,255	685	570	1,623	956	500	456	668	
Without income	1,754	173	105	67	38	68	57	35	23	11	
With income	11,961	2,705	1,150	618	532	1,555	898	465	433	657	
Under $10,000	4,825	1,477	475	235	242	1,002	536	243	293	466	
$10,000 to $19,999	3,158	640	292	149	143	348	218	128	92	129	
$20,000 to $29,999	1,946	275	160	92	69	115	80	53	27	35	
$30,000 to $39,999	1,053	117	88	54	33	29	17	13	3	11	
$40,000 to $49,999	468	81	53	33	20	28	24	17	6	4	
$50,000 to $74,999	414	88	63	46	17	25	15	9	6	10	
$75,000 to $99,999	57	15	13	6	7	2	2	2	–	–	
$100,000 or more	41	9	5	5	–	4	4	–	4	–	
Median income of women with income	$13,048	$9,868	$12,447	$14,731	$11,252	$7,874	$8,433	$9,622	$7,434	$7,366	
Median income of full-time workers	22,764	24,881	23,494	23,642	23,176	25,953	25,705	25,239	39,434	30,414	
Percent working full-time	38.7%	17.3%	36.2%	44.4%	26.3%	2.8%	4.2%	6.6%	1.5%	0.7%	

(continued)

(continued from previous page)

	total	aged 55 to 64			aged 55 or older	aged 65 or older		aged 65 to 74		75+
		total	55–59	60–64	total	total		65–69	70–74	
Total black women	100.0%	100.0%	100.0%	100.0%	100.0%	100.0%		100.0%	100.0%	100.0%
Without income	12.8	8.4	9.8	6.7	4.2	6.0		7.0	5.0	1.6
With income	87.2	91.6	90.2	93.3	95.8	93.9		93.0	95.0	98.4
Under $10,000	35.2	37.8	34.3	42.5	61.7	56.1		48.6	64.3	69.8
$10,000 to $19,999	23.0	23.3	21.8	25.1	21.4	22.8		25.6	20.2	19.3
$20,000 to $29,999	14.2	12.7	13.4	12.1	7.1	8.4		10.6	5.9	5.2
$30,000 to $39,999	7.7	7.0	7.9	5.8	1.8	1.8		2.6	0.7	1.6
$40,000 to $49,999	3.4	4.2	4.8	3.5	1.7	2.5		3.4	1.3	0.6
$50,000 to $74,999	3.0	5.0	6.7	3.0	1.5	1.6		1.8	1.3	1.5
$75,000 to $99,999	0.4	1.0	0.9	1.2	0.1	0.2		0.4	–	–
$100,000 or more	0.3	0.4	0.7	–	0.2	0.4		–	0.9	–

Note: (–) means sample is too small to make a reliable estimate.
Source: Bureau of the Census, unpublished data from the 1998 Current Population Survey, Internet web site <http://www.bls.census.gov/cps/ads/1998/sdata.htm>; calculations by New Strategist

Income Distribution of Women Aged 55 or Older, 1997: Hispanic Women

(number and percent distribution of Hispanic women aged 16 or older and Hispanic women aged 55 or older by income, 1997; women in thousands as of 1998)

			aged 55 or older								
				aged 55 to 64			aged 65 or older				
								aged 65 to 74			
	total	total	total	55-59	60-64	total	total	65-69	70-74	75+
Total Hispanic women	**10,485**	**1,802**	**865**	**522**	**343**	**937**	**586**	**332**	**254**	**351**
Without income	2,430	248	174	113	61	74	50	35	15	24
With income	8,055	1,554	691	409	282	863	536	297	239	327
Under $10,000	3,934	1,000	361	189	172	639	385	216	169	253
$10,000 to $19,999	2,210	309	148	87	62	161	100	51	48	61
$20,000 to $29,999	973	133	91	71	21	42	35	19	16	6
$30,000 to $39,999	502	61	45	30	14	16	11	8	3	5
$40,000 to $49,999	223	22	19	14	5	3	3	3	–	–
$50,000 to $74,999	150	18	16	13	4	2	2	1	1	–
$75,000 to $99,999	31	7	7	4	3	–	–	–	–	–
$100,000 or more	29	4	3	3	–	1	1	1	–	–
Median income of women with income	$10,260	$8,108	$9,460	$11,116	$7,369	$6,859	$6,849	$6,921	$6,737	$6,873
Median income of full-time workers	19,676	18,335	22,050	22,194	20,862	14,905	20,125	20,364	18,429	11,931
Percent working full-time	30.0%	16.1%	29.1%	34.9%	20.4%	4.2%	5.3%	8.4%	1.2%	2.0%

(continued)

(continued from previous page)

			aged 55 or older				aged 65 or older			
	total	aged 55 to 64					aged 65 to 74			
	total	total	55–59	60–64	total	total	65–69	70–74	75+
Total Hispanic women	100.0%	100.0%	100.0%	100.0%	100.0%	100.0%	100.0%	100.0%	100.0%
Without income	23.2	20.1	21.6	17.8	7.9	8.5	10.5	5.9	6.8
With income	76.8	79.9	78.4	82.2	92.1	91.5	89.5	94.1	93.2
Under $10,000	55.5	41.7	36.2	50.1	68.2	65.7	65.1	66.5	72.1
$10,000 to $19,999	17.1	17.1	16.7	18.1	17.2	17.1	15.4	18.9	17.4
$20,000 to $29,999	7.4	10.5	13.6	6.1	4.5	6.0	5.7	6.3	1.7
$30,000 to $39,999	3.4	5.2	5.7	4.1	1.7	1.9	2.4	1.2	1.4
$40,000 to $49,999	1.2	2.2	2.7	1.5	0.3	0.5	0.9	–	–
$50,000 to $74,999	1.0	1.8	2.5	1.2	0.2	0.3	0.3	0.4	–
$75,000 to $99,999	0.4	0.8	0.8	0.9	–	–	–	–	–
$100,000 or more	0.2	0.3	0.6	–	0.1	0.2	0.3	–	–

Note: (–) means sample is too small to make a reliable estimate.
Source: Bureau of the Census, unpublished data from the 1998 Current Population Survey, Internet web site <http://www.bls.census.gov/cps/ads/1998/sdata.htm>; calculations by New Strategist

Income Distribution of Women Aged 55 or Older, 1997: White Women

(number and percent distribution of white women aged 16 or older and white women aged 55 or older by income, 1997; women in thousands as of 1998)

	total	aged 55 or older	aged 55 to 64			aged 65 or older	aged 65 to 74			
		total	total	55–59	60–64	total	total	65–69	70–74	75+
Total white women	89,489	26,372	9,882	5,383	4,499	16,490	8,651	4,413	4,238	7,839
Without income	8,137	1,136	801	488	313	335	199	108	91	136
With income	81,352	25,236	9,081	4,895	4,187	16,155	8,452	4,305	4,147	7,703
Under $10,000	31,098	11,100	3,349	1,587	1,760	7,751	4,060	2,050	2,012	3,690
$10,000 to $19,999	20,616	7,514	2,244	1,184	1,061	5,270	2,530	1,221	1,309	2,740
$20,000 to $29,999	12,728	3,017	1,385	842	543	1,632	923	484	438	710
$30,000 to $39,999	7,554	1,493	885	507	377	608	383	229	154	225
$40,000 to $49,999	3,899	815	468	285	181	347	237	125	112	110
$50,000 to $74,999	3,728	833	501	320	180	332	195	125	69	138
$75,000 to $99,999	905	222	117	81	35	105	60	41	19	44
$100,000 or more	826	246	135	88	48	111	63	30	33	48
Median income of women with income	$13,792	$11,991	$14,640	$16,880	$12,285	$10,403	$10,452	$10,592	$10,325	$10,362
Median income of full-time workers	26,470	30,155	27,074	26,728	28,094	32,002	32,976	32,785	34,412	27,406
Percent working full-time	34.2%	14.9%	34.3%	41.7%	25.5%	3.3%	5.3%	8.3%	2.1%	1.2%

(continued)

(continued from previous page)

Total white women	total	aged 55 or older								
		total	aged 55 to 64			aged 65 or older				
			total	55–59	60–64	total	aged 65 to 74			75+
							total	65–69	70–74	
	100.0%	100.0%	100.0%	100.0%	100.0%	100.0%	100.0%	100.0%	100.0%	100.0%
Without income	9.1	4.3	8.1	9.1	7.0	2.0	2.3	2.4	2.1	1.7
With income	90.9	95.7	91.9	90.9	93.1	98.0	97.7	97.6	97.9	98.3
Under $10,000	34.8	42.1	33.9	29.5	39.1	47.0	46.9	46.5	47.5	47.1
$10,000 to $19,999	23.0	28.5	22.7	22.0	23.6	32.0	29.2	27.7	30.9	35.0
$20,000 to $29,999	14.2	11.4	14.0	15.6	12.1	9.9	10.7	11.0	10.3	9.1
$30,000 to $39,999	8.4	5.7	9.0	9.4	8.4	3.7	4.4	5.2	3.6	2.9
$40,000 to $49,999	4.4	3.1	4.7	5.3	4.0	2.1	2.7	2.8	2.6	1.4
$50,000 to $74,999	4.2	3.2	5.1	5.9	4.0	2.0	2.3	2.8	1.6	1.8
$75,000 to $99,999	1.0	0.8	1.2	1.5	0.8	0.6	0.7	0.9	0.4	0.6
$100,000 or more	0.9	0.9	1.4	1.6	1.1	0.7	0.7	0.7	0.8	0.6

Source: Bureau of the Census, unpublished data from the 1998 Current Population Survey, Internet web site <http://www.bls.census.gov/cps/ads/1998/sdata.htm>; calculations by New Strategist

Income Distribution of Women Aged 55 or Older, 1997: Non-Hispanic White Women

(number and percent distribution of total non-Hispanic white women aged 16 or older and non-Hispanic white women aged 55 or older by income, 1997; women in thousands as of 1998)

	total	aged 55 or older				aged 65 or older				
		total	aged 55 to 64			*total*	aged 65 to 74			*75+*
			total	*55–59*	*60–64*		*total*	*65–69*	*70–74*	
Total non-Hispanic white women	**79,502**	**24,632**	**9,040**	**4,874**	**4,166**	**15,592**	**8,091**	**4,088**	**4,002**	**7,501**
Without income	5,793	893	629	378	252	264	151	75	76	114
With income	73,709	23,738	8,411	4,496	3,914	15,327	7,940	4,014	3,926	7,387
Under $10,000	27,336	10,137	3,000	1,404	1,595	7,137	3,694	1,840	1,854	3,444
$10,000 to $19,999	18,523	7,215	2,100	1,097	1,002	5,115	2,435	1,170	1,265	2,681
$20,000 to $29,999	11,809	2,887	1,294	773	521	1,593	888	465	425	704
$30,000 to $39,999	7,096	1,432	840	478	362	592	374	222	151	219
$40,000 to $49,999	3,687	793	450	272	178	343	234	122	112	110
$50,000 to $74,999	3,588	814	484	308	175	330	193	124	68	138
$75,000 to $99,999	875	217	112	78	32	105	60	41	19	44
$100,000 or more	800	244	134	86	48	110	62	29	33	48
Median income of women with income	$14,389	$12,314	$15,147	$17,412	$12,713	$10,672	$10,794	$11,011	$10,598	$10,574
Median income of full-time workers	27,149	31,199	27,449	27,110	28,674	33,373	34,019	33,929	34,696	28,620
Percent working full-time	34.8%	14.8%	34.8%	42.4%	25.8%	3.3%	5.3%	8.2%	2.2%	1.1%

(continued)

(continued from previous page)

Total non-Hispanic white women	aged 55 or older								
		aged 55 to 64			aged 65 or older				
						aged 65 to 74			
	total	total	55–59	60–64	total	total	65–69	70–74	75+
Total non-Hispanic white women	100.0%	100.0%	100.0%	100.0%	100.0%	100.0%	100.0%	100.0%	100.0%
Without income	7.3	7.0	7.8	6.0	1.7	1.9	1.8	1.9	1.5
With income	92.7	93.0	92.2	94.0	98.3	98.1	98.2	98.1	98.5
Under $10,000	34.4	33.2	28.8	38.3	45.8	45.7	45.0	46.3	45.9
$10,000 to $19,999	23.3	23.2	22.5	24.1	32.8	30.1	28.6	31.6	35.7
$20,000 to $29,999	14.9	14.3	15.9	12.5	10.2	11.0	11.4	10.6	9.4
$30,000 to $39,999	8.9	9.3	9.8	8.7	3.8	4.6	5.4	3.8	2.9
$40,000 to $49,999	4.6	5.0	5.6	4.3	2.2	2.9	3.0	2.8	1.5
$50,000 to $74,999	4.5	5.4	6.3	4.2	2.1	2.4	3.0	1.7	1.8
$75,000 to $99,999	1.1	1.2	1.6	0.8	0.7	0.7	1.0	0.5	0.6
$100,000 or more	1.0	1.5	1.8	1.2	0.7	0.8	0.7	0.8	0.6

Source: Bureau of the Census, unpublished data from the 1998 Current Population Survey, Internet web site <http://www.bls.census.gov/cps/ads/1998/sdata.htm>; calculations by New Strategist

Education Boosts Earnings of Older Men and Women

Men aged 55 to 64 with a college degree earned more than $50,000 in 1997.

College-educated men aged 55 to 64 earned a median of $51,601 in 1997, much higher than the $32,395 median for all men in the age group. Women aged 55 to 64 with college degrees earned a median of $30,643, versus just $18,203 for the average woman in the age group.

Having an education boosts earnings among older Americans not only because the college-educated command higher salaries, but also because they are more likely to work full-time. Among college-educated men aged 55 to 64, 65 percent were full-time workers in 1997. Only 54 percent of men in the age group who went no further than high school had full-time jobs. The same is true for women aged 55 to 64: 44 percent of those with a college education worked full-time, versus 35 percent of those who did not go beyond high school.

Even in the 65-plus age group, education still plays a role. The median earnings of men aged 65 or older with a college degree stood at $21,743 in 1997, versus $12,317 for all men in the age group. Fourteen percent of college-educated men aged 65 or older worked full-time in 1997 versus only 7 percent of all men in the age group. For their female counterparts, the proportions were 8 and 4 percent, respectively.

♦ The rising affluence of older Americans is guaranteed because the highly educated baby-boom generation will enter the age group, boosting the proportion of older Americans with college degrees and driving up earnings.

Earnings Distribution of Men by Education, 1997: Aged 55 to 64

(number and percent distribution of men aged 55 to 64 by earnings and education, 1997; men in thousands as of 1998)

	total	less than 9th grade	9th to 12th grade, no degree	high school graduate, inc. GED	some college, no degree	associate's degree	bachelor's degree or more				
							total	bachelor's degree	master's degree	professional degree	doctoral degree
Total men aged 55 to 64	**10,673**	**1,017**	**1,091**	**3,661**	**1,589**	**493**	**2,821**	**1,550**	**744**	**266**	**261**
Without earnings	2,874	500	386	997	399	111	481	308	128	10	36
With earnings	7,799	517	705	2,664	1,190	383	2,339	1,242	616	256	225
Under $10,000	1,073	131	122	405	147	56	212	130	63	13	6
$10,000 to $19,999	1,117	144	157	439	144	37	196	140	39	13	5
$20,000 to $29,999	1,234	111	148	502	202	74	195	130	48	12	6
$30,000 to $39,999	1,304	81	124	565	215	61	258	153	63	24	17
$40,000 to $49,999	827	28	62	316	160	46	214	111	65	15	23
$50,000 to $74,999	1,201	13	66	311	197	73	539	262	161	32	81
$75,000 to $99,999	499	5	11	80	57	19	325	167	84	39	35
$100,000 or more	545	3	14	48	66	14	400	145	94	110	51
Median earnings of men with earnings	$32,395	$18,362	$24,474	$29,562	$35,271	$33,962	$51,601	$45,191	$52,288	$81,448	$65,636
Median earnings of full-time workers	37,904	22,784	28,666	32,395	38,259	39,920	60,270	51,860	61,744	90,518	70,888
Percent working full-time	54.9%	34.1%	47.8%	54.3%	56.3%	56.0%	65.1%	63.0%	60.6%	83.1%	72.4%

(continued)

(continued from previous page)

Total men aged 55 to 64	total	less than 9th grade	9th to 12th grade, no degree	high school graduate, inc. GED	some college, no degree	associate's degree	bachelor's degree or more				
							total	bachelor's degree	master's degree	professional degree	doctoral degree
	100.0%	100.0%	100.0%	100.0%	100.0%	100.0%	100.0%	100.0%	100.0%	100.0%	100.0%
Without earnings	26.9	49.2	35.4	27.2	25.1	22.5	17.1	19.9	17.2	3.8	13.8
With earnings	73.1	50.8	64.6	72.8	74.9	77.7	82.9	80.1	82.8	96.2	86.2
Under $10,000	10.1	12.9	11.2	11.1	9.3	11.4	7.5	8.4	8.5	4.9	2.3
$10,000 to $19,999	10.5	14.2	14.4	12.0	9.1	7.5	6.9	9.0	5.2	4.9	1.9
$20,000 to $29,999	11.6	10.9	13.6	13.7	12.7	15.0	6.9	8.4	6.5	4.5	2.3
$30,000 to $39,999	12.2	8.0	11.4	15.4	13.5	12.4	9.1	9.9	8.5	9.0	6.5
$40,000 to $49,999	7.7	2.8	5.7	8.6	10.1	9.3	7.6	7.2	8.7	5.6	8.8
$50,000 to $74,999	11.3	1.3	6.0	8.5	12.4	14.8	19.1	16.9	21.6	12.0	31.0
$75,000 to $99,999	4.7	0.5	1.0	2.2	3.6	3.9	11.5	10.8	11.3	14.7	13.4
$100,000 or more	5.1	0.3	1.3	1.3	4.2	2.8	14.2	9.4	12.6	41.4	19.5

Source: Bureau of the Census, unpublished tables from the 1998 Current Population Survey, Internet web site <http://www.bls.census.gov/cps/ads/1998/sdata.htm>; calculations by New Strategist

Earnings Distribution of Men by Education, 1997: Aged 65 or Older

(number and percent distribution of men aged 65 or older by earnings and education, 1997; men in thousands as of 1998)

	total	less than 9th grade	9th to 12th grade, no degree	high school graduate, inc. GED	some college, no degree	associate's degree	bachelor's degree or more				
							total	bachelor's degree	master's degree	professional degree	doctoral degree
Total men aged 65 or older	**13,524**	**2,478**	**1,908**	**4,084**	**1,986**	**393**	**2,675**	**1,549**	**560**	**317**	**250**
Without earnings	10,790	2,155	1,668	3,325	1,536	295	1,810	1,096	394	176	144
With earnings	2,735	324	240	759	450	98	865	453	165	141	105
Under $10,000	1,156	176	122	345	182	40	290	159	83	22	24
$10,000 to $19,999	560	72	55	179	105	25	124	57	23	24	17
$20,000 to $29,999	245	21	21	76	48	5	75	42	12	9	10
$30,000 to $39,999	188	13	13	55	37	4	67	41	8	13	5
$40,000 to $49,999	148	20	13	27	29	4	55	31	12	11	2
$50,000 to $74,999	239	13	4	66	36	16	102	57	12	15	19
$75,000 to $99,999	60	3	5	–	3	–	50	25	5	13	5
$100,000 or more	142	6	5	10	13	5	104	40	9	35	21
Median earnings of men with earnings	$12,317	$8,334	$9,439	$10,951	$13,068	$15,299	$21,743	$21,335	$9,579	$40,775	$26,988
Median earnings of full-time workers	35,892	17,488	21,671	25,404	31,244	40,976	51,752	42,011	49,631	76,491	66,877
Percent working full-time	7.4%	4.3%	4.2%	6.3%	7.4%	10.7%	13.6%	13.0%	8.8%	20.2%	20.0%

(continued)

(continued from previous page)

Total men aged 65 or older	total	less than 9th grade	9th to 12th grade, no degree	high school graduate, inc. GED	some college, no degree	associate's degree	bachelor's degree or more				
							total	bachelor's degree	master's degree	professional degree	doctoral degree
	100.0%	100.0%	100.0%	100.0%	100.0%	100.0%	100.0%	100.0%	100.0%	100.0%	100.0%
Without earnings	79.8	87.0	87.4	81.4	77.3	75.1	67.7	70.8	70.4	55.5	57.6
With earnings	20.2	13.1	12.6	18.6	22.7	24.9	32.3	29.2	29.5	44.5	42.0
Under $10,000	8.5	7.1	6.4	8.4	9.2	10.2	10.8	10.3	14.8	6.9	9.6
$10,000 to $19,999	4.1	2.9	2.9	4.4	5.3	6.4	4.6	3.7	4.1	7.6	6.8
$20,000 to $29,999	1.8	0.8	1.1	1.9	2.4	1.3	2.8	2.7	2.1	2.8	4.0
$30,000 to $39,999	1.4	0.5	0.7	1.3	1.9	1.0	2.5	2.6	1.4	4.1	2.0
$40,000 to $49,999	1.1	0.8	0.7	0.7	1.5	1.0	2.1	2.0	2.1	3.5	0.8
$50,000 to $74,999	1.8	0.5	0.2	1.6	1.8	4.1	3.8	3.7	2.1	4.7	7.6
$75,000 to $99,999	0.4	0.1	0.3	–	0.2	–	1.9	1.6	0.9	4.1	2.0
$100,000 or more	1.0	0.2	0.3	0.2	0.7	1.3	3.9	2.6	1.6	11.0	8.4

Note: (–) means sample is too small to make a reliable estimate.
Source: Bureau of the Census, unpublished tables from the 1998 Current Population Survey, Internet web site <http://www.bls.census.gov/cps/ads/1998/sdata.htm>; calculations by New Strategist

Earnings Distribution of Women by Education, 1997: Aged 55 to 64

(number and percent distribution of women aged 55 to 64 by earnings and education, 1997; women in thousands as of 1998)

	total	less than 9th grade	9th to 12th grade, no degree	high school graduate, inc. GED	some college, no degree	associate's degree	bachelor's degree or more				
							total	bachelor's degree	master's degree	professional degree	doctoral degree
Total women aged 55 to 64	11,582	931	1,519	4,650	1,737	669	2,077	1,340	601	78	58
Without earnings	4,985	661	841	2,033	630	214	607	450	128	15	14
With earnings	6,597	270	678	2,617	1,108	455	1,470	890	473	63	44
Under $10,000	1,720	103	287	715	253	88	272	189	73	5	5
$10,000 to $19,999	1,825	117	230	866	290	109	215	151	57	4	2
$20,000 to $29,999	1,323	34	108	603	231	122	224	155	65	1	3
$30,000 to $39,999	814	12	27	249	183	65	277	187	70	10	11
$40,000 to $49,999	390	1	12	107	60	39	171	85	65	13	6
$50,000 to $74,999	402	1	14	50	63	23	250	91	132	16	11
$75,000 to $99,999	71	–	–	6	25	8	35	21	7	4	1
$100,000 or more	53	–	–	21	5	–	27	9	4	8	5
Median earnings of women with earnings	$18,203	$11,675	$11,351	$16,192	$20,345	$21,251	$30,643	$25,746	$35,296	$48,397	$41,450
Median earnings of full-time workers	24,602	16,013	17,248	21,513	26,077	29,039	37,862	34,191	41,836	49,636	46,082
Percent working full-time	34.6%	18.0%	23.0%	34.9%	40.2%	39.2%	43.7%	39.1%	49.1%	61.5%	69.0%

(continued)

(continued from previous page)

Total women aged 55 to 64	total	less than 9th grade	9th to 12th grade, no degree	high school graduate, inc. GED	some college, no degree	associate's degree	bachelor's degree or more				
							total	bachelor's degree	master's degree	professional degree	doctoral degree
	100.0%	100.0%	100.0%	100.0%	100.0%	100.0%	100.0%	100.0%	100.0%	100.0%	100.0%
Without earnings	43.0	71.0	55.4	43.7	36.3	32.0	29.2	33.6	21.3	19.2	24.1
With earnings	57.0	29.0	44.6	56.3	63.8	68.0	70.8	66.4	78.7	80.8	75.9
Under $10,000	14.9	11.1	18.9	15.4	14.6	13.2	13.1	14.1	12.1	6.4	8.6
$10,000 to $19,999	15.8	12.6	15.1	18.6	16.7	16.3	10.4	11.3	9.5	5.1	3.4
$20,000 to $29,999	11.4	3.7	7.1	13.0	13.3	18.2	10.8	11.6	10.8	1.3	5.2
$30,000 to $39,999	7.0	1.3	1.8	5.4	10.5	9.7	13.3	14.0	11.6	12.8	19.0
$40,000 to $49,999	3.4	0.1	0.8	2.3	3.5	5.8	8.2	6.3	10.8	16.7	10.3
$50,000 to $74,999	3.5	0.1	0.9	1.1	3.6	3.4	12.0	6.8	22.0	20.5	19.0
$75,000 to $99,999	0.6	–	–	0.1	1.4	1.2	1.7	1.6	1.2	5.1	1.7
$100,000 or more	0.5	–	–	0.5	0.3	–	1.3	0.7	0.7	10.3	8.6

Note: (–) means sample is too small to make a reliable estimate.
Source: Bureau of the Census, unpublished tables from the 1998 Current Population Survey, Internet web site <http://www.bls.census.gov/cps/ads/1998/sdata.htm>; calculations by New Strategist

Earnings Distribution of Women by Education, 1997: Aged 65 or Older

(number and percent distribution of women aged 65 or older by earnings and education, 1997; women in thousands as of 1998)

	total	less than 9th grade	9th to 12th grade, no degree	high school graduate, inc. GED	some college, no degree	associate's degree	bachelor's degree or more				
							total	bachelor's degree	master's degree	professional degree	doctoral degree
Total women aged 65 or older	**18,558**	**3,325**	**2,867**	**7,131**	**2,328**	**825**	**2,083**	**1,396**	**544**	**96**	**47**
Without earnings	16,370	3,144	2,603	6,258	2,014	709	1,643	1,136	409	70	28
With earnings	2,188	181	264	873	313	117	440	260	135	27	18
Under $10,000	1,325	141	176	545	198	73	194	112	66	10	4
$10,000 to $19,999	435	28	59	213	48	15	73	48	15	5	5
$20,000 to $29,999	160	3	20	66	28	9	38	30	7	1	0
$30,000 to $39,999	121	5	7	31	18	10	51	23	25	3	0
$40,000 to $49,999	68	3	3	4	12	8	38	23	10	3	3
$50,000 to $74,999	53	–	–	9	11	4	30	12	10	3	5
$75,000 to $99,999	13	–	–	2	–	–	11	8	–	2	1
$100,000 or more	13	–	1	6	–	–	6	2	2	–	2
Median earnings of women with earnings	$7,272	$5,539	$6,933	$7,172	$6,257	$7,106	$11,882	$12,086	$10,197	$13,353	$40,741
Median earnings of full-time workers	21,717	10,896	13,228	16,362	26,879	31,093	35,822	32,043	36,190	45,962	60,815
Percent working full-time	3.3%	0.8%	2.4%	3.1%	4.2%	3.3%	8.4%	7.2%	10.7%	8.3%	17.0%

(continued)

(continued from previous page)

Total women aged 65 or older	total	less than 9th grade	9th to 12th grade, no degree	high school graduate, inc. GED	some college, no degree	associate's degree	bachelor's degree or more total	bachelor's degree	master's degree	professional degree	doctoral degree
	100.0%	100.0%	100.0%	100.0%	100.0%	100.0%	100.0%	100.0%	100.0%	100.0%	100.0%
Without earnings	88.2	94.6	90.8	87.8	86.5	85.9	78.9	81.4	75.2	72.9	59.6
With earnings	11.8	5.4	9.2	12.2	13.4	14.2	21.1	18.6	24.8	28.1	38.3
Under $10,000	7.1	4.2	6.1	7.6	8.5	8.8	9.3	8.0	12.1	10.4	8.5
$10,000 to $19,999	2.3	0.8	2.1	3.0	2.1	1.8	3.5	3.4	2.8	5.2	10.6
$20,000 to $29,999	0.9	0.1	0.7	0.9	1.2	1.1	1.8	2.1	1.3	1.0	0.0
$30,000 to $39,999	0.7	0.2	0.2	0.4	0.8	1.2	2.4	1.6	4.6	3.1	0.0
$40,000 to $49,999	0.4	0.1	0.1	0.1	0.5	1.0	1.8	1.6	1.8	3.1	6.4
$50,000 to $74,999	0.3	–	–	0.1	0.5	0.5	1.4	0.9	1.8	3.1	10.6
$75,000 to $99,999	0.1	–	–	0.0	–	–	0.5	0.6	–	2.1	2.1
$100,000 or more	0.1	–	0.0	0.1	–	–	0.3	0.1	0.4	–	4.3

Note: (–) means sample is too small to make a reliable estimate.
Source: Bureau of the Census, unpublished tables from the 1998 Current Population Survey, Internet web site <http://www.bls.census.gov/cps/ads/1998/sdata.htm>; calculations by New Strategist

One-Third of Elderly Receive Pensions

For those with pensions, annual amount surpasses $10,000.

Of the 31 million Americans aged 65 or older, 29 million receive Social Security benefits—averaging $8,690 per person in 1997. Social Security is the most common source of income for Americans aged 65 or older. The only other source of income the majority of people aged 65 or older received is interest. The 62 percent with interest income in 1997 received an average of $3,971. One in three elderly Americans received pensions, the average amount having been $10,831 in 1997.

Few older Americans work, but those who do receive the largest amount of income from this source rather than from Social Security, interest, or pensions. The 13 percent of older Americans with wage or salary income received an average of $21,044 from this source. Similarly, the 2 percent with nonfarm self-employment income received an average of $21,709.

♦ In the years ahead, the proportion of older Americans with wage, salary, or self-employment income will increase, boosting the economic well-being of the elderly.

♦ Because baby boomers save much more for retirement than the current older generation did, they are likely to receive more interest income than today's elderly.

Sources of Income for People Aged 65 or Older, 1997

(number and percent of people aged 65 or older with income and average income for those with income, by selected sources of income, 1997; ranked by number with income; people in thousands as of 1998)

	number	percent	average income
Total people aged 65 or older	**31,401**	**100.0%**	**$19,788**
Social Security	28,841	91.8	8,690
Interest	19,329	61.6	3,971
Pensions	10,212	32.5	10,831
Dividends	6,350	20.2	4,786
Wages and salary	4,174	13.3	21,044
Rents, royalties, estates, or trusts	3,032	9.7	5,414
Survivor benefits	1,534	4.9	8,268
Veteran benefits	1,113	3.5	6,332
Nonfarm self-employment	734	2.3	21,709
Disability benefits	219	0.7	10,577
Public assistance	107	0.3	1,748

Source: Bureau of the Census, Money Income in the United States: 1997, *Current Population Reports, P60-200, 1998; calculations by New Strategist*

Older Americans Less Likely to Be Poor

Only 10 percent of people aged 55 or older are poor, versus 13 percent of all Americans.

Of the nation's 36 million poor in 1997, 5.6 million were aged 55 or older. Older blacks and Hispanics are nearly three times as likely to be poor as older whites—24 and 23 percent, respectively, versus just 9 percent of whites. But older blacks and Hispanics are less likely to be poor than the average black (27 percent) or Hispanic (27 percent).

Older women are much more likely to be poor than older men—13 percent of women aged 55 or older are poor versus just 7 percent of men. But older women and men are less likely to be poor than the average female (15 percent) or male (12 percent). Black and Hispanic women are much more likely to be poor than their male counterparts. Among blacks aged 75 or older, 31 percent of women and 26 of men are poor. Among Hispanics aged 75 or older, 33 percent of women and 22 percent of men are poor.

♦ American children are much more likely to be poor than the nation's elderly. The disparity between the well-being of older and younger Americans may increase in the future as the more affluent baby-boom generation ages.

People in Poverty by Sex, Race, and Hispanic Origin, 1997

(number and percent of total people and people aged 55 or older in poverty, by sex, race, and Hispanic origin, 1997; people in thousands as of 1998)

	total	white	black	Hispanic
TOTAL PEOPLE				
Number in poverty, total	**35,574**	**24,396**	**9,116**	**8,308**
Aged 55 or older	5,595	4,204	1,192	736
Aged 65 or older	3,376	2,569	700	384
Aged 75 or older	1,735	1,370	316	170
Aged 55 to 59	1,092	778	270	191
Aged 60 to 64	1,127	857	222	161
Aged 65 to 74	1,641	1,198	383	214
Percent in poverty, total	**13.3%**	**11.0%**	**26.5%**	**27.1%**
Aged 55 or older	10.3	8.8	24.3	22.6
Aged 65 or older	10.5	9.0	26.0	23.8
Aged 75 or older	12.2	10.7	29.3	28.2
Aged 55 to 59	9.0	7.4	22.2	20.5
Aged 60 to 64	11.2	9.9	22.1	22.9
Aged 65 to 74	9.2	7.6	23.8	21.1
FEMALES				
Number in poverty, total	**20,387**	**13,944**	**5,317**	**4,463**
Aged 55 or older	3,794	2,906	775	461
Aged 65 or older	2,423	1,889	467	246
Aged 75 or older	1,318	1,077	209	116
Aged 55 to 59	723	529	175	130
Aged 60 to 64	648	488	133	85
Aged 65 to 74	1,105	812	257	130
Percent in poverty, total	**14.9%**	**12.4%**	**28.9%**	**29.8%**
Aged 55 or older	12.6	11.0	26.9	25.6
Aged 65 or older	13.1	11.5	28.8	26.3
Aged 75 or older	15.2	13.7	33.4	33.0
Aged 55 to 59	11.4	9.8	25.5	24.8
Aged 60 to 64	12.3	10.8	23.4	24.8
Aged 65 to 74	11.2	9.4	26.9	22.2

(continued)

(continued from previous page)

	total	white	black	Hispanic
MALES				
Number in poverty, total	**15,187**	**10,452**	**3,799**	**3,845**
Aged 55 or older	1,802	1,298	418	275
Aged 65 or older	953	680	233	138
Aged 75 or older	417	294	107	54
Aged 55 to 59	370	249	96	61
Aged 60 to 64	479	369	89	76
Aged 65 to 74	536	386	126	84
Percent in poverty, total	**11.6%**	**9.6%**	**23.6%**	**24.5%**
Aged 55 or older	7.4	6.1	20.5	19.0
Aged 65 or older	7.0	5.6	21.8	20.3
Aged 75 or older	7.5	5.9	26.0	21.5
Aged 55 to 59	6.3	4.9	17.9	15.0
Aged 60 to 64	10.0	8.8	20.5	21.2
Aged 65 to 74	6.7	5.4	19.2	19.5

Note: Numbers will not add to total because Hispanics may be of any race and not all races are shown.
Source: Bureau of the Census, Poverty in the United States: 1997, *Current Population Reports, P60-201, 1998; calculations by New Strategist*

5

Labor Force

♦ The labor force participation rate of older men has fallen sharply during the past five decades. The biggest drop has been among men aged 65 or older—down 29 percentage points between 1950 and 1998.

♦ The labor force participation rate of older women has increased substantially during the past few decades. The biggest gain has been among women aged 55 to 59—up 35 percentage points between 1950 and 1998.

♦ The proportion of couples in which neither husband nor wife works becomes the majority in the 65-to-74 age group.

♦ Nineteen percent of employed men aged 55 or older work part-time, compared with 11 percent of all employed men.

♦ The job tenure of older Americans is declining. In 1998, men aged 55 to 64 had been with their current employer a median of 11 years, down from 15 years in 1983.

♦ Twenty-two percent of working men and 14 percent of working women aged 65 or older are self-employed, a much higher share than the 7 percent of all workers who are self-employed.

♦ The early retirement trend is coming to an end. The labor force participation rate of men aged 55 to 59 is projected to climb slightly from 78 to 79 percent between 1996 and 2006.

Fewer Men, More Women at Work

Only 68 percent of men aged 55 to 64 were in the labor force in 1998, down from 87 percent in 1950.

In contrast to men, older women are much more likely to work than they were in 1950. More than half the women aged 55 to 64 were in the labor force in 1998, up from just 27 percent in 1950.

Several factors account for the divergent labor force trends of men and women. Generous pensions and the provision of retiree health insurance has allowed many men to retire before age 65. For women, the labor force participation rate has increased in all but the oldest age group as younger working women have replaced older housewives.

Among older men, the biggest drop in the labor force participation rate has been for those aged 65 or older—down 29 percentage points in the past five decades. In 1950, nearly half (46 percent) the men aged 65 or older worked; by 1998 the figure was just 17 percent. For women, the biggest increase in the labor force participation rate has been among those aged 55 to 59, rising from 26 to 61 percent between 1950 and 1998.

◆ Unlike their parents, baby boomers are not likely to benefit from generous employer-provided pensions or to receive employer-provided retiree health care coverage. Consequently, the labor force participation rate of older men will rise as boomers enter the 55-or-older age group after the turn of the century.

Older men are less likely to work today than in 1950

(percent of men aged 65 or older in the labor force, 1950 and 1998)

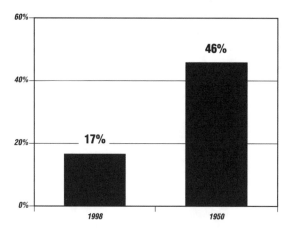

Labor Force Participation Rate for
People Aged 55 or Older by Sex, 1950 to 1998

(labor force participation rate for people aged 16 or older and aged 55 or older, by sex, 1950 to 1998; percentage point change, 1950–98)

	1998	1990	1980	1970	1960	1950	percentage point change 1950–1998
Men aged 16 or older	**74.9%**	**76.1%**	**77.4%**	**79.7%**	**83.3%**	**86.4%**	**–11.5**
Aged 55 to 64	68.1	67.7	72.1	83.0	86.8	86.9	–18.8
Aged 55 to 59	78.4	78.7	80.6	86.8	87.7	86.7	–8.3
Aged 60 to 64	55.4	55.1	60.4	73.0	77.6	79.4	–24.0
Aged 65 or older	16.5	16.4	19.0	26.8	33.1	45.8	–29.3
Women aged 16 or older	**59.8**	**57.5**	**51.5**	**43.3**	**37.7**	**33.9**	**25.9**
Aged 55 to 64	51.2	45.3	41.3	43.0	37.2	27.0	24.2
Aged 55 to 59	61.3	55.4	48.4	47.4	39.7	25.9	35.4
Aged 60 to 64	39.1	36.1	34.0	36.1	29.5	20.5	18.6
Aged 65 or older	8.6	8.7	8.1	9.7	10.8	9.7	–1.1

Sources: Bureau of Labor Statistics, Employment and Earnings, *January 1999 and January 1991;* Handbook of Labor Statistics, *Bulletin 2340, 1989; calculations by New Strategist*

Most People Aged 60 or Older Do Not Work

The majority of men drop out of the labor force during their sixties.

The late fifties and early sixties are an age of transition for most Americans, when their roles change from worker to retiree. The labor force participation rate drops sharply with age. Among men aged 55 to 59, 78 percent are in the labor force. The figure falls to 55 percent among those aged 60 to 64, then drops to 28 percent among those aged 65 to 69. Only 8 percent of men aged 75 or older are in the labor force.

The 61 percent majority of women aged 55 to 59 are in the labor force, a figure that falls to a 39 percent minority among women aged 60 to 64. Only 18 percent of women aged 65 to 69 and 3 percent of those aged 75 or older are in the labor force.

◆ The labor force participation of people aged 55 to 64 will rise in the coming decade as baby boomers enter the age group.

Labor force participation falls with age

(percent of people aged 55 or older in the labor force by age and sex, 1998)

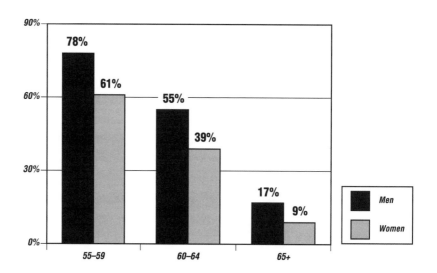

Employment Status of People Aged 55 or Older by Sex, 1998

(number and percent of people aged 16 or older and aged 55 or older in the civilian labor force by sex and employment status, 1998; numbers in thousands)

| | | civilian labor force | | | unemployed | |
	civilian noninstitutional population	total	percent of population	employed	number	percent of labor force
Total aged 16 or older	**205,220**	**137,673**	**67.1%**	**131,463**	**6,210**	**4.5%**
Aged 55 or older	54,533	17,062	31.3	16,598	464	2.7
Aged 65 or older	32,237	3,847	11.9	3,725	121	3.1
Aged 75 or older	14,290	668	4.7	647	21	3.2
Aged 55 to 59	12,219	8,494	69.5	8,279	216	2.5
Aged 60 to 64	10,077	4,721	46.8	4,594	127	2.7
Aged 65 to 69	9,387	2,111	22.5	2,042	69	3.3
Aged 70 to 74	8,560	1,068	12.5	1,036	31	2.9
Men aged 16 or older	**98,758**	**73,959**	**74.9**	**70,693**	**3,266**	**4.4**
Aged 55 or older	24,263	9,493	39.1	9,223	270	2.8
Aged 65 or older	13,613	2,240	16.5	2,171	69	3.1
Aged 75 or older	5,539	413	7.5	400	13	3.2
Aged 55 to 59	5,879	4,609	78.4	4,484	125	2.7
Aged 60 to 64	4,771	2,644	55.4	2,568	76	2.9
Aged 65 to 69	4,304	1,204	28.0	1,165	39	3.2
Aged 70 to 74	3,770	623	16.5	606	17	2.7
Women aged 16 or older	**106,462**	**63,714**	**59.8**	**60,771**	**2,944**	**4.6**
Aged 55 or older	30,272	7,569	25.0	7,374	195	2.6
Aged 65 or older	18,626	1,607	8.6	1,554	54	3.4
Aged 75 or older	8,752	255	2.9	247	8	3.1
Aged 55 to 59	6340	3885	61.3	3795	90	2.3
Aged 60 to 64	5306	2077	39.1	2025	51	2.5
Aged 65 to 69	5084	907	17.8	877	31	3.4
Aged 70 to 74	4790	445	9.3	430	15	3.3

Source: Bureau of Labor Statistics, Employment and Earnings, *January 1999; calculations by New Strategist*

Labor Force Rates Differ by Race and Hispanic Origin

Many Hispanic men work in old age.

Older Hispanic men are more likely to work than older whites and blacks. Among men aged 55 or older, only 39 percent of whites and 35 percent of blacks are in the labor force. Among Hispanic men in the age group, 44 percent are working. In the 65-or-older age group, the labor force participation rate of black, white, and Hispanic men is more similar, with 14 percent of blacks, 15 percent of Hispanics, and 17 percent of whites working. Among older women, Hispanics are slightly less likely to work than their white and black counterparts.

Among women aged 55 or older, 26 percent of blacks, 25 percent of whites, and 23 percent of Hispanics are in the labor force. The difference is about the same in the 65-or-older age group, with 9 percent of white women, 8 percent of black women, and 7 percent of Hispanic women in the labor force.

◆ The labor force participation of Hispanic men aged 55 or older is higher than that of whites and blacks because many are immigrants. They are less likely than both whites and blacks to have pension or Social Security benefits. They remain in the labor force longer because they cannot afford to retire.

Older Hispanic men are more likely to work

(percent of men aged 55 or older in the civilian labor force, by race and Hispanic origin, 1998)

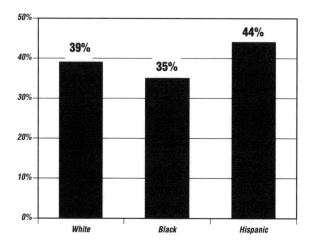

Employment Status of Men Aged 55 or Older by Race and Hispanic Origin, 1998

(number and percent of men aged 16 or older and aged 55 or older in the civilian labor force by race, Hispanic origin, and employment status, 1998; numbers in thousands)

| | civilian noninstitutional population | civilian labor force | | | unemployed | |
		total	percent of population	employed	number	percent of labor force
White men	**83,352**	**63,034**	**75.6%**	**60,604**	**2,431**	**3.9%**
Aged 55 or older	21,442	8,428	39.3	8,206	222	2.6
Aged 65 or older	12,155	2,013	16.6	1,955	58	2.9
Aged 75 or older	4,996	373	7.5	362	11	2.9
Aged 55 to 59	5,120	4,078	79.7	3,976	102	2.5
Aged 60 to 64	4,167	2,337	56.1	2,275	62	2.7
Aged 65 to 69	3,785	1,072	28.3	1,039	33	3.1
Aged 70 to 74	3,374	568	16.8	554	14	2.5
Black men	**10,927**	**7,542**	**69.0**	**6,871**	**671**	**8.9**
Aged 55 or older	2,024	699	34.5	666	32	4.6
Aged 65 or older	1,068	150	14.0	142	8	4.7
Aged 75 or older	400	34	8.4	31	2	–
Aged 55 to 59	533	353	66.1	339	14	3.9
Aged 60 to 64	423	196	46.3	185	11	5.5
Aged 65 to 69	365	80	21.9	77	3	4.1
Aged 70 to 74	303	36	12.0	34	2	6.6
Hispanic men*	**10,734**	**8,571**	**79.8**	**8,018**	**552**	**6.4**
Aged 55 or older	1,485	647	43.6	613	34	5.2
Aged 55 to 64	771	541	70.2	512	29	5.3
Aged 65 or older	714	106	14.9	101	5	5.0

* Employment status by detailed age group is not available for Hispanics.
Source: Bureau of Labor Statistics, Employment and Earnings, *January 1999*

Employment Status of Women Aged 55 or Older by Race and Hispanic Origin, 1998

(number and percent of women aged 16 or older and aged 55 or older in the civilian labor force by race, Hispanic origin, and employment status, 1998; numbers in thousands)

| | civilian noninstitutional population | civilian labor force | | | unemployed | |
		total	percent of population	employed	number	percent of labor force
White women	**88,126**	**52,380**	**59.4%**	**50,327**	**2,053**	**3.9%**
Aged 55 or older	26,431	6,569	24.9	6,413	156	2.4
Aged 65 or older	16,486	1,435	8.7	1,392	43	3.0
Aged 75 or older	7,885	225	2.9	218	7	3.1
Aged 55 to 59	5,412	3,350	61.9	3,282	69	2.1
Aged 60 to 64	4,532	1,783	39.3	1,739	44	2.4
Aged 65 to 69	4,377	808	18.5	783	24	3.0
Aged 70 to 74	4,225	403	9.5	391	12	2.9
Black women	**13,446**	**8,441**	**62.8**	**7,685**	**756**	**9.0**
Aged 55 or older	2,893	743	25.7	715	29	3.9
Aged 65 or older	1,626	128	7.9	120	8	6.3
Aged 75 or older	683	22	3.2	21	1	–
Aged 55 to 59	688	396	57.6	382	15	3.7
Aged 60 to 64	579	219	37.8	213	6	2.7
Aged 65 to 69	515	72	14.1	67	5	7.4
Aged 70 to 74	428	34	7.9	32	2	–
Hispanic women*	**10,335**	**5,746**	**55.6**	**5,273**	**473**	**8.2**
Aged 55 or older	1,792	416	23.2	391	24	5.9
Aged 55 to 64	844	353	41.9	334	19	5.4
Aged 65 or older	948	62	6.6	57	5	8.8

* Employment status by detailed age group is not available for Hispanics.
Source: Bureau of Labor Statistics, Employment and Earnings, *January 1999; calculations by New Strategist*

Few Older Couples Are Dual Earners

Neither husband nor wife is in the labor force in 49 percent of couples aged 55 or older.

While 56 percent of all married couples are dual earners—meaning that both husband and wife are in the labor force—the proportion is just 25 percent among those aged 55 or older. Dual-earner couples are a minority among older Americans because most older men are retired.

Among couples headed by 55-to-59-year-olds, however, dual earners are the 55 percent majority. This proportion falls to 33 percent among couples aged 60 to 64. In this age group, the wife is the sole wage earner in 18 percent of couples—a larger share than in any other age group. Behind this figure is the fact that most women marry men who are slightly older. When men retire in their early sixties, their younger wives are still in the labor force.

The proportion of couples in which neither husband nor wife is in the labor force rises from a 29 percent minority in the 60-to-64 age group to the 66 percent majority in the 65-to-74 age group.

♦ The dual-earner share of older couples will rise in the years ahead as baby boomers enter the age group. Expect to see a substantial increase in the dual-earner share of couples aged 60 to 64 within 10 years.

Dual-Income Couples Aged 55 or Older, 1998

(number and percent distribution of total married couples and couples headed by people aged 55 or older, by labor force status of husband and wife, 1998; numbers in thousands)

	total married couples	husband and wife in labor force	husband only in labor force	wife only in labor force	husband and wife not in labor force
Total couples, number	**54,317**	**30,591**	**11,582**	**3,087**	**9,057**
Aged 55 or older	17,145	4,226	2,693	1,889	8,337
Aged 65 or older	9,209	666	902	782	6,857
Aged 55 to 59	4,192	2,312	1,045	427	408
Aged 60 to 64	3,744	1,248	746	680	1,072
Aged 65 to 74	5,841	600	718	649	3,873
Aged 75 to 84	3,003	66	171	129	2,637
Aged 85 or older	365	—	13	4	347
Total couples, percent	**100.0%**	**56.3%**	**21.3%**	**5.7%**	**16.7%**
Aged 55 or older	100.0	24.6	15.7	11.0	48.6
Aged 65 or older	100.0	7.2	9.8	8.5	74.5
Aged 55 to 59	100.0	55.2	24.9	10.2	9.7
Aged 60 to 64	100.0	33.3	19.9	18.2	28.6
Aged 65 to 74	100.0	10.3	12.3	11.1	66.3
Aged 75 to 84	100.0	2.2	5.7	4.3	87.8
Aged 85 or older	100.0	—	3.6	1.1	95.1

Note: (–) means sample is too small to make a reliable estimate.
Source: Bureau of the Census, detailed tables from Household and Family Characteristics: March 1998, *Current Population Reports, P20-515, 1998; calculations by New Strategist*

Few Working Americans Are Aged 55 or Older

Only 13 percent of the nation's 131 million employed are aged 55 or older.

The share of workers aged 55 or older varies by occupation. Only 7 percent of technicians are aged 55 or older, for example, because of the rapid technological change that has occurred since older Americans began their careers. Among the nation's computer system analysts, only 6 percent are aged 55 or older. But older workers account for 39 percent of farm operators and managers—three times their share of the total labor force. Older workers account for a disproportionate share of agricultural workers because changes in the industry over the past few decades have made it more difficult for younger people to take up farming.

Thirty-two percent of workers aged 55 or older are managers or professionals, a slightly greater share than the 30 percent of all employed workers. But 46 percent of legislators, chief executives, and general administrators in public administration are aged 55 or older. For government bureaucrats, it takes decades to reach the top.

Workers aged 55 or older are overrepresented among the nation's funeral directors (26 percent), authors (23 percent), clergy (29 percent), real estate sales-people (31 percent), barbers (30 percent), tailors (38 percent), and shoe repairers (44 percent). They are underrepresented among the nation's actors and directors (7 percent), computer programmers (4 percent), and waiters and waitresses (5 percent).

◆ As boomers age into their fifties, expect to see a growing share of older workers in technical jobs.

Occupations of Workers Aged 55 or Older, 1998

(number of employed workers aged 16 or older and aged 55 or older by occupation, 1998; numbers in thousands)

	total	aged 55 or older		
		total	55 to 64	65 or older
Total workers	**131,463**	**16,597**	**12,872**	**3,725**
Managerial and professional specialty	38,937	5,286	4,211	1,075
Executive, administrative, and managerial	19,054	2,767	2,211	556
Professional specialty	19,883	2,519	2,000	519
Technical, sales, and administrative support	38,521	4,844	3,720	1,124
Technicians and related support	4,261	303	260	43
Sales	15,850	2,186	1,604	582
Administrative support, including clerical	18,410	2,355	1,856	499
Service	17,836	2,160	1,551	609
Private household	847	160	92	68
Protective services	2,417	304	204	100
Other services	14,572	1,696	1,255	441
Precision production, craft, and repair	14,411	1,572	1,322	250
Mechanics and repairers	4,786	513	421	92
Construction trades	5,594	525	451	74
Extractive occupations	125	9	8	1
Precision production	3,907	524	442	82
Operators, fabricators, and laborers	18,256	2,046	1,674	372
Machine operators, assemblers, and inspectors	7,791	827	721	106
Transport and material moving	5,363	812	642	170
Handlers, equipment cleaners, helpers, and laborers	5,102	406	311	95
Farming, forestry, and fishing	3,502	690	394	296
Farm operators and managers	1,187	458	242	216
Other agricultural and related occupations	2,171	212	139	73
Forestry and logging	91	13	8	5
Fishing, hunting, and trapping	53	6	5	1

Source: Bureau of Labor Statistics, unpublished tables from the 1998 Current Population Survey

Distribution of Workers Aged 55 or Older by Occupation, 1998

(percent distribution of employed people aged 16 or older and aged 55 or older by occupation, 1998)

	total	aged 55 or older		
		total	55 to 64	65 or older
Total workers	**100.0%**	**100.0%**	**100.0%**	**100.0%**
Managerial and professional specialty	29.6	31.8	32.7	28.9
Executive, administrative, and managerial	14.5	16.7	17.2	14.9
Professional specialty	15.1	15.2	15.5	13.9
Technical, sales, and administrative support	29.3	29.2	28.9	30.2
Technicians and related support	3.2	1.8	2.0	1.2
Sales	12.1	13.2	12.5	15.6
Administrative support, including clerical	14.0	14.2	14.4	13.4
Service	13.6	13.0	12.0	16.3
Private household	0.6	1.0	0.7	1.8
Protective services	1.8	1.8	1.6	2.7
Other services	11.1	10.2	9.7	11.8
Precision production, craft, and repair	11.0	9.5	10.3	6.7
Mechanics and repairers	3.6	3.1	3.3	2.5
Construction trades	4.3	3.2	3.5	2.0
Extractive occupations	0.1	0.1	0.1	0.0
Precision production	3.0	3.2	3.4	2.2
Operators, fabricators, and laborers	13.9	12.3	13.0	10.0
Machine operators, assemblers, and inspectors	5.9	5.0	5.6	2.8
Transport and material moving	4.1	4.9	5.0	4.6
Handlers, equipment cleaners, helpers, and laborers	3.9	2.4	2.4	2.6
Farming, forestry, and fishing	2.7	4.2	3.1	7.9
Farm operators and managers	0.9	2.8	1.9	5.8
Other agricultural and related occupations	1.7	1.3	1.1	2.0
Forestry and logging	0.1	0.1	0.1	0.1
Fishing, hunting, and trapping	0.0	0.0	0.0	0.0

Source: Bureau of Labor Statistics, unpublished data from the 1998 Current Population Survey; calculations by New Strategist

Share of Workers Aged 55 or Older by Occupation, 1998

(employed persons aged 55 or older as a percent of total employed people aged 16 or older by occupation, 1998)

	total	aged 55 or older		
		total	55 to 64	65 or older
Total workers	**100.0%**	**12.6%**	**9.8%**	**2.8%**
Managerial and professional specialty	100.0	13.6	10.8	2.8
Executive, administrative, and managerial	100.0	14.5	11.6	2.9
Professional specialty	100.0	12.7	10.1	2.6
Technical, sales, and administrative support	100.0	12.6	9.7	2.9
Technicians and related support	100.0	7.1	6.1	1.0
Sales	100.0	13.8	10.1	3.7
Administrative support, including clerical	100.0	12.8	10.1	2.7
Service	100.0	12.1	8.7	3.4
Private household	100.0	18.9	10.9	8.0
Protective services	100.0	12.6	8.4	4.1
Other services	100.0	11.6	8.6	3.0
Precision production, craft, and repair	100.0	10.9	9.2	1.7
Mechanics and repairers	100.0	10.7	8.8	1.9
Construction trades	100.0	9.4	8.1	1.3
Extractive occupations	100.0	7.2	6.4	0.8
Precision production	100.0	13.4	11.3	2.1
Operators, fabricators, and laborers	100.0	11.2	9.2	2.0
Machine operators, assemblers, and inspectors	100.0	10.6	9.3	1.4
Transport and material moving	100.0	15.1	12.0	3.2
Handlers, equipment cleaners, helpers, and laborers	100.0	8.0	6.1	1.9
Farming, forestry, and fishing	100.0	19.7	11.3	8.5
Farm operators and managers	100.0	38.6	20.4	18.2
Other agricultural and related occupations	100.0	9.8	6.4	3.4
Forestry and logging	100.0	14.3	8.8	5.5
Fishing, hunting, and trapping	100.0	11.3	9.4	1.9

Source: Bureau of Labor Statistics, unpublished data from the 1998 Current Population Survey; calculations by New Strategist

Workers Aged 55 or Older by Detailed Occupation, 1998

(number of employed workers aged 16 or older and number and percent aged 55 or older by selected detailed occupation; 1998; numbers in thousands)

	total	aged 55 or older	
		number	percent of total
Total workers	**131,463**	**16,597**	**12.6%**
Legislators, chief exec., and gen admin., public admin.	28	13	46.4
Officials and administrators, public admin.	630	132	21.0
Financial managers	705	69	9.8
Managers, marketing, advertising, public relations	772	66	8.5
Administrators, education	752	142	18.9
Managers, medicine and health	725	104	14.3
Funeral directors	38	10	26.3
Architects	158	26	16.5
Engineers	2,052	269	13.1
Computer system analysts and scientists	1,471	83	5.6
Natural scientists	519	51	9.8
Physicians	740	139	18.8
Registered nurses	2,032	237	11.7
Teachers, postsecondary	919	181	19.7
Teachers, except postsecondary	4,962	577	11.6
Psychologists	232	39	16.8
Clergy	325	94	28.9
Lawyers	912	138	15.1
Authors	130	30	23.1
Designers	692	89	12.9
Actors and directors	130	9	6.9
Editors and reporters	274	31	11.3
Public relations specialists	170	18	10.6
Airplane pilots and navigators	113	16	14.2
Computer programmers	613	26	4.2
Insurance sales	592	103	17.4
Real estate sales	749	230	30.7
Securities and financial service sales	477	61	12.8
Advertising sales	186	18	9.7
Sales workers, motor vehicles and boats	309	45	14.6
Sales workers, apparel	447	63	14.1
Cashiers	3,025	242	8.0

(continued)

(continued from previous page)

	total	aged 55 or older	
		number	percent of total
Secretaries	2,914	511	17.5%
Receptionists	1,006	131	13.0
File clerks	348	31	8.9
Bookkeepers	1,726	333	19.3
Telephone operators	159	20	12.6
Bank tellers	416	27	6.5
Teachers' aides	633	89	14.1
Firefighters	250	14	5.6
Police and detectives	1,062	68	6.4
Waiters and waitresses	1,379	63	4.6
Cooks	2,135	189	8.9
Nursing aides	1,913	254	13.3
Janitors and cleaners	2,233	438	19.6
Barbers	66	20	˙30.3
Hairdressers and cosmetologists	763	96	12.6
Automobile mechanics	877	80	9.1
Carpenters	1,346	105	7.8
Electricians	806	81	10.0
Plumbers	531	70	13.2
Machinists	535	66	12.3
Tailors	50	19	38.0
Shoe repairers	16	7	43.8
Machine operators, assemblers, and inspectors	7,791	827	10.6
Truck drivers	3,012	434	14.4
Bus drivers	471	115	24.4
Taxicab drivers	273	76	27.8
Construction laborers	821	53	6.5
Garbage collectors	44	3	6.8
Farm operators and managers	1,187	458	38.6
Farm workers	835	91	10.9
Groundskeepers and gardeners	924	90	9.7

Source: Bureau of Labor Statistics, unpublished tables from the 1998 Current Population Survey; calculations by New Strategist

Part-Time Work Appeals to Many

Workers aged 65 or older are much more likely to work part-time than the average worker.

While only 11 percent of all employed men work part-time, the proportion is 48 percent among working men aged 65 or older. The majority of men aged 75 or older who are in the labor force work only part-time. While 26 percent of all working women work part-time, the majority of working women aged 65 or older have part-time jobs.

Because so many older Americans work part-time, they account for a disproportionate share of part-time workers. Men aged 55 or older account for one in four men with part-time jobs.

♦ Many older Americans work part-time because they enjoy the flexibility it provides. It's likely that more older Americans would opt for part-time work if employers redesigned jobs and schedules to appeal to retirees.

Full-Time and Part-Time Workers Aged 55 or Older, 1998

(number and percent distribution of employed people aged 16 or older and aged 55 or older by full- and part-time employment status, by sex, 1998; numbers in thousands)

	men			women		
	total	*full-time*	*part-time*	*total*	*full-time*	*part-time*
NUMBER						
Total employed	**70,693**	**63,189**	**7,504**	**60,771**	**45,014**	**15,757**
Aged 55 or older	9,223	7,452	1,771	7,374	4,885	2,489
Aged 65 or older	2,171	1,127	1,044	1,554	588	966
Aged 75 or older	400	174	226	247	80	167
Aged 55 to 64	7,052	6,325	727	5,820	4,297	1,523
Aged 65 to 69	1,165	666	499	876	377	499
Aged 70 to 74	606	287	319	431	131	300
PERCENT DISTRIBUTION BY EMPLOYMENT STATUS						
Total employed	**100.0%**	**89.4%**	**10.6%**	**100.0%**	**74.1%**	**25.9%**
Aged 55 or older	100.0	80.8	19.2	100.0	66.2	33.8
Aged 65 or older	100.0	51.9	48.1	100.0	37.8	62.2
Aged 75 or older	100.0	43.5	56.5	100.0	32.4	67.6
Aged 55 to 64	100.0	89.7	10.3	100.0	73.8	26.2
Aged 65 to 69	100.0	57.2	42.8	100.0	43.0	57.0
Aged 70 to 74	100.0	47.4	52.6	100.0	30.4	69.6
PERCENT DISTRIBUTION BY AGE						
Total employed	**100.0%**	**100.0%**	**100.0%**	**100.0%**	**100.0%**	**100.0%**
Aged 55 or older	13.0	11.8	23.6	12.1	10.9	15.8
Aged 65 or older	3.1	1.8	13.9	2.6	1.3	6.1
Aged 75 or older	0.6	0.3	3.0	0.4	0.2	1.1
Aged 55 to 64	10.0	10.0	9.7	9.6	9.5	9.7
Aged 65 to 69	1.6	1.1	6.6	1.4	0.8	3.2
Aged 70 to 74	0.9	0.5	4.3	0.7	0.3	1.9

Source: Bureau of Labor Statistics, unpublished data from the 1998 Current Population Survey; calculations by New Strategist

Job Tenure Down for Older Workers

Men aged 55 to 64 saw the steepest decline.

The number of years workers have been with their current employer is on the decline—particularly among older men. In 1983, men aged 55 to 64 had been with their current employer a median of 15 years. By 1998, job tenure for this age group had fallen to 11 years—a loss of more than four years. Men aged 65 or older saw their median job tenure decline one year.

Median job tenure has not declined as much among older women, dropping one year among women aged 65 or older and just 0.2 years among women aged 55 to 64. The greater stability in the job tenure of women is due to their increasing attachment to the labor force as career-oriented younger women replace older just-a-job women.

◆ Job tenure can decline when workers voluntarily switch jobs or when they are laid off and forced to find new jobs. The decline in job tenure among older men is primarily due to layoffs rather than job hopping.

Job Tenure of Workers Aged 55 or Older by Sex, 1983 and 1998

(median number of years workers aged 16 or older and aged 55 or older have been with their current employer by sex, 1983 and 1998; change in years, 1983–98)

	1998	1983	change in years 1983–98
Total workers	**3.6**	**3.5**	**0.1**
Aged 55 to 64	10.1	12.2	–2.1
Aged 65 or older	7.8	9.6	–1.8
Total working men	**3.8**	**4.1**	**–0.3**
Aged 55 to 64	11.2	15.3	–4.1
Aged 65 or older	7.1	8.3	–1.2
Total working women	**3.4**	**3.1**	**0.3**
Aged 55 to 64	9.6	9.8	–0.2
Aged 65 or older	8.7	10.1	–1.4

Source: Bureau of Labor Statistics, Internet web site <http://www.bls.gov/news.release/tenure.t01.htm>; calculations by New Strategist

Many Older Americans Are Self-Employed

Men and women aged 65 or older are more likely than those younger to work for themselves.

While only 7 percent of all nonagricultural workers aged 16 or older are self-employed, 19 percent of workers aged 65 or older work for themselves. Self-employment usually requires specialized skills, and those most likely to have such skills are older workers with decades of experience. Men and women aged 55 or older account for 23 percent of all self-employed workers, a much greater proportion than their 12 percent share of all employed workers.

Older men are more likely to be self-employed than older women. While 15 percent of men aged 55 or older work for themselves, the proportion is just 10 percent among women in the age group. Twenty-two percent of men aged 65 or older are self-employed, versus 14 percent of their female counterparts.

◆ As boomers enter the 55-or-older age group, the number of self-employed Americans will rise sharply.

◆ Older Americans will be an increasingly important segment of the market for home-based business products and services.

Self-employment is much more common among older than younger men

(percent of men employed in nonagricultural work aged 16 or older and aged 55 or older who are self-employed, 1998)

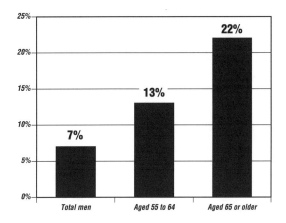

Self-Employed Workers Aged 55 or Older by Sex, 1998

(number of employed nonagricultural workers aged 16 or older and aged 55 or older, number and percent whose longest job in 1998 was self-employment, and percent of total self-employed accounted for by age group, by sex, 1998; numbers in thousands)

	total	self-employed number	self-employed percent	percent of total self-employed
Total workers	**128,084**	**8,962**	**7.0%**	**100.0%**
Total aged 55 or older	15,925	2,038	12.8	22.7
Aged 55 to 64	12,477	1,399	11.2	15.6
Aged 65 or older	3,448	639	18.5	7.1
Total working men	**68,139**	**5,480**	**8.0**	**100.0**
Total aged 55 or older	8,718	1,330	15.3	24.3
Aged 55 to 64	6,769	898	13.3	16.4
Aged 65 or older	1,949	432	22.2	7.9
Total working women	**59,945**	**3,482**	**5.8**	**100.0**
Total aged 55 or older	7,207	709	9.8	20.4
Aged 55 to 64	5,708	501	8.8	14.4
Aged 65 or older	1,499	208	13.9	6.0

Source: Bureau of Labor Statistics, Employment and Earnings, *January 1999; calculations by New Strategist*

Many Older Workers Are Independent Contractors

One in five working men aged 65 or older is an independent contractor.

Retirement does not appeal to everyone, but job flexibility does. This may explain why such a large proportion of workers aged 65 or older are independent contractors. Independent contracting is practiced by 21 percent of working men and 11 percent of working women aged 65 or older. Independent contractors include most of the nation's self-employed.

Independent contracting is just one type of alternative work arrangement, according to the Bureau of Labor Statistics. The others are on-call work (such as substitute teaching), temporary help, and working for a contract firm (such as a firm that provides lawn service). Few older workers are employed by temporary-help agencies or contract firms. But a significant share of older working women (5 percent) are on-call workers.

♦ Older workers are much more likely to be independent contractors than younger workers because of the job flexibility it offers.

♦ As entrepreneurial baby boomers enter the 55-or-older age group, the number of independent contractors will surge.

Workers Aged 55 or Older in Alternative Work Arrangements, 1997

(number of workers aged 16 or older and aged 55 or older, and number and percent employed in alternative work arrangements, by sex, 1997; numbers in thousands)

		alternative workers				
	total	total	independent contractors	on-call workers	temporary-help agency workers	workers provided by contract firms
Total employed	**126,742**	**12,561**	**8,456**	**1,996**	**1,300**	**809**
Total aged 55 or older	15,678	2,298	1,768	322	124	84
Aged 55 to 64	12,032	1,515	1,173	193	87	62
Aged 65 or older	3,646	783	595	129	37	22
Total men	**67,931**	**7,758**	**5,633**	**979**	**581**	**565**
Total aged 55 or older	8,669	1,499	1,270	129	52	48
Aged 55 to 64	6,558	985	838	77	29	41
Aged 65 or older	2,111	514	432	52	23	7
Total women	**58,811**	**4,804**	**2,824**	**1,017**	**719**	**244**
Total aged 55 or older	7,009	800	498	194	72	36
Aged 55 to 64	5,474	530	335	116	58	21
Aged 65 or older	1,535	270	163	78	14	15
Total employed	**100.0%**	**9.9%**	**6.7%**	**1.6%**	**1.0%**	**0.6%**
Total aged 55 or older	100.0	14.7	11.3	2.1	0.8	0.5
Aged 55 to 64	100.0	12.6	9.7	1.6	0.7	0.5
Aged 65 or older	100.0	21.5	16.3	3.5	1.0	0.6
Total men	**100.0**	**11.4**	**8.3**	**1.4**	**0.9**	**0.8**
Total aged 55 or older	100.0	17.3	14.6	1.5	0.6	0.6
Aged 55 to 64	100.0	15.0	12.8	1.2	0.4	0.6
Aged 65 or older	100.0	24.3	20.5	2.5	1.1	0.3
Total women	**100.0**	**8.2**	**4.8**	**1.7**	**1.2**	**0.4**
Total aged 55 or older	100.0	11.4	7.1	2.8	1.0	0.5
Aged 55 to 64	100.0	9.7	6.1	2.1	1.1	0.4
Aged 65 or older	100.0	17.6	10.6	5.1	0.9	1.0

Note: Independent contractors are workers who obtain customers on their own to provide a product or service, including the self-employed. On-call workers are in a pool of workers who are called to work only as needed, such as substitute teachers and construction workers supplied by a union hiring hall. Temporary-help agency workers are those who said they are paid by a temporary-help agency. Workers provided by contract firms are those employed by a company that provides employees or their services to others under contract, such as security, landscaping, and computer programming.
Source: Bureau of Labor Statistics, Contingent and Alternative Employment Arrangements, *February 1997, Internet web site <http://stats.bls.gov/newsrels.htm>; calculations by New Strategist*

Nearly 3 Million Older Workers Work at Home

Older workers account for a large share of the home-based self-employed.

Among the 14.5 million Americans aged 55 or older who work in nonagricultural industries, 2.7 million spend some of their time working at home. The largest number (1.3 million) are wage and salary workers who are not paid for the time they spend working at home—they are the ones lugging home a briefcase full of papers to finish a project after hours. Another 945,000 are self-employed people who work out of their home. The remaining 488,000 are wage and salary workers who are paid to work at home.

Workers aged 55 or older account for a disproportionate share of the home-based self-employed. While 12 percent of all nonagricultural workers are aged 55 or older, the proportion is nearly twice as high among the self-employed, at 23 percent. Older workers make up a large share of the self-employed because it often takes years to develop the expertise to run a business.

♦ Because older workers are the ones most likely to be self-employed, they are the best customers of home office products and services.

People Who Work at Home by Age, 1997

(number and percent distribution of workers aged 16 or older in nonagricultural industries by work-at-home status for primary job, by age, 1997; numbers in thousands)

	total workers	working at home total	working at home — wage and salary unpaid	working at home — wage and salary paid	home-based self-employed
NUMBER					
Total workers	**121,629**	**18,836**	**11,067**	**3,644**	**4,125**
Under age 35	47,899	5,127	3,142	1,173	812
Aged 35 to 54	59,203	11,084	6,734	1,982	2,368
Aged 55 or older	14,526	2,714	1,281	488	945
PERCENT DISTRIBUTION BY AGE					
Total workers	**100.0%**	**100.0%**	**100.0%**	**100.0%**	**100.0%**
Under age 35	39.4	27.2	28.4	32.2	19.7
Aged 35 to 54	48.7	58.8	60.8	54.4	57.4
Aged 55 or older	11.9	14.4	11.6	13.4	22.9
PERCENT DISTRIBUTION BY WORK STATUS					
Total workers	**100.0%**	**15.5%**	**9.1%**	**3.0%**	**3.4%**
Under age 35	100.0	10.7	6.6	2.4	1.7
Aged 35 to 54	100.0	18.7	11.4	3.3	4.0
Aged 55 or older	100.0	18.7	8.8	3.4	6.5

Source: Bureau of Labor Statistics, Work at Home in 1997, *USDL 98-93, Internet web site <http://stats.bls.gov/>; calculations by New Strategist*

Older Labor Force Projected to Grow Rapidly

The number of working women aged 55 to 59 should expand 74 percent between 1996 and 2006.

As the women of the baby-boom generation age into their late fifties and early sixties, the number of working women aged 55 to 59 will expand by more than 3 million. The labor force participation rate for women in this age group is projected to climb from 60 percent in 1996 to 67 percent in 2006. The participation rate for women aged 60 to 64 will also rise, climbing from 38 to 41 percent. In contrast, the rate for women aged 65 or older will remain stable during the decade.

The number of working men aged 55 to 59 will also climb more than 3 million between 1996 and 2006 as boomers enter the age group. And, in a reversal of the early retirement trend of the past several decades, the labor force participation rate for men in the age group will rise slightly, climbing from 77.9 to 78.7 percent. The participation rate of men aged 60 to 61 will continue to fall, while the rate for men aged 62 or older will rise slightly.

♦ As employers become increasingly stingy with pension benefits, and as the age of Social Security eligibility is rising, boomers won't be able to retire as early as the current generation of older Americans.

Projections of the Labor Force Aged 55 or Older by Sex, 1996 to 2006

(number and percent of people aged 16 or older and aged 55 or older in the civilian labor force by sex; 1996 and 2006; percent change in number and percentage point change in rate 1996–2006; numbers in thousands)

	number			participation rate		
	1996	2006	percent change 1996–2006	1996	2006	percentage point change 1996–2006
Total labor force	**133,943**	**148,847**	**11.1%**	**66.8%**	**67.1%**	**0.3**
Total men in labor force	**72,087**	**78,226**	**8.5**	**74.9**	**73.1**	**–1.8**
Aged 55 to 59	4,184	6,622	58.3	77.9	78.7	0.8
Aged 60 to 64	2,510	3,297	31.4	54.3	54.0	–0.3
Aged 60 to 61	1,276	1,627	27.5	66.2	65.0	–1.2
Aged 62 to 64	1,233	1,671	35.5	45.7	46.3	0.6
Aged 65 or older	2,247	2,551	13.5	16.9	17.3	0.9
Total women in labor force	**61,857**	**70,620**	**14.2**	**59.3**	**61.4**	**2.1**
Aged 55 to 59	3,474	6,047	74.1	59.8	66.6	6.8
Aged 60 to 64	1,978	2,787	40.9	38.2	41.3	3.1
Aged 60 to 61	1,011	1,376	36.1	47.2	49.7	2.5
Aged 62 to 64	967	1,411	45.9	31.8	35.4	3.6
Aged 65 or older	1,581	1,670	5.6	8.6	8.7	0.1

Source: Bureau of Labor Statistics, Internet web site <http://www.bls.gov/>; calculations by New Strategist

6

Living Arrangements

♦ Only half the 35 million households headed by people aged 55 or older are married couples.

♦ Among older householders, Hispanics are much more likely to be family heads than whites or blacks are.

♦ Single-person households are the most common household type among householders aged 75 or older.

♦ Eighteen percent of householders aged 55 or older have children living with them, most of whom are adults. Among Hispanic householders in this age group, fully 35 percent have children at home.

♦ One-third of women aged 55 or older live alone, a proportion that rises to 53 percent among women aged 75 or older. Among older men, the proportion of those who live alone peaks at 22 percent.

♦ Seventy-seven percent of women aged 85 or older are widows. Among their male counterparts, a much smaller 42 percent are widowers.

Married Couples Lose Ground with Age

Only 43 percent of householders aged 65 or older are married couples.

Of the nation's 103 million households in 1998, the 53 percent majority were married couples. But among the 21 million households headed by people aged 65 or older, a 43 percent minority are couples. Older people are less likely than the average American to live with their spouse because an important transition in living arrangements occurs in the 65-plus age group. While married couples account for an above-average share of households headed by 55-to-64-year-olds (61 percent), this proportion falls to just 33 percent among householders aged 75 or older.

The married-couple share of older households falls as older women become widowed and begin to live alone. Women who live alone or with nonrelatives account for 29 percent of all households headed by people aged 55 or older, ranging from just 18 percent of those headed by 55-to-64-year-olds to 46 percent of households headed by people aged 75 or older. In the oldest age group, the most common household type is women who live alone.

♦ Marketers targeting older householders must consider the unique consumer profile of each age group. While couples dominate households headed by 55-to-64-year-olds, women who live alone are the decision makers among householders aged 75 or older.

Households Headed by People Aged 55 or Older by Household Type, 1998: Total Households

(number and percent distribution of total households and households headed by people aged 55 or older, by household type; numbers in thousands, 1998)

| | | aged 55 or older | | | | |
| | | | | aged 65 or older | | |
	total	total	55 to 64	total	65 to 74	75 or older
Total households	**102,528**	**34,569**	**13,072**	**21,497**	**11,272**	**10,226**
Family households	**70,880**	**20,657**	**9,387**	**11,270**	**6,989**	**4,282**
Married couples	54,317	17,144	7,936	9,208	5,841	3,368
Female householder, no spouse present	12,652	2,775	1,099	1,676	938	738
Male householder, no spouse present	3,911	738	352	386	210	176
Nonfamily households	**31,648**	**13,912**	**3,685**	**10,227**	**4,283**	**5,944**
Female householder	17,516	10,081	2,337	7,744	3,080	4,665
Living alone	15,317	9,725	2,148	7,577	2,987	4,590
Male householder	14,133	3,831	1,348	2,483	1,203	1,279
Living alone	11,010	3,498	1,153	2,345	1,111	1,234
Total households	**100.0%**	**100.0%**	**100.0%**	**100.0%**	**100.0%**	**100.0%**
Family households	**69.1**	**59.8**	**71.8**	**52.4**	**62.0**	**41.9**
Married couples	53.0	49.6	60.7	42.8	51.8	32.9
Female householder, no spouse present	12.3	8.0	8.4	7.8	8.3	7.2
Male householder, no spouse present	3.8	2.1	2.7	1.8	1.9	1.7
Nonfamily households	**30.9**	**40.2**	**28.2**	**47.6**	**38.0**	**58.1**
Female householder	17.1	29.2	17.9	36.0	27.3	45.6
Living alone	14.9	28.1	16.4	35.2	26.5	44.9
Male householder	13.8	11.1	10.3	11.6	10.7	12.5
Living alone	10.7	10.1	8.8	10.9	9.9	12.1

Source: Bureau of the Census, unpublished data from the 1998 Current Population Survey, Internet web site <http://www.bls.census.gov/cps>; calculations by New Strategist

Households of Older Americans Differ by Race and Hispanic Origin

Among older households, married couples are a much larger share of white and Hispanic households than black households.

The differences in household composition among older people by race and ethnicity are so great that marketers who do not account for them are likely to miss their target. Married couples account for more than 4 out of 10 households headed by whites and Hispanics aged 65 or older, but for just 28 percent of those headed by older blacks. Female-headed families are more common among older blacks than whites. Eighteen percent of black householders aged 65 or older are female family heads versus only 7 percent of their white counterparts.

Older Hispanics are much more likely to live with family members than whites or blacks are. Sixty percent of Hispanic householders aged 65 or older are family heads versus 53 percent of white and 49 percent of black householders in the age group. Only 39 percent of Hispanic householders aged 65 or older live alone compared with a much higher 46 percent of whites and 50 percent of blacks.

♦ Many Hispanics are immigrants from Mexico and other Spanish-speaking countries who bring with them a traditional family structure that persists into old age.

Households Headed by People Aged 55 or Older by Household Type, 1998: Black Households

(number and percent distribution of total black households and black households headed by people aged 55 or older, by household type; numbers in thousands, 1998)

| | | aged 55 or older | | | | |
| | | | | aged 65 or older | | |
	total	total	55 to 64	total	65 to 74	75 or older
Total black households	**12,474**	**3,319**	**1,441**	**1,878**	**1,123**	**755**
Family households	**8,409**	**1,777**	**861**	**916**	**607**	**308**
Married couples	3,921	1,003	485	518	369	149
Female householder, no spouse present	3,926	659	314	345	214	131
Male householder, no spouse present	562	115	62	53	24	28
Nonfamily households	**4,066**	**1,543**	**580**	**963**	**516**	**446**
Female householder	2,190	1,049	365	684	369	315
Living alone	1,982	998	335	663	359	304
Male householder	1,876	494	215	279	147	131
Living alone	1,594	442	176	266	142	124
Total black households	**100.0%**	**100.0%**	**100.0%**	**100.0%**	**100.0%**	**100.0%**
Family households	**67.4**	**53.5**	**59.8**	**48.8**	**54.1**	**40.8**
Married couples	31.4	30.2	33.7	27.6	32.9	19.7
Female householder, no spouse present	31.5	19.9	21.8	18.4	19.1	17.4
Male householder, no spouse present	4.5	3.5	4.3	2.8	2.1	3.7
Nonfamily households	**32.6**	**46.5**	**40.2**	**51.3**	**45.9**	**59.1**
Female householder	17.6	31.6	25.3	36.4	32.9	41.7
Living alone	15.9	30.1	23.2	35.3	32.0	40.3
Male householder	15.0	14.9	14.9	14.9	13.1	17.4
Living alone	12.8	13.3	12.2	14.2	12.6	16.4

Source: Bureau of the Census, unpublished data from the 1998 Current Population Survey, Internet web site <http://www.bls.census.gov/cps>; calculations by New Strategist

Households Headed by People Aged 55 or Older by Household Type, 1998: Hispanic Households

(number and percent distribution of total Hispanic households and Hispanic households headed by people aged 55 or older, by household type; numbers in thousands, 1998)

	total	aged 55 or older		aged 65 or older		
		total	55 to 64	total	65 to 74	75 or older
Total Hispanic households	**8,590**	**1,805**	**889**	**916**	**566**	**350**
Family households	**6,961**	**1,222**	**675**	**547**	**372**	**175**
Married couples	4,804	919	507	412	282	130
Female householder,						
no spouse present	1,612	252	135	117	78	39
Male householder,						
no spouse present	545	51	33	18	12	6
Nonfamily households	**1,629**	**583**	**213**	**370**	**193**	**175**
Female householder	754	400	137	263	131	131
Living alone	617	371	115	256	127	129
Male householder	875	183	76	107	62	44
Living alone	623	160	65	95	55	40
Total Hispanic households	**100.0%**	**100.0%**	**100.0%**	**100.0%**	**100.0%**	**100.0%**
Family households	**81.0**	**67.7**	**75.9**	**59.7**	**65.7**	**50.0**
Married couples	55.9	50.9	57.0	45.0	49.8	37.1
Female householder,						
no spouse present	18.8	14.0	15.2	12.8	13.8	11.1
Male householder,						
no spouse present	6.3	2.8	3.7	2.0	2.1	1.7
Nonfamily households	**19.0**	**32.3**	**24.0**	**40.4**	**34.1**	**50.0**
Female householder	8.8	22.2	15.4	28.7	23.1	37.4
Living alone	7.2	20.6	12.9	27.9	22.4	36.9
Male householder	10.2	10.1	8.5	11.7	11.0	12.6
Living alone	7.3	8.9	7.3	10.4	9.7	11.4

Source: Bureau of the Census, unpublished data from the 1998 Current Population Survey, Internet web site <http://www.bls.census.gov/cps>; calculations by New Strategist

Households Headed by People Aged 55 or Older by Household Type, 1998: White Households

(number and percent distribution of total white households and white households headed by people aged 55 or older, by household type; numbers in thousands, 1998)

| | | aged 55 or older | | | | |
| | | | | aged 65 or older | | |
	total	total	55 to 64	total	65 to 74	75 or older
Total white households	**86,106**	**30,359**	**11,163**	**19,196**	**9,917**	**9,279**
Family households	**59,511**	**18,217**	**8,145**	**10,072**	**6,222**	**3,850**
Married couples	48,066	15,581	7,125	8,456	5,338	3,118
Female householder, no spouse present	8,308	2,049	748	1,301	710	591
Male householder, no spouse present	3,137	587	272	315	174	141
Nonfamily households	**26,596**	**12,142**	**3,018**	**9,124**	**3,695**	**5,429**
Female householder	14,871	8,891	1,937	6,954	2,660	4,294
Living alone	12,980	8,585	1,778	6,807	2,577	4,230
Male householder	11,725	3,251	1,081	2,170	1,035	1,135
Living alone	9,018	2,989	939	2,050	951	1,099
Total white households	**100.0%**	**100.0%**	**100.0%**	**100.0%**	**100.0%**	**100.0%**
Family households	**69.1**	**60.0**	**73.0**	**52.5**	**62.7**	**41.5**
Married couples	55.8	51.3	63.8	44.1	53.8	33.6
Female householder, no spouse present	9.6	6.7	6.7	6.8	7.2	6.4
Male householder, no spouse present	3.6	1.9	2.4	1.6	1.8	1.5
Nonfamily households	**30.9**	**40.0**	**27.0**	**47.5**	**37.3**	**58.5**
Female householder	17.3	29.3	17.4	36.2	26.8	46.3
Living alone	15.1	28.3	15.9	35.5	26.0	45.6
Male householder	13.6	10.7	9.7	11.3	10.4	12.2
Living alone	10.5	9.8	8.4	10.7	9.6	11.8

Source: Bureau of the Census, unpublished data from the 1998 Current Population Survey, Internet web site <http://www.bls.census.gov/cps>; calculations by New Strategist

Older Households Are Small

Households headed by people aged 55 or older average only 1.95 people.

The average U.S. household is home to 2.62 people. Household size peaks in middle age, when couples are raising children. It falls steadily in the 55-plus age groups, from an average of 2.26 people in households headed by 55-to-64-year-olds to just 1.41 people in households headed by people aged 85 or older.

The two-person household is most common among householders aged 55 to 74. Among householders aged 75 or older, single-person households are most common. Fully 71 percent of households headed by Americans aged 85 or older are home to just one person—most of them widows. Overall, householders aged 55 or older account for more than half the nation's single-person households.

♦ The wants and needs of married couples are different from those of people who live alone. Businesses targeting older Americans must segment the market by lifestyle to find receptive consumers.

Average household size shrinks with age

(average number of persons per household by age of householder, 1998)

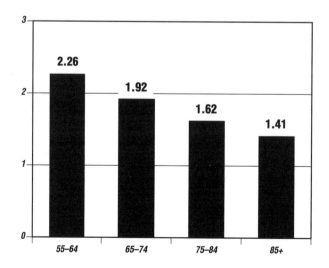

Households Headed by People Aged 55 or Older by Size, 1998

(number and percent distribution of total households and households headed by people aged 55 or older by size of household, 1998; numbers in thousands)

| | total | aged 55 or older | | aged 65 or older | | | |
		total	55 to 64	total	65 to 74	75 to 84	85 or older
Total households	**102,528**	**34,569**	**13,072**	**21,497**	**11,272**	**8,090**	**2,135**
One person	26,327	13,224	3,301	9,923	4,098	4,301	1,524
Two persons	32,965	15,874	6,499	9,375	5,667	3,214	494
Three persons	17,331	3,315	1,891	1,424	944	403	77
Four persons	15,358	1,295	855	440	331	79	30
Five persons	7,048	506	310	196	143	44	9
Six persons	2,232	198	126	72	47	23	2
Seven or more persons	1,267	160	91	69	42	27	–
Average number of people per household	2.62	1.95	2.26	1.76	1.92	1.62	1.41
Total households	**100.0%**	**100.0%**	**100.0%**	**100.0%**	**100.0%**	**100.0%**	**100.0%**
One person	25.7	38.3	25.3	46.2	36.4	53.2	71.4
Two persons	32.2	45.9	49.7	43.6	50.3	39.7	23.1
Three persons	16.9	9.6	14.5	6.6	8.4	5.0	3.6
Four persons	15.0	3.7	6.5	2.0	2.9	1.0	1.4
Five persons	6.9	1.5	2.4	0.9	1.3	0.5	0.4
Six persons	2.2	0.7	1.0	0.3	0.4	0.3	0.1
Seven or more persons	1.2	0.5	0.7	0.3	0.4	0.3	–

Note: (–) means sample is too small to make a reliable estimate.
Source: Bureau of the Census, detailed tables from Household and Family Characteristics: March 1998, *Current Population Reports, P20-515, 1998; calculations by New Strategist*

Many Older Americans Have Children at Home

Six million householders aged 55 or older share their homes with children.

Eighteen percent of householders aged 55 or older have children in their home. Among householders aged 55 to 64, the figure is a substantial 27 percent. Most of these children are adults, many of them living with mom and dad while they attend college, hunt for a job, or recover from divorce. Despite the rise in the number of older parents in the past few decades, only 6 percent of householders aged 55 to 64 have children under age 18 at home.

Blacks and Hispanics are much more likely than whites to have children at home. One-third of black householders aged 55 to 64 live with children, as do an even greater 46 percent of Hispanics in the age group. In contrast, only 24 percent of white householders aged 55 to 64 have children at home.

◆ The nest is slow to empty, particularly for Hispanics and blacks. With the lives of many older Americans still revolving around their children, marketers should not assume that the older market is free of the constraints of parenting.

Householders aged 55 to 64 are most likely to have children at home

(percent of households headed by people aged 55 or older with children of any age at home, 1998)

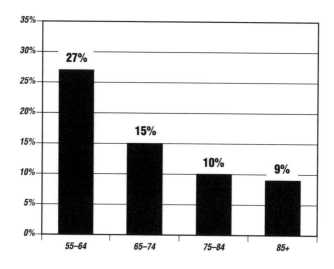

Households Headed by People Aged 55 or Older by Presence and Age of Children at Home, 1998: Total Households

(number and percent distribution of total households and households headed by people aged 55 or older, by presence and age of own children at home, 1998; numbers in thousands)

| | total | aged 55 or older | | aged 65 or older | | | |
		total	55 to 64	total	65 to 74	75 to 84	85 or older
Total households	102,528	34,569	13,072	21,497	11,272	8,090	2,135
With children of any age	44,979	6,149	3,469	2,680	1,687	810	183
Under age 25	40,006	2,092	1,802	290	240	48	2
Under age 18	34,760	899	760	139	112	25	2
Under age 6	15,532	98	71	27	22	5	–
Total households	100.0%	100.0%	100.0%	100.0%	100.0%	100.0%	100.0%
With children of any age	43.9	17.8	26.5	12.5	15.0	10.0	8.6
Under age 25	39.0	6.1	13.8	1.3	2.1	0.6	0.1
Under age 18	33.9	2.6	5.8	0.6	1.0	0.3	0.1
Under age 6	15.1	0.3	0.5	0.1	0.2	0.1	–

Note: (–) means sample is too small to make a reliable estimate.
Source: Bureau of the Census, detailed tables from Household and Family Characteristics: March 1998; *Current Population Reports, P20-515, 1998; calculations by New Strategist*

Households Headed by People Aged 55 or Older by Presence and Age of Children at Home, 1998: Black Households

(number and percent distribution of total black households and black households headed by people aged 55 or older, by presence and age of own children at home, 1998; numbers in thousands)

| | | aged 55 or older | | | | | |
| | | | | aged 65 or older | | | |
	total	*total*	*55 to 64*	*total*	*65 to 74*	*75 to 84*	*85 or older*
Total black households	**12,474**	**3,319**	**1,441**	**1,878**	**1,123**	**562**	**193**
With children of any age	**6,383**	**907**	**512**	**395**	**245**	**119**	**31**
Under age 25	5,538	238	179	59	44	15	–
Under age 18	4,847	119	80	39	31	8	–
Under age 6	2,101	21	9	12	9	3	–
Total black households	**100.0%**	**100.0%**	**100.0%**	**100.0%**	**100.0%**	**100.0%**	**100.0%**
With children of any age	**51.2**	**27.3**	**35.5**	**21.0**	**21.8**	**21.2**	**16.1**
Under age 25	44.4	7.2	12.4	3.1	3.9	2.7	–
Under age 18	38.9	3.6	5.6	2.1	2.8	1.4	–
Under age 6	16.8	0.6	0.6	0.6	0.8	0.5	–

Note: (–) means sample is too small to make a reliable estimate.
Source: Bureau of the Census, detailed tables from Household and Family Characteristics: March 1998*; Current Population Reports, P20-515, 1998; calculations by New Strategist*

Households Headed by People Aged 55 or Older by Presence and Age of Children at Home, 1998: Hispanic Households

(number and percent distribution of total Hispanic households and Hispanic households headed by people aged 55 or older, by presence and age of own children at home, 1998; numbers in thousands)

| | | aged 55 or older | | | | | |
| | | | | aged 65 or older | | | |
	total	*total*	*55 to 64*	*total*	*65 to 74*	*75 to 84*	*85 or older*
Total Hispanic households	**8,590**	**1,805**	**889**	**916**	**566**	**292**	**58**
With children of any age	**5,421**	**635**	**412**	**223**	**160**	**53**	**10**
Under age 25	5,004	283	257	26	20	4	2
Under age 18	4,475	125	113	12	7	3	2
Under age 6	2,399	13	11	2	2	–	–
Total Hispanic households	**100.0%**	**100.0%**	**100.0%**	**100.0%**	**100.0%**	**100.0%**	**100.0%**
With children of any age	**63.1**	**35.2**	**46.3**	**24.3**	**28.3**	**18.2**	**17.2**
Under age 25	58.3	15.7	28.9	2.8	3.5	1.4	3.4
Under age 18	52.1	6.9	12.7	1.3	1.2	1.0	3.4
Under age 6	27.9	0.7	1.2	0.2	0.4	–	–

Note: (–) means sample is too small to make a reliable estimate.
Source: Bureau of the Census, detailed tables from Household and Family Characteristics: March 1998;
Current Population Reports, P20-515, 1998; calculations by New Strategist

Households Headed by People Aged 55 or Older by Presence and Age of Children at Home, 1998: White Households

(number and percent distribution of total white households and white households headed by people aged 55 or older, by presence and age of own children at home, 1998; numbers in thousands)

| | | aged 55 or older | | | | | |
| | | | | aged 65 or older | | | |
	total	*total*	*55 to 64*	*total*	*65 to 74*	*75 to 84*	*85 or older*
Total white households	**86,106**	**30,359**	**11,163**	**19,196**	**9,917**	**7,371**	**1,908**
With children of any age	**36,520**	**4,898**	**2,717**	**2,181**	**1,381**	**649**	**151**
Under age 25	32,632	1,702	1,488	214	179	33	2
Under age 18	28,336	721	625	96	76	18	2
Under age 6	12,710	70	55	15	13	2	–
Total white households	**100.0%**	**100.0%**	**100.0%**	**100.0%**	**100.0%**	**100.0%**	**100.0%**
With children of any age	**42.4**	**16.1**	**24.3**	**11.4**	**13.9**	**8.8**	**7.9**
Under age 25	37.9	5.6	13.3	1.1	1.8	0.4	0.1
Under age 18	32.9	2.4	5.6	0.5	0.8	0.2	0.1
Under age 6	14.8	0.2	0.5	0.1	0.1	0.0	–

Note: (–) means sample is too small to make a reliable estimate.
Source: Bureau of the Census, detailed tables from Household and Family Characteristics: March 1998;
Current Population Reports, P20-515, 1998; calculations by New Strategist

Lifestyles of Men and Women Diverge in Old Age

Most older men live with a wife, while most older women live alone.

The lifestyles of men and women become increasingly different with age. Because men die at a younger age than women, and because women tend to marry men who are slightly older, most women spend the end of their lives alone while most men die while still married.

In the 55-to-64 age group, 64 percent of women and 76 percent of men live with a spouse. This 12 percentage point gap in living arrangements grows to a 39 percentage point chasm in the 75-plus age group—when a substantial 66 percent of men, but only 27 percent of women, still live with a spouse. Fifty-three percent of women aged 75 or older live alone, versus only 22 percent of their male counterparts.

◆ Married couples dominate consumers aged 55 to 64, but in older age groups single women are the dominant consumers. Businesses targeting older Americans must design their products and services and craft their messages accordingly.

Most older men are married

(percent of people aged 75 or older who live with a spouse or live alone, by sex, 1998)

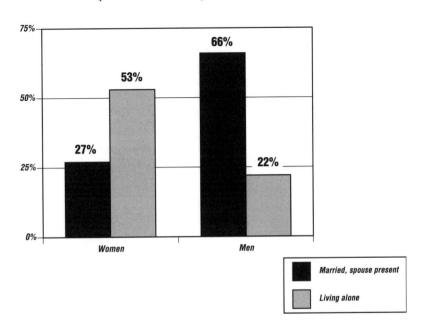

Living Arrangements of Men Aged 55 or Older, 1998

(number and percent distribution of men aged 15 or older and aged 55 or older by living arrangement, 1998; numbers in thousands)

	total	aged 55 or older total	55 to 64	aged 65 or older total	65 to 74	75 or older
Total men	**101,123**	**24,198**	**10,673**	**13,525**	**7,992**	**5,533**
Living with spouse	55,304	17,975	8,154	9,821	6,146	3,675
Other family householder	3,911	738	352	386	210	176
Living with parents	18,421	221	199	22	22	–
Other family member	3,678	822	279	543	237	306
Living alone	11,010	3,498	1,153	2,345	1,111	1,234
Living with nonrelatives	8,799	943	536	407	266	141
Total men	**100.0%**	**100.0%**	**100.0%**	**100.0%**	**100.0%**	**100.0%**
Living with spouse	54.7	74.3	76.4	72.6	76.9	66.4
Other family householder	3.9	3.0	3.3	2.9	2.6	3.2
Living with parents	18.2	0.9	1.9	0.2	0.3	–
Other family member	3.6	3.4	2.6	4.0	3.0	5.5
Living alone	10.9	14.5	10.8	17.3	13.9	22.3
Living with nonrelatives	8.7	3.9	5.0	3.0	3.3	2.5

Note: (–) means sample is too small to make a reliable estimate.
Source: Bureau of the Census, Marital Status and Living Arrangements: March 1998, Current Population Reports, P20-514, 1998; and unpublished tables from the 1998 Current Population Survey, Internet web site <http://www.bls.census.gov/cps>; calculations by New Strategist

Living Arrangements of Women Aged 55 or Older, 1998

(number and percent distribution of women aged 15 or older and aged 55 or older by living arrangement, 1998; numbers in thousands)

| | total | aged 55 or older | | aged 65 or older | | |
		total	55 to 64	total	65 to 74	75 or older
Total women	**108,168**	**30,141**	**11,582**	**18,559**	**9,882**	**8,677**
Living with spouse	55,304	15,012	7,451	7,561	5,181	2,380
Other family householder	12,652	2,775	1,099	1,676	938	738
Living with parents	14,224	134	110	24	21	3
Other family member	4,116	1,790	375	1,415	579	836
Living alone	15,317	9,725	2,148	7,577	2,987	4,590
Living with nonrelatives	6,555	706	400	306	176	130
Total women	**100.0%**	**100.0%**	**100.0%**	**100.0%**	**100.0%**	**100.0%**
Living with spouse	51.1	49.8	64.3	40.7	52.4	27.4
Other family householder	11.7	9.2	9.5	9.0	9.5	8.5
Living with parents	13.1	0.4	0.9	0.1	0.2	0.0
Other family member	3.8	5.9	3.2	7.6	5.9	9.6
Living alone	14.2	32.3	18.5	40.8	30.2	52.9
Living with nonrelatives	6.1	2.3	3.5	1.6	1.8	1.5

Source: Bureau of the Census, Marital Status and Living Arrangements: March 1998, Current Population Reports, P20-514, 1998; and unpublished tables from the 1998 Current Population Survey, Internet web site <http://www.bls.census.gov/cps>; calculations by New Strategist

People Aged 55 or Older Who Live Alone by Sex, 1998

(number and percent of people aged 15 or older and aged 55 or older who live alone by age and sex, 1998; numbers in thousands)

	total	living alone	
		number	percent
Total people	**209,291**	**26,327**	**12.6%**
Aged 55 or older	54,338	13,224	24.3
Aged 65 or older	32,083	9,923	30.9
Aged 75 or older	14,209	5,824	41.0
Aged 55 to 64	22,255	3,301	14.8
Aged 65 to 74	17,874	4,099	22.9
Aged 75 or older	14,209	5,824	41.0
Aged 55 to 59	12,190	1,653	13.6
Aged 60 to 64	10,065	1,648	16.4
Aged 65 to 69	9,361	1,905	20.4
Aged 70 to 74	8,513	2,194	25.8
Aged 75 or older	14,209	5,824	41.0
Total men	**101,123**	**11,010**	**10.9**
Aged 55 or older	24,197	3,498	14.5
Aged 65 or older	13,524	2,345	17.3
Aged 75 or older	5,532	1,234	22.3
Aged 55 to 64	10,673	1,153	10.8
Aged 65 to 74	7,992	1,111	13.9
Aged 75 or older	5,532	1,234	22.3
Aged 55 to 59	5,869	656	11.2
Aged 60 to 64	4,804	497	10.3
Aged 65 to 69	4,286	528	12.3
Aged 70 to 74	3,706	583	15.7
Aged 75 or older	5,532	1,234	22.3

(continued)

(continued from previous page)

		living alone	
	total	**number**	**percent**
Total women	**108,168**	**15,317**	**14.2%**
Aged 55 or older	30,141	9,726	32.3
Aged 65 or older	18,559	7,578	40.8
Aged 75 or older	8,677	4,590	52.9
Aged 55 to 64	11,582	2,148	18.5
Aged 65 to 74	9,882	2,988	30.2
Aged 75 or older	8,677	4,590	52.9
Aged 55 to 59	6,321	997	15.8
Aged 60 to 64	5,261	1,151	21.9
Aged 65 to 69	5,075	1,377	27.1
Aged 70 to 74	4,807	1,611	33.5
Aged 75 or older	8,677	4,590	52.9

*Source: Bureau of the Census, unpublished tables from the 1998 Current Population Survey, Internet web site
<http://www.bls.census.gov/cps>; calculations by New Strategist*

Among Women Aged 65 or Older, Married Are in the Minority

Widows outnumber wives among women aged 65 or older.

While 53 percent of women aged 55 or older are currently married, the proportion among men is a much higher 77 percent. Reasons for this difference include the facts that women tend to marry men who are a few years older and that men die at a younger age than women. Consequently, women are much more likely than men to be widowed in old age.

The percentage of women who are widows stood at 33 percent among women aged 55 or older in 1998, ranging from a low of 13 percent among those aged 55 to 64 to a high of 77 percent among those aged 85 or older. Only 10 percent of men aged 55 or older are widowed, but 42 percent of those aged 85 or older are.

Marital-status trends are the same regardless of race and ethnicity. The married far outnumber the widowed among whites, blacks, and Hispanics aged 55 to 64. But in the 85-plus age group, more than three out of four black, Hispanic, and white women are widows. For white and Hispanic men, the married outnumber the widowed even in the oldest age group. The only exception are black men aged 85 or older, among whom widowers outnumber the married.

♦ Many older Americans are coping with the loss of a spouse, a lifestyle transition of importance to many marketers.

Marital Status of People Aged 55 or Older by Sex, 1998: Total People

(number and percent distribution of people aged 15 or older and aged 55 or older by sex and marital status, 1998; numbers in thousands)

| | | aged 55 or older | | | aged 65 or older | | |
	total	total	55 to 64	total	65 to 74	75 to 84	85 or older
Total men	**101,123**	**24,198**	**10,673**	**13,525**	**7,992**	**4,527**	**1,006**
Never married	31,591	1,090	572	518	328	145	45
Married	58,633	18,719	8,559	10,160	6,331	3,327	502
Divorced	8,331	2,094	1,266	828	626	166	36
Widowed	2,569	2,293	275	2,018	707	888	423
Total women	**108,168**	**30,141**	**11,582**	**18,559**	**9,882**	**6,754**	**1,923**
Never married	26,713	1,409	538	871	425	340	106
Married	59,333	15,825	7,847	7,978	5,420	2,300	258
Divorced	11,093	2,986	1,671	1,315	882	362	71
Widowed	11,029	9,920	1,526	8,394	3,155	3,752	1,487
Total men	**100.0%**	**100.0%**	**100.0%**	**100.0%**	**100.0%**	**100.0%**	**100.0%**
Never married	31.2	4.5	5.4	3.8	4.1	3.2	4.5
Married	58.0	77.4	80.2	75.1	79.2	73.5	49.9
Divorced	8.2	8.7	11.9	6.1	7.8	3.7	3.6
Widowed	2.5	9.5	2.6	14.9	8.8	19.6	42.0
Total women	**100.0**	**100.0**	**100.0**	**100.0**	**100.0**	**100.0**	**100.0**
Never married	24.7	4.7	4.6	4.7	4.3	5.0	5.5
Married	54.9	52.5	67.8	43.0	54.8	34.1	13.4
Divorced	10.3	9.9	14.4	7.1	8.9	5.4	3.7
Widowed	10.2	32.9	13.2	45.2	31.9	55.6	77.3

Source: Bureau of the Census, Marital Status and Living Arrangements: March 1998, *Current Population Reports, P20-514, 1998; calculations by New Strategist*

Marital Status of People Aged 55 or Older by Sex, 1998: Blacks

(number and percent distribution of blacks aged 15 or older and aged 55 or older by sex and marital status, 1998; numbers in thousands)

| | total | aged 55 or older | | aged 65 or older | | | |
		total	55 to 64	total	65 to 74	75 to 84	85 or older
Total black men	**11,283**	**2,036**	**968**	**1,068**	**657**	**295**	**116**
Never married	5,191	163	104	59	36	16	7
Married	4,675	1,248	640	608	420	157	31
Divorced	1,035	293	154	139	106	26	7
Widowed	382	334	71	263	97	95	71
Total black women	**13,715**	**2,879**	**1,255**	**1,624**	**956**	**494**	**174**
Never married	5,689	248	136	112	63	45	4
Married	4,983	1,057	580	477	344	118	15
Divorced	1,673	426	275	151	105	36	10
Widowed	1,370	1,148	263	885	444	296	145
Total black men	**100.0%**	**100.0%**	**100.0%**	**100.0%**	**100.0%**	**100.0%**	**100.0%**
Never married	46.0	8.0	10.7	5.5	5.5	5.4	6.0
Married	41.4	61.3	66.1	56.9	63.9	53.2	26.7
Divorced	9.2	14.4	15.9	13.0	16.1	8.8	6.0
Widowed	3.4	16.4	7.3	24.6	14.8	32.2	61.2
Total black women	**100.0**	**100.0**	**100.0**	**100.0**	**100.0**	**100.0**	**100.0**
Never married	41.5	8.6	10.8	6.9	6.6	9.1	2.3
Married	36.3	36.7	46.2	29.4	36.0	23.9	8.6
Divorced	12.2	14.8	21.9	9.3	11.0	7.3	5.7
Widowed	10.0	39.9	21.0	54.5	46.4	59.9	83.3

Source: Bureau of the Census, Marital Status and Living Arrangements: March 1998, *Current Population Reports, P20-514, 1998; calculations by New Strategist*

Marital Status of People Aged 55 or Older by Sex, 1998: Hispanics

(number and percent distribution of Hispanics aged 15 or older and aged 55 or older by sex and marital status, 1998; numbers in thousands)

		aged 55 or older					
				aged 65 or older			
	total	*total*	*55 to 64*	*total*	*65 to 74*	*75 to 84*	*85 or older*
Total Hispanic men	**10,944**	**1,449**	**768**	**681**	**429**	**199**	**53**
Never married	4,370	74	44	30	23	4	3
Married	5,797	1,128	629	499	331	143	25
Divorced	647	130	77	53	37	15	1
Widowed	131	113	18	95	37	36	22
Total Hispanic women	**10,485**	**1,802**	**865**	**937**	**586**	**281**	**70**
Never married	3,072	127	75	52	35	11	6
Married	5,911	965	565	400	296	95	9
Divorced	885	227	133	94	73	21	–
Widowed	617	481	91	390	182	153	55
Total Hispanic men	**100.0%**	**100.0%**	**100.0%**	**100.0%**	**100.0%**	**100.0%**	**100.0%**
Never married	39.9	5.1	5.7	4.4	5.4	2.0	5.7
Married	53.0	77.8	81.9	73.3	77.2	71.9	47.2
Divorced	5.9	9.0	10.0	7.8	8.6	7.5	1.9
Widowed	1.2	7.8	2.3	14.0	8.6	18.1	41.5
Total Hispanic women	**100.0**	**100.0**	**100.0**	**100.0**	**100.0**	**100.0**	**100.0**
Never married	29.3	7.0	8.7	5.5	6.0	3.9	8.6
Married	56.4	53.6	65.3	42.7	50.5	33.8	12.9
Divorced	8.4	12.6	15.4	10.0	12.5	7.5	–
Widowed	5.9	26.7	10.5	41.6	31.1	54.4	78.6

Note: (–) means sample is too small to make a reliable estimate.
Source: Bureau of the Census, Marital Status and Living Arrangements: March 1998, *Current Population Reports, P20-514, 1998; calculations by New Strategist*

Marital Status of People Aged 55 or Older by Sex, 1998: Whites

(number and percent distribution of whites aged 15 or older and aged 55 or older by sex and marital status, 1998; numbers in thousands)

| | | aged 55 or older | | | | | |
| | | | | aged 65 or older | | | |
	total	total	55 to 64	total	65 to 74	75 to 84	85 or older
Total white men	**85,219**	**21,321**	**9,258**	**12,063**	**7,109**	**4,103**	**851**
Never married	24,775	902	451	451	285	129	37
Married	51,299	16,795	7,559	9,236	5,730	3,060	446
Divorced	7,038	1,734	1,060	674	507	138	29
Widowed	2,106	1,891	189	1,702	587	775	340
Total white women	**89,489**	**26,372**	**9,882**	**16,490**	**8,651**	**6,108**	**1,731**
Never married	19,614	1,129	387	742	351	290	101
Married	51,410	14,210	6,927	7,283	4,920	2,127	236
Divorced	9,115	2,497	1,362	1,135	755	318	62
Widowed	9,351	8,536	1,206	7,330	2,625	3,373	1,332
Total white men	**100.0%**	**100.0%**	**100.0%**	**100.0%**	**100.0%**	**100.0%**	**100.0%**
Never married	29.1	4.2	4.9	3.7	4.0	3.1	4.3
Married	60.2	78.8	81.6	76.6	80.6	74.6	52.4
Divorced	8.3	8.1	11.4	5.6	7.1	3.4	3.4
Widowed	2.5	8.9	2.0	14.1	8.3	18.9	40.0
Total white women	**100.0**	**100.0**	**100.0**	**100.0**	**100.0**	**100.0**	**100.0**
Never married	21.9	4.3	3.9	4.5	4.1	4.7	5.8
Married	57.4	53.9	70.1	44.2	56.9	34.8	13.6
Divorced	10.2	9.5	13.8	6.9	8.7	5.2	3.6
Widowed	10.4	32.4	12.2	44.5	30.3	55.2	76.9

Source: Bureau of the Census, Marital Status and Living Arrangements: March 1998, *Current Population Reports, P20–514, 1998; calculations by New Strategist*

7

Population

◆ Most older Americans are women. Among 65-to-69-year-olds, only 46 percent are men. This figure drops to 31 percent among 85-to-89-year-olds and to just 17 percent among people aged 100 or older.

◆ The number of 55-to-64-year-olds will grow 27 percent between 1999 and 2005, while the number of people aged 85 or older will climb 19 percent. In contrast, the 65-to-74 age group will increase only 1 percent.

◆ Although 11 percent of all Americans are Hispanic, only 6 percent of people aged 55 or older are Hispanic.

◆ The number of 65-to-74-year-olds is projected to decline 6 percent in New England between 2000 and 2005 and grow 12 percent in the Mountain states.

◆ In Nevada, the number of people aged 55 or older is projected to grow 25 percent between 2000 and 2005.

◆ In 24 states, the elderly population will number more than 1 million by 2025, up from only 9 states today.

◆ People aged 55 or older are far less likely to move than younger people. When they do move, however, they are more likely to move to a different state.

More Women Than Men in 55-plus Population

There are only 78 men aged 55 or older for every 100 women in the age group.

At birth males outnumber females, but by the early thirties women are in the majority. This trend gains strength with age because, at every age, men are more likely to die than women. The average life expectancy of newborn boys is 74 years, but for newborn girls it is 79. By age 55, women can expect to live 27 more years, men just 23. Thus, women increasingly outnumber men in the older age groups. In the 65-to-69 age group, there are 85 men per 100 women—in other words, men account for 46 percent of the population. This figure falls to 31 percent in the 85-to-89 age group, and only 17 percent of the nation's centenarians are men.

◆ The older market is increasingly a women's market—especially among the very old, aged 85 or older.

◆ Because men die younger than women, many older women are widows. The figure rises from 13 percent among women aged 55 to 64 to 78 percent among women aged 85 or older. Marketers should keep in mind that many, if not most, older women are independent consumers.

Women increasingly outnumber men with age

(males per 100 females, by age, 1999)

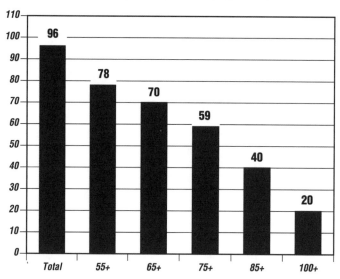

Population Aged 55 or Older by Sex, 1999

(number of total people and people aged 55 or older by age and sex, and sex ratio by age, 1999; numbers in thousands)

	total	men	women	males per 100 females
Total people	**272,330**	**133,039**	**139,291**	**96**
Total aged 55 or older	**57,817**	**25,340**	**32,479**	**78**
Aged 65 or older	34,439	14,190	20,251	70
Aged 75 or older	16,253	6,018	10,235	59
Aged 55 to 64	23,378	11,150	12,228	91
Aged 65 to 74	18,186	8,172	10,016	82
Aged 75 to 84	12,129	4,839	7,290	66
Aged 85 or older	4,124	1,179	2,945	40
Aged 55 to 59	12,870	6,183	6,687	92
Aged 60 to 64	10,508	4,967	5,541	90
Aged 65 to 69	9,428	4,323	5,106	85
Aged 70 to 74	8,758	3,849	4,910	78
Aged 75 to 79	7,323	3,045	4,278	71
Aged 80 to 84	4,806	1,794	3,012	60
Aged 85 to 89	2,600	816	1,784	46
Aged 90 to 94	1,121	283	838	34
Aged 95 to 99	337	69	267	26
Aged 100 or older	66	11	56	20

Source: Bureau of the Census, Population Projections of the United States by Age, Sex, Race, and Hispanic Origin: 1995 to 2050, *Current Population Reports, P25-1130, 1996; calculations by New Strategist*

Big Gain Forecast for People Aged 55 to 59

The number of people aged 55 to 59 is projected to increase by nearly 4 million between 1999 and 2005 as boomers enter the age group.

While the number of people in their late fifties is projected to grow the most during the next few years, in percentage terms the oldest old should grow the fastest. The number of people aged 100 or older is projected to grow 53 percent between 1999 and 2005. This figure represents a gain of just 35,000 people, however.

Because of baby booms and busts over most of this century, the growth of the population aged 55 or older during the next decade will vary sharply by age group. The number of people aged 55 to 64 will grow 27 percent, for example, but the number of those aged 70 to 74 will decline 5 percent as the small generation born during the Depression enters the age group.

◆ Businesses looking for growth in the older market should target the extremes. The younger (55 to 64) and older (85+) ends of the market will experience rapid growth, while the number of people in the middle will expand little, if at all.

◆ The split in the older market suggests a two-tiered marketing strategy. On the one hand, businesses targeting the very old can continue with their traditional approach. But businesses targeting the expanding number of Americans in their fifties should craft a new strategy to appeal to the very different baby-boom generation.

Increase in older Americans will vary by age

(percent change in population, by age, 1999 to 2005)

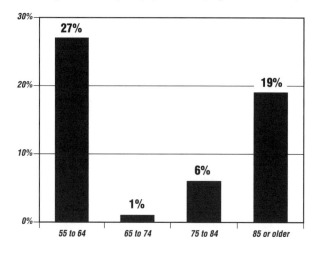

Population Aged 55 or Older, 1999 to 2005

(number of total people and people aged 55 or older, 1999 to 2005; numerical and percent change, 1999–2005; numbers in thousands)

	1999	2000	2005	change, 1999–2005 number	change, 1999–2005 percent
Total people	**272,330**	**274,634**	**285,981**	**13,651**	**5.0%**
Total aged 55 or older	**57,817**	**58,673**	**65,770**	**7,954**	**13.8**
Aged 65 or older	34,439	34,711	36,165	1,726	5.0
Aged 75 or older	16,253	16,575	17,796	1,543	9.5
Aged 55 to 64	23,378	23,961	29,606	6,228	26.6
Aged 65 to 74	18,186	18,136	18,369	183	1.0
Aged 75 to 84	12,129	12,315	12,898	769	6.3
Aged 85 or older	4,124	4,260	4,898	774	18.8
Aged 55 to 59	12,870	13,307	16,798	3,928	30.5
Aged 60 to 64	10,508	10,654	12,807	2,300	21.9
Aged 65 to 69	9,428	9,410	10,037	609	6.5
Aged 70 to 74	8,758	8,726	8,332	–426	–4.9
Aged 75 to 79	7,323	7,415	7,393	70	1.0
Aged 80 to 84	4,806	4,900	5,505	699	14.5
Aged 85 to 89	2,600	2,679	2,993	393	15.1
Aged 90 to 94	1,121	1,153	1,373	252	22.5
Aged 95 to 99	337	356	431	94	27.9
Aged 100 or older	66	72	101	35	53.0

Source: Bureau of the Census, Population Projections of the United States by Age, Sex, Race, and Hispanic Origin: 1995 to 2050, *Current Population Report, P25-1130, 1996; calculations by New Strategist*

Little Diversity among Older Americans

Fully 82 percent of people aged 55 or older are non-Hispanic white.

Although the population of younger Americans is becoming increasingly diverse, older Americans are still homogeneous. While only 72 percent of all Americans are non-Hispanic white, the proportion is 84 percent among people aged 65 or older and 87 percent among those aged 85 or older. Just 9 percent of older Americans are non-Hispanic black, while fewer than 2 percent are non-Hispanic Asian.

Among the population as a whole, 11 percent are Hispanic. But among people aged 55 or older, only 6 percent are Hispanic. This figure falls to 4 percent among people aged 85 or older.

◆ As boomers enter their fifties and sixties in the next few years, the diversity of the older market will begin to increase. But not until Generation X reaches its fifties will diversity be the rule.

Number of Non-Hispanics Aged 55 or Older by Race, 1999

(number of total people and people aged 55 or older who are non-Hispanics by race, 1999; numbers in thousands)

	total	non-Hispanic total	white	black	Asian	Native American	Hispanic
Total people	**272,330**	**241,869**	**196,441**	**33,180**	**10,219**	**2,029**	**30,461**
Total aged 55 or older	**57,817**	**54,383**	**47,642**	**4,993**	**1,471**	**277**	**3,435**
Aged 65 or older	34,439	32,650	29,010	2,752	743	145	1,789
Aged 75 or older	16,253	15,544	14,061	1,156	263	64	708
Aged 55 to 64	23,378	21,733	18,632	2,241	728	132	1,646
Aged 65 to 74	18,186	17,106	14,949	1,596	480	81	1,081
Aged 75 to 84	12,129	11,592	10,478	853	216	45	536
Aged 85 or older	4,124	3,952	3,583	303	47	19	172
Aged 55 to 59	12,870	11,957	10,249	1,231	403	74	914
Aged 60 to 64	10,508	9,776	8,383	1,010	325	58	732
Aged 65 to 69	9,428	8,829	7,626	890	268	45	599
Aged 70 to 74	8,758	8,277	7,323	706	212	36	482
Aged 75 to 79	7,323	6,981	6,276	534	143	28	342
Aged 80 to 84	4,806	4,611	4,202	319	73	17	194
Aged 85 to 89	2,600	2,493	2,274	177	32	10	108
Aged 90 to 94	1,121	1,075	973	86	10	6	46
Aged 95 to 99	337	321	283	32	4	2	15
Aged 100 or older	66	63	53	8	1	1	3

Source: Bureau of the Census, Population Projections of the United States, by Age, Sex, Race, and Hispanic Origin: 1995 to 2050, *Current Population Reports, P25-1130, 1996*

Percent Distribution of Non-Hispanics
Aged 55 or Older by Race, 1999

(percent distribution of total people and people aged 55 or older who are non-Hispanics by race, 1999; numbers in thousands)

	total	non-Hispanic total	white	black	Asian	Native American	Hispanic
Total people	**100.0%**	**88.8%**	**72.1%**	**12.2%**	**3.8%**	**0.7%**	**11.2%**
Total aged 55 or older	**100.0**	**94.1**	**82.4**	**8.6**	**2.5**	**0.5**	**5.9**
Aged 65 or older	100.0	94.8	84.2	8.0	2.2	0.4	5.2
Aged 75 or older	100.0	95.6	86.5	7.1	1.6	0.4	4.4
Aged 55 to 64	100.0	93.0	79.7	9.6	3.1	0.6	7.0
Aged 65 to 74	100.0	94.1	82.2	8.8	2.6	0.4	5.9
Aged 75 to 84	100.0	95.6	86.4	7.0	1.8	0.4	4.4
Aged 85 or older	100.0	95.8	86.9	7.3	1.1	0.5	4.2
Aged 55 to 59	100.0	92.9	79.6	9.6	3.1	0.6	7.1
Aged 60 to 64	100.0	93.0	79.8	9.6	3.1	0.6	7.0
Aged 65 to 69	100.0	93.6	80.9	9.4	2.8	0.5	6.4
Aged 70 to 74	100.0	94.5	83.6	8.1	2.4	0.4	5.5
Aged 75 to 79	100.0	95.3	85.7	7.3	2.0	0.4	4.7
Aged 80 to 84	100.0	95.9	87.4	6.6	1.5	0.4	4.0
Aged 85 to 89	100.0	95.9	87.5	6.8	1.2	0.4	4.2
Aged 90 to 94	100.0	95.9	86.8	7.7	0.9	0.5	4.1
Aged 95 to 99	100.0	95.3	84.0	9.5	1.2	0.6	4.5
Aged 100 or older	100.0	95.5	80.3	12.1	1.5	1.5	4.5

Source: Bureau of the Census, Population Projections of the United States, by Age, Sex, Race, and Hispanic Origin: 1995 to 2050, *Current Population Reports, P25-1130, 1996*

Number of Hispanics Aged 55 or Older by Race, 1999

(number of total people and Hispanics aged 55 or older by race, 1999; numbers in thousands)

	total	Hispanic total	white	black	Asian	Native American	non-Hispanic
Total people	**272,330**	**30,461**	**27,662**	**1,816**	**642**	**340**	**241,869**
Total aged 55 or older	**57,817**	**3,435**	**3,141**	**195**	**66**	**32**	**54,382**
Aged 65 or older	34,439	1,789	1,642	95	34	16	32,650
Aged 75 or older	16,253	709	656	32	14	6	15,544
Aged 55 to 64	23,378	1,646	1,499	100	32	16	21,732
Aged 65 to 74	18,186	1,081	986	63	20	10	17,105
Aged 75 to 84	12,129	536	495	26	11	4	11,593
Aged 85 or older	4,124	173	161	6	3	2	3,951
Aged 55 to 59	12,870	914	832	55	18	9	11,956
Aged 60 to 64	10,508	732	667	45	14	7	9,776
Aged 65 to 69	9,428	599	545	37	11	6	8,829
Aged 70 to 74	8,758	482	441	26	9	4	8,276
Aged 75 to 79	7,323	342	315	17	7	2	6,981
Aged 80 to 84	4,806	194	180	9	4	2	4,612
Aged 85 to 89	2,600	108	100	4	1	1	2,492
Aged 90 to 94	1,121	46	43	2	1	0	1,075
Aged 95 to 99	337	15	15	0	0	1	322
Aged 100 or older	66	4	3	0	1	0	62

Source: Bureau of the Census, Population Projections of the United States, by Age, Sex, Race, and Hispanic Origin: 1995 to 2050, *Current Population Reports, P25-1130, 1996; calculations by New Strategist*

Percent Distribution of Hispanics
Aged 55 or Older by Race, 1999

(percent distribution of total people and Hispanics aged 55 or older by race, 1999)

	total	Hispanic total	white	black	Asian	Native American	non-Hispanic
Total people	**100.0%**	**11.2%**	**10.2%**	**0.7%**	**0.2%**	**0.1%**	**88.8%**
Total aged 55 or older	**100.0**	**5.9**	**5.4**	**0.3**	**0.1**	**0.1**	**94.1**
Aged 65 or older	100.0	5.2	4.8	0.3	0.1	0.0	94.8
Aged 75 or older	100.0	4.4	4.0	0.2	0.1	0.0	95.6
Aged 55 to 64	100.0	7.0	6.4	0.4	0.1	0.1	93.0
Aged 65 to 74	100.0	5.9	5.4	0.3	0.1	0.1	94.1
Aged 75 to 84	100.0	4.4	4.1	0.2	0.1	0.0	95.6
Aged 85 or older	100.0	4.2	3.9	0.1	0.1	0.0	95.8
Aged 55 to 59	100.0	7.1	6.5	0.4	0.1	0.1	92.9
Aged 60 to 64	100.0	7.0	6.3	0.4	0.1	0.1	93.0
Aged 65 to 69	100.0	6.4	5.8	0.4	0.1	0.1	93.6
Aged 70 to 74	100.0	5.5	5.0	0.3	0.1	0.0	94.5
Aged 75 to 79	100.0	4.7	4.3	0.2	0.1	0.0	95.3
Aged 80 to 84	100.0	4.1	3.7	0.2	0.1	0.0	95.9
Aged 85 to 89	100.0	4.1	3.8	0.2	0.0	0.0	95.9
Aged 90 to 94	100.0	4.1	3.8	0.2	0.1	0.0	95.9
Aged 95 to 99	100.0	4.7	4.5	0.0	0.0	0.3	95.3
Aged 100 or older	100.0	6.1	4.5	0.0	1.5	0.0	93.9

Source: Bureau of the Census, Population Projections of the United States, by Age, Sex, Race, and Hispanic Origin: 1995 to 2050, *Current Population Reports, P25-1130, 1996; calculations by New Strategist*

Two Growth Markets among Older Americans in Every Region

The 55-to-64 and 85-or-older age groups will see sharp gains.

Nationally, the number of Americans aged 55 to 64 is projected to grow 24 percent between 2000 and 2005, while the number of those aged 85 or older should grow 15 percent. In contrast, the number of people aged 65 to 74 will rise just 1 percent during those years, while 75-to-84-year-olds will gain 5 percent.

This pattern is found in every region, with much less growth (or even decline) forecast for the 65-to-84 age group than for those younger and older. In the Middle Atlantic, New England, and East North Central divisions, the number of people aged 65 to 74 will decline between 2000 and 2005. But in the Mountain states, the number of 65-to-74-year-olds will rise 12 percent. The Mountain division will also see a 32 percent increase in 55-to-64-year-olds between 2000 and 2005. No other division will experience such rapid growth in this age group.

Women's share of the population aged 55 or older by region ranges from 54 to 57 percent. The share rises with age to between 68 and 73 percent of people aged 85 or older.

♦ Businesses looking for growth in the older market must target specific age groups and areas of the country.

♦ Whether businesses are national or regional in scope, the fundamentals of marketing to the older population are the same. The majority of customers are women.

Population Aged 55 or Older by Region, Division, and Sex, 2000

(number of total people and people aged 55 or older by region, division, and sex; women's share of people aged 55 or older by region and division, 2000; numbers in thousands)

	total	men	women	percent women
UNITED STATES, TOTAL	**274,634**	**134,181**	**140,453**	**51.1%**
Total aged 55 or older	**58,671**	**25,778**	**32,893**	**56.1**
Aged 55 to 64	23,961	11,432	12,529	52.3
Aged 65 to 74	18,136	8,180	9,956	54.9
Aged 75 to 84	12,315	4,938	7,377	59.9
Aged 85 or older	4,259	1,228	3,031	71.2
NORTHEAST, TOTAL	**52,107**	**25,180**	**26,927**	**51.7**
Total aged 55 or older	**11,836**	**5,105**	**6,732**	**56.9**
Aged 55 to 64	4,648	2,196	2,452	52.8
Aged 65 to 74	3,668	1,637	2,031	55.4
Aged 75 to 84	2,609	1,019	1,590	60.9
Aged 85 or older	912	253	659	72.3
New England, total	**13,581**	**6,599**	**6,982**	**51.4**
Total aged 55 or older	**3,007**	**1,305**	**1,702**	**56.6**
Aged 55 to 64	1,167	559	608	52.1
Aged 65 to 74	907	409	498	54.9
Aged 75 to 84	678	267	411	60.6
Aged 85 or older	255	70	185	72.5
Middle Atlantic, total	**38,526**	**18,581**	**19,945**	**51.8**
Total aged 55 or older	**8,829**	**3,799**	**5,030**	**57.0**
Aged 55 to 64	3,481	1,636	1,845	53.0
Aged 65 to 74	2,760	1,228	1,532	55.5
Aged 75 to 84	1,931	752	1,179	61.1
Aged 85 or older	657	183	474	72.1
MIDWEST, TOTAL	**63,502**	**30,970**	**32,532**	**51.2**
Total aged 55 or older	**13,812**	**6,056**	**7,756**	**56.2**
Aged 55 to 64	5,539	2,655	2,884	52.1
Aged 65 to 74	4,251	1,938	2,313	54.4
Aged 75 to 84	2,939	1,165	1,774	60.4
Aged 85 or older	1,083	298	785	72.5

(continued)

(continued from previous page)

	total	men	women	percent women
East North Central, total	**44,419**	**21,631**	**22,788**	**51.3%**
Total aged 55 or older	**9,551**	**4,183**	**5,368**	**56.2**
Aged 55 to 64	3,877	1,854	2,023	52.2
Aged 65 to 74	2,948	1,340	1,608	54.5
Aged 75 to 84	2,021	796	1,225	60.6
Aged 85 or older	705	193	512	72.6
West North Central, total	**19,082**	**9,338**	**9,744**	**51.1**
Total aged 55 or older	**4,261**	**1,874**	**2,387**	**56.0**
Aged 55 to 64	1,662	801	861	51.8
Aged 65 to 74	1,304	600	704	54.0
Aged 75 to 84	917	368	549	59.9
Aged 85 or older	378	105	273	72.2
SOUTH, TOTAL	**97,613**	**47,462**	**50,151**	**51.4**
Total aged 55 or older	**21,257**	**9,282**	**11,975**	**56.3**
Aged 55 to 64	8,809	4,168	4,641	52.7
Aged 65 to 74	6,648	2,968	3,680	55.4
Aged 75 to 84	4,342	1,728	2,614	60.2
Aged 85 or older	1,458	418	1,040	71.3
South Atlantic, total	**50,147**	**24,341**	**25,806**	**51.5**
Total aged 55 or older	**11,467**	**5,015**	**6,452**	**56.3**
Aged 55 to 64	4,634	2,192	2,442	52.7
Aged 65 to 74	3,591	1,602	1,989	55.4
Aged 75 to 84	2,443	984	1,459	59.7
Aged 85 or older	799	237	562	70.3
East South Central, total	**16,918**	**8,164**	**8,754**	**51.7**
Total aged 55 or older	**3,727**	**1,601**	**2,126**	**57.0**
Aged 55 to 64	1,586	744	842	53.1
Aged 65 to 74	1,164	514	650	55.8
Aged 75 to 84	728	276	452	62.1
Aged 85 or older	249	67	182	73.1
West South Central, total	**30,548**	**14,957**	**15,591**	**51.0**
Total aged 55 or older	**6,062**	**2,668**	**3,394**	**56.0**
Aged 55 to 64	2,589	1,232	1,357	52.4
Aged 65 to 74	1,892	852	1,040	55.0
Aged 75 to 84	1,170	468	702	60.0
Aged 85 or older	411	116	295	71.8

(continued)

(continued from previous page)

	total	men	women	percent women
WEST, TOTAL	**61,412**	**30,569**	**30,843**	**50.2%**
Total aged 55 or older	**11,765**	**5,336**	**6,429**	**54.6**
Aged 55 to 64	4,965	2,415	2,550	51.4
Aged 65 to 74	3,569	1,637	1,932	54.1
Aged 75 to 84	2,425	1,025	1,400	57.7
Aged 85 or older	806	259	547	67.9
Mountain, total	**17,725**	**8,797**	**8,928**	**50.4**
Total aged 55 or older	**3,606**	**1,654**	**1,952**	**54.1**
Aged 55 to 64	1,545	753	792	51.3
Aged 65 to 74	1,118	521	597	53.4
Aged 75 to 84	711	305	406	57.1
Aged 85 or older	232	75	157	67.7
Pacific, total	**43,687**	**21,772**	**21,915**	**50.2**
Total aged 55 or older	**8,159**	**3,683**	**4,476**	**54.9**
Aged 55 to 64	3,420	1,662	1,758	51.4
Aged 65 to 74	2,451	1,116	1,335	54.5
Aged 75 to 84	1,714	721	993	57.9
Aged 85 or older	574	184	390	67.9

Source: Bureau of the Census, Population Projections for States by Age, Sex, Race and Hispanic Origin: 1995 to 2025, *PPL-47, 1996; calculations by New Strategist*

Population Aged 55 or Older
by Region and Division, 2000 and 2005

(number of total people and people aged 55 or older by region and division, 2000 and 2005; percent change 2000–2005; numbers in thousands)

	2000	2005	percent change 2000–2005
UNITED STATES, TOTAL	274,634	285,981	4.1%
Total aged 55 or older	58,671	65,772	12.1
Aged 55 to 64	23,961	29,606	23.6
Aged 65 to 74	18,136	18,369	1.3
Aged 75 to 84	12,315	12,898	4.7
Aged 85 or older	4,259	4,899	15.0
NORTHEAST, TOTAL	52,107	52,767	1.3
Total aged 55 or older	11,836	12,650	6.9
Aged 55 to 64	4,648	5,546	19.3
Aged 65 to 74	3,668	3,454	−5.8
Aged 75 to 84	2,609	2,635	1.0
Aged 85 or older	912	1,015	11.3
New England, total	13,581	13,843	1.9
Total aged 55 or older	3,007	3,270	8.7
Aged 55 to 64	1,167	1,447	24.0
Aged 65 to 74	907	852	−6.1
Aged 75 to 84	678	682	0.6
Aged 85 or older	255	289	13.3
Middle Atlantic, total	38,526	38,923	1.0
Total aged 55 or older	8,829	9,380	6.2
Aged 55 to 64	3,481	4,099	17.8
Aged 65 to 74	2,760	2,602	−5.7
Aged 75 to 84	1,931	1,953	1.1
Aged 85 or older	657	726	10.5
MIDWEST, TOTAL	63,502	64,825	2.1
Total aged 55 or older	13,812	15,114	9.4
Aged 55 to 64	5,539	6,646	20.0
Aged 65 to 74	4,251	4,225	−0.6
Aged 75 to 84	2,939	3,025	2.9
Aged 85 or older	1,083	1,218	12.5

(continued)

(continued from previous page)

	2000	2005	percent change 2000–2005
East North Central, total	**44,419**	**45,151**	**1.6%**
Total aged 55 or older	**9,551**	**10,398**	**8.9**
Aged 55 to 64	3,877	4,614	19.0
Aged 65 to 74	2,948	2,904	−1.5
Aged 75 to 84	2,021	2,079	2.9
Aged 85 or older	705	801	13.6
West North Central, total	**19,082**	**19,673**	**3.1**
Total aged 55 or older	**4,261**	**4,717**	**10.7**
Aged 55 to 64	1,662	2,032	22.3
Aged 65 to 74	1,304	1,321	1.3
Aged 75 to 84	917	946	3.2
Aged 85 or older	378	418	10.6
SOUTH, TOTAL	**97,613**	**102,788**	**5.3**
Total aged 55 or older	**21,257**	**24,384**	**14.7**
Aged 55 to 64	8,809	11,075	25.7
Aged 65 to 74	6,648	6,948	4.5
Aged 75 to 84	4,342	4,661	7.3
Aged 85 or older	1,458	1,700	16.6
South Atlantic, total	**50,147**	**52,921**	**5.5**
Total aged 55 or older	**11,467**	**13,180**	**14.9**
Aged 55 to 64	4,634	5,903	27.4
Aged 65 to 74	3,591	3,712	3.4
Aged 75 to 84	2,443	2,608	6.8
Aged 85 or older	799	957	19.8
East South Central, total	**16,918**	**17,604**	**4.1**
Total aged 55 or older	**3,727**	**4,236**	**13.7**
Aged 55 to 64	1,586	1,962	23.7
Aged 65 to 74	1,164	1,226	5.3
Aged 75 to 84	728	772	6.0
Aged 85 or older	249	276	10.8
West South Central, total	**30,548**	**32,263**	**5.6**
Total aged 55 or older	**6,062**	**6,968**	**14.9**
Aged 55 to 64	2,589	3,210	24.0
Aged 65 to 74	1,892	2,010	6.2
Aged 75 to 84	1,170	1,281	9.5
Aged 85 or older	411	467	13.6

(continued)

(continued from previous page)

	2000	2005	percent change 2000–2005
WEST, TOTAL	**61,412**	**65,603**	**6.8%**
Total aged 55 or older	**11,765**	**13,624**	**15.8**
Aged 55 to 64	4,965	6,338	27.7
Aged 65 to 74	3,569	3,742	4.8
Aged 75 to 84	2,425	2,578	6.3
Aged 85 or older	806	966	19.9
Mountain, total	**17,725**	**19,249**	**8.6**
Total aged 55 or older	**3,606**	**4,380**	**21.5**
Aged 55 to 64	1,545	2,037	31.8
Aged 65 to 74	1,118	1,249	11.7
Aged 75 to 84	711	799	12.4
Aged 85 or older	232	295	27.2
Pacific, total	**43,687**	**46,354**	**6.1**
Total aged 55 or older	**8,159**	**9,245**	**13.3**
Aged 55 to 64	3,420	4,302	25.8
Aged 65 to 74	2,451	2,493	1.7
Aged 75 to 84	1,714	1,779	3.8
Aged 85 or older	574	671	16.9

Source: Bureau of the Census, Population Projections for States by Age, Sex, Race and Hispanic Origin: 1995 to 2025, *PPL-47, 1996; calculations by New Strategist*

Wide Variation in Growth of Older Population Projected for States

While the number of people aged 55 or older will grow 12 percent nationally between 2000 and 2005, the figure is much higher in some states.

Between 2000 and 2005, the greatest growth in the number of people aged 55 or older is projected for Nevada, up 25 percent. In contrast, in New York the number of people in this age group is projected to rise only 5.5 percent during those years.

In every state, growth in the older population will be greatest for 55-to-64-year-olds and for those aged 85 or older. Many states—including California, Connecticut, Michigan, Ohio, and Pennsylvania—will see a decline in the number of people aged 65 to 74 as the small generation born during the Depression enters the age group.

Women are the majority of the 55-or-older population in every state except Alaska, and that majority increases with age. Women account for more than 70 percent of people aged 85 or older in many states.

♦ As the oldest boomers turn 55 years old beginning in 2001, businesses in every state will have to adjust their strategies to target boomers' very different wants and needs.

States with fastest growth in 55+ population

(percent change in number of persons aged 55 or older, top five states, 2000–2005)

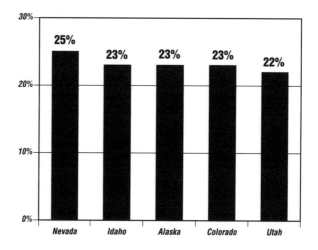

Population Aged 55 or Older by State and Sex, 2000

(number of total people and people aged 55 or older by state and sex, women's share of people aged 55 or older by state; 2000; numbers in thousands)

	total	men	women	percent women
United States, total	**274,634**	**134,181**	**140,453**	**51.1%**
Total aged 55 or older	**58,671**	**25,878**	**32,793**	**55.9**
Aged 55 to 64	23,961	11,432	12,529	52.3
Aged 65 to 74	18,136	8,180	9,956	54.9
Aged 75 to 84	12,315	5,038	7,277	59.1
Aged 85 or older	4,259	1,228	3,031	71.2
Alabama, total	**4,451**	**2,140**	**2,311**	**51.9**
Total aged 55 or older	**1,003**	**429**	**574**	**57.2**
Aged 55 to 64	421	196	225	53.4
Aged 65 to 74	317	139	178	56.2
Aged 75 to 84	198	76	122	61.6
Aged 85 or older	67	18	49	73.1
Alaska, total	**653**	**339**	**314**	**48.1**
Total aged 55 or older	**83**	**42**	**41**	**49.4**
Aged 55 to 64	45	24	21	46.7
Aged 65 to 74	25	13	12	48.0
Aged 75 to 84	11	5	6	54.5
Aged 85 or older	2	0	2	100.0
Arizona, total	**4,798**	**2,368**	**2,430**	**50.6**
Total aged 55 or older	**1,062**	**481**	**581**	**54.7**
Aged 55 to 64	427	205	222	52.0
Aged 65 to 74	339	155	184	54.3
Aged 75 to 84	226	97	129	57.1
Aged 85 or older	70	24	46	65.7
Arkansas, total	**2,631**	**1,270**	**1,361**	**51.7**
Total aged 55 or older	**644**	**281**	**363**	**56.4**
Aged 55 to 64	267	126	141	52.8
Aged 65 to 74	200	89	111	55.5
Aged 75 to 84	130	52	78	60.0
Aged 85 or older	47	14	33	70.2

(continued)

(continued from previous page)

	total	men	women	percent women
California, total	**32,521**	**16,216**	**16,305**	**50.1%**
Total aged 55 or older	**5,817**	**2,610**	**3,207**	**55.1**
Aged 55 to 64	2,430	1,174	1,256	51.7
Aged 65 to 74	1,757	795	962	54.8
Aged 75 to 84	1,226	513	713	58.2
Aged 85 or older	404	128	276	68.3
Colorado, total	**4,168**	**2,066**	**2,102**	**50.4**
Total aged 55 or older	**815**	**371**	**444**	**54.5**
Aged 55 to 64	363	178	185	51.0
Aged 65 to 74	246	114	132	53.7
Aged 75 to 84	152	63	89	58.6
Aged 85 or older	54	16	38	70.4
Connecticut, total	**3,284**	**1,596**	**1,688**	**51.4**
Total aged 55 or older	**753**	**329**	**424**	**56.3**
Aged 55 to 64	292	140	152	52.1
Aged 65 to 74	224	102	122	54.5
Aged 75 to 84	173	69	104	60.1
Aged 85 or older	64	18	46	71.9
Delaware, total	**768**	**375**	**393**	**51.2**
Total aged 55 or older	**164**	**73**	**91**	**55.5**
Aged 55 to 64	67	32	35	52.2
Aged 65 to 74	51	23	28	54.9
Aged 75 to 84	35	15	20	57.1
Aged 85 or older	11	3	8	72.7
District of Columbia, total	**523**	**246**	**277**	**53.0**
Total aged 55 or older	**115**	**48**	**67**	**58.3**
Aged 55 to 64	46	21	25	54.3
Aged 65 to 74	36	15	21	58.3
Aged 75 to 84	24	9	15	62.5
Aged 85 or older	9	3	6	66.7
Florida, total	**15,233**	**7,367**	**7,866**	**51.6**
Total aged 55 or older	**4,281**	**1,890**	**2,391**	**55.9**
Aged 55 to 64	1,526	717	809	53.0
Aged 65 to 74	1,384	619	765	55.3
Aged 75 to 84	1,028	437	591	57.5
Aged 85 or older	343	117	226	65.9

(continued)

(continued from previous page)

	total	men	women	percent women
Georgia, total	**7,875**	**3,831**	**4,044**	**51.4%**
Total aged 55 or older	**1,433**	**620**	**813**	**56.7**
Aged 55 to 64	654	311	343	52.4
Aged 65 to 74	429	189	240	55.9
Aged 75 to 84	263	99	164	62.4
Aged 85 or older	87	21	66	75.9
Hawaii, total	**1,257**	**633**	**624**	**49.6**
Total aged 55 or older	**264**	**121**	**143**	**54.2**
Aged 55 to 64	107	51	56	52.3
Aged 65 to 74	83	37	46	55.4
Aged 75 to 84	56	25	31	55.4
Aged 85 or older	18	8	10	55.6
Idaho, total	**1,347**	**672**	**675**	**50.1**
Total aged 55 or older	**275**	**128**	**147**	**53.5**
Aged 55 to 64	118	58	60	50.8
Aged 65 to 74	82	39	43	52.4
Aged 75 to 84	55	24	31	56.4
Aged 85 or older	20	7	13	65.0
Illinois, total	**12,051**	**5,878**	**6,173**	**51.2**
Total aged 55 or older	**2,509**	**1,091**	**1,418**	**56.5**
Aged 55 to 64	1,025	488	537	52.4
Aged 65 to 74	767	346	421	54.9
Aged 75 to 84	529	206	323	61.1
Aged 85 or older	188	51	137	72.9
Indiana, total	**6,045**	**2,945**	**3,100**	**51.3**
Total aged 55 or older	**1,304**	**570**	**734**	**56.3**
Aged 55 to 64	541	260	281	51.9
Aged 65 to 74	402	181	221	55.0
Aged 75 to 84	268	104	164	61.2
Aged 85 or older	93	25	68	73.1
Iowa, total	**2,900**	**1,413**	**1,487**	**51.3**
Total aged 55 or older	**708**	**309**	**399**	**56.4**
Aged 55 to 64	266	128	138	51.9
Aged 65 to 74	217	100	117	53.9
Aged 75 to 84	158	63	95	60.1
Aged 85 or older	67	18	49	73.1

(continued)

(continued from previous page)

	total	*men*	*women*	*percent women*
Kansas, total	**2,668**	**1,314**	**1,354**	**50.7%**
Total aged 55 or older	**581**	**255**	**326**	**56.1**
Aged 55 to 64	222	107	115	51.8
Aged 65 to 74	179	82	97	54.2
Aged 75 to 84	128	51	77	60.2
Aged 85 or older	52	15	37	71.2
Kentucky, total	**3,995**	**1,940**	**2,055**	**51.4**
Total aged 55 or older	**891**	**388**	**503**	**56.5**
Aged 55 to 64	382	182	200	52.4
Aged 65 to 74	279	125	154	55.2
Aged 75 to 84	173	66	107	61.8
Aged 85 or older	57	15	42	73.7
Louisiana, total	**4,425**	**2,131**	**2,294**	**51.8**
Total aged 55 or older	**910**	**392**	**518**	**56.9**
Aged 55 to 64	387	180	207	53.5
Aged 65 to 74	289	128	161	55.7
Aged 75 to 84	176	68	108	61.4
Aged 85 or older	58	16	42	72.4
Maine, total	**1,259**	**614**	**645**	**51.2**
Total aged 55 or older	**289**	**128**	**161**	**55.7**
Aged 55 to 64	117	57	60	51.3
Aged 65 to 74	89	40	49	55.1
Aged 75 to 84	61	25	36	59.0
Aged 85 or older	22	6	16	72.7
Maryland, total	**5,275**	**2,563**	**2,712**	**51.4**
Total aged 55 or older	**1,039**	**459**	**580**	**55.8**
Aged 55 to 64	450	217	233	51.8
Aged 65 to 74	312	141	171	54.8
Aged 75 to 84	211	83	128	60.7
Aged 85 or older	66	18	48	72.7
Massachusetts, total	**6,199**	**3,001**	**3,198**	**51.6**
Total aged 55 or older	**1,365**	**585**	**780**	**57.1**
Aged 55 to 64	522	248	274	52.5
Aged 65 to 74	413	184	229	55.4
Aged 75 to 84	311	121	190	61.1
Aged 85 or older	119	32	87	73.1

(continued)

(continued from previous page)

	total	men	women	percent women
Michigan, total	**9,679**	**4,714**	**4,965**	**51.3%**
Total aged 55 or older	**2,036**	**900**	**1,136**	**55.8**
Aged 55 to 64	839	402	437	52.1
Aged 65 to 74	627	287	340	54.2
Aged 75 to 84	427	170	257	60.2
Aged 85 or older	143	41	102	71.3
Minnesota, total	**4,830**	**2,378**	**2,452**	**50.8**
Total aged 55 or older	**1,001**	**447**	**554**	**55.3**
Aged 55 to 64	405	198	207	51.1
Aged 65 to 74	296	138	158	53.4
Aged 75 to 84	211	86	125	59.2
Aged 85 or older	89	25	64	71.9
Mississippi, total	**2,816**	**1,351**	**1,465**	**52.0**
Total aged 55 or older	**593**	**250**	**343**	**57.8**
Aged 55 to 64	249	115	134	53.8
Aged 65 to 74	187	81	106	56.7
Aged 75 to 84	116	43	73	62.9
Aged 85 or older	41	11	30	73.2
Missouri, total	**5,540**	**2,685**	**2,855**	**51.5**
Total aged 55 or older	**1,260**	**548**	**712**	**56.5**
Aged 55 to 64	505	241	264	52.3
Aged 65 to 74	391	177	214	54.7
Aged 75 to 84	263	103	160	60.8
Aged 85 or older	101	27	74	73.3
Montana, total	**950**	**471**	**479**	**50.4**
Total aged 55 or older	**221**	**101**	**120**	**54.3**
Aged 55 to 64	93	46	47	50.5
Aged 65 to 74	66	31	35	53.0
Aged 75 to 84	45	19	26	57.8
Aged 85 or older	17	5	12	70.6
Nebraska, total	**1,705**	**835**	**870**	**51.0**
Total aged 55 or older	**383**	**168**	**215**	**56.1**
Aged 55 to 64	144	69	75	52.1
Aged 65 to 74	120	56	64	53.3
Aged 75 to 84	83	33	50	60.2
Aged 85 or older	36	10	26	72.2

(continued)

(continued from previous page)

	total	men	women	percent women
Nevada, total	**1,871**	**942**	**929**	**49.7%**
Total aged 55 or older	**407**	**194**	**213**	**52.3**
Aged 55 to 64	188	94	94	50.0
Aged 65 to 74	129	62	67	51.9
Aged 75 to 84	72	32	40	55.6
Aged 85 or older	18	6	12	66.7
New Hampshire, total	**1,224**	**602**	**622**	**50.8**
Total aged 55 or older	**242**	**109**	**133**	**55.0**
Aged 55 to 64	100	50	50	50.0
Aged 65 to 74	72	33	39	54.2
Aged 75 to 84	51	21	30	58.8
Aged 85 or older	19	5	14	73.7
New Jersey, total	**8,178**	**3,963**	**4,215**	**51.5**
Total aged 55 or older	**1,827**	**796**	**1,031**	**56.4**
Aged 55 to 64	737	350	387	52.5
Aged 65 to 74	565	254	311	55.0
Aged 75 to 84	395	155	240	60.8
Aged 85 or older	130	37	93	71.5
New Mexico, total	**1,860**	**917**	**943**	**50.7**
Total aged 55 or older	**364**	**165**	**199**	**54.7**
Aged 55 to 64	158	75	83	52.5
Aged 65 to 74	114	53	61	53.5
Aged 75 to 84	70	30	40	57.1
Aged 85 or older	22	7	15	68.2
New York, total	**18,146**	**8,740**	**9,406**	**51.8**
Total aged 55 or older	**3,980**	**1,708**	**2,272**	**57.1**
Aged 55 to 64	1,622	757	865	53.3
Aged 65 to 74	1,239	549	690	55.7
Aged 75 to 84	826	320	506	61.3
Aged 85 or older	293	82	211	72.0
North Carolina, total	**7,777**	**3,776**	**4,001**	**51.4**
Total aged 55 or older	**1,714**	**738**	**976**	**56.9**
Aged 55 to 64	723	339	384	53.1
Aged 65 to 74	539	239	300	55.7
Aged 75 to 84	341	131	210	61.6
Aged 85 or older	111	29	82	73.9

(continued)

(continued from previous page)

	total	men	women	percent women
North Dakota, total	**662**	**329**	**333**	**50.3%**
Total aged 55 or older	**155**	**69**	**86**	**55.5**
Aged 55 to 64	56	27	29	51.8
Aged 65 to 74	48	22	26	54.2
Aged 75 to 84	35	15	20	57.1
Aged 85 or older	16	5	11	68.8
Ohio, total	**11,319**	**5,480**	**5,839**	**51.6**
Total aged 55 or older	**2,536**	**1,103**	**1,433**	**56.5**
Aged 55 to 64	1,011	480	531	52.5
Aged 65 to 74	795	359	436	54.8
Aged 75 to 84	547	215	332	60.7
Aged 85 or older	183	49	134	73.2
Oklahoma, total	**3,373**	**1,648**	**1,725**	**51.1**
Total aged 55 or older	**795**	**349**	**446**	**56.1**
Aged 55 to 64	323	154	169	52.3
Aged 65 to 74	249	113	136	54.6
Aged 75 to 84	160	64	96	60.0
Aged 85 or older	63	18	45	71.4
Oregon, total	**3,397**	**1,674**	**1,723**	**50.7**
Total aged 55 or older	**796**	**361**	**435**	**54.6**
Aged 55 to 64	325	159	166	51.1
Aged 65 to 74	236	109	127	53.8
Aged 75 to 84	173	73	100	57.8
Aged 85 or older	62	20	42	67.7
Pennsylvania, total	**12,202**	**5,879**	**6,323**	**51.8**
Total aged 55 or older	**3,021**	**1,293**	**1,728**	**57.2**
Aged 55 to 64	1,122	529	593	52.9
Aged 65 to 74	956	424	532	55.6
Aged 75 to 84	709	276	433	61.1
Aged 85 or older	234	64	170	72.6
Rhode Island, total	**998**	**482**	**516**	**51.7**
Total aged 55 or older	**230**	**97**	**133**	**57.8**
Aged 55 to 64	82	38	44	53.7
Aged 65 to 74	70	31	39	55.7
Aged 75 to 84	57	22	35	61.4
Aged 85 or older	21	6	15	71.4

(continued)

(continued from previous page)

	total	men	women	percent women
South Carolina, total	**3,858**	**1,863**	**1,995**	**51.7%**
Total aged 55 or older	**837**	**361**	**476**	**56.9**
Aged 55 to 64	359	168	191	53.2
Aged 65 to 74	263	116	147	55.9
Aged 75 to 84	165	64	101	61.2
Aged 85 or older	50	13	37	74.0
South Dakota, total	**777**	**383**	**394**	**50.7**
Total aged 55 or older	**174**	**78**	**96**	**55.2**
Aged 55 to 64	64	31	33	51.6
Aged 65 to 74	54	26	28	51.9
Aged 75 to 84	39	16	23	59.0
Aged 85 or older	17	5	12	70.6
Tennessee, total	**5,657**	**2,734**	**2,923**	**51.7**
Total aged 55 or older	**1,242**	**535**	**707**	**56.9**
Aged 55 to 64	535	252	283	52.9
Aged 65 to 74	382	169	213	55.8
Aged 75 to 84	242	92	150	62.0
Aged 85 or older	83	22	61	73.5
Texas, total	**20,119**	**9,908**	**10,211**	**50.8**
Total aged 55 or older	**3,714**	**1,647**	**2,067**	**55.7**
Aged 55 to 64	1,613	772	841	52.1
Aged 65 to 74	1,154	522	632	54.8
Aged 75 to 84	704	284	420	59.7
Aged 85 or older	243	69	174	71.6
Utah, total	**2,207**	**1,099**	**1,108**	**50.2**
Total aged 55 or older	**352**	**162**	**190**	**54.0**
Aged 55 to 64	150	73	77	51.3
Aged 65 to 74	107	50	57	53.3
Aged 75 to 84	71	31	40	56.3
Aged 85 or older	24	8	16	66.7
Vermont, total	**617**	**304**	**313**	**50.7**
Total aged 55 or older	**127**	**56**	**71**	**55.9**
Aged 55 to 64	54	26	28	51.9
Aged 65 to 74	38	17	21	55.3
Aged 75 to 84	25	10	15	60.0
Aged 85 or older	10	3	7	70.0

(continued)

(continued from previous page)

	total	men	women	percent women
Virginia, total	6,997	3,433	3,564	50.9%
Total aged 55 or older	1,405	620	785	55.9
Aged 55 to 64	617	298	319	51.7
Aged 65 to 74	422	190	232	55.0
Aged 75 to 84	276	108	168	60.9
Aged 85 or older	90	24	66	73.3
Washington, total	**5,858**	**2,909**	**2,949**	**50.3**
Total aged 55 or older	**1,198**	**549**	**649**	**54.2**
Aged 55 to 64	513	255	258	50.3
Aged 65 to 74	350	162	188	53.7
Aged 75 to 84	248	105	143	57.7
Aged 85 or older	87	27	60	69.0
West Virginia, total	**1,841**	**886**	**955**	**51.9**
Total aged 55 or older	**481**	**207**	**274**	**57.0**
Aged 55 to 64	194	91	103	53.1
Aged 65 to 74	155	69	86	55.5
Aged 75 to 84	100	38	62	62.0
Aged 85 or older	32	9	23	71.9
Wisconsin, total	**5,326**	**2,616**	**2,710**	**50.9**
Total aged 55 or older	**1,166**	**519**	**647**	**55.5**
Aged 55 to 64	461	225	236	51.2
Aged 65 to 74	357	166	191	53.5
Aged 75 to 84	250	101	149	59.6
Aged 85 or older	98	27	71	72.4
Wyoming, total	**525**	**263**	**262**	**49.9**
Total aged 55 or older	**109**	**51**	**58**	**53.2**
Aged 55 to 64	47	23	24	51.1
Aged 65 to 74	34	17	17	50.0
Aged 75 to 84	21	9	12	57.1
Aged 85 or older	7	2	5	71.4

Source: Bureau of the Census, Population Projections for States by Age, Sex, Race and Hispanic Origin: 1995 to 2025, *PPL-47, 1996; calculations by New Strategist*

Population Aged 55 or Older by State, 2000 and 2005

(number of total people and people aged 55 or older by state, 2000 and 2005; percent change 2000–2005; numbers in thousands)

	2000	2005	percent change 2000–2005
United States, total	**274,634**	**285,981**	**4.1%**
Total aged 55 or older	**58,671**	**65,772**	**12.1**
Aged 55 to 64	23,961	29,606	23.6
Aged 65 to 74	18,136	18,369	1.3
Aged 75 to 84	12,315	12,898	4.7
Aged 85 or older	4,259	4,899	15.0
Alabama, total	**4,451**	**4,631**	**4.0**
Total aged 55 or older	**1,003**	**1,130**	**12.7**
Aged 55 to 64	421	517	22.8
Aged 65 to 74	317	330	4.1
Aged 75 to 84	198	209	5.6
Aged 85 or older	67	74	10.4
Alaska, total	**653**	**700**	**7.2**
Total aged 55 or older	**83**	**102**	**22.9**
Aged 55 to 64	45	56	24.4
Aged 65 to 74	25	29	16.0
Aged 75 to 84	11	14	27.3
Aged 85 or older	2	3	50.0
Arizona, total	**4,798**	**5,230**	**9.0**
Total aged 55 or older	**1,062**	**1,275**	**20.1**
Aged 55 to 64	427	568	33.0
Aged 65 to 74	339	371	9.4
Aged 75 to 84	226	248	9.7
Aged 85 or older	70	88	25.7
Arkansas, total	**2,631**	**2,750**	**4.5**
Total aged 55 or older	**644**	**739**	**14.8**
Aged 55 to 64	267	337	26.2
Aged 65 to 74	200	216	8.0
Aged 75 to 84	130	135	3.8
Aged 85 or older	47	51	8.5

(continued)

(continued from previous page)

	2000	2005	percent change 2000–2005
California, total	**32,521**	**34,441**	**5.9%**
Total aged 55 or older	**5,817**	**6,443**	**10.8**
Aged 55 to 64	2,430	2,989	23.0
Aged 65 to 74	1,757	1,742	–0.9
Aged 75 to 84	1,226	1,254	2.3
Aged 85 or older	404	458	13.4
Colorado, total	**4,168**	**4,468**	**7.2**
Total aged 55 or older	**815**	**998**	**22.5**
Aged 55 to 64	363	475	30.9
Aged 65 to 74	246	279	13.4
Aged 75 to 84	152	176	15.8
Aged 85 or older	54	68	25.9
Connecticut, total	**3,284**	**3,317**	**1.0**
Total aged 55 or older	**753**	**803**	**6.6**
Aged 55 to 64	292	347	18.8
Aged 65 to 74	224	209	–6.7
Aged 75 to 84	173	172	–0.6
Aged 85 or older	64	75	17.2
Delaware, total	**768**	**800**	**4.2**
Total aged 55 or older	**164**	**184**	**12.2**
Aged 55 to 64	67	83	23.9
Aged 65 to 74	51	51	0.0
Aged 75 to 84	35	37	5.7
Aged 85 or older	11	13	18.2
District of Columbia, total	**523**	**529**	**1.1**
Total aged 55 or older	**115**	**117**	**1.7**
Aged 55 to 64	46	52	13.0
Aged 65 to 74	36	33	–8.3
Aged 75 to 84	24	23	–4.2
Aged 85 or older	9	9	0.0
Florida, total	**15,233**	**16,279**	**6.9**
Total aged 55 or older	**4,281**	**4,899**	**14.4**
Aged 55 to 64	1,526	1,988	30.3
Aged 65 to 74	1,384	1,405	1.5
Aged 75 to 84	1,028	1,091	6.1
Aged 85 or older	343	415	21.0

(continued)

(continued from previous page)

	2000	*2005*	*percent change 2000–2005*
Georgia, total	**7,875**	**8,413**	**6.8%**
Total aged 55 or older	**1,433**	**1,696**	**18.4**
Aged 55 to 64	654	844	29.1
Aged 65 to 74	429	468	9.1
Aged 75 to 84	263	282	7.2
Aged 85 or older	87	102	17.2
Hawaii, total	**1,257**	**1,342**	**6.8**
Total aged 55 or older	**264**	**298**	**12.9**
Aged 55 to 64	107	134	25.2
Aged 65 to 74	83	80	−3.6
Aged 75 to 84	56	60	7.1
Aged 85 or older	18	24	33.3
Idaho, total	**1,347**	**1,480**	**9.9**
Total aged 55 or older	**275**	**339**	**23.3**
Aged 55 to 64	118	157	33.1
Aged 65 to 74	82	96	17.1
Aged 75 to 84	55	61	10.9
Aged 85 or older	20	25	25.0
Illinois, total	**12,051**	**12,266**	**1.8**
Total aged 55 or older	**2,509**	**2,690**	**7.2**
Aged 55 to 64	1,025	1,196	16.7
Aged 65 to 74	767	755	−1.6
Aged 75 to 84	529	532	0.6
Aged 85 or older	188	207	10.1
Indiana, total	**6,045**	**6,215**	**2.8**
Total aged 55 or older	**1,304**	**1,444**	**10.7**
Aged 55 to 64	541	650	20.1
Aged 65 to 74	402	407	1.2
Aged 75 to 84	268	282	5.2
Aged 85 or older	93	105	12.9
Iowa, total	**2,900**	**2,941**	**1.4**
Total aged 55 or older	**708**	**769**	**8.6**
Aged 55 to 64	266	317	19.2
Aged 65 to 74	217	218	0.5
Aged 75 to 84	158	160	1.3
Aged 85 or older	67	74	10.4

(continued)

(continued from previous page)

	2000	2005	percent change 2000–2005
Kansas, total	**2,668**	**2,761**	**3.5%**
Total aged 55 or older	**581**	**640**	**10.2**
Aged 55 to 64	222	274	23.4
Aged 65 to 74	179	179	0.0
Aged 75 to 84	128	131	2.3
Aged 85 or older	52	56	7.7
Kentucky, total	**3,995**	**4,098**	**2.6**
Total aged 55 or older	**891**	**1,009**	**13.2**
Aged 55 to 64	382	471	23.3
Aged 65 to 74	279	293	5.0
Aged 75 to 84	173	183	5.8
Aged 85 or older	57	62	8.8
Louisiana, total	**4,425**	**4,535**	**2.5**
Total aged 55 or older	**910**	**1,019**	**12.0**
Aged 55 to 64	387	464	19.9
Aged 65 to 74	289	299	3.5
Aged 75 to 84	176	190	8.0
Aged 85 or older	58	66	13.8
Maine, total	**1,259**	**1,285**	**2.1**
Total aged 55 or older	**289**	**325**	**12.5**
Aged 55 to 64	117	152	29.9
Aged 65 to 74	89	87	−2.2
Aged 75 to 84	61	63	3.3
Aged 85 or older	22	23	4.5
Maryland, total	**5,275**	**5,467**	**3.6**
Total aged 55 or older	**1,039**	**1,162**	**11.8**
Aged 55 to 64	450	551	22.4
Aged 65 to 74	312	313	0.3
Aged 75 to 84	211	220	4.3
Aged 85 or older	66	78	18.2
Massachusetts, total	**6,199**	**6,310**	**1.8**
Total aged 55 or older	**1,365**	**1,470**	**7.7**
Aged 55 to 64	522	643	23.2
Aged 65 to 74	413	384	−7.0
Aged 75 to 84	311	309	−0.6
Aged 85 or older	119	134	12.6

(continued)

(continued from previous page)

	2000	2005	percent change 2000–2005
Michigan, total	**9,679**	**9,763**	**0.9%**
Total aged 55 or older	**2,036**	**2,211**	**8.6**
Aged 55 to 64	839	1,000	19.2
Aged 65 to 74	627	607	−3.2
Aged 75 to 84	427	439	2.8
Aged 85 or older	143	165	15.4
Minnesota, total	**4,830**	**5,005**	**3.6**
Total aged 55 or older	**1,001**	**1,131**	**13.0**
Aged 55 to 64	405	504	24.4
Aged 65 to 74	296	307	3.7
Aged 75 to 84	211	218	3.3
Aged 85 or older	89	102	14.6
Mississippi, total	**2,816**	**2,908**	**3.3**
Total aged 55 or older	**593**	**667**	**12.5**
Aged 55 to 64	249	304	22.1
Aged 65 to 74	187	196	4.8
Aged 75 to 84	116	122	5.2
Aged 85 or older	41	45	9.8
Missouri, total	**5,540**	**5,718**	**3.2**
Total aged 55 or older	**1,260**	**1,387**	**10.1**
Aged 55 to 64	505	613	21.4
Aged 65 to 74	391	393	0.5
Aged 75 to 84	263	272	3.4
Aged 85 or older	101	109	7.9
Montana, total	**950**	**1,006**	**5.9**
Total aged 55 or older	**221**	**265**	**19.9**
Aged 55 to 64	93	122	31.2
Aged 65 to 74	66	74	12.1
Aged 75 to 84	45	47	4.4
Aged 85 or older	17	22	29.4
Nebraska, total	**1,705**	**1,761**	**3.3**
Total aged 55 or older	**383**	**425**	**11.0**
Aged 55 to 64	144	177	22.9
Aged 65 to 74	120	121	0.8
Aged 75 to 84	83	88	6.0
Aged 85 or older	36	39	8.3

(continued)

(continued from previous page)

	2000	2005	percent change 2000–2005
Nevada, total	**1,871**	**2,070**	**10.6%**
Total aged 55 or older	**407**	**510**	**25.3**
Aged 55 to 64	188	253	34.6
Aged 65 to 74	129	147	14.0
Aged 75 to 84	72	86	19.4
Aged 85 or older	18	24	33.3
New Hampshire, total	**1,224**	**1,281**	**4.7**
Total aged 55 or older	**242**	**280**	**15.7**
Aged 55 to 64	100	132	32.0
Aged 65 to 74	72	71	−1.4
Aged 75 to 84	51	55	7.8
Aged 85 or older	19	22	15.8
New Jersey, total	**8,178**	**8,392**	**2.6**
Total aged 55 or older	**1,827**	**1,970**	**7.8**
Aged 55 to 64	737	877	19.0
Aged 65 to 74	565	543	−3.9
Aged 75 to 84	395	403	2.0
Aged 85 or older	130	147	13.1
New Mexico, total	**1,860**	**2,016**	**8.4**
Total aged 55 or older	**364**	**432**	**18.7**
Aged 55 to 64	158	204	29.1
Aged 65 to 74	114	124	8.8
Aged 75 to 84	70	77	10.0
Aged 85 or older	22	27	22.7
New York, total	**18,146**	**18,250**	**0.6**
Total aged 55 or older	**3,980**	**4,197**	**5.5**
Aged 55 to 64	1,622	1,876	15.7
Aged 65 to 74	1,239	1,176	−5.1
Aged 75 to 84	826	835	1.1
Aged 85 or older	293	310	5.8
North Carolina, total	**7,777**	**8,227**	**5.8**
Total aged 55 or older	**1,714**	**2,002**	**16.8**
Aged 55 to 64	723	921	27.4
Aged 65 to 74	539	572	6.1
Aged 75 to 84	341	375	10.0
Aged 85 or older	111	134	20.7

(continued)

(continued from previous page)

	2000	2005	percent change 2000–2005
North Dakota, total	**662**	**677**	**2.3%**
Total aged 55 or older	**155**	**171**	**10.3**
Aged 55 to 64	56	68	21.4
Aged 65 to 74	48	48	0.0
Aged 75 to 84	35	36	2.9
Aged 85 or older	16	19	18.8
Ohio, total	**11,319**	**11,428**	**1.0**
Total aged 55 or older	**2,536**	**2,754**	**8.6**
Aged 55 to 64	1,011	1,200	18.7
Aged 65 to 74	795	775	–2.5
Aged 75 to 84	547	567	3.7
Aged 85 or older	183	212	15.8
Oklahoma, total	**3,373**	**3,491**	**3.5**
Total aged 55 or older	**795**	**896**	**12.7**
Aged 55 to 64	323	392	21.4
Aged 65 to 74	249	262	5.2
Aged 75 to 84	160	172	7.5
Aged 85 or older	63	70	11.1
Oregon, total	**3,397**	**3,613**	**6.4**
Total aged 55 or older	**796**	**961**	**20.7**
Aged 55 to 64	325	439	35.1
Aged 65 to 74	236	258	9.3
Aged 75 to 84	173	186	7.5
Aged 85 or older	62	78	25.8
Pennsylvania, total	**12,202**	**12,281**	**0.6**
Total aged 55 or older	**3,021**	**3,213**	**6.4**
Aged 55 to 64	1,122	1,346	20.0
Aged 65 to 74	956	883	–7.6
Aged 75 to 84	709	715	0.8
Aged 85 or older	234	269	15.0
Rhode Island, total	**998**	**1,012**	**1.4**
Total aged 55 or older	**230**	**245**	**6.5**
Aged 55 to 64	82	102	24.4
Aged 65 to 74	70	62	–11.4
Aged 75 to 84	57	57	0.0
Aged 85 or older	21	24	14.3

(continued)

(continued from previous page)

	2000	2005	percent change 2000–2005
South Carolina, total	**3,858**	**4,033**	**4.5%**
Total aged 55 or older	**837**	**974**	**16.4**
Aged 55 to 64	359	457	27.3
Aged 65 to 74	263	277	5.3
Aged 75 to 84	165	178	7.9
Aged 85 or older	50	62	24.0
South Dakota, total	**777**	**810**	**4.2**
Total aged 55 or older	**174**	**193**	**10.9**
Aged 55 to 64	64	79	23.4
Aged 65 to 74	54	54	0.0
Aged 75 to 84	39	41	5.1
Aged 85 or older	17	19	11.8
Tennessee, total	**5,657**	**5,966**	**5.5**
Total aged 55 or older	**1,242**	**1,430**	**15.1**
Aged 55 to 64	535	670	25.2
Aged 65 to 74	382	407	6.5
Aged 75 to 84	242	258	6.6
Aged 85 or older	83	95	14.5
Texas, total	**20,119**	**21,487**	**6.8**
Total aged 55 or older	**3,714**	**4,314**	**16.2**
Aged 55 to 64	1,613	2,017	25.0
Aged 65 to 74	1,154	1,234	6.9
Aged 75 to 84	704	784	11.4
Aged 85 or older	243	279	14.8
Utah, total	**2,207**	**2,411**	**9.2**
Total aged 55 or older	**352**	**431**	**22.4**
Aged 55 to 64	150	197	31.3
Aged 65 to 74	107	122	14.0
Aged 75 to 84	71	80	12.7
Aged 85 or older	24	32	33.3
Vermont, total	**617**	**638**	**3.4**
Total aged 55 or older	**127**	**148**	**16.5**
Aged 55 to 64	54	71	31.5
Aged 65 to 74	38	39	2.6
Aged 75 to 84	25	27	8.0
Aged 85 or older	10	11	10.0

(continued)

Virginia, total	**6,997**	**7,324**	**4.7%**
Total aged 55 or older	**1,405**	**1,616**	**15.0**
Aged 55 to 64	617	771	25.0
Aged 65 to 74	422	439	4.0
Aged 75 to 84	276	297	7.6
Aged 85 or older	90	109	21.1
Washington, total	**5,858**	**6,258**	**6.8**
Total aged 55 or older	**1,198**	**1,440**	**20.2**
Aged 55 to 64	513	683	33.1
Aged 65 to 74	350	384	9.7
Aged 75 to 84	248	265	6.9
Aged 85 or older	87	108	24.1
West Virginia, total	**1,841**	**1,849**	**0.4**
Total aged 55 or older	**481**	**533**	**10.8**
Aged 55 to 64	194	237	22.2
Aged 65 to 74	155	156	0.6
Aged 75 to 84	100	105	5.0
Aged 85 or older	32	35	9.4
Wisconsin, total	**5,326**	**5,479**	**2.9**
Total aged 55 or older	**1,166**	**1,297**	**11.2**
Aged 55 to 64	461	567	23.0
Aged 65 to 74	357	360	0.8
Aged 75 to 84	250	259	3.6
Aged 85 or older	98	111	13.3
Wyoming, total	**525**	**568**	**8.2**
Total aged 55 or older	**109**	**132**	**21.1**
Aged 55 to 64	47	61	29.8
Aged 65 to 74	34	37	8.8
Aged 75 to 84	21	25	19.0
Aged 85 or older	7	9	28.6

Source: Bureau of the Census, Population Projections for States by Age, Sex, Race and Hispanic Origin: 1995 to 2025, *PPL-47, 1996; calculations by New Strategist*

In Most States, Older Americans Are Not Diverse

Non-Hispanic whites are the majority in all but one state.

Hawaii is the only state in which non-Hispanic whites do not account for the majority of the population aged 55 or older. In California, where no racial or ethnic group can claim the majority of the total population, fully two out of three people aged 55 or older are non-Hispanic white.

Older Americans are far less diverse than the nation's children and young adults because of immigration. During the past few decades, millions of Hispanic and Asian young adults have come to the U.S. to work, many of them bringing their families. The higher fertility rates of blacks and immigrants has also contributed to the rapid rise of diversity among the young.

In fully 23 states, more than 90 percent of the population aged 55 or older is non-Hispanic white. The minority share of this age group reaches at least 25 percent in only the District of Columbia and seven states—California, Hawaii, Louisiana, Maryland, Mississippi, New Mexico, and Texas.

◆ Marketers targeting older consumers should prepare for change. As younger generations age, the diversity of older Americans will grow, requiring new marketing approaches.

State Populations Aged 55 or Older by Race and Hispanic Origin, 2000

(number and percent distribution of total people and people aged 55 or older by race and Hispanic origin, 2000)

		non-Hispanic					non-Hispanic				
	total	white	black	Native American	Asian	Hispanic	white	black	Native American	Asian	Hispanic
Alabama, total	**4,450,583**	**3,231,301**	**1,133,242**	**17,243**	**32,502**	**36,295**	**72.6%**	**25.5%**	**0.4%**	**0.7%**	**0.8%**
Total, aged 55 or older	**1,001,709**	**807,773**	**182,557**	**3,081**	**4,078**	**4,220**	**80.6**	**18.2**	**0.3**	**0.4**	**0.4**
Aged 55–59	229,332	184,597	41,096	886	1,454	1,299	80.5	17.9	0.4	0.6	0.6
Aged 60–64	191,354	153,829	34,845	675	1,050	955	80.4	18.2	0.4	0.5	0.5
Aged 65–69	169,676	135,697	32,091	473	699	716	80.0	18.9	0.3	0.4	0.4
Aged 70–74	146,827	119,287	26,235	318	446	541	81.2	17.9	0.2	0.3	0.4
Aged 75 or older	264,520	214,363	48,290	729	429	709	81.0	18.3	0.3	0.2	0.3
Alaska, total	**653,293**	**461,334**	**26,766**	**90,940**	**44,412**	**29,841**	**70.6**	**4.1**	**13.9**	**6.8**	**4.6**
Total, aged 55 or older	**83,515**	**65,440**	**1,675**	**10,305**	**4,290**	**1,805**	**78.4**	**2.0**	**12.3**	**5.1**	**2.2**
Aged 55–59	26,842	21,627	495	2,835	1,261	624	80.6	1.8	10.6	4.7	2.3
Aged 60–64	18,631	14,531	405	2,282	976	437	78.0	2.2	12.2	5.2	2.3
Aged 65–69	14,271	10,806	328	1,960	826	351	75.7	2.3	13.7	5.8	2.5
Aged 70–74	10,272	7,943	202	1,322	593	212	77.3	2.0	12.9	5.8	2.1
Aged 75 or older	13,499	10,533	245	1,906	634	181	78.0	1.8	14.1	4.7	1.3
Arizona, total	**4,797,526**	**3,253,086**	**150,088**	**232,236**	**91,649**	**1,070,467**	**67.8**	**3.1**	**4.8**	**1.9**	**22.3**
Total, aged 55 or older	**1,061,311**	**888,971**	**20,888**	**23,747**	**13,431**	**114,274**	**83.8**	**2.0**	**2.2**	**1.3**	**10.8**
Aged 55–59	232,162	185,152	5,542	6,489	3,781	31,198	79.8	2.4	2.8	1.6	13.4
Aged 60–64	194,650	156,888	4,691	5,191	3,164	24,716	80.6	2.4	2.7	1.6	12.7
Aged 65–69	174,038	142,590	4,073	4,242	2,715	20,418	81.9	2.3	2.4	1.6	11.7
Aged 70–74	164,639	139,885	2,855	3,262	1,969	16,668	85.0	1.7	2.0	1.2	10.1
Aged 75 or older	295,822	264,456	3,727	4,563	1,802	21,274	89.4	1.3	1.5	0.6	7.2

(continued)

(continued from previous page)

	total	non-Hispanic white	black	Native American	Asian	Hispanic	non-Hispanic white	black	Native American	Asian	Hispanic
Arkansas, total	**2,631,383**	**2,154,759**	**407,431**	**15,187**	**18,604**	**35,402**	**81.9%**	**15.5%**	**0.6%**	**0.7%**	**1.3%**
Total, aged 55 or older	**644,348**	**572,295**	**62,467**	**3,015**	**2,529**	**4,042**	**88.8**	**9.7**	**0.5**	**0.4**	**0.6**
Aged 55–59	145,812	128,821	14,252	788	812	1,139	88.3	9.8	0.5	0.6	0.8
Aged 60–64	120,877	106,937	11,899	605	580	856	88.5	9.8	0.5	0.5	0.7
Aged 65–69	107,415	95,144	10,620	474	460	717	88.6	9.9	0.4	0.4	0.7
Aged 70–74	92,949	83,030	8,609	395	371	544	89.3	9.3	0.4	0.4	0.6
Aged 75 or older	177,295	158,363	17,087	753	306	786	89.3	9.6	0.4	0.2	0.4
California, total	**32,521,102**	**15,561,848**	**2,137,541**	**169,997**	**4,005,991**	**10,645,725**	**47.9**	**6.6**	**0.5**	**12.3**	**32.7**
Total, aged 55 or older	**5,816,353**	**3,857,064**	**326,388**	**30,633**	**622,124**	**980,144**	**66.3**	**5.6**	**0.5**	**10.7**	**16.9**
Aged 55–59	1,372,485	850,784	83,819	8,040	159,072	270,770	62.0	6.1	0.6	11.6	19.7
Aged 60–64	1,057,562	647,013	68,539	5,940	133,087	202,983	61.2	6.5	0.6	12.6	19.2
Aged 65–69	895,582	560,207	55,894	4,505	112,461	162,515	62.6	6.2	0.5	12.6	18.1
Aged 70–74	861,231	578,579	44,399	4,095	95,593	138,565	67.2	5.2	0.5	11.1	16.1
Aged 75 or older	1,629,493	1,220,481	73,737	8,053	121,911	205,311	74.9	4.5	0.5	7.5	12.6
Colorado, total	**4,168,224**	**3,267,777**	**178,393**	**30,168**	**97,742**	**594,144**	**78.4**	**4.3**	**0.7**	**2.3**	**14.3**
Total, aged 55 or older	**814,739**	**702,309**	**23,639**	**3,610**	**12,881**	**72,300**	**86.2**	**2.9**	**0.4**	**1.6**	**8.9**
Aged 55–59	204,296	173,482	6,347	1,114	3,479	19,874	84.9	3.1	0.5	1.7	9.7
Aged 60–64	158,612	133,811	5,413	804	2,828	15,756	84.4	3.4	0.5	1.8	9.9
Aged 65–69	135,934	115,062	4,740	592	2,537	13,003	84.6	3.5	0.4	1.9	9.6
Aged 70–74	110,236	95,432	2,972	373	1,937	9,522	86.6	2.7	0.3	1.8	8.6
Aged 75 or older	205,661	184,522	4,167	727	2,100	14,145	89.7	2.0	0.4	1.0	6.9

(continued)

(continued from previous page)

	total	non-Hispanic					non-Hispanic				
		white	black	Native American	Asian	Hispanic	white	black	Native American	Asian	Hispanic
Connecticut, total	**3,284,142**	**2,622,264**	**292,778**	**5,759**	**76,019**	**287,322**	**79.8%**	**8.9%**	**0.2%**	**2.3%**	**8.7%**
Total, aged 55 or older	**753,543**	**672,915**	**41,732**	**964**	**8,481**	**29,451**	**89.3**	**5.5**	**0.1**	**1.1**	**3.9**
Aged 55–59	167,258	144,450	11,306	242	2,652	8,608	86.4	6.8	0.1	1.6	5.1
Aged 60–64	124,685	107,049	9,044	180	2,038	6,374	85.9	7.3	0.1	1.6	5.1
Aged 65–69	112,093	98,645	7,137	148	1,407	4,756	88.0	6.4	0.1	1.3	4.2
Aged 70–74	111,898	101,638	5,564	133	1,086	3,477	90.8	5.0	0.1	1.0	3.1
Aged 75 or older	237,609	221,133	8,681	261	1,298	6,236	93.1	3.7	0.1	0.5	2.6
Delaware, total	**767,559**	**582,611**	**142,599**	**2,079**	**14,887**	**25,383**	**75.9**	**18.6**	**0.3**	**1.9**	**3.3**
Total, aged 55 or older	**163,601**	**138,563**	**20,224**	**391**	**2,022**	**2,401**	**84.7**	**12.4**	**0.2**	**1.2**	**1.5**
Aged 55–59	37,408	30,443	5,500	102	653	710	81.4	14.7	0.3	1.7	1.9
Aged 60–64	29,564	24,138	4,234	87	561	544	81.6	14.3	0.3	1.9	1.8
Aged 65–69	26,460	22,136	3,490	69	327	438	83.7	13.2	0.3	1.2	1.7
Aged 70–74	24,820	21,580	2,676	53	191	320	86.9	10.8	0.2	0.8	1.3
Aged 75 or older	45,349	40,266	4,324	80	290	389	88.8	9.5	0.2	0.6	0.9
District of Columbia, total	**523,328**	**152,409**	**315,434**	**851**	**13,845**	**40,789**	**29.1**	**60.3**	**0.2**	**2.6**	**7.8**
Total, aged 55 or older	**114,385**	**32,190**	**75,011**	**246**	**2,097**	**4,841**	**28.1**	**65.6**	**0.2**	**1.8**	**4.2**
Aged 55–59	25,308	8,467	14,850	49	581	1,361	33.5	58.7	0.2	2.3	5.4
Aged 60–64	20,641	5,720	13,339	36	477	1,069	27.7	64.6	0.2	2.3	5.2
Aged 65–69	18,409	4,406	12,777	40	372	814	23.9	69.4	0.2	2.0	4.4
Aged 70–74	17,542	4,346	12,202	34	320	640	24.8	69.6	0.2	1.8	3.6
Aged 75 or older	32,485	9,251	21,843	87	347	957	28.5	67.2	0.3	1.1	2.9

(continued)

(continued from previous page)

		non-Hispanic					non-Hispanic				
	total	white	black	Native American	Asian	Hispanic	white	black	Native American	Asian	Hispanic
Florida, total	**15,233,224**	**10,404,927**	**2,159,717**	**38,913**	**238,797**	**2,390,870**	**68.3%**	**14.2%**	**0.3%**	**1.6%**	**15.7%**
Total, aged 55 or older	**4,280,271**	**3,416,547**	**315,509**	**8,121**	**39,300**	**500,794**	**79.8**	**7.4**	**0.2**	**0.9**	**11.7**
Aged 55–59	813,548	606,871	80,450	2,161	12,035	112,031	74.6	9.9	0.3	1.5	13.8
Aged 60–64	711,977	530,915	68,516	1,688	9,539	101,319	74.6	9.6	0.2	1.3	14.2
Aged 65–69	676,106	522,731	57,270	1,307	7,332	87,466	77.3	8.5	0.2	1.1	12.9
Aged 70–74	707,953	577,045	45,984	1,069	5,310	78,545	81.5	6.5	0.2	0.8	11.1
Aged 75 or older	1,370,687	1,178,985	63,289	1,896	5,084	121,433	86.0	4.6	0.1	0.4	8.9
Georgia, total	**7,874,792**	**5,269,997**	**2,262,068**	**15,340**	**137,045**	**190,342**	**66.9**	**28.7**	**0.2**	**1.7**	**2.4**
Total, aged 55 or older	**1,433,894**	**1,115,882**	**283,480**	**2,519**	**15,160**	**16,853**	**77.8**	**19.8**	**0.2**	**1.1**	**1.2**
Aged 55–59	372,068	285,097	76,054	755	5,331	4,831	76.6	20.4	0.2	1.4	1.3
Aged 60–64	281,677	215,605	58,112	538	3,804	3,618	76.5	20.6	0.2	1.4	1.3
Aged 65–69	234,220	180,835	47,367	371	2,708	2,939	77.2	20.2	0.2	1.2	1.3
Aged 70–74	195,269	155,232	35,980	290	1,656	2,111	79.5	18.4	0.1	0.8	1.1
Aged 75 or older	350,660	279,113	65,967	565	1,661	3,354	79.6	18.8	0.2	0.5	1.0
Hawaii, total	**1,257,404**	**362,790**	**26,579**	**4,624**	**755,738**	**107,673**	**28.9**	**2.1**	**0.4**	**60.1**	**8.6**
Total, aged 55 or older	**263,584**	**78,281**	**1,516**	**572**	**172,116**	**11,099**	**29.7**	**0.6**	**0.2**	**65.3**	**4.2**
Aged 55–59	60,279	20,070	466	212	36,299	3,232	33.3	0.8	0.4	60.2	5.4
Aged 60–64	46,318	14,097	335	129	29,370	2,387	30.4	0.7	0.3	63.4	5.2
Aged 65–69	42,134	11,516	237	83	28,309	1,989	27.3	0.6	0.2	67.2	4.7
Aged 70–74	41,156	10,410	186	51	28,915	1,594	25.3	0.5	0.1	70.3	3.9
Aged 75 or older	73,697	22,188	292	97	49,223	1,897	30.1	0.4	0.1	66.8	2.6

(continued)

(continued from previous page)

		non-Hispanic					non-Hispanic				
	total	white	black	Native American	Asian	Hispanic	white	black	Native American	Asian	Hispanic
Idaho, total	1,346,506	1,211,465	6,101	17,747	14,834	96,359	90.0%	0.5%	1.3%	1.1%	7.2%
Total, aged 55 or older	**274,818**	**262,902**	**515**	**2,047**	**1,661**	**7,693**	**95.7**	**0.2**	**0.7**	**0.6**	**2.8**
Aged 55–59	65,360	61,688	157	641	461	2,413	94.4	0.2	1.0	0.7	3.7
Aged 60–64	52,665	50,032	116	473	303	1,741	95.0	0.2	0.9	0.6	3.3
Aged 65–69	44,952	42,768	75	353	313	1,443	95.1	0.2	0.8	0.7	3.2
Aged 70–74	37,291	35,776	64	237	252	962	95.9	0.2	0.6	0.7	2.6
Aged 75 or older	74,550	72,638	103	343	332	1,134	97.4	0.1	0.5	0.4	1.5
Illinois, total	12,050,818	8,553,616	1,812,651	18,191	398,270	1,268,090	71.0	15.0	0.2	3.3	10.5
Total, aged 55 or older	**2,507,825**	**2,044,690**	**279,302**	**3,258**	**58,126**	**122,449**	**81.5**	**11.1**	**0.1**	**2.3**	**4.9**
Aged 55–59	567,905	445,582	69,210	883	17,463	34,767	78.5	12.2	0.2	3.1	6.1
Aged 60–64	456,812	356,619	58,887	620	13,728	26,958	78.1	12.9	0.1	3.0	5.9
Aged 65–69	400,777	317,450	50,704	486	10,539	21,598	79.2	12.7	0.1	2.6	5.4
Aged 70–74	365,857	303,160	39,488	425	7,289	15,495	82.9	10.8	0.1	2.0	4.2
Aged 75 or older	716,474	621,879	61,013	844	9,107	23,631	86.8	8.5	0.1	1.3	3.3
Indiana, total	6,044,528	5,337,906	494,936	13,378	57,857	140,451	88.3	8.2	0.2	1.0	2.3
Total, aged 55 or older	**1,303,971**	**1,201,417**	**77,032**	**2,546**	**6,390**	**16,586**	**92.1**	**5.9**	**0.2**	**0.5**	**1.3**
Aged 55–59	299,325	273,556	18,784	665	2,006	4,314	91.4	6.3	0.2	0.7	1.4
Aged 60–64	241,926	220,920	15,626	503	1,606	3,271	91.3	6.5	0.2	0.7	1.4
Aged 65–69	210,472	191,789	14,295	375	1,202	2,811	91.1	6.8	0.2	0.6	1.3
Aged 70–74	191,721	177,057	11,175	301	757	2,431	92.4	5.8	0.2	0.4	1.3
Aged 75 or older	360,527	338,095	17,152	702	819	3,759	93.8	4.8	0.2	0.2	1.0

(continued)

(continued from previous page)

| | | non-Hispanic | | | | | non-Hispanic | | | | |
	total	white	black	Native American	Asian	Hispanic	white	black	Native American	Asian	Hispanic
Iowa, total	**2,899,829**	**2,736,647**	**60,432**	**8,072**	**41,610**	**53,068**	**94.4%**	**2.1%**	**0.3%**	**1.4%**	**1.8%**
Total, aged 55 or older	**708,078**	**691,058**	**7,349**	**1,001**	**3,562**	**5,108**	**97.6**	**1.0**	**0.1**	**0.5**	**0.7**
Aged 55–59	142,908	138,408	1,790	273	1,097	1,340	96.9	1.3	0.2	0.8	0.9
Aged 60–64	123,262	119,727	1,492	222	865	956	97.1	1.2	0.2	0.7	0.8
Aged 65–69	113,170	110,247	1,318	140	629	836	97.4	1.2	0.1	0.6	0.7
Aged 70–74	103,982	101,721	1,025	116	406	714	97.8	1.0	0.1	0.4	0.7
Aged 75 or older	224,756	220,955	1,724	250	565	1,262	98.3	0.8	0.1	0.3	0.6
Kansas, total	**2,668,263**	**2,292,993**	**166,801**	**22,701**	**47,339**	**138,429**	**85.9**	**6.3**	**0.9**	**1.8**	**5.2**
Total, aged 55 or older	**580,291**	**537,104**	**22,045**	**3,086**	**4,980**	**13,076**	**92.6**	**3.8**	**0.5**	**0.9**	**2.3**
Aged 55–59	122,125	110,846	5,258	826	1,634	3,561	90.8	4.3	0.7	1.3	2.9
Aged 60–64	99,995	91,143	4,342	672	1,196	2,642	91.1	4.3	0.7	1.2	2.6
Aged 65–69	92,949	85,170	3,984	535	972	2,288	91.6	4.3	0.6	1.0	2.5
Aged 70–74	85,659	79,863	3,096	346	557	1,797	93.2	3.6	0.4	0.7	2.1
Aged 75 or older	179,563	170,082	5,365	707	621	2,788	94.7	3.0	0.4	0.3	1.6
Kentucky, total	**3,994,566**	**3,643,538**	**284,955**	**6,293**	**27,201**	**32,579**	**91.2**	**7.1**	**0.2**	**0.7**	**0.8**
Total, aged 55 or older	**891,156**	**837,087**	**46,039**	**1,216**	**3,116**	**3,698**	**93.9**	**5.2**	**0.1**	**0.3**	**0.4**
Aged 55–59	209,346	196,247	10,589	324	1,084	1,102	93.7	5.1	0.2	0.5	0.5
Aged 60–64	172,279	161,553	8,936	233	777	780	93.8	5.2	0.1	0.5	0.5
Aged 65–69	149,589	140,056	8,202	188	529	614	93.6	5.5	0.1	0.4	0.4
Aged 70–74	129,574	121,978	6,589	164	378	465	94.1	5.1	0.1	0.3	0.4
Aged 75 or older	230,368	217,253	11,723	307	348	737	94.3	5.1	0.1	0.2	0.3

(continued)

(continued from previous page)

		non-Hispanic					non-Hispanic				
	total	white	black	Native American	Asian	Hispanic	white	black	Native American	Asian	Hispanic
Louisiana, total	4,424,618	2,791,582	1,438,366	17,941	57,812	118,917	63.1%	32.5%	0.4%	1.3%	2.7%
Total, aged 55 or older	**909,809**	**665,273**	**212,559**	**2,984**	**7,050**	**21,943**	**73.1**	**23.4**	**0.3**	**0.8**	**2.4**
Aged 55–59	211,462	151,197	52,134	804	2,229	5,098	71.5	24.7	0.4	1.1	2.4
Aged 60–64	175,042	125,331	43,053	621	1,723	4,314	71.6	24.6	0.4	1.0	2.5
Aged 65–69	155,295	112,031	37,794	430	1,242	3,798	72.1	24.3	0.3	0.8	2.4
Aged 70–74	133,226	99,501	29,377	378	885	3,085	74.7	22.1	0.3	0.7	2.3
Aged 75 or older	234,784	177,213	50,201	751	971	5,648	75.5	21.4	0.3	0.4	2.4
Maine, total	1,259,170	1,230,020	4,517	5,768	9,451	9,414	97.7	0.4	0.5	0.8	0.7
Total, aged 55 or older	**288,370**	**285,464**	**393**	**696**	**935**	**882**	**99.0**	**0.1**	**0.2**	**0.3**	**0.3**
Aged 55–59	65,729	64,773	129	239	320	268	98.5	0.2	0.4	0.5	0.4
Aged 60–64	50,881	50,245	85	154	209	188	98.8	0.2	0.3	0.4	0.4
Aged 65–69	45,630	45,161	65	115	154	135	99.0	0.1	0.3	0.3	0.3
Aged 70–74	43,745	43,396	47	78	110	114	99.2	0.1	0.2	0.3	0.3
Aged 75 or older	82,385	81,889	67	110	142	177	99.4	0.1	0.1	0.2	0.2
Maryland, total	5,274,608	3,370,473	1,462,797	13,474	212,224	215,640	63.9	27.7	0.3	4.0	4.1
Total, aged 55 or older	**1,039,067**	**770,514**	**213,496**	**2,304**	**30,167**	**22,586**	**74.2**	**20.5**	**0.2**	**2.9**	**2.2**
Aged 55–59	257,483	180,794	59,916	640	9,666	6,467	70.2	23.3	0.2	3.8	2.5
Aged 60–64	192,193	134,518	45,400	472	7,153	4,650	70.0	23.6	0.2	3.7	2.4
Aged 65–69	161,571	115,398	36,996	378	5,188	3,611	71.4	22.9	0.2	3.2	2.2
Aged 70–74	150,841	115,869	28,015	279	3,883	2,795	76.8	18.6	0.2	2.6	1.9
Aged 75 or older	276,979	223,935	43,169	535	4,277	5,063	80.8	15.6	0.2	1.5	1.8

(continued)

(continued from previous page)

| | | non-Hispanic | | | | | | non-Hispanic | | | |
	total	white	black	Native American	Asian	Hispanic	white	black	Native American	Asian	Hispanic
Massachusetts, total	**6,198,746**	**5,182,035**	**331,601**	**10,336**	**238,368**	**436,406**	**83.6%**	**5.3%**	**0.2%**	**3.8%**	**7.0%**
Total, aged 55 or older	**1,364,977**	**1,257,497**	**43,391**	**1,939**	**24,608**	**37,542**	**92.1**	**3.2**	**0.1**	**1.8**	**2.8**
Aged 55–59	297,926	267,466	11,963	466	7,133	10,898	89.8	4.0	0.2	2.4	3.7
Aged 60–64	224,316	202,027	8,662	352	5,508	7,767	90.1	3.9	0.2	2.5	3.5
Aged 65–69	205,195	187,457	7,264	281	4,515	5,678	91.4	3.5	0.1	2.2	2.8
Aged 70–74	207,929	193,809	6,200	278	3,317	4,325	93.2	3.0	0.1	1.6	2.1
Aged 75 or older	429,611	406,738	9,302	562	4,135	8,874	94.7	2.2	0.1	1.0	2.1
Michigan, total	**9,678,943**	**7,789,804**	**1,417,504**	**55,157**	**156,781**	**259,697**	**80.5**	**14.6**	**0.6**	**1.6**	**2.7**
Total, aged 55 or older	**2,036,253**	**1,762,237**	**220,577**	**6,525**	**17,747**	**29,167**	**86.5**	**10.8**	**0.3**	**0.9**	**1.4**
Aged 55–59	470,951	401,365	53,959	2,106	6,011	7,510	85.2	11.5	0.4	1.3	1.6
Aged 60–64	368,140	315,963	40,754	1,553	4,201	5,669	85.8	11.1	0.4	1.1	1.5
Aged 65–69	322,225	275,252	37,991	1,071	2,992	4,919	85.4	11.8	0.3	0.9	1.5
Aged 70–74	305,037	265,460	32,476	803	2,036	4,262	87.0	10.6	0.3	0.7	1.4
Aged 75 or older	569,900	504,197	55,397	992	2,507	6,807	88.5	9.7	0.2	0.4	1.2
Minnesota, total	**4,829,798**	**4,387,552**	**151,933**	**60,493**	**135,380**	**94,440**	**90.8**	**3.1**	**1.3**	**2.8**	**2.0**
Total, aged 55 or older	**1,001,645**	**965,425**	**12,079**	**5,258**	**11,422**	**7,461**	**96.4**	**1.2**	**0.5**	**1.1**	**0.7**
Aged 55–59	225,963	215,496	3,528	1,625	3,257	2,057	95.4	1.6	0.7	1.4	0.9
Aged 60–64	179,271	171,468	2,520	1,258	2,526	1,499	95.6	1.4	0.7	1.4	0.8
Aged 65–69	154,704	148,550	2,008	854	2,058	1,234	96.0	1.3	0.6	1.3	0.8
Aged 70–74	141,084	136,536	1,567	582	1,502	897	96.8	1.1	0.4	1.1	0.6
Aged 75 or older	300,623	293,375	2,456	939	2,079	1,774	97.6	0.8	0.3	0.7	0.6

(continued)

(continued from previous page)

	total	non-Hispanic				Hispanic	non-Hispanic				Hispanic
		white	black	Native American	Asian		white	black	Native American	Asian	
Mississippi, total	**2,815,743**	**1,754,438**	**1,009,938**	**8,649**	**19,946**	**22,772**	**62.3%**	**35.9%**	**0.3%**	**0.7%**	**0.8%**
Total, aged 55 or older	**592,969**	**439,911**	**145,829**	**1,156**	**2,387**	**3,686**	**74.2**	**24.6**	**0.2**	**0.4**	**0.6**
Aged 55–59	134,249	98,931	33,356	342	780	840	73.7	24.8	0.3	0.6	0.6
Aged 60–64	114,709	84,613	28,448	288	583	777	73.8	24.8	0.3	0.5	0.7
Aged 65–69	100,323	74,187	24,862	194	416	664	73.9	24.8	0.2	0.4	0.7
Aged 70–74	86,178	64,960	20,243	150	332	493	75.4	23.5	0.2	0.4	0.6
Aged 75 or older	157,510	117,220	38,920	182	276	912	74.4	24.7	0.1	0.2	0.6
Missouri, total	**5,540,378**	**4,745,409**	**621,746**	**22,207**	**61,038**	**89,978**	**85.7**	**11.2**	**0.4**	**1.1**	**1.6**
Total, aged 55 or older	**1,260,095**	**1,143,548**	**95,047**	**3,902**	**7,043**	**10,555**	**90.8**	**7.5**	**0.3**	**0.6**	**0.8**
Aged 55–59	278,152	248,952	22,993	1,034	2,414	2,759	89.5	8.3	0.4	0.9	1.0
Aged 60–64	226,612	202,856	19,081	789	1,774	2,112	89.5	8.4	0.3	0.8	0.9
Aged 65–69	204,425	183,696	17,057	643	1,238	1,791	89.9	8.3	0.3	0.6	0.9
Aged 70–74	186,212	169,520	13,698	534	890	1,570	91.0	7.4	0.3	0.5	0.8
Aged 75 or older	364,694	338,524	22,218	902	727	2,323	92.8	6.1	0.2	0.2	0.6
Montana, total	**949,657**	**860,423**	**3,469**	**58,124**	**7,172**	**20,469**	**90.6**	**0.4**	**6.1**	**0.8**	**2.2**
Total, aged 55 or older	**221,388**	**212,276**	**361**	**5,776**	**822**	**2,153**	**95.9**	**0.2**	**2.6**	**0.4**	**1.0**
Aged 55–59	51,299	48,656	84	1,739	219	601	94.8	0.2	3.4	0.4	1.2
Aged 60–64	41,666	39,374	79	1,489	186	538	94.5	0.2	3.6	0.4	1.3
Aged 65–69	36,211	34,496	74	1,092	169	380	95.3	0.2	3.0	0.5	1.0
Aged 70–74	30,284	29,227	42	630	127	258	96.5	0.1	2.1	0.4	0.9
Aged 75 or older	61,928	60,523	82	826	121	376	97.7	0.1	1.3	0.2	0.6

(continued)

(continued from previous page)

	total	white	black	Native American	Asian	Hispanic	white	black	Native American	Asian	Hispanic
			non-Hispanic						*non-Hispanic*		
Nebraska, total	1,705,467	1,539,408	69,984	14,222	21,711	60,142	90.3%	4.1%	0.8%	1.3%	3.5%
Total, aged 55 or older	**382,838**	**364,384**	**8,948**	**1,312**	**2,181**	**6,013**	**95.2**	**2.3**	**0.3**	**0.6**	**1.6**
Aged 55–59	78,509	73,811	2,284	406	625	1,383	94.0	2.9	0.5	0.8	1.8
Aged 60–64	65,970	62,153	1,908	293	487	1,129	94.2	2.9	0.4	0.7	1.7
Aged 65–69	62,711	59,389	1,663	195	417	1,047	94.7	2.7	0.3	0.7	1.7
Aged 70–74	56,821	54,280	1,240	141	290	870	95.5	2.2	0.2	0.5	1.5
Aged 75 or older	118,827	114,751	1,853	277	362	1,584	96.6	1.6	0.2	0.3	1.3
Nevada, total	1,871,299	1,365,753	127,830	24,867	76,899	275,950	73.0	6.8	1.3	4.1	14.7
Total, aged 55 or older	**407,646**	**339,951**	**18,934**	**4,136**	**13,729**	**30,896**	**83.4**	**4.6**	**1.0**	**3.4**	**7.6**
Aged 55–59	104,786	85,309	5,350	1,194	3,958	8,975	81.4	5.1	1.1	3.8	8.6
Aged 60–64	83,571	67,891	4,533	907	3,336	6,904	81.2	5.4	1.1	4.0	8.3
Aged 65–69	68,406	56,045	3,646	723	2,661	5,331	81.9	5.3	1.1	3.9	7.8
Aged 70–74	60,739	51,549	2,521	539	1,970	4,160	84.9	4.2	0.9	3.2	6.8
Aged 75 or older	90,144	79,157	2,884	773	1,804	5,526	87.8	3.2	0.9	2.0	6.1
New Hampshire, total	1,224,230	1,183,300	7,215	2,345	14,213	17,157	96.7	0.6	0.2	1.2	1.4
Total, aged 55 or older	**241,952**	**238,171**	**806**	**337**	**1,439**	**1,199**	**98.4**	**0.3**	**0.1**	**0.6**	**0.5**
Aged 55–59	57,687	56,437	261	105	455	429	97.8	0.5	0.2	0.8	0.7
Aged 60–64	41,898	41,049	187	57	330	275	98.0	0.4	0.1	0.8	0.7
Aged 65–69	36,145	35,545	126	41	260	173	98.3	0.3	0.1	0.7	0.5
Aged 70–74	36,070	35,634	97	43	154	142	98.8	0.3	0.1	0.4	0.4
Aged 75 or older	70,152	69,506	135	91	240	180	99.1	0.2	0.1	0.3	0.3

(continued)

(continued from previous page)

		non-Hispanic					non-Hispanic				
	total	white	black	Native American	Asian	Hispanic	white	black	Native American	Asian	Hispanic
New Jersey, total	8,177,791	5,557,637	1,104,522	14,298	456,050	1,045,284	68.0%	13.5%	0.2%	5.6%	12.8%
Total, aged 55 or older	**1,827,169**	**1,446,623**	**179,588**	**2,580**	**60,332**	**138,046**	**79.2**	**9.8**	**0.1**	**3.3**	**7.6**
Aged 55–59	414,788	309,049	47,168	604	19,371	38,596	74.5	11.4	0.1	4.7	9.3
Aged 60–64	322,132	237,531	38,962	493	14,243	30,903	73.7	12.1	0.2	4.4	9.6
Aged 65–69	288,358	221,139	32,359	418	10,464	23,978	76.7	11.2	0.1	3.6	8.3
Aged 70–74	276,523	226,356	24,419	378	7,290	18,080	81.9	8.8	0.1	2.6	6.5
Aged 75 or older	525,368	452,548	36,680	687	8,964	26,489	86.1	7.0	0.1	1.7	5.0
New Mexico, total	1,860,397	911,758	34,026	156,717	21,335	736,561	49.0	1.8	8.4	1.1	39.6
Total, aged 55 or older	**364,304**	**234,536**	**5,207**	**16,542**	**2,839**	**105,180**	**64.4**	**1.4**	**4.5**	**0.8**	**28.9**
Aged 55–59	87,014	53,358	1,278	4,525	868	26,985	61.3	1.5	5.2	1.0	31.0
Aged 60–64	71,100	43,277	1,129	3,694	694	22,306	60.9	1.6	5.2	1.0	31.4
Aged 65–69	62,319	38,312	1,033	2,840	540	19,594	61.5	1.7	4.6	0.9	31.4
Aged 70–74	51,776	33,777	756	2,003	370	14,870	65.2	1.5	3.9	0.7	28.7
Aged 75 or older	92,095	65,812	1,011	3,480	367	21,425	71.5	1.1	3.8	0.4	23.3
New York, total	18,146,185	11,640,203	2,668,358	52,425	980,588	2,804,611	64.1	14.7	0.3	5.4	15.5
Total, aged 55 or older	**3,980,299**	**2,987,763**	**446,079**	**8,599**	**147,448**	**390,410**	**75.1**	**11.2**	**0.2**	**3.7**	**9.8**
Aged 55–59	902,443	630,014	119,728	2,145	43,439	107,117	69.8	13.3	0.2	4.8	11.9
Aged 60–64	719,801	501,756	95,683	1,566	35,336	85,460	69.7	13.3	0.2	4.9	11.9
Aged 65–69	639,055	464,460	77,620	1,321	26,994	68,660	72.7	12.1	0.2	4.2	10.7
Aged 70–74	599,847	465,829	61,817	1,129	19,211	51,861	77.7	10.3	0.2	3.2	8.6
Aged 75 or older	1,119,153	925,704	91,231	2,438	22,468	77,312	82.7	8.2	0.2	2.0	6.9

(continued)

(continued from previous page)

		non-Hispanic					non-Hispanic			
	total	white	black	Native American	Asian	Hispanic	white	black	Native American	Asian	Hispanic
North Carolina, total	**7,777,253**	**5,747,974**	**1,725,731**	**91,637**	**92,074**	**119,837**	**73.9%**	**22.2%**	**1.2%**	**1.2%**	**1.5%**
Total, aged 55 or older	**1,713,487**	**1,402,873**	**274,451**	**12,675**	**11,350**	**12,138**	**81.9**	**16.0**	**0.7**	**0.7**	**0.7**
Aged 55–59	398,565	322,181	65,533	3,674	3,799	3,378	80.8	16.4	0.9	1.0	0.8
Aged 60–64	323,979	261,920	54,055	2,676	2,737	2,591	80.8	16.7	0.8	0.8	0.8
Aged 65–69	285,423	231,846	47,465	1,987	2,046	2,079	81.2	16.6	0.7	0.7	0.7
Aged 70–74	253,441	210,046	38,947	1,609	1,278	1,561	82.9	15.4	0.6	0.5	0.6
Aged 75 or older	452,079	376,880	68,451	2,729	1,490	2,529	83.4	15.1	0.6	0.3	0.6
North Dakota, total	**661,689**	**611,587**	**4,711**	**32,145**	**5,694**	**7,552**	**92.4**	**0.7**	**4.9**	**0.9**	**1.1**
Total, aged 55 or older	**154,616**	**150,526**	**264**	**2,686**	**598**	**542**	**97.4**	**0.2**	**1.7**	**0.4**	**0.4**
Aged 55–59	30,064	28,908	72	754	197	133	96.2	0.2	2.5	0.7	0.4
Aged 60–64	25,754	24,826	48	651	129	100	96.4	0.2	2.5	0.5	0.4
Aged 65–69	25,188	24,563	43	445	90	47	97.5	0.2	1.8	0.4	0.2
Aged 70–74	22,884	22,345	30	349	77	83	97.6	0.1	1.5	0.3	0.4
Aged 75 or older	50,726	49,884	71	487	105	179	98.3	0.1	1.0	0.2	0.4
Ohio, total	**11,318,718**	**9,672,043**	**1,305,993**	**20,519**	**136,359**	**183,804**	**85.5**	**11.5**	**0.2**	**1.2**	**1.6**
Total, aged 55 or older	**2,536,278**	**2,272,760**	**219,108**	**3,943**	**17,025**	**23,442**	**89.6**	**8.6**	**0.2**	**0.7**	**0.9**
Aged 55–59	552,142	491,454	48,633	1,030	5,371	5,654	89.0	8.8	0.2	1.0	1.0
Aged 60–64	459,197	406,542	43,328	764	4,063	4,500	88.5	9.4	0.2	0.9	1.0
Aged 65–69	408,660	360,378	40,753	632	2,952	3,945	88.2	10.0	0.2	0.7	1.0
Aged 70–74	385,885	345,912	33,980	509	2,138	3,346	89.6	8.8	0.1	0.6	0.9
Aged 75 or older	730,394	668,474	52,414	1,008	2,501	5,997	91.5	7.2	0.1	0.3	0.8

(continued)

(continued from previous page)

	non-Hispanic					non-Hispanic				
total	white	black	Native American	Asian	Hispanic	white	black	Native American	Asian	Hispanic
Oklahoma, total 3,372,514	2,653,074	276,109	272,606	47,184	123,541	78.7%	8.2%	8.1%	1.4%	3.7%
Total, aged 55 or older 794,620	**691,620**	**39,867**	**46,596**	**5,615**	**10,922**	**87.0**	**5.0**	**5.9**	**0.7**	**1.4**
Aged 55–59 175,640	150,146	9,822	10,514	1,690	3,468	85.5	5.6	6.0	1.0	2.0
Aged 60–64 147,035	126,439	8,017	8,593	1,258	2,728	86.0	5.5	5.8	0.9	1.9
Aged 65–69 133,571	116,110	7,173	7,252	1,062	1,974	86.9	5.4	5.4	0.8	1.5
Aged 70–74 115,823	102,203	5,337	6,191	746	1,346	88.2	4.6	5.3	0.6	1.2
Aged 75 or older 222,551	196,722	9,518	14,046	859	1,406	88.4	4.3	6.3	0.4	0.6
Oregon, total 3,397,161	2,989,829	59,602	44,738	109,680	193,312	88.0	1.8	1.3	3.2	5.7
Total, aged 55 or older 796,286	**749,291**	**8,081**	**6,707**	**14,530**	**17,677**	**94.1**	**1.0**	**0.8**	**1.8**	**2.2**
Aged 55–59 183,261	170,170	2,098	1,950	3,914	5,129	92.9	1.1	1.1	2.1	2.8
Aged 60–64 141,971	131,668	1,745	1,458	3,176	3,924	92.7	1.2	1.0	2.2	2.8
Aged 65–69 121,774	113,658	1,385	1,081	2,713	2,937	93.3	1.1	0.9	2.2	2.4
Aged 70–74 113,897	107,670	1,073	774	2,156	2,224	94.5	0.9	0.7	1.9	2.0
Aged 75 or older 235,383	226,125	1,780	1,444	2,571	3,463	96.1	0.8	0.6	1.1	1.5
Pennsylvania, total 12,202,050	10,460,455	1,181,047	15,818	210,419	334,311	85.7	9.7	0.1	1.7	2.7
Total, aged 55 or older 3,021,460	**2,747,649**	**208,018**	**3,034**	**26,978**	**35,781**	**90.9**	**6.9**	**0.1**	**0.9**	**1.2**
Aged 55–59 616,118	550,120	46,587	749	8,593	10,069	89.3	7.6	0.1	1.4	1.6
Aged 60–64 505,393	451,281	39,634	532	6,475	7,471	89.3	7.8	0.1	1.3	1.5
Aged 65–69 474,350	426,205	36,940	465	4,734	6,006	89.9	7.8	0.1	1.0	1.3
Aged 70–74 482,113	441,995	31,862	378	3,307	4,571	91.7	6.6	0.1	0.7	0.9
Aged 75 or older 943,486	878,048	52,995	910	3,869	7,664	93.1	5.6	0.1	0.4	0.8

(continued)

(continued from previous page)

		non-Hispanic						non-Hispanic			
	total	white	black	Native American	Asian	Hispanic	white	black	Native American	Asian	Hispanic
Rhode Island, total	**997,607**	**850,536**	**40,634**	**4,233**	**26,457**	**75,747**	**85.3%**	**4.1%**	**0.4%**	**2.7%**	**7.6%**
Total, aged 55 or older	**230,876**	**216,002**	**4,609**	**566**	**2,434**	**7,265**	**93.6**	**2.0**	**0.2**	**1.1**	**3.1**
Aged 55–59	46,477	42,492	1,227	122	750	1,886	91.4	2.6	0.3	1.6	4.1
Aged 60–64	35,822	32,827	994	105	561	1,335	91.6	2.8	0.3	1.6	3.7
Aged 65–69	32,990	30,652	828	92	402	1,016	92.9	2.5	0.3	1.2	3.1
Aged 70–74	37,229	35,136	735	83	300	975	94.4	2.0	0.2	0.8	2.6
Aged 75 or older	78,358	74,895	825	164	421	2,053	95.6	1.1	0.2	0.5	2.6
South Carolina, total	**3,858,023**	**2,624,084**	**1,151,436**	**8,264**	**30,906**	**43,333**	**68.0**	**29.8**	**0.2**	**0.8**	**1.1**
Total, aged 55 or older	**836,892**	**645,884**	**180,613**	**1,379**	**4,084**	**4,932**	**77.2**	**21.6**	**0.2**	**0.5**	**0.6**
Aged 55–59	199,219	151,447	44,505	414	1,372	1,481	76.0	22.3	0.2	0.7	0.7
Aged 60–64	159,659	122,198	34,971	331	1,094	1,065	76.5	21.9	0.2	0.7	0.7
Aged 65–69	140,404	107,988	30,551	243	815	807	76.9	21.8	0.2	0.6	0.6
Aged 70–74	122,138	95,815	25,137	135	448	603	78.4	20.6	0.1	0.4	0.5
Aged 75 or older	215,472	168,436	45,449	256	355	976	78.2	21.1	0.1	0.2	0.5
South Dakota, total	**777,073**	**697,922**	**5,032**	**59,881**	**5,409**	**8,829**	**89.8**	**0.6**	**7.7**	**0.7**	**1.1**
Total, aged 55 or older	**173,805**	**167,306**	**411**	**4,847**	**441**	**800**	**96.3**	**0.2**	**2.8**	**0.3**	**0.5**
Aged 55–59	34,534	32,700	115	1,380	132	207	94.7	0.3	4.0	0.4	0.6
Aged 60–64	29,286	27,863	84	1,104	102	133	95.1	0.3	3.8	0.3	0.5
Aged 65–69	28,136	27,014	62	872	67	121	96.0	0.2	3.1	0.2	0.4
Aged 70–74	25,833	25,033	47	585	61	107	96.9	0.2	2.3	0.2	0.4
Aged 75 or older	56,016	54,696	103	906	79	232	97.6	0.2	1.6	0.1	0.4

(continued)

(continued from previous page)

	total	white	black	Native American	Asian	Hispanic	non-Hispanic white	black	Native American	Asian	Hispanic
Tennessee, total	5,657,161	4,607,340	925,022	12,546	54,584	57,669	81.4%	16.4%	0.2%	1.0%	1.0%
Total, aged 55 or older	1,241,767	1,094,525	132,517	2,350	6,078	6,297	88.1	10.7	0.2	0.5	0.5
Aged 55–59	296,512	259,360	32,513	641	2,111	1,887	87.5	11.0	0.2	0.7	0.6
Aged 60–64	238,458	208,611	26,659	464	1,499	1,225	87.5	11.2	0.2	0.6	0.5
Aged 65–69	206,275	180,539	23,250	410	1,086	990	87.5	11.3	0.2	0.5	0.5
Aged 70–74	175,908	156,006	18,124	266	728	784	88.7	10.3	0.2	0.4	0.4
Aged 75 or older	324,614	290,009	31,971	569	654	1,411	89.3	9.8	0.2	0.2	0.4
Texas, total	20,119,335	11,272,203	2,406,384	60,215	505,300	5,875,233	56.0	12.0	0.3	2.5	29.2
Total, aged 55 or older	3,713,207	2,643,677	335,656	11,749	57,523	664,602	71.2	9.0	0.3	1.5	17.9
Aged 55–59	899,587	612,481	84,746	3,039	18,702	180,619	68.1	9.4	0.3	2.1	20.1
Aged 60–64	713,414	490,006	67,931	2,318	13,842	139,317	68.7	9.5	0.3	1.9	19.5
Aged 65–69	624,625	434,047	60,947	1,833	10,731	117,067	69.5	9.8	0.3	1.7	18.7
Aged 70–74	529,231	381,490	45,919	1,509	7,263	93,050	72.1	8.7	0.3	1.4	17.6
Aged 75 or older	946,350	725,653	76,113	3,050	6,985	134,549	76.7	8.0	0.3	0.7	14.2
Utah, total	2,207,013	1,960,830	17,743	33,315	58,588	136,537	88.8	0.8	1.5	2.7	6.2
Total, aged 55 or older	353,011	330,760	1,826	2,370	5,833	12,222	93.7	0.5	0.7	1.7	3.5
Aged 55–59	83,626	77,484	483	690	1,621	3,348	92.7	0.6	0.8	1.9	4.0
Aged 60–64	66,843	62,033	407	487	1,311	2,605	92.8	0.6	0.7	2.0	3.9
Aged 65–69	57,789	53,845	300	398	1,037	2,209	93.2	0.5	0.7	1.8	3.8
Aged 70–74	49,622	46,565	226	317	787	1,727	93.8	0.5	0.6	1.6	3.5
Aged 75 or older	95,131	90,833	410	478	1,077	2,333	95.5	0.4	0.5	1.1	2.5

(continued)

(continued from previous page)

		non-Hispanic					non-Hispanic				
	total	white	black	Native American	Asian	Hispanic	white	black	Native American	Asian	Hispanic
Vermont, total	**616,803**	**600,653**	**2,777**	**1,793**	**5,717**	**5,863**	**97.4%**	**0.5%**	**0.3%**	**0.9%**	**1.0%**
Total, aged 55 or older	**128,086**	**126,482**	**241**	**251**	**504**	**608**	**98.7**	**0.2**	**0.2**	**0.4**	**0.5**
Aged 55–59	31,446	30,980	63	69	145	189	98.5	0.2	0.2	0.5	0.6
Aged 60–64	22,984	22,657	59	55	116	97	98.6	0.3	0.2	0.5	0.4
Aged 65–69	20,006	19,740	38	45	104	79	98.7	0.2	0.2	0.5	0.4
Aged 70–74	18,419	18,207	24	31	76	81	98.8	0.1	0.2	0.4	0.4
Aged 75 or older	35,231	34,898	57	51	63	162	99.1	0.2	0.1	0.2	0.5
Virginia, total	**6,997,006**	**5,061,303**	**1,394,404**	**15,579**	**257,517**	**268,203**	**72.3**	**19.9**	**0.2**	**3.7**	**3.8**
Total, aged 55 or older	**1,405,309**	**1,127,040**	**216,921**	**2,770**	**34,455**	**24,123**	**80.2**	**15.4**	**0.2**	**2.5**	**1.7**
Aged 55–59	350,724	278,387	52,458	810	11,487	7,582	79.4	15.0	0.2	3.3	2.2
Aged 60–64	266,163	209,481	42,473	588	8,378	5,243	78.7	16.0	0.2	3.1	2.0
Aged 65–69	221,487	174,336	37,254	412	5,878	3,607	78.7	16.8	0.2	2.7	1.6
Aged 70–74	200,337	161,435	31,197	328	4,245	3,132	80.6	15.6	0.2	2.1	1.6
Aged 75 or older	366,598	303,401	53,539	632	4,467	4,559	82.8	14.6	0.2	1.2	1.2
Washington, total	**5,858,392**	**4,881,702**	**179,147**	**95,553**	**342,268**	**359,722**	**83.3**	**3.1**	**1.6**	**5.8**	**6.1**
Total, aged 55 or older	**1,198,997**	**1,087,514**	**22,037**	**11,901**	**48,342**	**29,203**	**90.7**	**1.8**	**1.0**	**4.0**	**2.4**
Aged 55–59	292,873	260,978	6,142	3,585	13,397	8,771	89.1	2.1	1.2	4.6	3.0
Aged 60–64	219,881	195,797	4,564	2,680	10,484	6,356	89.0	2.1	1.2	4.8	2.9
Aged 65–69	184,549	164,742	3,802	2,034	8,834	5,137	89.3	2.1	1.1	4.8	2.8
Aged 70–74	165,916	150,992	2,851	1,405	6,897	3,771	91.0	1.7	0.8	4.2	2.3
Aged 75 or older	335,778	315,005	4,678	2,197	8,730	5,168	93.8	1.4	0.7	2.6	1.5

(continued)

(continued from previous page)

	total	non-Hispanic white	non-Hispanic black	non-Hispanic Native American	non-Hispanic Asian	Hispanic	non-Hispanic white	non-Hispanic black	non-Hispanic Native American	non-Hispanic Asian	Hispanic
West Virginia, total	1,840,983	1,757,908	57,362	2,389	10,895	12,429	95.5%	3.1%	0.1%	0.6%	0.7%
Total, aged 55 or older	480,774	464,396	11,794	673	1,716	2,195	96.6	2.5	0.1	0.4	0.5
Aged 55–59	103,878	100,332	2,278	161	619	488	96.6	2.2	0.2	0.6	0.5
Aged 60–64	90,053	87,008	2,019	137	507	382	96.6	2.2	0.2	0.6	0.4
Aged 65–69	80,559	77,865	1,910	95	294	395	96.7	2.4	0.1	0.4	0.5
Aged 70–74	74,371	71,865	1,942	83	141	340	96.6	2.6	0.1	0.2	0.5
Aged 75 or older	131,913	127,326	3,645	197	155	590	96.5	2.8	0.1	0.1	0.4
Wisconsin, total	5,326,324	4,731,293	318,392	44,971	97,068	134,600	88.8	6.0	0.8	1.8	2.5
Total, aged 55 or older	1,166,501	1,107,187	33,643	4,937	8,079	12,655	94.9	2.9	0.4	0.7	1.1
Aged 55–59	253,989	237,677	9,206	1,409	2,305	3,392	93.6	3.6	0.6	0.9	1.3
Aged 60–64	206,687	193,699	7,514	1,111	1,791	2,572	93.7	3.6	0.5	0.9	1.2
Aged 65–69	185,357	174,797	6,090	865	1,536	2,069	94.3	3.3	0.5	0.8	1.1
Aged 70–74	171,658	163,620	4,631	578	1,107	1,722	95.3	2.7	0.3	0.6	1.0
Aged 75 or older	348,810	337,394	6,202	974	1,340	2,900	96.7	1.8	0.3	0.4	0.8
Wyoming, total	524,700	469,445	4,418	11,790	4,702	34,345	89.5	0.8	2.2	0.9	6.5
Total, aged 55 or older	109,085	102,928	445	1,155	600	3,957	94.4	0.4	1.1	0.6	3.6
Aged 55–59	26,338	24,595	100	373	171	1,099	93.4	0.4	1.4	0.6	4.2
Aged 60–64	20,927	19,527	90	261	141	908	93.3	0.4	1.2	0.7	4.3
Aged 65–69	17,998	16,898	72	218	120	690	93.9	0.4	1.2	0.7	3.8
Aged 70–74	15,684	14,920	61	123	70	510	95.1	0.4	0.8	0.4	3.3
Aged 75 or older	28,138	26,988	122	180	98	750	95.9	0.4	0.6	0.3	2.7

Source: Bureau of the Census, unpublished tables from Internet web site <http://www.census.gov>; calculations by New Strategist

Older Americans Not Likely to Move

Each year, only 6 percent of people aged 55 or older move.

Despite the perception that older Americans move en masse to Florida and other warm states upon retirement, people aged 55 or older are far less likely to move than younger Americans. Overall, 16 percent of Americans moved between March 1996 and March 1997, nearly three times the proportion of those aged 55 or older who moved.

Only 7 percent of people aged 60 to 64 move in a year's time, as do 5 percent of those aged 65 to 69. Mobility bottoms out in the 70-to-74 age group at 3.8 percent, then rises above 6 percent at ages 85 or older. The higher mobility among the very old occurs as women become widowed and move from retirement locales to areas closer to their families.

Older Americans who do move are more likely to move out-of-state than movers in general. Among all movers, only 15 percent moved to a different state between 1996 and 1997. But among movers aged 55 or older, 19 percent moved to a different state. Older Americans who move are also more likely to settle in a different region than movers in general.

While young adults are more mobile than their elders, this has always been the case. The popular notion that middle-aged and younger adults are more mobile than older generations were in their youth is a myth. The proportion of Americans who live in the same community in which they lived at age 16 does not vary much by age among those aged 45 or older.

♦ Between 1996 and 1997, 582,000 Americans aged 55 or older moved to a different state. As the large baby-boom generation ages into its late fifties, the number of older interstate movers should surge, surpassing 1 million per year.

Geographical Mobility of People Aged 55 or Older, 1996 to 1997

(number and percent of people aged 1 or older and aged 55 or older who moved between March 1996 and March 1997, by type of move; numbers in thousands)

		same house (non-movers)	different house in the U.S.							movers from abroad
					different county					
							different state			
	total		total	same county	total	same state	total	same region	different region	
Total, 1 or older	262,976	219,585	42,088	27,740	14,348	7,960	6,389	3,220	3,168	1,303
Aged 55 or older	53,353	50,170	3,117	1,852	1,266	682	582	291	291	67
Aged 65 or older	31,878	30,361	1,486	893	593	307	285	125	160	36
Aged 55 to 59	11,579	10,629	928	573	356	193	162	92	70	22
Aged 60 to 64	9,896	9,180	703	386	317	182	135	74	61	13
Aged 65 to 69	9,501	9,015	480	277	203	108	95	50	45	6
Aged 70 to 74	8,514	8,182	326	218	109	59	49	16	33	7
Aged 75 to 79	6,743	6,439	297	183	113	52	61	24	36	7
Aged 80 to 84	4,211	4,002	204	124	80	32	48	14	34	5
Aged 85 or older	2,909	2,723	179	91	88	56	32	21	12	7
Median age	34.7	37.0	26.6	26.3	27.3	27.2	27.4	27.0	27.9	27.3
Total, 1 or older	100.0%	83.5%	16.0%	10.5%	5.5%	3.0%	2.4%	1.2%	1.2%	0.5%
Aged 55 or older	100.0	94.0	5.8	3.5	2.4	1.3	1.1	0.5	0.5	0.1
Aged 65 or older	100.0	95.2	4.7	2.8	1.9	1.0	0.9	0.4	0.5	0.1
Aged 55 to 59	100.0	91.8	8.0	4.9	3.1	1.7	1.4	0.8	0.6	0.2
Aged 60 to 64	100.0	92.8	7.1	3.9	3.2	1.8	1.4	0.7	0.6	0.1
Aged 65 to 69	100.0	94.9	5.1	2.9	2.1	1.1	1.0	0.5	0.5	0.1
Aged 70 to 74	100.0	96.1	3.8	2.6	1.3	0.7	0.6	0.2	0.4	0.1
Aged 75 to 79	100.0	95.5	4.4	2.7	1.7	0.8	0.9	0.4	0.5	0.1
Aged 80 to 84	100.0	95.0	4.8	2.9	1.9	0.8	1.1	0.3	0.8	0.1
Aged 85 or older	100.0	93.6	6.2	3.1	3.0	1.9	1.1	0.7	0.4	0.2

Source: Bureau of the Census, Geographical Mobility: March 1996 to March 1997, *Current Population Reports, P20-510, 1998; calculations by New Strategist*

Mobility Since Age 16, 1996

"When you were 16 years old, were you living in this same city?"

(percent of people aged 18 or older responding by age, 1996)

	same place	different city	different state
Total people	**38%**	**24%**	**38%**
Aged 18 to 24	55	25	20
Aged 25 to 34	43	22	35
Aged 35 to 44	37	25	38
Aged 45 to 54	30	26	44
Aged 55 to 64	34	22	44
Aged 65 to 74	31	27	41
Aged 75 or older	31	25	43

Note: Numbers may not add to 100 because no answer is not shown.
Source: 1996 General Social Survey, National Opinion Research Center, University of Chicago; calculations by New Strategist

Where Boomers Will Live in Retirement

The South and the West should gain the most older Americans as boomers age.

Overall, the number of Americans aged 65 or older is projected to increase an enormous 79 percent between 2000 and 2025 as the large baby-boom generation enters the age group. By 2025, boomers will be aged 61 to 79.

The Census Bureau's projections of the elderly population by state in 2025 reveal where the boomer hot spots will be. Not surprisingly, states in the South and the West will see above-average growth in their elderly populations, while states in the Midwest and the Northeast will see below-average growth. The elderly populations of 15 states will more than double, including the western states of Utah, Alaska, Idaho, Wyoming, and Colorado. The southern states that will see their elderly populations double are Georgia, Texas, North Carolina, and South Carolina. By 2025, fully 24 states will be home to more than 1 million people aged 65 or older, up from just 9 states in 2000.

◆ In retirement, boomers will create prosperity wherever they go, driving up demand for a variety of services ranging from entertainment to home health care.

Population Aged 65 or Older by State, 2000 and 2025

(number of people aged 65 or older by state, 2000 and 2025; percent change, 2000–2025; numbers in thousands; ranked by percent change)

	2000	2025	percent change 2000–2025
Utah	202	495	145.0%
Alaska	38	92	142.1
Idaho	157	374	138.2
Wyoming	62	145	133.9
Colorado	452	1,044	131.0
Washington	685	1,580	130.7
Oregon	471	1,054	123.8
Nevada	219	486	121.9
Arizona	635	1,368	115.4
Georgia	779	1,668	114.1
New Mexico	206	441	114.1
Montana	128	274	114.1
Texas	2,101	4,364	107.7
North Carolina	991	2,004	102.2
South Carolina	478	963	101.5
Florida	2,755	5,453	97.9
Arkansas	377	731	93.9
Virginia	788	1,515	92.3
New Hampshire	142	273	92.3
Tennessee	707	1,355	91.7
California	3,387	6,424	89.7
Vermont	73	138	89.0
Oklahoma	472	888	88.1
Minnesota	596	1,099	84.4
Hawaii	157	289	84.1
Alabama	582	1,069	83.7
Louisiana	523	945	80.7
Kentucky	509	917	80.2
Mississippi	344	615	78.8
United States total	**34,710**	**61,952**	**78.5**
Maine	172	304	76.7
Maryland	589	1,029	74.7
South Dakota	110	188	70.9
Wisconsin	705	1,200	70.2

(continued)

(continued from previous page)

	2000	2025	percent change 2000–2025
Delaware	97	165	70.1%
Nebraska	239	405	69.5
Kansas	359	605	68.5
North Dakota	99	166	67.7
Missouri	755	1,258	66.6
Indiana	763	1,260	65.1
West Virginia	287	460	60.3
Iowa	442	686	55.2
Michigan	1,197	1,821	52.1
New Jersey	1,090	1,654	51.7
Ohio	1,525	2,305	51.1
Illinois	1,484	2,234	50.5
Massachusetts	843	1,252	48.5
Connecticut	461	671	45.6
Rhode Island	148	214	44.6
Pennsylvania	1,899	2,659	40.0
New York	2,358	3,263	38.4
District of Columbia	69	92	33.3

Source: Bureau of the Census, Population Projections for States by Age, Sex, Race and Hispanic Origin: 1995 to 2025, *PPL-47, 1996; calculations by New Strategist*

8

Spending

◆ While the average household spent less in 1997 than in 1990, householders aged 65 or older spent significantly more, after adjusting for inflation.

◆ Retirees spend only 69 percent of what the average household spends because their households are smaller than average—1.8 people versus 2.5 people in the average household.

◆ Despite their lower spending, households headed by retirees spend more than average on postage and stationery, floor coverings, cash contributions, and gifts of major appliances and toys.

◆ Householders aged 55 to 64 spend much more than the average household on such items as coffee, whiskey, owned vacation homes, office furniture for home use, airfares, and gifts.

◆ Householders aged 65 to 74 spend much more than the average household on such things as coffee, owned vacation homes, lawn and garden services, ship fares, and radios.

◆ The spending of householders aged 75 or older is becoming more like that of the average household. They spend more than average on a variety of items such as home security services, gardening supplies, and magazine subscriptions.

Note: The Bureau of Labor Statistics' Consumer Expenditure Survey, on which the spending tables are based, presents average spending data for all households in a segment, not just for the purchasers of an item. When examining the spending data that follow, it is important to remember that by including purchasers and nonpurchasers in the calculation of the average, the average spending amount is diluted for items that are not purchased universally. Consequently, for categories purchased by few consumers, the average spending figures are less revealing than the indexes. For universally purchased items such as soaps and detergents, the average spending figures give a more accurate picture of actual spending.

Older Householders Are Spending More

Householders aged 65 or older spent significantly more in 1997 than in 1990, after adjusting for inflation.

Between 1990 and 1997, householders aged 65 to 74 boosted their spending 8 percent, after adjusting for inflation. Those aged 75 or older spent 7 percent more in 1997 than in 1990. In contrast, spending by the average household fell 0.1 percent during those years. Because of these diverging trends, the spending of older householders is approaching that of the average household—despite the fact that older households are much smaller. Householders aged 65 to 74 spent just 74 percent as much as the average household in 1990, but the figure had risen to 80 percent by 1997. For the oldest householders, spending rose from 54 to 58 percent of the average during those years.

Unlike their older counterparts, householders aged 55 to 64 did not boost their spending much during the 1990s—the increase amounted to just 0.1 percent, after adjusting for inflation. One factor accounting for the lack of growth in spending

Spending by older householders is growing

(percent change in average annual spending of householders by age, 1990 to 1997; in 1997 dollars)

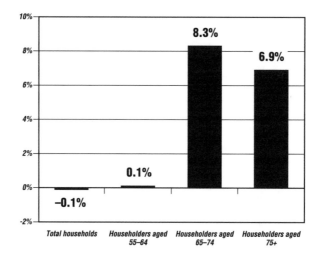

among 55-to-64-year-olds was the 4 percent decline in before-tax income for this group.

Older householders spent more than before on a number of items for which the average household's spending decreased. While the average household spent 14 percent less on alcoholic beverages in 1997 than in 1990, householders aged 65 to 74 and those aged 75 or older spent 32 and 27 percent more on alcohol, respectively. Householders aged 75 or older spent 34 percent more on women's clothes in 1997 than in 1990 while the average household spent 20 percent less. Householders aged 65 to 74 spent 9 percent more on new cars and trucks, while the average household spent 14 percent less. Entertainment spending by older householder soared during the 1990s; those aged 65 to 74 spent 16 percent more on entertainment and those aged 75 or older spent fully 66 percent more in 1997 than in 1990. Spending on entertainment by the average household rose only 4 percent.

♦ The income and spending of householders aged 55 to 64 is likely to rise in the years ahead as early retirement becomes less common.

♦ The spending of older Americans will continue to approach that of the average household as the well-educated baby-boom generation enters the 65-or-older age group, boosting the affluence of the elderly.

Average Spending of Householders Aged 55 or Older, 1990 and 1997

(average annual spending of total consumer units and consumer units aged 55 or older, 1990 and 1997; percent change, 1990–97; in 1997 dollars)

	total consumer units			aged 55–64			aged 65–74			aged 75 or older		
	1990	1997	percent change 1990–97	1990	1997	percent change 1990–97	1990	1997	percent change 1990–97	1990	1997	percent change 1990–97
Number of consumer units (in 000s)	96,968	105,576	8.9%	12,162	12,316	1.3%	11,318	12,109	7.0%	8,761	9,827	12.2%
Average before-tax income	$39,160	$39,926	2.0	$43,359	$41,734	-3.7	$26,403	$27,492	4.1	$18,954	$19,425	2.5
Average annual spending	34,852	34,819	-0.1	35,935	35,954	0.1	25,666	27,792	8.3	18,973	20,279	6.9
FOOD	**5,275**	**4,801**	**-9.0**	**5,440**	**5,085**	**-6.5**	**4,059**	**4,066**	**0.2**	**2,955**	**2,786**	**-5.7**
FOOD AT HOME	3,052	2,880	-5.6	3,194	3,139	-1.7	2,586	2,600	0.5	2,031	1,924	-5.3
Cereals and bakery products	**452**	**453**	**0.2**	**464**	**470**	**1.3**	**398**	**402**	**1.0**	**329**	**309**	**-6.1**
Cereals and cereal products	158	161	1.6	158	160	1.0	126	130	2.8	108	103	-4.7
Bakery products	295	292	-0.9	306	310	1.4	271	272	0.2	220	207	-5.8
Meats, poultry, fish, and eggs	**820**	**743**	**-9.4**	**917**	**830**	**-9.5**	**734**	**676**	**-7.9**	**497**	**465**	**-6.5**
Beef	268	224	-16.3	284	231	-18.6	254	190	-25.3	142	128	-10.1
Pork	162	157	-3.1	188	187	-0.5	144	148	3.0	104	115	10.2
Other meats	122	96	-21.0	141	110	-22.1	101	92	-8.6	68	60	-11.2
Poultry	133	145	9.3	154	150	-2.3	120	135	12.2	86	81	-5.8
Fish and seafood	101	89	-11.6	111	114	3.1	81	77	-5.0	70	54	-22.9
Eggs	37	33	-10.4	41	37	-8.7	33	33	-0.5	27	27	-0.1
Dairy products	**362**	**314**	**-13.3**	**357**	**325**	**-9.1**	**303**	**284**	**-6.4**	**247**	**212**	**-14.1**
Fresh milk and cream	172	128	-25.5	157	122	-22.4	150	118	-21.2	124	91	-26.6
Other dairy products	190	186	-2.3	200	203	1.4	155	167	7.9	124	121	-2.4

(continued)

(continued from previous page)

	total consumer units			aged 55–64			aged 65–74			aged 75 or older		
	1990	1997	percent change 1990–97	1990	1997	percent change 1990–97	1990	1997	percent change 1990–97	1990	1997	percent change 1990–97
Fruits and vegetables	$501	$476	-5.0%	$549	$549	0.0%	$481	$472	-1.9%	$426	$386	-9.4%
Fresh fruits	156	150	-3.8	190	169	-11.2	157	151	-3.9	147	143	-3.0
Fresh vegetables	145	143	-1.3	161	185	15.0	141	143	1.3	104	109	4.4
Processed fruits	114	102	-10.7	108	108	-0.1	109	101	-7.6	111	82	-25.8
Processed vegetables	86	80	-6.9	88	87	-1.6	75	76	1.5	64	52	-18.6
Other food at home	916	895	-2.3	905	965	6.6	669	766	14.5	532	550	3.4
Sugar and other sweets	115	114	-1.2	117	131	12.3	97	111	14.4	85	79	-6.8
Fats and oils	84	81	-3.0	88	99	12.0	79	82	4.3	59	68	15.4
Miscellaneous foods	413	403	-2.3	372	403	8.3	271	299	10.2	223	252	12.8
Nonalcoholic beverages	262	245	-6.3	265	267	0.7	189	217	14.7	152	130	-14.6
Food prepared by householder on trips	43	52	21.0	63	65	3.8	33	57	71.9	12	21	71.0
FOOD AWAY FROM HOME	2,224	1,921	-13.6	2,247	1,946	-13.4	1,472	1,466	-0.4	923	863	-6.5
ALCOHOLIC BEVERAGES	360	309	-14.1	312	283	-9.3	204	268	31.5	87	111	27.3
HOUSING	10,687	11,272	5.5	10,388	11,090	6.8	7,919	8,876	12.1	6,716	7,107	5.8
Shelter	5,939	6,344	6.8	5,182	5,783	11.6	3,915	4,365	11.5	3,432	3,557	3.6
Owned dwellings	3,626	3,935	8.5	3,527	4,059	15.1	2,555	3,021	18.2	1,988	2,109	6.1
Mortgage interest and charges	2,231	2,225	-0.3	1,534	1,927	25.6	698	779	11.7	131	260	97.9
Property taxes	733	971	32.4	1,044	1,195	14.5	1,012	1,197	18.3	831	891	7.2
Maintenance, repairs, insurance, etc.	663	738	11.3	948	936	-1.3	846	1,045	23.5	1,025	957	-6.7
Rented dwellings	1,883	1,983	5.3	1,072	1,145	6.8	901	911	1.1	1,196	1,223	2.3

(continued)

(continued from previous page)

	total consumer units			aged 55–64			aged 65–74			aged 75 or older		
	1990	1997	percent change 1990–97	1990	1997	percent change 1990–97	1990	1997	percent change 1990–97	1990	1997	percent change 1990–97
Other lodging	**$429**	**$426**	**–0.6%**	**$585**	**$579**	**–0.9%**	**$458**	**$432**	**–5.7%**	**$248**	**$226**	**–8.9%**
UTILITIES, FUELS, PUBLIC SERVICES	**2,321**	**2,412**	**3.9**	**2,652**	**2,654**	**0.1**	**2,257**	**2,321**	**2.8**	**1,860**	**1,954**	**5.0**
Natural gas	302	301	–0.4	357	342	–4.3	351	341	–2.9	264	334	26.5
Electricity	931	909	–2.3	1,127	1,013	–10.1	900	911	1.2	744	751	0.9
Fuel oil and other fuels	123	108	–12.1	158	126	–20.5	158	134	–15.4	182	127	–30.1
Telephone services	727	809	11.3	725	842	16.2	585	627	7.3	462	458	–0.8
Water and other public services	237	286	20.7	285	331	16.2	264	309	17.0	208	283	36.4
HOUSEHOLD SERVICES	**548**	**548**	**0.1**	**474**	**402**	**–15.2**	**420**	**392**	**–6.7**	**565**	**526**	**–6.9**
Personal services	269	263	–2.2	70	59	–15.7	36	75	110.6	232	149	–35.8
Other household expenses	279	285	2.2	403	343	–14.8	384	317	–17.5	333	377	13.3
HOUSEKEEPING SUPPLIES	**499**	**455**	**–8.7**	**599**	**523**	**–12.7**	**445**	**449**	**1.0**	**335**	**368**	**9.8**
Laundry and cleaning supplies	139	116	–16.4	154	130	–15.3	106	105	–0.6	86	73	–15.1
Other household products	210	210	0.0	276	245	–11.3	181	207	14.7	129	170	31.8
Postage and stationery	150	129	–13.9	169	148	–12.7	160	138	–13.6	120	124	3.0
HOUSEHOLD FURNISHINGS AND EQUIPMENT	**1,382**	**1,512**	**9.4**	**1,480**	**1,728**	**16.8**	**882**	**1,349**	**53.0**	**522**	**703**	**34.7**
Household textiles	122	79	–35.0	150	100	–33.3	111	72	–34.9	42	33	–21.0
Furniture	381	387	1.7	454	390	–14.2	179	268	49.5	112	95	–15.0
Floor coverings	113	78	–31.0	112	101	–9.6	69	142	106.5	65	102	56.7

(continued)

(continued from previous page)

	total consumer units			aged 55–64			aged 65–74			aged 75 or older		
	1990	1997	percent change 1990–97	1990	1997	percent change 1990–97	1990	1997	percent change 1990–97	1990	1997	percent change 1990–97
Major appliances	$181	$169	–6.4%	$231	$246	6.6%	$141	$167	18.3%	$109	$109	–0.3%
Small appliances, misc. housewares	92	92	–0.1	111	123	11.3	75	79	5.5	49	49	–0.2
Miscellaneous household equipment	494	707	43.2	424	768	81.3	307	622	102.6	144	316	119.9
APPAREL AND SERVICES	**1,987**	**1,729**	**–13.0**	**1,916**	**1,656**	**–13.6**	**1,194**	**1,302**	**9.1**	**600**	**735**	**22.4**
Men and boys	**483**	**407**	**–15.7**	**440**	**357**	**–18.8**	**214**	**295**	**38.1**	**92**	**128**	**39.0**
Men, 16 and over	398	323	–18.8	399	318	–20.3	187	262	40.4	87	120	37.6
Boys, 2 to 15	86	84	–2.3	42	39	–6.6	27	33	22.1	5	8	62.9
Women and girls	**826**	**680**	**–17.7**	**847**	**684**	**–19.3**	**637**	**552**	**–13.4**	**296**	**393**	**32.8**
Women, 16 and over	720	574	–20.2	810	633	–21.9	602	521	–13.4	284	381	34.3
Girls, 2 to 15	107	106	–0.8	37	51	38.4	36	31	–13.0	12	12	–2.3
Children under 2	**86**	**77**	**–10.4**	**63**	**34**	**–45.7**	**23**	**25**	**7.1**	**16**	**18**	**12.8**
Footwear	**276**	**315**	**14.0**	**266**	**337**	**26.5**	**165**	**232**	**41.0**	**107**	**138**	**29.2**
Other apparel products, services	**317**	**250**	**–21.1**	**298**	**243**	**–18.6**	**156**	**199**	**27.6**	**90**	**58**	**–35.3**
TRANSPORTATION	**6,287**	**6,457**	**2.7**	**6,505**	**6,708**	**3.1**	**4,253**	**4,645**	**9.2**	**2,617**	**2,785**	**6.4**
Vehicle purchases	2,614	2,736	4.7	2,473	2,641	6.8	1,428	1,826	27.9	1,131	1,059	–6.4
Cars and trucks, new	1,423	1,229	–13.6	1,405	1,374	–2.2	862	942	9.3	690	574	–16.8
Cars and trucks, used	1,164	1,464	25.8	1,047	1,267	21.0	566	850	50.1	441	485	10.0
Other vehicles	27	43	59.2	20	–	–	1	34	2,668.7	–	–	–
Gasoline and motor oil	1,286	1,098	–14.6	1,393	1,188	–14.7	973	801	–17.6	486	461	–5.2
Other vehicle expenses	2,016	2,230	10.6	2,132	2,369	11.1	1,520	1,641	7.9	776	1,050	35.3

(continued)

(continued from previous page)

	total consumer units			aged 55–64			aged 65–74			aged 75 or older		
	1990	1997	percent change 1990–97	1990	1997	percent change 1990–97	1990	1997	percent change 1990–97	1990	1997	percent change 1990–97
Vehicle finance charges	$368	$293	–20.5%	$322	$260	–19.2%	$174	$137	–21.4%	$34	$43	25.1%
Maintenance and repairs	723	682	–5.7	807	760	–5.8	602	571	–5.1	305	393	29.0
Vehicle insurance	691	755	9.2	793	851	7.3	577	661	14.5	363	411	13.1
Vehicle rental, leases, licenses, other	233	501	114.7	209	499	139.0	166	272	64.1	74	202	174.2
Public transportation	371	393	6.0	508	509	0.1	333	378	13.6	223	216	–3.4
HEALTH CARE	**1,817**	**1,841**	**1.3**	**2,199**	**2,187**	**–0.6**	**2,698**	**2,900**	**7.5**	**2,730**	**2,799**	**2.5**
Health insurance	713	881	23.5	860	965	12.3	1,245	1,547	24.2	1,179	1,494	26.7
Medical services	690	531	–23.1	803	664	–17.3	806	636	–21.0	828	475	–42.6
Drugs	309	320	3.4	418	407	–2.5	559	594	6.3	615	691	12.3
Medical supplies	104	108	3.5	118	151	28.1	90	123	37.2	108	138	27.7
ENTERTAINMENT	**1,746**	**1,813**	**3.8**	**1,851**	**1,900**	**2.7**	**1,122**	**1,300**	**15.8**	**519**	**861**	**65.8**
Fees and admissions	456	471	3.4	448	451	0.6	404	390	–3.5	188	180	–4.2
Television, radio, sound equipment	558	577	3.5	479	561	17.1	377	470	24.7	198	314	58.8
Pets, toys, playground equipment	339	327	–3.5	313	376	20.1	198	237	19.9	102	128	25.6
Other entertainment supplies, equipment, services	394	439	11.4	610	512	–16.1	142	203	42.5	32	239	648.6
PERSONAL CARE PRODUCTS AND SERVICES	**447**	**528**	**18.1**	**506**	**541**	**6.9**	**375**	**494**	**31.9**	**268**	**376**	**40.5**
READING	**188**	**164**	**–12.7**	**200**	**198**	**–1.1**	**192**	**195**	**1.8**	**138**	**148**	**7.6**

(continued)

(continued from previous page)

	total consumer units			aged 55–64			aged 65–74			aged 75 or older		
	1990	1997	percent change 1990–97	1990	1997	percent change 1990–97	1990	1997	percent change 1990–97	1990	1997	percent change 1990–97
EDUCATION	**$499**	**$571**	**14.5%**	**$462**	**$281**	**–39.1%**	**$59**	**$227**	**285.1%**	**$75**	**$61**	**–18.6%**
TOBACCO PRODUCTS AND SMOKING SUPPLIES	336	264	–21.5	400	292	–27.1	257	213	–17.0	112	87	–22.1
MISCELLANEOUS	**1,034**	**847**	**–18.1**	**1,017**	**1,061**	**4.3**	**869**	**745**	**–14.3**	**433**	**463**	**6.8**
Cash contributions	1,002	1,001	–0.1	1,109	1,208	8.9	1,151	1,196	3.9	1,401	1,485	6.0
Personal insurance and pensions	3,183	3,223	1.3	3,632	3,466	–4.6	1,315	1,362	3.6	321	473	47.6
Life and other personal insurance	424	379	–10.5	573	523	–8.8	419	406	–3.0	161	244	51.7
Pensions and Social Security	2,761	2,844	3.0	3,059	2,943	–3.8	896	956	6.6	160	229	43.4
PERSONAL TAXES	**3,625**	**3,241**	**–10.6**	**4,307**	**3,500**	**–18.7**	**1,692**	**1,706**	**0.8**	**1,018**	**835**	**–18.0**
Federal income taxes	2,848	2,468	–13.3	3,416	2,663	–22.1	1,327	1,257	–5.3	766	617	–19.5
State and local income taxes	685	645	–5.9	774	669	–13.5	260	245	–5.9	138	79	–42.6
Other taxes	92	129	40.1	117	169	44.9	104	204	95.4	114	139	21.7
GIFTS	**1,119**	**1,059**	**–5.3**	**1,402**	**1,272**	**–9.3**	**901**	**1,083**	**20.2**	**664**	**652**	**–1.9**
FOOD	117	68	–41.7	162	77	–52.5	71	47	–34.0	69	36	–47.7
HOUSING	285	273	–4.2	318	328	3.1	228	215	–5.9	178	166	–6.8
HOUSEKEEPING SUPPLIES	**43**	**37**	**–13.9**	**53**	**44**	**–16.7**	**45**	**41**	**–9.8**	**23**	**24**	**2.9**
Household textiles	17	8	–53.5	20	15	–23.7	26	11	–57.3	4	7	90.0
Appliances, misc. housewares	33	27	–18.6	54	55	1.8	34	25	–27.3	25	12	–51.1
Major appliances	9	6	–30.2	10	13	32.3	10	8	–18.6	7	2	–72.9
Small appliances, misc. housewares	25	21	–14.5	44	41	–7.3	25	17	–30.8	17	10	–41.8

(continued)

(continued from previous page)

	total consumer units			aged 55–64			aged 65–74			aged 75 or older		
	1990	1997	percent change 1990–97	1990	1997	percent change 1990–97	1990	1997	percent change 1990–97	1990	1997	percent change 1990–97
Misc. household equipment	$61	$66	7.5%	$72	$95	31.1%	$48	$58	21.1%	$10	$29	195.2%
Other housing	131	135	2.7	119	119	-0.1	76	80	5.1	117	94	-19.4
APPAREL AND SERVICES	**290**	**252**	**-13.0**	**340**	**332**	**-2.4**	**295**	**260**	**-11.8**	**92**	**132**	**43.3**
Males, 2 and over	75	61	-18.6	120	87	-27.7	61	73	18.9	37	46	24.9
Females, 2 and over	117	81	-30.6	106	101	-4.4	161	99	-38.5	37	48	30.3
Children under 2	38	33	-13.3	45	32	-29.6	21	23	10.2	7	17	130.7
Other apparel products, services	**59**	**77**	**30.6**	**70**	**112**	**60.0**	**50**	**64**	**27.1**	**11**	**22**	**99.1**
Jewelry and watches	31	49	59.6	36	56	57.3	22	45	103.6	6	10	62.9
All other apparel products and services	28	29	2.7	34	55	60.0	28	19	-32.7	5	12	144.3
TRANSPORTATION	**65**	**57**	**-12.4**	**128**	**56**	**-56.2**	**42**	**119**	**185.0**	**16**	**78**	**388.6**
HEALTH CARE	**55**	**30**	**-45.7**	**45**	**60**	**32.1**	**65**	**27**	**-58.5**	**126**	**53**	**-58.1**
ENTERTAINMENT	**81**	**99**	**22.1**	**126**	**138**	**9.1**	**70**	**114**	**62.9**	**36**	**49**	**37.6**
Toys, games, hobbies, tricycles	31	41	33.6	60	65	8.0	29	40	35.7	14	31	129.5
Other entertainment	50	58	15.2	66	74	11.6	41	74	82.6	22	18	-18.6
EDUCATION	**118**	**155**	**31.5**	**185**	**98**	**-47.1**	**17**	**163**	**848.1**	**56**	**50**	**-11.5**
ALL OTHER GIFTS	**108**	**125**	**15.7**	**98**	**183**	**86.3**	**113**	**138**	**22.1**	**91**	**88**	**-3.2**

Note: The Bureau of Labor Statistics uses consumer units rather than households as the sampling unit in the Consumer Expenditure Survey. For the definition of consumer unit, see the Glossary. (–) means sample is too small to make a reliable estimate. Spending on gifts is also included in the preceding product and service categories.
Source: Bureau of Labor Statistics, 1990 and 1997 Consumer Expenditure Surveys; calculations by New Strategist

Retiree Spending Is below Average

Retirees spend just 69 percent as much as the average household.

Households headed by retirees spent $24,019 in 1997, 31 percent less than the $34,819 spent by the average household. The spending of retirees is below average in part because their households are small, with only 1.8 people compared with 2.5 people in the average household.

On some items, retiree spending is above average. They spend 9 percent more than the average household on postage and stationery, for example. They spend 47 percent more on floor coverings. Not surprisingly, households headed by retirees spend 49 percent more than the average household on health care.

Retirees spend an average amount on reading material (books, newspapers, and magazines) and 17 percent more than average on cash contributions. They also spend more than average on housing maintenance, repairs, and insurance as well as property taxes. Behind this higher spending is the fact that retirees are more likely than average to be homeowners.

♦ As better-educated and more affluent generations of Americans reach retirement age, the spending of retirees is likely to rise. This higher spending, combined with growth in the segment, will make retirees an important market for most businesses in the decades ahead.

Average and Indexed Spending of Retirees, 1997

(average annual and indexed spending of consumer units headed by retirees, 1997)

	average spending of total consumer units	consumer units headed by retirees	
		average spending	indexed spending
Number of consumer units (in 000s)	105,576	19,145	–
Average before-tax income	$39,926	$21,717	54
Average annual spending	34,819	24,019	69
FOOD	**$4,801**	**$3,539**	**74**
FOOD AT HOME	2,880	2,424	84
Cereals and bakery products	**453**	**377**	**83**
Cereals and cereal products	161	128	80
Bakery products	292	249	85
Meats, poultry, fish, and eggs	**743**	**634**	**85**
Beef	224	181	81
Pork	157	139	89
Other meats	96	84	88
Poultry	145	121	83
Fish and seafood	89	77	87
Eggs	33	32	97
Dairy products	**314**	**253**	**81**
Fresh milk and cream	128	106	83
Other dairy products	186	147	79
Fruits and vegetables	**476**	**444**	**93**
Fresh fruits	150	149	99
Fresh vegetables	143	133	93
Processed fruits	102	94	92
Processed vegetables	80	68	85
Other food at home	**895**	**717**	**80**
Sugar and other sweets	114	101	89
Fats and oils	81	80	99
Miscellaneous foods	403	298	74
Nonalcoholic beverages	245	196	80
Food prepared by household on trips	52	42	81
FOOD AWAY FROM HOME	1,921	1,115	58
ALCOHOLIC BEVERAGES	**$309**	**$223**	**72**

(continued)

(continued from previous page)

	average spending of total consumer units	consumer units headed by retirees	
		average spending	indexed spending
HOUSING	**$11,272**	**$8,009**	**71**
SHELTER	**6,344**	**3,858**	**61**
Owned dwellings	**3,935**	**2,513**	**64**
Mortgage interest and charges	2,225	561	25
Property taxes	971	1,016	105
Maintenance, repairs, insurance, other	738	936	127
Rented dwellings	**1,983**	**1,047**	**53**
Other lodging	**426**	**297**	**70**
UTILITIES, FUELS, PUBLIC SERVICES	**2,412**	**2,163**	**90**
Natural gas	301	340	113
Electricity	909	839	92
Fuel oil and other fuels	108	120	111
Telephone services	809	560	69
Water and other public services	286	303	106
HOUSEHOLD OPERATIONS	**548**	**415**	**76**
Personal services	263	102	39
Other household expenses	285	313	110
HOUSEKEEPING SUPPLIES	**455**	**415**	**91**
Laundry and cleaning supplies	116	96	83
Other household products	210	179	85
Postage and stationery	129	140	109
HOUSEHOLD FURNISHINGS			
AND EQUIPMENT	**1,512**	**1,158**	**77**
Household textiles	79	56	71
Furniture	387	232	60
Floor coverings	78	115	147
Major appliances	169	156	92
Small appliances, miscellaneous housewares	92	78	85
Miscellaneous household equipment	707	522	74
APPAREL AND SERVICES	**$1,729**	**$1,057**	**61**
Men and boys	**407**	**187**	**46**
Men, 16 and over	323	164	51
Boys, 2 to 15	84	24	29
Women and girls	**680**	**488**	**72**
Women, 16 and over	574	447	78
Girls, 2 to 15	106	41	39

(continued)

(continued from previous page)

	average spending of total consumer units	consumer units headed by retirees	
		average spending	indexed spending
Children under 2	$77	$26	34
Footwear	315	211	67
Other apparel products, services	250	145	58
TRANSPORTATION	**$6,457**	**$3,976**	**62**
Vehicle purchases	2,736	1,590	58
Cars and trucks, new	1,229	814	66
Cars and trucks, used	1,464	776	53
Other vehicles	43	–	–
Gasoline and motor oil	**1,098**	**692**	**63**
Other vehicle expenses	**2,230**	**1,429**	**64**
Vehicle finance charges	293	116	40
Maintenance and repairs	**682**	**505**	**74**
Vehicle insurance	**755**	**587**	**78**
Vehicle rental, leases, licenses, other	**501**	**221**	**44**
Public transportation	**393**	**264**	**67**
HEALTH CARE	**$1,841**	**$2,742**	**149**
Health insurance	881	1,421	161
Medical services	531	582	110
Drugs	320	605	189
Medical supplies	108	133	123
ENTERTAINMENT	**$1,813**	**$1,157**	**64**
Fees and admissions	471	286	61
Television, radio, sound equipment	577	386	67
Pets, toys, playground equipment	327	202	62
Other entertainment supplies, equipment, services	439	283	64
PERSONAL CARE PRODUCTS AND SERVICES	**$528**	**$434**	**82**
READING	**$164**	**$166**	**101**
EDUCATION	**$571**	**$177**	**31**
TOBACCO PRODUCTS AND SMOKING SUPPLIES	**$264**	**$171**	**65**
MISCELLANEOUS	**$847**	**$571**	**67**
Cash contributions	1,001	1,170	117
Personal insurance and pensions	3,223	628	19
Life and other personal insurance	379	298	79
Pensions and Social Security	2,844	329	12

(continued)

(continued from previous page)

	average spending of total consumer units	consumer units headed by retirees	
		average spending	indexed spending
PERSONAL TAXES	**$3,241**	**$1,072**	**33**
Federal income taxes	2,468	760	31
State and local income taxes	645	159	25
Other taxes	129	153	119
GIFTS	**$1,059**	**$897**	**85**
Food	**68**	**53**	**78**
Housing	**273**	**201**	**74**
Housekeeping supplies	37	36	97
Household textiles	8	8	100
Appliances and miscellaneous housewares	27	24	89
Major appliances	6	8	133
Small appliances, miscellaneous housewares	21	15	71
Miscellaneous household equipment	66	52	79
Other housing	135	82	61
Apparel and services	**252**	**196**	**78**
Males, 2 and over	61	53	87
Females, 2 and over	81	71	88
Children under 2	33	23	70
Other apparel products, services	77	50	65
Jewelry and watches	49	29	59
All other apparel products, services	29	21	72
Transportation	**57**	**78**	**137**
Health care	**30**	**52**	**173**
Entertainment	**99**	**85**	**86**
Toys, games, hobbies, tricycles	41	45	110
Other entertainment	58	40	69
Education	**155**	**122**	**79**
All other gifts	**125**	**110**	**88**

Note: The Bureau of Labor Statistics uses consumer units rather than households as the sampling unit in the Consumer Expenditure Survey. For the definition of consumer unit, see the Glossary. An index of 100 is the average for all households. An index of 132 means retirees spend 32 percent more than the average household. An index of 75 means retirees spend 25 percent less than the average household. (–) means sample is too small to make a reliable estimate.
Source: Bureau of Labor Statistics 1997 Consumer Expenditure Survey; calculations by New Strategist

Spending of Householders Aged 55 to 64 Is Average

Householders aged 55 to 64 spent $35,954 in 1997.

The spending of householders aged 55 to 64 was just 3 percent above average in 1997. Behind the average spending of this age group are two very different lifestyles. Many householders aged 55 to 64 are still working and enjoying peak earnings. Their spending is well above average. Others are retired and have cut their spending as they adjust to lower retirement incomes.

On many items, householders aged 55 to 64 spend well above average. They spend 39 percent more on coffee than the average household, because older Americans are the most devoted coffee drinkers. They spend 46 percent more than average on whiskey—another generational preference. Householders aged 55 to 64 spend 87 percent more than average on owned vacation homes, 67 percent more on office furniture for home use, 52 percent more on satellite dishes, 32 percent more on airfares, 25 percent more on medical services, 21 percent more on reading material, and 20 percent more on gifts.

This age group spends significantly less than average on personal services such as day care. They spend less on computer online services, children's clothes, sports equipment, and education.

◆ Many marketers pursue young adults and ignore older consumers because they think older people are not willing to spend. In fact, householders aged 55 to 64 spend more than young adults in most product and service categories.

Average and Indexed Spending of Householders Aged 55 to 64, 1997

(average annual spending of total consumer units and average annual and indexed spending of consumer units headed by 55-to-64-year-olds, 1997)

	average spending of total consumer units	consumer units headed by 55-to-64-year-olds	
		average spending	indexed spending*
Number of consumer units (in 000s)	105,576	12,316	–
Average before-tax income	$39,926.00	$41,734.00	105
Average annual spending	34,819.38	35,954.38	103
FOOD	**$4,801.35**	**$5,085.08**	**106**
FOOD AT HOME	2,880.00	3,139.41	109
Cereals and bakery products	**453.00**	**470.50**	**104**
Cereals and cereal products	161.39	160.01	99
Flour	8.79	10.82	123
Prepared flour mixes	15.04	14.01	93
Ready-to-eat and cooked cereals	91.15	83.87	92
Rice	18.37	23.62	129
Pasta, cornmeal, and other cereal products	28.03	27.70	99
Bakery products	291.60	310.49	106
Bread	83.43	93.33	112
White bread	40.89	41.84	102
Bread, other than white	42.55	51.49	121
Crackers and cookies	68.27	75.40	110
Cookies	45.01	47.60	106
Crackers	23.26	27.80	120
Frozen and refrigerated bakery products	23.35	21.34	91
Other bakery products	116.56	120.42	103
Biscuits and rolls	40.96	41.92	102
Cakes and cupcakes	34.51	30.13	87
Bread and cracker products	4.45	4.88	110
Sweetrolls, coffee cakes, doughnuts	23.13	26.03	113
Pies, tarts, turnovers	13.50	17.46	129
Meats, poultry, fish, and eggs	**743.12**	**830.10**	**112**
Beef	223.55	231.02	103
Ground beef	82.77	84.43	102

(continued)

(continued from previous page)

	average spending of total consumer units	consumer units headed by 55-to-64-year-olds	
		average spending	indexed spending*
Roast	$40.48	$46.04	114
Chuck roast	13.02	12.45	96
Round roast	12.85	11.97	93
Other roast	14.61	21.62	148
Steak	87.48	84.53	97
Round steak	16.70	17.68	106
Sirloin steak	23.01	22.23	97
Other steak	47.76	44.62	93
Other beef	12.81	16.02	125
Pork	157.13	187.46	119
Bacon	25.42	32.31	127
Pork chops	39.23	38.33	98
Ham	37.28	49.20	132
Ham, not canned	35.12	45.98	131
Canned ham	2.16	3.22	149
Sausage	24.12	33.52	139
Other pork	31.07	34.10	110
Other meats	96.03	110.35	115
Frankfurters	22.83	23.47	103
Lunch meats (cold cuts)	65.55	75.36	115
Bologna, liverwurst, salami	23.82	27.09	114
Other lunch meats	41.73	48.27	116
Lamb, organ meats, and others	7.92	11.52	145
Lamb and organ meats	7.34	11.34	154
Mutton, goat, and game	0.58	0.18	31
Poultry	145.01	149.87	103
Fresh and frozen chickens	113.38	111.15	98
Fresh and frozen whole chickens	29.77	34.33	115
Fresh and frozen chicken parts	83.61	76.83	92
Other poultry	31.63	38.71	122
Fish and seafood	88.54	114.06	129
Canned fish and seafood	14.18	17.41	123
Fresh fish and shellfish	50.95	74.22	146
Frozen fish and shellfish	23.41	22.42	96
Eggs	32.59	37.34	115

(continued)

(continued from previous page)

	average spending of total consumer units	consumer units headed by 55-to-64-year-olds	
		average spending	indexed spending*
Dairy products	**$313.68**	**$324.93**	**104**
Fresh milk and cream	128.12	121.85	95
Fresh milk, all types	118.78	112.93	95
Cream	9.34	8.92	96
Other dairy products	185.56	203.08	109
Butter	14.63	16.98	116
Cheese	94.33	100.60	107
Ice cream and related products	52.91	60.52	114
Miscellaneous dairy products	23.69	24.97	105
Fruits and vegetables	**475.62**	**548.74**	**115**
Fresh fruits	150.47	168.56	112
Apples	28.47	31.14	109
Bananas	31.44	34.58	110
Oranges	17.62	18.49	105
Citrus fruits, excluding oranges	13.42	14.78	110
Other fresh fruits	59.52	69.57	117
Fresh vegetables	142.75	185.04	130
Potatoes	26.15	33.72	129
Lettuce	19.27	27.61	143
Tomatoes	23.87	28.83	121
Other fresh vegetables	73.46	94.89	129
Processed fruits	102.28	108.18	106
Frozen fruits and fruit juices	15.02	17.71	118
Frozen orange juice	8.44	11.07	131
Frozen fruits	2.02	2.82	140
Frozen fruit juices, excluding orange juice	4.57	3.83	84
Canned fruits	13.97	16.47	118
Dried fruits	6.03	6.58	109
Fresh fruit juice	19.82	21.60	109
Canned and bottled fruit juice	47.43	45.83	97
Processed vegetables	80.13	86.95	109
Frozen vegetables	26.57	25.99	98
Canned and dried vegetables and juices	53.56	60.96	114
Canned beans	11.79	14.86	126
Canned corn	7.26	7.99	110
Canned miscellaneous vegetables	16.80	20.37	121
Dried peas	0.23	0.19	83

(continued)

(continued from previous page)

	average spending of total consumer units	consumer units headed by 55-to-64-year-olds	
		average spending	indexed spending*
Dried beans	$2.58	$2.13	83
Dried miscellaneous vegetables	7.18	6.30	88
Dried processed vegetables	0.22	0.10	45
Frozen vegetable juices	0.28	0.14	50
Fresh and canned vegetable juices	7.22	8.87	123
Other food at home	**894.58**	**965.15**	**108**
Sugar and other sweets	114.30	130.72	114
Candy and chewing gum	69.26	79.66	115
Sugar	18.93	20.07	106
Artificial sweeteners	3.48	4.65	134
Jams, preserves, other sweets	22.63	26.34	116
Fats and oils	81.05	98.63	122
Margarine	11.74	14.91	127
Fats and oils	24.50	29.24	119
Salad dressings	24.68	32.10	130
Nondairy cream and imitation milk	8.50	10.20	120
Peanut butter	11.63	12.18	105
Miscellaneous foods	403.06	403.43	100
Frozen prepared foods	77.61	79.14	102
Frozen meals	20.73	26.91	130
Other frozen prepared foods	56.88	52.23	92
Canned and packaged soups	32.87	37.87	115
Potato chips, nuts, and other snacks	84.53	89.36	106
Potato chips and other snacks	66.83	65.12	97
Nuts	17.70	24.23	137
Condiments and seasonings	86.12	93.23	108
Salt, spices, and other seasonings	19.07	20.77	109
Olives, pickles, relishes	10.54	12.01	114
Sauces and gravies	39.86	38.66	97
Baking needs and miscellaneous products	16.65	21.78	131
Other canned/packaged prepared foods	121.94	103.85	85
Prepared salads	15.05	14.81	98
Prepared desserts	9.95	11.46	115
Baby food	27.86	10.30	37
Miscellaneous prepared foods	68.44	66.60	97
Vitamin supplements	0.64	0.67	105

(continued)

(continued from previous page)

	average spending of total consumer units	consumer units headed by 55-to-64-year-olds	
		average spending	indexed spending*
Nonalcoholic beverages	$244.51	$267.24	109
Cola	90.51	101.06	112
Other carbonated drinks	42.94	42.32	99
Coffee	48.80	67.99	139
Roasted coffee	32.65	45.45	139
Instant and freeze-dried coffee	16.15	22.53	140
Noncarbonated fruit flavored drinks, including nonfrozen lemonade	19.22	15.46	80
Tea	14.76	20.30	138
Nonalcoholic beer	0.34	0.21	62
Other nonalcoholic beverages and ice	27.93	19.90	71
Food prepared by household on out-of-town trips	51.65	65.14	126
FOOD AWAY FROM HOME	**$1,921.35**	**$1,945.66**	**101**
Meals at restaurants, carry-outs, other	**1,477.51**	**1,428.89**	**97**
Lunch	501.92	434.30	87
Dinner	740.70	779.05	105
Snacks and nonalcoholic beverages	119.38	101.08	85
Breakfast and brunch	115.51	114.47	99
Board (including at school)	**51.88**	**28.44**	**55**
Catered affairs	**83.52**	**150.21**	**180**
Food on out-of-town trips	**223.90**	**300.86**	**134**
School lunches	**54.03**	**15.94**	**30**
Meals as pay	**30.51**	**21.32**	**70**
ALCOHOLIC BEVERAGES	**$309.22**	**$283.33**	**92**
At home	**180.13**	**176.85**	**98**
Beer and ale	90.92	82.66	91
Whiskey	13.40	19.56	146
Wine	55.32	51.46	93
Other alcoholic beverages	20.50	23.18	113
Away from home	**129.09**	**106.47**	**82**
Beer and ale	39.50	32.46	82
Wine	24.30	17.61	72
Other alcoholic beverages	32.81	21.80	66
Alcoholic beverages purchased on trips	32.48	34.61	107

(continued)

(continued from previous page)

	average spending of total consumer units	consumer units headed by 55-to-64-year-olds	
		average spending	indexed spending*
HOUSING	**$11,272.04**	**$11,089.96**	**98**
SHELTER	**6,343.87**	**5,782.90**	**91**
Owned dwellings**	**3,934.87**	**4,058.63**	**103**
Mortgage interest and charges	2,225.26	1,927.08	87
Mortgage interest	2,109.06	1,778.23	84
Interest paid, home equity loan	57.21	68.01	119
Interest paid, home equity line of credit	58.84	80.77	137
Prepayment penalty charges	0.16	0.08	50
Property taxes	971.15	1,195.34	123
Maintenance, repairs, insurance, other expenses	738.46	936.20	127
Homeowner's and related insurance	230.91	255.53	111
Fire and extended coverage	8.02	10.92	136
Homeowner's insurance	222.88	244.61	110
Ground rent	37.16	59.07	159
Maintenance and repair services	365.61	496.81	136
Painting and papering	45.31	62.08	137
Plumbing and water heating	36.61	46.60	127
Heat, air conditioning, electrical work	63.28	77.92	123
Roofing and gutters	72.99	83.87	115
Other repair and maintenance services	124.47	196.68	158
Repair/replacement of hard surface flooring	21.17	27.00	128
Repair of built-in appliances	1.79	2.67	149
Maintenance and repair materials	83.91	105.57	126
Paints, wallpaper, and supplies	18.33	19.94	109
Tools/equipment for painting, wallpapering	1.97	2.14	109
Plumbing supplies and equipment	6.87	11.42	166
Electrical supplies, heating/cooling equipment	4.55	4.73	104
Hard surface flooring, repair and replacement	7.13	13.13	184
Roofing and gutters	7.77	8.95	115
Plaster, paneling, siding, windows, doors, screens, awnings	14.97	23.51	157
Patio, walk, fence, driveway, masonry, brick, and stucco work	0.92	1.60	174
Landscape maintenance	5.19	4.72	91
Miscellaneous supplies and equipment	16.21	15.42	95
Insulation, other maintenance/repair	9.22	9.49	103

(continued)

(continued from previous page)

	average spending of total consumer units	consumer units headed by 55-to-64-year-olds	
		average spending	indexed spending*
Finish basement, remodel rooms, build patios, walks, etc.	$6.99	$5.93	85
Property management and security	19.58	18.29	93
Property management	16.49	13.56	82
Management and upkeep services for security	3.09	4.73	153
Parking	1.30	0.93	72
Rented dwellings	**1,983.18**	**1,144.79**	**58**
Rent	1,876.81	1,042.51	56
Rent as pay	72.36	63.51	88
Maintenance, insurance, and other expenses	34.02	38.78	114
Tenant's insurance	9.76	8.16	84
Maintenance and repair services	16.62	22.94	138
Repair or maintenance services	15.42	22.00	143
Repair and replacement of hard surface flooring	1.17	0.94	80
Repair of built-in appliances	0.03	–	–
Maintenance and repair materials	7.63	7.68	101
Paint, wallpaper, and supplies	1.57	1.58	101
Painting and wallpapering	0.17	0.17	100
Plastering, paneling, roofing, gutters, etc.	1.22	5.04	413
Patio, walk, fence, driveway, masonry, brick, and stucco work	0.02	–	–
Plumbing supplies and equipment	0.36	0.01	3
Electrical supplies, heating and cooling equipment	0.08	0.02	25
Miscellaneous supplies and equipment	2.94	0.85	29
Insulation, other maintenance and repair	1.04	0.38	37
Materials for additions, finishing basements, remodeling rooms	1.65	0.47	28
Construction materials for jobs not started	0.25	–	–
Hard surface flooring	0.74	–	–
Landscape maintenance	0.53	–	–
Other lodging	**425.82**	**579.48**	**136**
Owned vacation homes	133.69	250.32	187
Mortgage interest and charges	58.02	99.55	172
Mortgage interest	56.46	92.57	164
Interest paid, home equity loan	0.66	2.68	406
Interest paid, home equity line of credit	0.89	4.30	483

(continued)

(continued from previous page)

	average spending of total consumer units	consumer units headed by 55-to-64-year-olds	
		average spending	indexed spending*
Property taxes	$54.83	$112.16	205
Maintenance, insurance, and other expenses	20.84	38.61	185
Homeowner's and related insurance	5.03	11.08	220
Homeowner's insurance	4.67	10.80	231
Fire and extended coverage	0.36	0.28	78
Ground rent	1.63	2.20	135
Maintenance and repair services	9.66	15.65	162
Maintenance and repair materials	0.81	2.54	314
Property management and security	3.41	6.10	179
Property management	2.96	5.03	170
Management and upkeep services for security	0.45	1.07	238
Parking	0.29	1.04	359
Housing while attending school	66.35	46.02	69
Lodging on out-of-town trips	225.77	283.15	125
UTILITIES, FUELS & PUBLIC SERVICES	**2,412.30**	**2,654.49**	**110**
Natural gas	**300.96**	**342.15**	**114**
Natural gas (renter)	60.81	34.66	57
Natural gas (owner)	238.55	304.95	128
Natural gas (vacation)	1.60	2.54	159
Electricity	**908.67**	**1,013.36**	**112**
Electricity (renter)	212.54	122.42	58
Electricity (owner)	687.53	872.12	127
Electricity (vacation)	8.60	18.81	219
Fuel oil and other fuels	**107.72**	**126.00**	**117**
Fuel oil	55.18	65.51	119
Fuel oil (renter)	4.92	2.70	55
Fuel oil (owner)	49.77	62.57	126
Fuel oil (vacation)	0.49	0.23	47
Coal	0.99	1.74	176
Coal (renter)	0.02	–	–
Coal (owner)	0.97	1.74	179
Bottled/tank gas	43.84	49.62	113
Gas (renter)	4.66	2.68	58
Gas (owner)	36.37	41.07	113
Gas (vacation)	2.81	5.87	209

(continued)

(continued from previous page)

	average spending of total consumer units	consumer units headed by 55-to-64-year-olds	
		average spending	indexed spending*
Wood and other fuels	$7.72	$9.13	118
Wood and other fuels (renter)	1.53	0.76	50
Wood and other fuels (owner)	5.80	8.09	139
Wood and other fuels (vacation)	0.39	0.29	74
Telephone services	**809.05**	**842.20**	**104**
Telephone services in home city, excluding mobile car phones	756.44	782.37	103
Telephone services for mobile car phones	52.61	59.83	114
Water and other public services	**285.90**	**330.79**	**116**
Water and sewerage maintenance	207.28	237.58	115
Water and sewerage maintenance (renter)	28.28	19.82	70
Water and sewerage maintenance (owner)	176.95	213.49	121
Water and sewerage maintenance (vacation)	2.06	4.28	208
Trash and garbage collection	76.00	88.39	116
Trash and garbage collection (renter)	8.78	5.97	68
Trash and garbage collection (owner)	65.66	78.51	120
Trash and garbage collection (vacation)	1.56	3.91	251
Septic tank cleaning	2.62	4.82	184
Septic tank cleaning (renter)	0.19	–	–
Septic tank cleaning (owner)	2.41	4.82	200
HOUSEHOLD OPERATIONS	**548.50**	**401.57**	**73**
Personal services	**263.10**	**58.93**	**22**
Baby-sitting and child care in your own home	34.39	2.83	8
Baby-sitting and child care in someone else's home	37.37	0.52	1
Care for elderly, invalids, handicapped, etc.	26.95	26.32	98
Adult day care centers	3.79	–	–
Day care centers, nurseries, and preschools	160.60	29.26	18
Other household expenses	**285.40**	**342.65**	**120**
Housekeeping services	75.34	71.29	95
Gardening, lawn care services	72.44	90.44	125
Water softening services	4.51	4.42	98
Nonclothing laundry and dry cleaning, sent out	10.20	9.80	96
Nonclothing laundry and dry cleaning, coin-operated	4.91	3.68	75
Termite/pest control services	11.55	12.66	110
Other home services	15.94	20.01	126
Termite/pest control products	0.12	0.36	300

(continued)

(continued from previous page)

	average spending of total consumer units	consumer units headed by 55-to-64-year-olds	
		average spending	indexed spending*
Moving, storage, and freight express	$34.75	$62.64	180
Appliance repair, including service center	13.50	22.32	165
Reupholstering and furniture repair	10.87	18.14	167
Repairs/rentals of lawn/garden equipment, hand/power tools, etc.	5.13	5.69	111
Appliance rental	1.05	–	–
Rental of office equipment for nonbusiness use	0.43	0.13	30
Repair of miscellaneous household equipment and furnishings	1.53	1.19	78
Repair of computer systems for nonbusiness use	2.47	2.57	104
Computer information services	20.65	17.31	84
HOUSEKEEPING SUPPLIES	**454.93**	**522.96**	**115**
Laundry and cleaning supplies	**115.85**	**129.90**	**112**
Soaps and detergents	65.05	73.71	113
Other laundry cleaning products	50.80	56.18	111
Other household products	**210.07**	**244.78**	**117**
Cleansing and toilet tissue, paper towels, and napkins	64.42	75.06	117
Miscellaneous household products	89.90	86.89	97
Lawn and garden supplies	55.74	82.83	149
Postage and stationery	**129.01**	**148.29**	**115**
Stationery, stationery supplies, giftwrap	62.61	59.18	95
Postage	62.53	79.94	128
Delivery services	3.88	9.16	236
HOUSEHOLD FURNISHINGS & EQUIPMENT	**1,512.44**	**1,728.03**	**114**
Household textiles	**79.12**	**99.72**	**126**
Bathroom linens	11.13	12.65	114
Bedroom linens	34.28	37.95	111
Kitchen and dining room linens	2.40	3.24	135
Curtains and draperies	16.73	25.72	154
Slipcovers and decorative pillows	2.10	2.60	124
Sewing materials for household items	11.20	16.29	145
Other linens	1.28	1.26	98
Furniture	**387.34**	**389.86**	**101**
Mattresses and springs	46.56	51.38	110
Other bedroom furniture	63.99	57.14	89

(continued)

(continued from previous page)

	average spending of total consumer units	consumer units headed by 55-to-64-year-olds	
		average spending	indexed spending*
Sofas	$93.81	$87.80	94
Living room chairs	47.42	52.12	110
Living room tables	20.60	16.96	82
Kitchen and dining room furniture	48.69	60.36	124
Infants' furniture	9.87	8.66	88
Outdoor furniture	13.61	17.33	127
Wall units, cabinets, and other furniture	42.81	38.11	89
Floor coverings	**77.74**	**101.47**	**131**
Wall-to-wall carpeting	38.82	72.71	187
Wall-to-wall carpeting (renter)	1.94	0.50	26
Wall-to-wall carpeting, installed	1.37	0.37	27
Wall-to-wall carpeting, not installed carpet squares	0.56	0.14	25
Wall-to-wall carpeting, replacement (owner)	36.88	72.21	196
Wall-to-wall carpeting, not installed carpet squares	2.68	4.98	186
Wall-to-wall carpeting, installed	34.20	67.22	197
Room-size rugs and other floor covering, nonpermanent	38.93	28.75	74
Major appliances	**169.18**	**246.04**	**145**
Dishwashers (built-in), garbage disposals, range hoods (renter)	0.82	–	–
Dishwashers (built-in), garbage disposals, range hoods (owner)	11.65	22.75	195
Refrigerators and freezers (renter)	9.52	6.16	65
Refrigerators and freezers (owner)	48.08	92.51	192
Washing machines (renter)	5.46	1.67	31
Washing machines (owner)	17.56	23.96	136
Clothes dryers (renter)	4.40	0.46	10
Clothes dryers (owner)	11.82	15.66	132
Cooking stoves, ovens (renter)	2.83	1.26	45
Cooking stoves, ovens (owner)	19.23	38.06	198
Microwave ovens (renter)	2.96	1.16	39
Microwave ovens (owner)	6.63	9.93	150
Portable dishwashers (renter)	0.41	–	–
Portable dishwashers (owner)	0.26	–	–
Window air conditioners (renter)	1.69	0.92	54
Window air conditioners (owner)	3.24	7.34	227

(continued)

(continued from previous page)

	average spending of total consumer units	consumer units headed by 55-to-64-year-olds	
		average spending	indexed spending*
Electric floor cleaning equipment	$15.68	$17.75	113
Sewing machines	3.55	5.64	159
Miscellaneous household appliances	**3.39**	**0.81**	**24**
Small appliances and miscellaneous housewares	91.91	123.05	134
Housewares	66.12	85.66	130
Plastic dinnerware	1.75	2.25	129
China and other dinnerware	8.86	5.91	67
Flatware	4.68	8.90	190
Glassware	8.25	12.14	147
Silver serving pieces	2.31	1.92	83
Other serving pieces	1.74	1.44	83
Nonelectric cookware	15.05	27.58	183
Tableware, nonelectric kitchenware	23.48	25.53	109
Small appliances	25.79	37.39	145
Small electric kitchen appliances	16.67	22.34	134
Portable heating and cooling equipment	9.12	15.06	165
Miscellaneous household equipment	**707.15**	**767.90**	**109**
Window coverings	13.71	33.01	241
Infants' equipment	7.05	6.97	99
Laundry and cleaning equipment	13.70	15.69	115
Outdoor equipment	18.42	11.66	63
Clocks	4.51	5.17	115
Lamps and lighting fixtures	12.53	11.33	90
Other household decorative items	134.12	137.95	103
Telephones and accessories	96.54	122.09	126
Lawn and garden equipment	39.37	54.16	138
Power tools	16.31	14.42	88
Office furniture for home use	10.61	17.71	167
Hand tools	9.29	12.59	136
Indoor plants and fresh flowers	52.33	65.14	124
Closet and storage items	8.94	6.08	68
Rental of furniture	3.41	0.98	29
Luggage	9.72	11.41	117
Computers and computer hardware, nonbusiness use	162.66	176.61	109
Computer software and accessories, nonbusiness use	24.72	21.00	85
Telephone answering devices	3.31	3.95	119

(continued)

(continued from previous page)

	average spending of total consumer units	consumer units headed by 55-to-64-year-olds	
		average spending	indexed spending*
Calculators	$1.92	$1.14	59
Business equipment for home use	2.33	5.19	223
Other hardware	23.27	2.92	13
Smoke alarms (owner)	0.86	0.99	115
Smoke alarms (renter)	0.19	0.02	11
Other household appliances (owner)	8.78	8.50	97
Other household appliances (renter)	1.47	0.42	29
Miscellaneous household equipment and parts	27.10	20.78	77
APPAREL AND SERVICES	**$1,729.06**	**$1,655.63**	**96**
Men's apparel	**322.98**	**318.05**	**98**
Suits	35.18	29.87	85
Sportcoats and tailored jackets	15.19	19.69	130
Coats and jackets	29.80	15.42	52
Underwear	12.52	17.47	140
Hosiery	9.91	8.97	91
Nightwear	2.93	7.43	254
Accessories	30.27	23.41	77
Sweaters and vests	15.84	19.94	126
Active sportswear	12.24	9.06	74
Shirts	75.81	75.80	100
Pants	64.52	75.99	118
Shorts and shorts sets	13.76	6.11	44
Uniforms	2.25	4.51	200
Costumes	2.79	4.38	157
Boys' (aged 2 to 15) apparel	**83.88**	**38.90**	**46**
Coats and jackets	8.33	2.70	32
Sweaters	2.81	2.05	73
Shirts	18.34	9.58	52
Underwear	3.08	1.49	48
Nightwear	1.94	0.61	31
Hosiery	3.66	0.67	18
Accessories	3.94	2.46	62
Suits, sportcoats, and vests	2.89	1.85	64
Pants	21.85	8.82	40
Shorts and shorts sets	8.66	4.12	48
Uniforms	4.41	2.64	60

(continued)

	average spending of total consumer units	consumer units headed by 55-to-64-year-olds	
		average spending	indexed spending*
Active sportswear	$2.65	$0.75	28
Costumes	1.33	1.16	87
Women's apparel	**574.26**	**633.07**	**110**
Coats and jackets	44.33	52.14	118
Dresses	84.25	77.27	92
Sportcoats and tailored jackets	2.77	4.50	162
Sweaters and vests	40.39	41.97	104
Shirts, blouses, and tops	93.73	102.15	109
Skirts	18.35	11.27	61
Pants	70.48	80.29	114
Shorts and shorts sets	22.34	26.36	118
Active sportswear	29.74	25.03	84
Nightwear	24.73	16.98	69
Undergarments	29.71	45.16	152
Hosiery	22.88	20.66	90
Suits	38.30	59.12	154
Accessories	45.42	62.98	139
Uniforms	3.20	–	–
Costumes	3.64	7.18	197
Girls' (aged 2 to 15) apparel	**106.01**	**51.01**	**48**
Coats and jackets	6.50	4.41	68
Dresses and suits	13.42	9.37	70
Shirts, blouses, and sweaters	25.74	8.75	34
Skirts and pants	19.49	7.85	40
Shorts and shorts sets	9.67	3.82	40
Active sportswear	6.86	5.51	80
Underwear and nightwear	6.75	2.75	41
Hosiery	5.29	2.55	48
Accessories	5.64	3.34	59
Uniforms	3.17	1.35	43
Costumes	3.48	1.31	38
Children under age 2	**77.05**	**33.83**	**44**
Coats, jackets, and snowsuits	3.28	4.09	125
Outerwear including dresses	15.01	8.46	56
Underwear	43.93	10.74	24
Nightwear and loungewear	4.38	5.22	119
Accessories	10.45	5.32	51

(continued)

(continued from previous page)

	average spending of total consumer units	consumer units headed by 55-to-64-year-olds	
		average spending	indexed spending*
Footwear	**$314.52**	**$337.40**	**107**
Men's	100.43	108.78	108
Boys'	27.90	19.72	71
Women's	157.11	197.83	126
Girls'	29.08	11.08	38
Other apparel products and services	**250.35**	**243.37**	**97**
Material for making clothes	4.07	6.22	153
Sewing patterns and notions	4.82	7.68	159
Watches	29.70	36.67	123
Jewelry	142.02	119.10	84
Shoe repair and other shoe services	2.38	2.74	115
Coin-operated apparel laundry and dry cleaning	20.79	20.79	100
Apparel alteration, repair, and tailoring services	6.10	7.30	120
Clothing rental	3.85	3.37	88
Watch and jewelry repair	5.08	6.58	130
Professional laundry, dry cleaning	31.24	32.50	104
Clothing storage	0.30	0.42	140
TRANSPORTATION	**$6,456.86**	**$6,707.56**	**104**
VEHICLE PURCHASES	**2,735.76**	**2,641.46**	**97**
Cars and trucks, new	**1,228.89**	**1,374.46**	**112**
New cars	700.22	744.40	106
New trucks	528.67	630.06	119
Cars and trucks, used	**1,463.52**	**1,266.97**	**87**
Used cars	895.31	807.91	90
Used trucks	568.22	459.06	81
Other vehicles	**43.35**	**0.03**	**0**
New motorcycles	26.39	–	–
Used motorcycles	15.32	0.03	0
GASOLINE AND MOTOR OIL	**1,097.52**	**1,188.28**	**108**
Gasoline	985.31	1,046.96	106
Diesel fuel	10.10	17.60	174
Gasoline on out-of-town trips	89.11	111.36	125
Motor oil	12.10	11.24	93
Motor oil on out-of-town trips	0.90	1.12	124

(continued)

(continued from previous page)

	average spending of total consumer units	consumer units headed by 55-to-64-year-olds	
		average spending	indexed spending*
OTHER VEHICLE EXPENSES	**$2,230.41**	**$2,369.05**	**106**
Vehicle finance charges	**292.81**	**259.54**	**89**
Automobile finance charges	161.70	147.18	91
Truck finance charges	116.10	82.60	71
Motorcycle and plane finance charges	1.52	0.69	45
Other vehicle finance charges	13.49	29.07	215
Maintenance and repairs	**681.62**	**759.53**	**111**
Coolant, additives, brake, transmission fluids	5.70	5.48	96
Tires	87.94	86.45	98
Parts, equipment, and accessories	51.31	59.98	117
Vehicle audio equipment	2.00	0.95	48
Vehicle products	6.95	4.41	63
Miscellaneous auto repair, servicing	51.74	26.46	51
Body work and painting	32.29	48.92	152
Clutch, transmission repair	47.92	62.07	130
Drive shaft and rear-end repair	5.73	3.99	70
Brake work	55.82	64.68	116
Repair to steering or front-end	17.41	16.29	94
Repair to engine cooling system	19.98	25.25	126
Motor tune-up	45.05	59.18	131
Lube, oil change, and oil filters	54.29	64.56	119
Front-end alignment, wheel balance, rotation	12.13	11.29	93
Shock absorber replacement	4.98	4.01	81
Gas tank repair, replacement	1.20	0.80	67
Tire repair and other repair work	29.63	38.05	128
Vehicle air conditioning repair	19.07	20.06	105
Exhaust system repair	18.52	17.05	92
Electrical system repair	29.34	29.03	99
Motor repair, replacement	75.45	99.55	132
Auto repair service policy	7.16	11.02	154
Vehicle insurance	**754.99**	**851.14**	**113**
Vehicle rental, leases, licenses, other charges	**500.99**	**498.85**	**100**
Leased and rented vehicles	331.25	313.93	95
Rented vehicles	41.03	61.26	149
Auto rental	7.73	14.06	182
Auto rental, out-of-town trips	26.78	34.62	129

(continued)

(continued from previous page)

	average spending of total consumer units	consumer units headed by 55-to-64-year-olds	
		average spending	indexed spending*
Truck rental	$1.85	$2.71	146
Truck rental, out-of-town trips	4.29	9.30	217
Leased vehicles	290.22	252.67	87
Car lease payments	162.28	174.29	107
Cash downpayment (car lease)	16.16	15.06	93
Termination fee (car lease)	1.81	0.20	11
Truck lease payments	98.37	53.71	55
Cash downpayment (truck lease)	10.63	8.85	83
Termination fee (truck lease)	0.97	0.56	58
State and local registration	94.62	107.27	113
Driver's license	7.42	7.57	102
Vehicle inspection	8.74	9.90	113
Parking fees	28.20	22.10	78
Parking fees in home city, excluding residence	24.37	16.29	67
Parking fees, out-of-town trips	3.83	5.81	152
Tolls	13.19	17.51	133
Tolls on out-of-town trips	4.32	4.76	110
Towing charges	5.04	3.74	74
Automobile service clubs	8.19	12.07	147
PUBLIC TRANSPORTATION	**393.16**	**508.77**	**129**
Airline fares	248.82	327.78	132
Intercity bus fares	10.51	14.25	136
Intracity mass transit fares	55.77	58.89	106
Local transportation on out-of-town trips	12.61	17.82	141
Taxi fares and limousine service on trips	7.40	10.46	141
Taxi fares and limousine service	9.51	6.80	72
Intercity train fares	21.19	32.09	151
Ship fares	26.40	40.51	153
School bus	0.95	0.17	18
HEALTH CARE	**$1,840.71**	**$2,186.72**	**119**
HEALTH INSURANCE	**881.28**	**965.48**	**110**
Commercial health insurance	**203.37**	**279.03**	**137**
Traditional fee-for-service health plan (not BCBS)	100.09	147.55	147
Preferred provider health plan (not BCBS)	103.29	131.48	127
Blue Cross, Blue Shield	**192.51**	**270.95**	**141**
Traditional fee-for-service health plan	$62.93	$98.37	156

(continued)

(continued from previous page)

	average spending of total consumer units	consumer units headed by 55-to-64-year-olds	
		average spending	indexed spending*
Preferred provider health plan	46.45	70.43	152
Health maintenance organization	47.39	77.75	164
Commercial Medicare supplement	31.92	15.81	50
Other BCBS health insurance	3.82	8.59	225
Health maintenance plans (HMOs)	**229.07**	**247.99**	**108**
Medicare payments	**160.92**	**91.64**	**57**
Commercial Medicare supplements/			
other health insurance	**95.40**	**75.87**	**80**
Commercial Medicare supplement (not BCBS)	60.66	21.82	36
Other health insurance (not BCBS)	34.74	54.05	156
MEDICAL SERVICES	**531.04**	**663.67**	**125**
Physician's services	133.59	168.03	126
Dental services	203.56	244.82	120
Eye care services	27.14	46.63	172
Service by professionals other than physicians	37.03	48.83	132
Lab tests, X-rays	22.93	48.61	212
Hospital room	35.07	49.94	142
Hospital services other than room	52.37	11.24	21
Care in convalescent or nursing home	13.09	34.37	263
Repair of medical equipment	0.62	–	–
Other medical services	5.64	11.20	199
DRUGS	**320.44**	**406.72**	**127**
Nonprescription drugs	75.43	96.36	128
Nonprescription vitamins	28.43	30.15	106
Prescription drugs	216.58	280.20	129
MEDICAL SUPPLIES	**107.95**	**150.86**	**140**
Eyeglasses and contact lenses	59.73	82.91	139
Hearing aids	11.42	28.02	245
Topicals and dressings	29.47	35.62	121
Medical equipment for general use	2.43	1.95	80
Supportive/convalescent medical equipment	2.62	1.10	42
Rental of medical equipment	0.60	1.12	187
Rental of supportive, convalescent medical equipment	1.67	0.13	8
ENTERTAINMENT	**$1,813.28**	**$1,900.04**	**105**
FEES AND ADMISSIONS	**470.74**	**451.21**	**96**

(continued)

(continued from previous page)

	average spending of total consumer units	consumer units headed by 55-to-64-year-olds	
		average spending	indexed spending*
Recreation expenses, out-of-town trips	$24.70	$33.21	134
Social, recreation, civic club membership	75.12	97.69	130
Fees for participant sports	72.62	68.92	95
Participant sports, out-of-town trips	30.30	32.56	107
Movie, theater, opera, ballet	86.71	67.74	78
Movie, other admissions, out-of-town trips	41.93	47.54	113
Admission to sports events	33.51	23.01	69
Admission to sports events, out-of-town trips	13.98	15.84	113
Fees for recreational lessons	67.17	31.49	47
Other entertainment services, out-of-town trips	24.70	33.21	134
TELEVISION, RADIO, SOUND EQUIPMENT	**577.33**	**560.69**	**97**
Television	**403.51**	**441.26**	**109**
Community antenna or cable TV	262.34	293.31	112
Black and white TV sets	0.67	0.75	112
Color TV, console	25.17	36.55	145
Color TV, portable/table model	39.96	38.87	97
VCRs and video disc players	26.58	29.55	111
Video cassettes, tapes, and discs	22.15	24.13	109
Video game hardware and software	19.74	11.15	56
Repair of TV, radio, and sound equipment	6.65	6.77	102
Rental of television sets	0.24	0.18	75
Radios and sound equipment	**173.81**	**119.43**	**69**
Radios	11.76	11.47	98
Tape recorders and players	6.57	–	–
Sound components and component systems	29.86	22.17	74
Miscellaneous sound equipment	0.63	–	–
Sound equipment accessories	5.23	11.73	224
Satellite dishes	3.41	5.17	152
Compact disc, tape, record, video mail order clubs	10.59	8.67	82
Records, CDs, audio tapes, needles	39.41	25.00	63
Rental of VCR, radio, sound equipment	0.45	0.27	60
Musical instruments and accessories	23.96	11.80	49
Rental and repair of musical instruments	1.64	0.51	31
Rental of video cassettes, tapes, discs, films	40.30	22.63	56
PETS, TOYS, PLAYGROUND EQUIPMENT	**326.53**	**375.74**	**115**
Pets	**198.03**	**250.03**	**126**

(continued)

(continued from previous page)

	average spending of total consumer units	consumer units headed by 55-to-64-year-olds	
		average spending	indexed spending*
Pet food	$87.23	$130.65	150
Pet purchase, supplies, and medicines	40.15	41.51	103
Pet services	17.17	19.10	111
Veterinary services	53.49	58.78	110
Toys, games, hobbies, and tricycles	**127.68**	**124.56**	**98**
Playground equipment	**0.82**	**1.15**	**140**
OTHER ENTERTAINMENT SUPPLIES, EQUIPMENT, SERVICES	**438.68**	**512.41**	**117**
Unmotored recreational vehicles	**37.97**	**89.84**	**237**
Boats without motor and boat trailers	8.48	13.06	154
Trailers and other attachable campers	29.49	76.78	260
Motorized recreational vehicles	**145.96**	**205.86**	**141**
Motorized campers	26.17	91.88	351
Other vehicles	10.62	19.47	183
Motor boats	109.17	94.51	87
Rental of recreational vehicles	**3.35**	**7.12**	**213**
Outboard motors	**3.27**	**3.69**	**113**
Docking and landing fees	**9.52**	**9.08**	**95**
Sports, recreation, exercise equipment	**128.96**	**107.34**	**83**
Athletic gear, game tables, exercise equipment	60.02	48.84	81
Bicycles	15.27	7.86	51
Camping equipment	9.34	2.69	29
Hunting and fishing equipment	16.11	27.91	173
Winter sports equipment	5.50	2.28	41
Water sports equipment	4.52	1.57	35
Other sports equipment	16.29	13.26	81
Rental and repair of miscellaneous sports equipment	1.91	2.92	153
Photographic equipment and supplies	**89.92**	**72.54**	**81**
Film	21.36	20.16	94
Other photographic supplies	1.07	5.48	512
Film processing	29.36	29.96	102
Repair and rental of photographic equipment	0.49	0.76	155
Photographic equipment	14.19	15.58	110
Photographer fees	23.45	0.61	3
Fireworks	**3.98**	**0.31**	**8**

(continued)

(continued from previous page)

	average spending of total consumer units	consumer units headed by 55-to-64-year-olds	
		average spending	indexed spending*
Souvenirs	$0.74	$2.28	308
Visual goods	3.15	–	–
Pinball, electronic video games	11.85	14.36	121

PERSONAL CARE PRODUCTS AND SERVICES

	average spending of total consumer units	consumer units headed by 55-to-64-year-olds	
PERSONAL CARE PRODUCTS AND SERVICES	**$527.62**	**$541.24**	**103**
Personal care products	**241.86**	**237.22**	**98**
Hair care products	51.00	45.52	89
Hair accessories	6.89	4.38	64
Wigs and hairpieces	1.22	2.26	185
Oral hygiene products	26.96	29.71	110
Shaving products	11.45	11.26	98
Cosmetics, perfume, and bath products	109.99	113.08	103
Deodorants, feminine hygiene, miscellaneous products	29.80	26.93	90
Electric personal care appliances	4.56	4.08	89
Personal care services	**285.76**	**304.02**	**106**
Personal care services (female)	188.30	215.67	115
Personal care services (male)	97.25	88.03	91
Repair of personal care appliances	0.20	0.32	160

READING

	average spending of total consumer units	consumer units headed by 55-to-64-year-olds	
READING	**$163.58**	**$197.86**	**121**
Newspaper subscriptions	51.70	68.18	132
Newspaper, nonsubscriptions	17.18	19.99	116
Magazine subscriptions	22.62	30.00	133
Magazines, nonsubscriptions	11.55	12.21	106
Books purchased through book clubs	10.18	11.73	115
Books not purchased through book clubs	49.50	55.41	112
Encyclopedia and other reference book sets	0.85	0.35	41

EDUCATION

	average spending of total consumer units	consumer units headed by 55-to-64-year-olds	
EDUCATION	**$570.70**	**$280.85**	**49**
College tuition	326.09	158.32	49
Elementary/high school tuition	90.14	28.26	31
Other school tuition	19.26	9.05	47
Other school expenses including rentals	27.44	19.70	72
Books, supplies for college	47.87	24.65	51
Books, supplies for elementary, high school	12.22	3.94	32
Books, supplies for day care, nursery school	3.13	2.05	65
Miscellaneous school expenses and supplies	44.55	34.88	78

(continued)

(continued from previous page)

	average spending of total consumer units	consumer units headed by 55-to-64-year-olds	
		average spending	indexed spending*
TOBACCO PRODUCTS AND SMOKING SUPPLIES	**$263.69**	**$291.74**	**111**
Cigarettes	232.31	260.95	112
Other tobacco products	28.78	29.30	102
Smoking accessories	2.60	1.49	57
FINANCIAL PRODUCTS AND SERVICES	**$847.31**	**$1,061.02**	**125**
Miscellaneous fees, gambling losses	53.32	114.95	216
Legal fees	135.79	191.07	141
Funeral expenses	63.05	172.26	273
Safe deposit box rental	6.69	10.13	151
Checking accounts, other bank service charges	24.51	21.80	89
Cemetery lots, vaults, and maintenance fees	19.65	15.79	80
Accounting fees	48.99	63.25	129
Miscellaneous personal services	39.17	15.44	39
Finance charges, except mortgage and vehicles	249.40	251.49	101
Occupational expenses	102.65	88.10	86
Expenses for other properties	99.61	109.59	110
Interest paid, home equity line of credit (other property)	0.49	0.29	59
Credit card memberships	3.98	6.86	172
CASH CONTRIBUTIONS	**$1,000.90**	**$1,207.61**	**121**
Cash contributions to nonhousehold members, including students, alimony, child support	253.98	306.14	121
Gifts of cash, stocks, bonds to nonhousehold members	225.03	236.53	105
Contributions to charities	101.95	126.73	124
Contributions to religious organizations	390.25	510.10	131
Contributions to educational organizations	16.88	11.00	65
Political contributions	6.20	10.12	163
Other contributions	6.61	7.00	106
PERSONAL INSURANCE AND PENSIONS	**$3,223.06**	**$3,465.75**	**108**
Life and other personal insurance	**378.63**	**522.55**	**138**
Life, endowment, annuity, other personal insurance	369.48	511.48	138
Other nonhealth insurance	9.15	11.07	121

(continued)

(continued from previous page)

	average spending of total consumer units	consumer units headed by 55-to-64-year-olds	
		average spending	indexed spending*
Pensions and Social Security	**$2,844.43**	**$2,943.20**	**103**
Deductions for government retirement	81.02	116.23	143
Deductions for railroad retirement	2.26	2.31	102
Deductions for private pensions	339.22	316.65	93
Nonpayroll deposit to retirement plans	376.65	617.06	164
Deductions for Social Security	2,045.27	1,890.94	92
PERSONAL TAXES	**$3,241.49**	**$3,500.08**	**108**
Federal income tax	2,467.90	2,662.70	108
State and local income tax	644.81	668.52	104
Other taxes	128.78	168.86	131
GIFTS*	**$1,059.44**	**$1,272.07**	**120**
FOOD	**67.73**	**77.17**	**114**
Cakes and cupcakes	2.73	1.79	66
Cheese	3.16	2.53	80
Fresh fruits	6.23	9.49	152
Candy and chewing gum	11.56	19.24	166
Board (including at school)	23.79	19.76	83
HOUSING	**273.22**	**327.72**	**120**
Housekeeping supplies	**36.73**	**44.02**	**120**
Miscellaneous household products	6.62	6.85	103
Lawn and garden supplies	2.04	2.62	128
Stationery, stationery supplies, giftwrap	20.71	23.31	113
Postage	4.08	5.80	142
Household textiles	**8.35**	**14.86**	**178**
Bedroom linens	4.18	7.10	170
Appliances and miscellaneous housewares	**27.34**	**54.76**	**200**
Major appliances	6.41	13.47	210
Small appliances and miscellaneous housewares	20.93	41.29	197
China and other dinnerware	2.46	0.47	19
Glassware	3.97	8.29	209
Nonelectric cookware	3.57	10.44	292
Tableware, nonelectric kitchenware	3.76	9.19	244
Small electric kitchen appliances	3.51	6.71	191

(continued)

	average spending of total consumer units	consumer units headed by 55-to-64-year-olds	
		average spending	indexed spending*
Miscellaneous household equipment	**$66.08**	**$95.09**	**144**
Infants' equipment	2.43	6.97	287
Other household decorative items	24.94	28.69	115
Telephones and accessories	3.14	11.31	360
Indoor plants, fresh flowers	16.63	21.03	126
Computers and hardware, nonbusiness use	7.19	7.19	100
Other housing	**134.72**	**118.99**	**88**
Repair or maintenance services	5.04	10.46	208
Housing while attending school	36.57	39.22	107
Natural gas (renter)	3.26	1.64	50
Electricity (renter)	13.58	8.33	61
Telephone services in home city, excluding mobile car phone	16.34	10.55	65
Water, sewerage maintenance (renter)	2.61	1.64	63
Baby-sitting and child care, someone else's home	3.73	–	–
Day care centers, nurseries, and preschools	19.65	9.68	49
Housekeeping services	4.07	0.64	16
Gardening, lawn care services	4.24	4.19	99
Moving, storage, freight express	2.59	3.43	132
Infants' furniture	2.07	2.41	116
APPAREL AND SERVICES	**252.24**	**332.11**	**132**
Men and boys, aged 2 or older	**61.29**	**87.32**	**142**
Men's coats and jackets	2.99	2.37	79
Men's accessories	4.73	3.23	68
Men's sweaters and vests	3.45	6.97	202
Men's active sportswear	3.31	0.77	23
Men's shirts	12.60	19.31	153
Men's pants	7.88	14.28	181
Boys' shirts	4.76	6.72	141
Boys' pants	3.25	5.23	161
Women and girls, aged 2 or older	**81.19**	**100.80**	**124**
Women's coats and jackets	3.17	1.83	58
Women's dresses	7.83	3.57	46
Women's vests and sweaters	6.06	5.52	91
Women's shirts, tops, blouses	12.70	16.91	133
Women's pants	6.09	4.00	66

(continued)

(continued from previous page)

	average spending of total consumer units	consumer units headed by 55-to-64-year-olds	
		average spending	indexed spending*
Women's shorts and shorts sets	$2.22	$5.94	268
Women's active sportswear	4.13	5.01	121
Women's nightwear	6.03	6.26	104
Women's hosiery	2.19	2.11	96
Women's suits	2.25	5.80	258
Women's accessories	5.86	4.67	80
Girls' dresses and suits	4.80	7.23	151
Girls' shirts, blouses, sweaters	5.38	4.93	92
Girls' skirts and pants	2.72	5.18	190
Children under age 2	**32.52**	**32.24**	**99**
Infant dresses, outerwear	7.54	8.46	112
Infant underwear	15.64	9.87	63
Infant nightwear, loungewear	2.94	4.95	168
Infant accessories	4.41	5.28	120
Other apparel products and services	**77.24**	**111.75**	**145**
Watches	7.41	1.20	16
Jewelry	41.18	55.08	134
Men's footwear	7.81	9.40	120
Boys' footwear	3.24	8.58	265
Women's footwear	11.83	27.79	235
Girls' footwear	3.81	6.19	162
TRANSPORTATION	**56.74**	**55.64**	**98**
New cars	7.05	–	–
New trucks	4.52	–	–
Used cars	9.67	7.52	78
Gasoline on out-of-town trips	13.52	21.30	158
Miscellaneous auto repair, servicing	2.94	0.12	4
Airline fares	6.89	9.27	135
Local transportation on out-of-town trips	2.25	4.52	201
Ship fares	3.09	5.36	173
HEALTH CARE	**30.35**	**59.79**	**197**
Physician services	2.23	0.37	17
Dental services	4.76	4.96	104
Hospital service other than room	2.79	1.06	38
Care in convalescent or nursing home	8.05	30.90	384
Prescription drugs	2.17	4.78	220

(continued)

(continued from previous page)

	average spending of total consumer units	consumer units headed by 55-to-64-year-olds	
		average spending	indexed spending*
ENTERTAINMENT	**$98.92**	**$138.45**	**140**
Toys, games, hobbies, tricycles	40.95	64.86	158
Movie, other admissions, out-of-town trips	7.77	10.82	139
Admission to sports events, out-of-town trips	2.59	3.61	139
Fees for recreational lessons	3.33	3.29	99
Community antenna or cable TV	3.96	2.25	57
Color TV, portable/table model	2.88	5.31	184
VCRs and video disc players	2.84	8.03	283
Video game hardware and software	2.17	4.77	220
Tape recorders and players	2.93	–	–
Sound components and component systems	2.09	2.32	111
Musical instruments and accessories	2.13	0.77	36
Veterinary services	2.18	1.62	74
Athletic gear, game tables, exercise equipment	5.97	5.08	85
EDUCATION	**155.44**	**97.81**	**63**
College tuition	119.23	55.83	47
Elementary, high school tuition	10.29	13.57	132
Other school expenses, including rentals	4.33	9.09	210
College books, supplies	9.80	6.28	64
Miscellaneous school supplies	8.35	10.44	125
ALL OTHER GIFTS	**124.80**	**183.40**	**147**
Out-of-town trip expenses	46.85	110.67	236

* The index compares the spending of consumer units headed by 55-to-64-year-olds with the spending of the average consumer unit by dividing the spending of 55-to-64-year-olds by average spending in each category and multiplying by 100. An index of 100 means the spending of 55-to-64-year-olds in the category equals average spending. An index of 132 means the spending of 55-to-64-year-olds is 32 percent above average, while an index of 75 means the spending of 55-to-64-year-olds is 25 percent below average.
** This figure does not include the amount paid for mortgage principle, which is considered an asset.
*** Expenditures on gifts are also included in the preceding product and service categories. Food spending, for example, includes the amount spent on food gifts. Only gift categories with spending of $2.00 or more by the average consumer unit are shown.
Note: The Bureau of Labor Statistics uses consumer units rather than households as the sampling unit in the Consumer Expenditure Survey. For the definition of consumer unit, see the Glossary. (–) means the sample is too small to make a reliable estimate.
Source: Bureau of Labor Statistics, unpublished data from the 1997 Consumer Expenditure Survey; calculations by New Strategist

Householders Aged 65 to 74 Spend More Than Average on Many Items

Householders aged 65 to 74 spend 80 percent as much as the average household.

In 1997, householders aged 65 to 74 spent $27,792, less than the $34,819 spent by the average household. The spending of householders in this age group is well below average because household size is small and most 65-to-74-year-olds are retired. Nevertheless, the spending of householders aged 65 to 74 is rising to meet the average. In 1997, they spent 20 percent less than the average household, while in 1990 they spent 27 percent less.

Householders aged 65 to 74 spend well above average on a number of items. They spend 49 percent more on coffee (reflecting the fact that older Americans are the biggest coffee drinkers). They spend 32 percent more on owned vacation homes, 37 percent more on lawn and garden services, 36 percent more on postage (reflecting the preferences of older Americans for letter writing rather than e-mailing). This age group spends 83 percent more than average on floor coverings, and more than twice the average amount on smoke alarms. Older Americans are the biggest spenders on travel, which accounts for the 80 percent above-average spending on ship fares. Not surprisingly, householders aged 65 to 74 spend much more than the average household on health care. They spend 19 percent more than average on reading materials, and they are the biggest spenders on radios. They spend twice as much as the average household on cash gifts to nonhousehold members.

♦ As better-educated and more affluent generations age into their sixties and seventies, older Americans aren't acting old anymore. Businesses must abandon their patronizing "mature market" campaigns and find new ways to reach older age groups.

Average and Indexed Spending of Householders Aged 65 to 74, 1997

(average annual spending of total consumer units and average annual and indexed spending of consumer units headed by 65-to-74-year-olds, 1997)

	average spending of total consumer units	consumer units headed by 65-to-74-year-olds	
		average spending	indexed spending*
Number of consumer units (in 000s)	105,576	12,109	–
Average before-tax income	$39,926.00	$27,492.00	69
Average annual spending	34,819.38	27,791.97	80
FOOD	**$4,801.35**	**$4,066.37**	**85**
FOOD AT HOME	2,880.00	2,599.98	90
Cereals and bakery products	453.00	402.21	89
Cereals and cereal products	161.39	130.15	81
Flour	8.79	8.22	94
Prepared flour mixes	15.04	13.60	90
Ready-to-eat and cooked cereals	91.15	74.67	82
Rice	18.37	12.73	69
Pasta, cornmeal, and other cereal products	28.03	20.93	75
Bakery products	291.60	272.07	93
Bread	83.43	85.75	103
White bread	40.89	39.64	97
Bread, other than white	42.55	46.11	108
Crackers and cookies	68.27	67.88	99
Cookies	45.01	44.43	99
Crackers	23.26	23.45	101
Frozen and refrigerated bakery products	23.35	22.86	98
Other bakery products	116.56	95.58	82
Biscuits and rolls	40.96	34.75	85
Cakes and cupcakes	34.51	24.94	72
Bread and cracker products	4.45	3.95	89
Sweetrolls, coffee cakes, doughnuts	23.13	20.85	90
Pies, tarts, turnovers	13.50	11.10	82
Meats, poultry, fish, and eggs	**743.12**	**675.96**	**91**
Beef	223.55	190.43	85
Ground beef	82.77	69.45	84

(continued)

(continued from previous page)

	average spending of total consumer units	consumer units headed by 65-to-74-year-olds	
		average spending	indexed spending*
Roast	$40.48	$37.33	92
Chuck roast	13.02	10.72	82
Round roast	12.85	12.91	100
Other roast	14.61	13.71	94
Steak	87.48	70.38	80
Round steak	16.70	10.59	63
Sirloin steak	23.01	24.39	106
Other steak	47.76	35.40	74
Other beef	12.81	13.26	104
Pork	157.13	148.00	94
Bacon	25.42	23.50	92
Pork chops	39.23	30.62	78
Ham	37.28	33.39	90
Ham, not canned	35.12	31.43	89
Canned ham	2.16	1.96	91
Sausage	24.12	21.36	89
Other pork	31.07	39.13	126
Other meats	96.03	91.68	95
Frankfurters	22.83	19.12	84
Lunch meats (cold cuts)	65.55	65.62	100
Bologna, liverwurst, salami	23.82	27.19	114
Other lunch meats	41.73	38.42	92
Lamb, organ meats, and others	7.92	6.95	88
Lamb and organ meats	7.34	6.95	95
Mutton, goat, and game	0.58	–	–
Poultry	145.01	135.42	93
Fresh and frozen chickens	113.38	103.78	92
Fresh and frozen whole chickens	29.77	26.05	88
Fresh and frozen chicken parts	83.61	77.73	93
Other poultry	31.63	31.64	100
Fish and seafood	88.54	77.32	87
Canned fish and seafood	14.18	14.52	102
Fresh fish and shellfish	50.95	41.06	81
Frozen fish and shellfish	23.41	21.75	93
Eggs	32.59	33.11	102

(continued)

(continued from previous page)

	average spending of total consumer units	consumer units headed by 65-to-74-year-olds	
		average spending	indexed spending*
Dairy products	**$313.68**	**$284.24**	**91**
Fresh milk and cream	128.12	117.64	92
Fresh milk, all types	118.78	110.23	93
Cream	9.34	7.41	79
Other dairy products	185.56	166.60	90
Butter	14.63	13.95	95
Cheese	94.33	78.69	83
Ice cream and related products	52.91	57.32	108
Miscellaneous dairy products	23.69	16.64	70
Fruits and vegetables	**475.62**	**471.62**	**99**
Fresh fruits	150.47	151.15	100
Apples	28.47	24.34	85
Bananas	31.44	33.10	105
Oranges	17.62	16.68	95
Citrus fruits, excluding oranges	13.42	13.05	97
Other fresh fruits	59.52	63.99	108
Fresh vegetables	142.75	143.46	100
Potatoes	26.15	26.99	103
Lettuce	19.27	19.73	102
Tomatoes	23.87	22.37	94
Other fresh vegetables	73.46	74.37	101
Processed fruits	102.28	100.75	99
Frozen fruits and fruit juices	15.02	14.39	96
Frozen orange juice	8.44	9.04	107
Frozen fruits	2.02	2.10	104
Frozen fruit juices, excluding orange juice	4.57	3.24	71
Canned fruits	13.97	14.86	106
Dried fruits	6.03	6.19	103
Fresh fruit juice	19.82	20.76	105
Canned and bottled fruit juice	47.43	44.55	94
Processed vegetables	80.13	76.25	95
Frozen vegetables	26.57	24.51	92
Canned and dried vegetables and juices	53.56	51.74	97
Canned beans	11.79	10.92	93
Canned corn	7.26	6.57	90
Canned miscellaneous vegetables	16.80	16.97	101
Dried peas	0.23	0.13	57

(continued)

(continued from previous page)

	average spending of total consumer units	consumer units headed by 65-to-74-year-olds	
		average spending	indexed spending*
Dried beans	$2.58	$2.62	102
Dried miscellaneous vegetables	7.18	7.41	103
Dried processed vegetables	0.22	0.38	173
Frozen vegetable juices	0.28	0.21	75
Fresh and canned vegetable juices	7.22	6.54	91
Other food at home	**894.58**	**765.94**	**86**
Sugar and other sweets	114.30	110.60	97
Candy and chewing gum	69.26	62.83	91
Sugar	18.93	19.48	103
Artificial sweeteners	3.48	5.07	146
Jams, preserves, other sweets	22.63	23.21	103
Fats and oils	81.05	82.15	101
Margarine	11.74	12.09	103
Fats and oils	24.50	25.12	103
Salad dressings	24.68	23.53	95
Nondairy cream and imitation milk	8.50	10.97	129
Peanut butter	11.63	10.44	90
Miscellaneous foods	403.06	299.17	74
Frozen prepared foods	77.61	48.02	62
Frozen meals	20.73	14.04	68
Other frozen prepared foods	56.88	33.98	60
Canned and packaged soups	32.87	35.86	109
Potato chips, nuts, and other snacks	84.53	71.02	84
Potato chips and other snacks	66.83	49.96	75
Nuts	17.70	21.06	119
Condiments and seasonings	86.12	68.08	79
Salt, spices, and other seasonings	19.07	16.96	89
Olives, pickles, relishes	10.54	9.41	89
Sauces and gravies	39.86	27.46	69
Baking needs and miscellaneous products	16.65	14.26	86
Other canned/packaged prepared foods	121.94	76.18	62
Prepared salads	15.05	11.73	78
Prepared desserts	9.95	8.68	87
Baby food	27.86	8.03	29
Miscellaneous prepared foods	68.44	47.32	69
Vitamin supplements	0.64	0.42	66

(continued)

(continued from previous page)

	average spending of total consumer units	consumer units headed by 65-to-74-year-olds	
		average spending	indexed spending*
Nonalcoholic beverages	$244.51	$217.24	89
Cola	90.51	66.96	74
Other carbonated drinks	42.94	32.57	76
Coffee	48.80	72.50	149
Roasted coffee	32.65	49.73	152
Instant and freeze-dried coffee	16.15	22.77	141
Noncarbonated fruit flavored drinks, including nonfrozen lemonade	19.22	8.62	45
Tea	14.76	17.40	118
Nonalcoholic beer	0.34	0.35	103
Other nonalcoholic beverages and ice	27.93	18.82	67
Food prepared by household on out-of-town trips	51.65	56.78	110
FOOD AWAY FROM HOME	**1,921.35**	**1,466.39**	**76**
Meals at restaurants, carry-outs, other	**1,477.51**	**1,177.32**	**80**
Lunch	501.92	354.99	71
Dinner	740.70	645.38	87
Snacks and nonalcoholic beverages	119.38	53.14	45
Breakfast and brunch	115.51	123.81	107
Board (including at school)	**51.88**	**17.76**	**34**
Catered affairs	**83.52**	**33.58**	**40**
Food on out-of-town trips	**223.90**	**222.79**	**100**
School lunches	**54.03**	**6.03**	**11**
Meals as pay	**30.51**	**8.92**	**29**
ALCOHOLIC BEVERAGES	**$309.22**	**$268.08**	**87**
At home	**180.13**	**153.25**	**85**
Beer and ale	90.92	60.05	66
Whiskey	13.40	11.55	86
Wine	55.32	59.95	108
Other alcoholic beverages	20.50	21.70	106
Away from home	**129.09**	**114.83**	**89**
Beer and ale	39.50	32.73	83
Wine	24.30	24.04	99
Other alcoholic beverages	32.81	33.76	103
Alcoholic beverages purchased on trips	32.48	24.30	75

(continued)

(continued from previous page)

	average spending of total consumer units	consumer units headed by 65-to-74-year-olds	
		average spending	indexed spending*
HOUSING	**$11,272.04**	**$8,876.48**	**79**
SHELTER	**6,343.87**	**4,364.95**	**69**
Owned dwellings**	**3,934.87**	**3,021.24**	**77**
Mortgage interest and charges	2,225.26	778.89	35
Mortgage interest	2,109.06	716.27	34
Interest paid, home equity loan	57.21	30.85	54
Interest paid, home equity line of credit	58.84	31.77	54
Prepayment penalty charges	0.16	–	–
Property taxes	971.15	1,197.12	123
Maintenance, repairs, insurance, other expenses	738.46	1,045.23	142
Homeowner's and related insurance	230.91	329.10	143
Fire and extended coverage	8.02	10.97	137
Homeowner's insurance	222.88	318.14	143
Ground rent	37.16	59.56	160
Maintenance and repair services	365.61	543.75	149
Painting and papering	45.31	56.55	125
Plumbing and water heating	36.61	64.30	176
Heat, air conditioning, electrical work	63.28	93.27	147
Roofing and gutters	72.99	116.75	160
Other repair and maintenance services	124.47	175.68	141
Repair/replacement of hard surface flooring	21.17	32.27	152
Repair of built-in appliances	1.79	4.93	275
Maintenance and repair materials	83.91	79.79	95
Paints, wallpaper, and supplies	18.33	11.44	62
Tools/equipment for painting, wallpapering	1.97	1.23	62
Plumbing supplies and equipment	6.87	6.48	94
Electrical supplies, heating/cooling equipment	4.55	10.01	220
Hard surface flooring, repair and replacement	7.13	9.49	133
Roofing and gutters	7.77	4.13	53
Plaster, paneling, siding, windows, doors, screens, awnings	14.97	21.45	143
Patio, walk, fence, driveway, masonry, brick, and stucco work	0.92	0.63	68
Landscape maintenance	5.19	4.76	92
Miscellaneous supplies and equipment	16.21	10.18	63
Insulation, other maintenance/repair	9.22	2.61	28

(continued)

(continued from previous page)

	average spending of total consumer units	consumer units headed by 65-to-74-year-olds	
		average spending	indexed spending*
Finish basement, remodel rooms, build patios, walks, etc.	$6.99	$7.57	108
Property management and security	19.58	30.63	156
Property management	16.49	24.99	152
Management and upkeep services for security	3.09	5.65	183
Parking	1.30	2.39	184
Rented dwellings	**1,983.18**	**911.21**	**46**
Rent	1,876.81	846.89	45
Rent as pay	72.36	37.50	52
Maintenance, insurance, and other expenses	34.02	26.83	79
Tenant's insurance	9.76	6.09	62
Maintenance and repair services	16.62	18.95	114
Repair or maintenance services	15.42	12.57	82
Repair and replacement of hard surface flooring	1.17	6.20	530
Repair of built-in appliances	0.03	0.17	567
Maintenance and repair materials	7.63	1.79	23
Paint, wallpaper, and supplies	1.57	0.40	25
Painting and wallpapering	0.17	0.04	24
Plastering, paneling, roofing, gutters, etc.	1.22	0.04	3
Patio, walk, fence, driveway, masonry, brick, and stucco work	0.02	–	–
Plumbing supplies and equipment	0.36	0.31	86
Electrical supplies, heating and cooling equipment	0.08	0.01	13
Miscellaneous supplies and equipment	2.94	0.85	29
Insulation, other maintenance and repair	1.04	0.08	8
Materials for additions, finishing basements, remodeling rooms	1.65	0.46	28
Construction materials for jobs not started	0.25	0.31	124
Hard surface flooring	0.74	0.14	19
Landscape maintenance	0.53	–	–
Other lodging	**425.82**	**432.49**	**102**
Owned vacation homes	133.69	177.11	132
Mortgage interest and charges	58.02	45.00	78
Mortgage interest	56.46	41.50	74
Interest paid, home equity loan	0.66	0.86	130
Interest paid, home equity line of credit	0.89	2.64	297

(continued)

(continued from previous page)

	average spending of total consumer units	consumer units headed by 65-to-74-year-olds	
		average spending	indexed spending*
Property taxes	$54.83	$90.59	165
Maintenance, insurance, and other expenses	20.84	41.52	199
Homeowner's and related insurance	5.03	15.85	315
Homeowner's insurance	4.67	14.86	318
Fire and extended coverage	0.36	0.99	275
Ground rent	1.63	1.48	91
Maintenance and repair services	9.66	17.59	182
Maintenance and repair materials	0.81	0.13	16
Property management and security	3.41	6.19	182
Property management	2.96	5.61	190
Management and upkeep services for security	0.45	0.58	129
Parking	0.29	0.27	93
Housing while attending school	66.35	13.65	21
Lodging on out-of-town trips	225.77	241.73	107
UTILITIES, FUELS & PUBLIC SERVICES	**2,412.30**	**2,321.32**	**96**
Natural gas	**300.96**	**341.20**	**113**
Natural gas (renter)	60.81	24.56	40
Natural gas (owner)	238.55	312.99	131
Natural gas (vacation)	1.60	3.65	228
Electricity	**908.67**	**910.88**	**100**
Electricity (renter)	212.54	97.06	46
Electricity (owner)	687.53	797.52	116
Electricity (vacation)	8.60	16.30	190
Fuel oil and other fuels	**107.72**	**133.88**	**124**
Fuel oil	55.18	74.89	136
Fuel oil (renter)	4.92	2.33	47
Fuel oil (owner)	49.77	72.03	145
Fuel oil (vacation)	0.49	0.53	108
Coal	0.99	–	–
Coal (renter)	0.02	–	–
Coal (owner)	0.97	–	–
Bottled/tank gas	43.84	53.87	123
Gas (renter)	4.66	5.02	108
Gas (owner)	36.37	46.87	129
Gas (vacation)	2.81	1.97	70

(continued)

(continued from previous page)

	average spending of total consumer units	consumer units headed by 65-to-74-year-olds	
		average spending	indexed spending*
Wood and other fuels	$7.72	$5.13	66
Wood and other fuels (renter)	1.53	0.67	44
Wood and other fuels (owner)	5.80	4.45	77
Wood and other fuels (vacation)	0.39	–	–
Telephone services	**809.05**	**626.80**	**77**
Telephone services in home city, excluding mobile car phones	756.44	601.41	80
Telephone services for mobile car phones	52.61	25.39	48
Water and other public services	**285.90**	**308.56**	**108**
Water and sewerage maintenance	207.28	222.19	107
Water and sewerage maintenance (renter)	28.28	14.49	51
Water and sewerage maintenance (owner)	176.95	204.37	115
Water and sewerage maintenance (vacation)	2.06	3.33	162
Trash and garbage collection	76.00	83.53	110
Trash and garbage collection (renter)	8.78	4.83	55
Trash and garbage collection (owner)	65.66	76.87	117
Trash and garbage collection (vacation)	1.56	1.84	118
Septic tank cleaning	2.62	2.83	108
Septic tank cleaning (renter)	0.19	–	–
Septic tank cleaning (owner)	2.41	2.83	117
HOUSEHOLD OPERATIONS	**548.50**	**391.53**	**71**
Personal services	**263.10**	**74.96**	**28**
Baby-sitting and child care in your own home	34.39	1.21	4
Baby-sitting and child care in someone else's home	37.37	0.16	0
Care for elderly, invalids, handicapped, etc.	26.95	53.43	198
Adult day care centers	3.79	15.09	398
Day care centers, nurseries, and preschools	160.60	5.08	3
Other household expenses	**285.40**	**316.57**	**111**
Housekeeping services	75.34	74.29	99
Gardening, lawn care services	72.44	99.57	137
Water softening services	4.51	6.29	139
Nonclothing laundry and dry cleaning, sent out	10.20	5.84	57
Nonclothing laundry and dry cleaning, coin-operated	4.91	2.47	50
Termite/pest control services	11.55	18.45	160
Other home services	15.94	18.59	117
Termite/pest control products	0.12	0.10	83

(continued)

(continued from previous page)

	average spending of total consumer units	consumer units headed by 65-to-74-year-olds	
		average spending	indexed spending*
Moving, storage, and freight express	$34.75	$29.83	86
Appliance repair, including service center	13.50	16.97	126
Reupholstering and furniture repair	10.87	20.69	190
Repairs/rentals of lawn/garden equipment, hand/power tools, etc.	5.13	7.80	152
Appliance rental	1.05	0.29	28
Rental of office equipment for nonbusiness use	0.43	0.13	30
Repair of miscellaneous household equipment and furnishings	1.53	4.25	278
Repair of computer systems for nonbusiness use	2.47	4.13	167
Computer information services	20.65	6.87	33
HOUSEKEEPING SUPPLIES	**454.93**	**449.46**	**99**
Laundry and cleaning supplies	**115.85**	**104.57**	**90**
Soaps and detergents	65.05	54.39	84
Other laundry cleaning products	50.80	50.18	99
Other household products	**210.07**	**207.20**	**99**
Cleansing and toilet tissue, paper towels, and napkins	64.42	67.92	105
Miscellaneous household products	89.90	64.61	72
Lawn and garden supplies	55.74	74.68	134
Postage and stationery	**129.01**	**137.69**	**107**
Stationery, stationery supplies, giftwrap	62.61	50.66	81
Postage	62.53	85.01	136
Delivery services	3.88	2.02	52
HOUSEHOLD FURNISHINGS & EQUIPMENT	**1,512.44**	**1,349.23**	**89**
Household textiles	**79.12**	**71.69**	**91**
Bathroom linens	11.13	10.71	96
Bedroom linens	34.28	29.61	86
Kitchen and dining room linens	2.40	2.40	100
Curtains and draperies	16.73	13.02	78
Slipcovers and decorative pillows	2.10	1.89	90
Sewing materials for household items	11.20	12.96	116
Other linens	1.28	1.10	86
Furniture	**387.34**	**268.08**	**69**
Mattresses and springs	46.56	30.47	65
Other bedroom furniture	63.99	21.79	34

(continued)

(continued from previous page)

	average spending of total consumer units	consumer units headed by 65-to-74-year-olds	
		average spending	indexed spending*
Sofas	$93.81	$53.10	57
Living room chairs	47.42	54.74	115
Living room tables	20.60	16.78	81
Kitchen and dining room furniture	48.69	37.34	77
Infants' furniture	9.87	3.41	35
Outdoor furniture	13.61	9.71	71
Wall units, cabinets, and other furniture	42.81	40.75	95
Floor coverings	**77.74**	**142.00**	**183**
Wall-to-wall carpeting	38.82	35.38	91
Wall-to-wall carpeting (renter)	1.94	0.02	1
Wall-to-wall carpeting, installed	1.37	–	–
Wall-to-wall carpeting, not installed carpet squares	0.56	0.02	4
Wall-to-wall carpeting, replacement (owner)	36.88	35.36	96
Wall-to-wall carpeting, not installed carpet squares	2.68	1.71	64
Wall-to-wall carpeting, installed	34.20	33.65	98
Room-size rugs and other floor covering, nonpermanent	38.93	106.62	274
Major appliances	**169.18**	**166.86**	**99**
Dishwashers (built-in), garbage disposals, range hoods (renter)	0.82	0.16	20
Dishwashers (built-in), garbage disposals, range hoods (owner)	11.65	15.15	130
Refrigerators and freezers (renter)	9.52	5.59	59
Refrigerators and freezers (owner)	48.08	47.89	100
Washing machines (renter)	5.46	1.20	22
Washing machines (owner)	17.56	27.78	158
Clothes dryers (renter)	4.40	0.86	20
Clothes dryers (owner)	11.82	11.97	101
Cooking stoves, ovens (renter)	2.83	0.84	30
Cooking stoves, ovens (owner)	19.23	19.21	100
Microwave ovens (renter)	2.96	1.45	49
Microwave ovens (owner)	6.63	7.10	107
Portable dishwashers (renter)	0.41	–	–
Portable dishwashers (owner)	0.26	0.80	308
Window air conditioners (renter)	1.69	–	–
Window air conditioners (owner)	3.24	2.27	70

(continued)

(continued from previous page)

	average spending of total consumer units	consumer units headed by 65-to-74-year-olds	
		average spending	indexed spending*
Electric floor cleaning equipment	$15.68	$18.09	115
Sewing machines	3.55	5.42	153
Miscellaneous household appliances	**3.39**	**1.09**	**32**
Small appliances and miscellaneous housewares	91.91	78.92	86
Housewares	66.12	50.57	76
Plastic dinnerware	1.75	0.93	53
China and other dinnerware	8.86	2.37	27
Flatware	4.68	4.35	93
Glassware	8.25	11.78	143
Silver serving pieces	2.31	2.26	98
Other serving pieces	1.74	1.20	69
Nonelectric cookware	15.05	14.67	97
Tableware, nonelectric kitchenware	23.48	13.00	55
Small appliances	25.79	28.35	110
Small electric kitchen appliances	16.67	18.04	108
Portable heating and cooling equipment	9.12	10.31	113
Miscellaneous household equipment	**707.15**	**621.68**	**88**
Window coverings	13.71	10.15	74
Infants' equipment	7.05	0.93	13
Laundry and cleaning equipment	13.70	17.02	124
Outdoor equipment	18.42	6.12	33
Clocks	4.51	2.21	49
Lamps and lighting fixtures	12.53	16.74	134
Other household decorative items	134.12	182.61	136
Telephones and accessories	96.54	86.81	90
Lawn and garden equipment	39.37	37.64	96
Power tools	16.31	11.28	69
Office furniture for home use	10.61	2.51	24
Hand tools	9.29	4.79	52
Indoor plants and fresh flowers	52.33	54.11	103
Closet and storage items	8.94	14.88	166
Rental of furniture	3.41	0.85	25
Luggage	9.72	11.06	114
Computers and computer hardware, nonbusiness use	162.66	94.28	58
Computer software and accessories, nonbusiness use	24.72	10.54	43
Telephone answering devices	3.31	1.50	45

(continued)

(continued from previous page)

	average spending of total consumer units	consumer units headed by 65-to-74-year-olds	
		average spending	indexed spending*
Calculators	$1.92	$0.25	13
Business equipment for home use	2.33	2.68	115
Other hardware	23.27	14.66	63
Smoke alarms (owner)	0.86	2.16	251
Smoke alarms (renter)	0.19	–	–
Other household appliances (owner)	8.78	14.94	170
Other household appliances (renter)	1.47	0.40	27
Miscellaneous household equipment and parts	27.10	20.56	76
APPAREL AND SERVICES	**$1,729.06**	**$1,302.46**	**75**
Men's apparel	**322.98**	**261.83**	**81**
Suits	35.18	22.85	65
Sportcoats and tailored jackets	15.19	18.54	122
Coats and jackets	29.80	15.84	53
Underwear	12.52	10.96	88
Hosiery	9.91	9.13	92
Nightwear	2.93	0.51	17
Accessories	30.27	28.68	95
Sweaters and vests	15.84	13.92	88
Active sportswear	12.24	14.36	117
Shirts	75.81	71.72	95
Pants	64.52	38.27	59
Shorts and shorts sets	13.76	14.66	107
Uniforms	2.25	–	–
Costumes	2.79	2.39	86
Boys' (aged 2 to 15) apparel	**83.88**	**32.71**	**39**
Coats and jackets	8.33	3.97	48
Sweaters	2.81	1.12	40
Shirts	18.34	7.78	42
Underwear	3.08	0.18	6
Nightwear	1.94	0.23	12
Hosiery	3.66	0.86	23
Accessories	3.94	0.39	10
Suits, sportcoats, and vests	2.89	2.68	93
Pants	21.85	7.77	36
Shorts and shorts sets	8.66	2.39	28
Uniforms	4.41	3.44	78

(continued)

(continued from previous page)

	average spending of total consumer units	consumer units headed by 65-to-74-year-olds	
		average spending	indexed spending*
Active sportswear	$2.65	$0.83	31
Costumes	1.33	1.08	81
Women's apparel	**574.26**	**521.12**	**91**
Coats and jackets	44.33	35.25	80
Dresses	84.25	67.26	80
Sportcoats and tailored jackets	2.77	3.49	126
Sweaters and vests	40.39	40.01	99
Shirts, blouses, and tops	93.73	90.68	97
Skirts	18.35	19.58	107
Pants	70.48	79.69	113
Shorts and shorts sets	22.34	22.33	100
Active sportswear	29.74	22.29	75
Nightwear	24.73	14.71	59
Undergarments	29.71	20.26	68
Hosiery	22.88	20.56	90
Suits	38.30	35.18	92
Accessories	45.42	47.13	104
Uniforms	3.20	–	–
Costumes	3.64	2.71	74
Girls' (aged 2 to 15) apparel	**106.01**	**31.38**	**30**
Coats and jackets	6.50	4.47	69
Dresses and suits	13.42	4.79	36
Shirts, blouses, and sweaters	25.74	2.02	8
Skirts and pants	19.49	7.09	36
Shorts and shorts sets	9.67	3.68	38
Active sportswear	6.86	1.62	24
Underwear and nightwear	6.75	3.10	46
Hosiery	5.29	1.78	34
Accessories	5.64	1.16	21
Uniforms	3.17	0.70	22
Costumes	3.48	0.98	28
Children under age 2	**77.05**	**24.54**	**32**
Coats, jackets, and snowsuits	3.28	1.82	55
Outerwear including dresses	15.01	4.73	32
Underwear	43.93	11.04	25
Nightwear and loungewear	4.38	2.96	68
Accessories	10.45	3.99	38

(continued)

	average spending of total consumer units	consumer units headed by 65-to-74-year-olds	
		average spending	indexed spending*
Footwear	**$314.52**	**$231.99**	**74**
Men's	100.43	83.29	83
Boys'	27.90	4.80	17
Women's	157.11	137.24	87
Girls'	29.08	6.66	23
Other apparel products and services	**250.35**	**198.90**	**79**
Material for making clothes	4.07	7.24	178
Sewing patterns and notions	4.82	5.18	107
Watches	29.70	20.83	70
Jewelry	142.02	129.51	91
Shoe repair and other shoe services	2.38	1.95	82
Coin-operated apparel laundry and dry cleaning	20.79	6.63	32
Apparel alteration, repair, and tailoring services	6.10	7.75	127
Clothing rental	3.85	0.67	17
Watch and jewelry repair	5.08	6.79	134
Professional laundry, dry cleaning	31.24	11.56	37
Clothing storage	0.30	0.79	263
TRANSPORTATION	**$6,456.86**	**$4,644.75**	**72**
VEHICLE PURCHASES	**2,735.76**	**1,825.52**	**67**
Cars and trucks, new	**1,228.89**	**942.16**	**77**
New cars	700.22	668.54	95
New trucks	528.67	273.62	52
Cars and trucks, used	**1,463.52**	**849.56**	**58**
Used cars	895.31	579.11	65
Used trucks	568.22	270.44	48
Other vehicles	**43.35**	**33.80**	**78**
New motorcycles	26.39	33.80	128
Used motorcycles	15.32	–	–
GASOLINE AND MOTOR OIL	**1,097.52**	**800.64**	**73**
Gasoline	985.31	705.02	72
Diesel fuel	10.10	6.83	68
Gasoline on out-of-town trips	89.11	82.04	92
Motor oil	12.10	5.93	49
Motor oil on out-of-town trips	0.90	0.83	92

(continued)

(continued from previous page)

	average spending of total consumer units	consumer units headed by 65-to-74-year-olds	
		average spending	indexed spending*
OTHER VEHICLE EXPENSES	**$2,230.41**	**$1,640.52**	**74**
Vehicle finance charges	**292.81**	**136.66**	**47**
Automobile finance charges	161.70	70.02	43
Truck finance charges	116.10	54.22	47
Motorcycle and plane finance charges	1.52	1.37	90
Other vehicle finance charges	13.49	11.06	82
Maintenance and repairs	**681.62**	**570.64**	**84**
Coolant, additives, brake, transmission fluids	5.70	3.55	62
Tires	87.94	68.88	78
Parts, equipment, and accessories	51.31	22.31	43
Vehicle audio equipment	2.00	–	–
Vehicle products	6.95	4.42	64
Miscellaneous auto repair, servicing	51.74	54.71	106
Body work and painting	32.29	21.72	67
Clutch, transmission repair	47.92	28.02	58
Drive shaft and rear-end repair	5.73	3.48	61
Brake work	55.82	59.75	107
Repair to steering or front-end	17.41	13.84	79
Repair to engine cooling system	19.98	20.63	103
Motor tune-up	45.05	40.77	90
Lube, oil change, and oil filters	54.29	53.82	99
Front-end alignment, wheel balance, rotation	12.13	13.47	111
Shock absorber replacement	4.98	7.63	153
Gas tank repair, replacement	1.20	0.26	22
Tire repair and other repair work	29.63	29.99	101
Vehicle air conditioning repair	19.07	20.36	107
Exhaust system repair	18.52	18.18	98
Electrical system repair	29.34	37.42	128
Motor repair, replacement	75.45	41.85	55
Auto repair service policy	7.16	5.57	78
Vehicle insurance	**754.99**	**661.03**	**88**
Vehicle rental, leases, licenses, other charges	**500.99**	**272.19**	**54**
Leased and rented vehicles	331.25	136.12	41
Rented vehicles	41.03	24.09	59
Auto rental	7.73	2.06	27
Auto rental, out-of-town trips	26.78	15.71	59

(continued)

(continued from previous page)

	average spending of total consumer units	consumer units headed by 65-to-74-year-olds	
		average spending	indexed spending*
Truck rental	$1.85	$1.43	77
Truck rental, out-of-town trips	4.29	4.89	114
Leased vehicles	290.22	112.02	39
Car lease payments	162.28	81.98	51
Cash downpayment (car lease)	16.16	4.62	29
Termination fee (car lease)	1.81	7.08	391
Truck lease payments	98.37	15.42	16
Cash downpayment (truck lease)	10.63	2.93	28
Termination fee (truck lease)	0.97	–	–
State and local registration	94.62	81.85	87
Driver's license	7.42	6.03	81
Vehicle inspection	8.74	8.51	97
Parking fees	28.20	13.86	49
Parking fees in home city, excluding residence	24.37	10.61	44
Parking fees, out-of-town trips	3.83	3.25	85
Tolls	13.19	6.89	52
Tolls on out-of-town trips	4.32	4.23	98
Towing charges	5.04	3.58	71
Automobile service clubs	8.19	11.12	136
PUBLIC TRANSPORTATION	**393.16**	**378.06**	**96**
Airline fares	248.82	226.35	91
Intercity bus fares	10.51	13.89	132
Intracity mass transit fares	55.77	34.54	62
Local transportation on out-of-town trips	12.61	15.31	121
Taxi fares and limousine service on trips	7.40	8.99	121
Taxi fares and limousine service	9.51	6.06	64
Intercity train fares	21.19	25.12	119
Ship fares	26.40	47.49	180
School bus	0.95	0.33	35
HEALTH CARE	**$1,840.71**	**$2,900.35**	**158**
HEALTH INSURANCE	**881.28**	**1,547.03**	**176**
Commercial health insurance	**203.37**	**226.02**	**111**
Traditional fee-for-service health plan (not BCBS)	100.09	111.55	111
Preferred provider health plan (not BCBS)	103.29	114.47	111
Blue Cross, Blue Shield	**192.51**	**273.20**	**142**
Traditional fee-for-service health plan	62.93	100.33	159

(continued)

(continued from previous page)

	average spending of total consumer units	consumer units headed by 65-to-74-year-olds	
		average spending	indexed spending*
Preferred provider health plan	$46.45	$29.76	64
Health maintenance organization	47.39	26.39	56
Commercial Medicare supplement	31.92	113.28	355
Other BCBS health insurance	3.82	3.44	90
Health maintenance plans (HMOs)	**229.07**	**126.92**	**55**
Medicare payments	**160.92**	**642.99**	**400**
Commercial Medicare supplements/			
other health insurance	**95.40**	**277.90**	**291**
Commercial Medicare supplement (not BCBS)	60.66	223.73	369
Other health insurance (not BCBS)	34.74	54.17	156
MEDICAL SERVICES	**531.04**	**636.26**	**120**
Physician's services	133.59	134.74	101
Dental services	203.56	274.25	135
Eye care services	27.14	32.61	120
Service by professionals other than physicians	37.03	24.37	66
Lab tests, X-rays	22.93	21.64	94
Hospital room	35.07	25.88	74
Hospital services other than room	52.37	107.37	205
Care in convalescent or nursing home	13.09	4.10	31
Repair of medical equipment	0.62	2.11	340
Other medical services	5.64	9.20	163
DRUGS	**320.44**	**594.18**	**185**
Nonprescription drugs	75.43	108.32	144
Nonprescription vitamins	28.43	55.07	194
Prescription drugs	216.58	430.80	199
MEDICAL SUPPLIES	**107.95**	**122.88**	**114**
Eyeglasses and contact lenses	59.73	52.08	87
Hearing aids	11.42	16.41	144
Topicals and dressings	29.47	34.77	118
Medical equipment for general use	2.43	3.82	157
Supportive/convalescent medical equipment	2.62	11.02	421
Rental of medical equipment	0.60	1.12	187
Rental of supportive, convalescent medical equipment	1.67	3.66	219
ENTERTAINMENT	**$1,813.28**	**$1,300.32**	**72**
FEES AND ADMISSIONS	**470.74**	**389.95**	**83**

(continued)

(continued from previous page)

	average spending of total consumer units	consumer units headed by 65-to-74-year-olds	
		average spending	indexed spending*
Recreation expenses, out-of-town trips	$24.70	$16.49	67
Social, recreation, civic club membership	75.12	98.87	132
Fees for participant sports	72.62	62.61	86
Participant sports, out-of-town trips	30.30	21.80	72
Movie, theater, opera, ballet	86.71	71.27	82
Movie, other admissions, out-of-town trips	41.93	45.69	109
Admission to sports events	33.51	23.98	72
Admission to sports events, out-of-town trips	13.98	15.23	109
Fees for recreational lessons	67.17	17.52	26
Other entertainment services, out-of-town trips	24.70	16.49	67
TELEVISION, RADIO, SOUND EQUIPMENT	**577.33**	**470.22**	**81**
Television	**403.51**	**359.25**	**89**
Community antenna or cable TV	262.34	266.65	102
Black and white TV sets	0.67	0.10	15
Color TV, console	25.17	16.44	65
Color TV, portable/table model	39.96	32.52	81
VCRs and video disc players	26.58	13.95	52
Video cassettes, tapes, and discs	22.15	16.68	75
Video game hardware and software	19.74	5.10	26
Repair of TV, radio, and sound equipment	6.65	7.81	117
Rental of television sets	0.24	–	–
Radios and sound equipment	**173.81**	**110.97**	**64**
Radios	11.76	27.70	236
Tape recorders and players	6.57	21.18	322
Sound components and component systems	29.86	6.92	23
Miscellaneous sound equipment	0.63	0.16	25
Sound equipment accessories	5.23	1.12	21
Satellite dishes	3.41	1.57	46
Compact disc, tape, record, video mail order clubs	10.59	5.07	48
Records, CDs, audio tapes, needles	39.41	18.01	46
Rental of VCR, radio, sound equipment	0.45	–	–
Musical instruments and accessories	23.96	18.15	76
Rental and repair of musical instruments	1.64	0.64	39
Rental of video cassettes, tapes, discs, films	40.30	10.45	26
PETS, TOYS, PLAYGROUND EQUIPMENT	**326.53**	**237.22**	**73**
Pets	**198.03**	**154.70**	**78**

(continued)

(continued from previous page)

	average spending of total consumer units	consumer units headed by 65-to-74-year-olds	
		average spending	indexed spending*
Pet food	$87.23	$81.84	94
Pet purchase, supplies, and medicines	40.15	18.93	47
Pet services	17.17	13.81	80
Veterinary services	53.49	40.12	75
Toys, games, hobbies, and tricycles	**127.68**	**82.29**	**64**
Playground equipment	**0.82**	**0.23**	**28**
OTHER ENTERTAINMENT SUPPLIES, EQUIPMENT, SERVICES	**438.68**	**202.94**	**46**
Unmotored recreational vehicles	**37.97**	**9.61**	**25**
Boats without motor and boat trailers	8.48	0.83	10
Trailers and other attachable campers	29.49	8.78	30
Motorized recreational vehicles	**145.96**	**71.81**	**49**
Motorized campers	26.17	55.35	212
Other vehicles	10.62	6.79	64
Motor boats	109.17	9.67	9
Rental of recreational vehicles	**3.35**	**0.86**	**26**
Outboard motors	**3.27**	**7.77**	**238**
Docking and landing fees	**9.52**	**11.24**	**118**
Sports, recreation, exercise equipment	**128.96**	**42.74**	**33**
Athletic gear, game tables, exercise equipment	60.02	16.32	27
Bicycles	15.27	1.49	10
Camping equipment	9.34	7.06	76
Hunting and fishing equipment	16.11	8.84	55
Winter sports equipment	5.50	0.60	11
Water sports equipment	4.52	0.69	15
Other sports equipment	16.29	5.33	33
Rental and repair of miscellaneous sports equipment	1.91	2.41	126
Photographic equipment and supplies	**89.92**	**45.80**	**51**
Film	21.36	15.69	73
Other photographic supplies	1.07	0.64	60
Film processing	29.36	19.94	68
Repair and rental of photographic equipment	0.49	0.34	69
Photographic equipment	14.19	7.62	54
Photographer fees	23.45	1.58	7
Fireworks	**3.98**	**–**	**–**

(continued)

(continued from previous page)

	average spending of total consumer units	consumer units headed by 65-to-74-year-olds	
		average spending	indexed spending*
Souvenirs	$0.74	–	–
Visual goods	3.15	$4.80	152
Pinball, electronic video games	11.85	8.30	70
PERSONAL CARE PRODUCTS AND SERVICES	**$527.62**	**$494.32**	**94**
Personal care products	**241.86**	**202.92**	**84**
Hair care products	51.00	34.56	68
Hair accessories	6.89	2.10	30
Wigs and hairpieces	1.22	0.83	68
Oral hygiene products	26.96	23.62	88
Shaving products	11.45	10.16	89
Cosmetics, perfume, and bath products	109.99	108.90	99
Deodorants, feminine hygiene, miscellaneous products	29.80	19.22	64
Electric personal care appliances	4.56	3.53	77
Personal care services	**285.76**	**291.40**	**102**
Personal care services (female)	188.30	218.87	116
Personal care services (male)	97.25	72.32	74
Repair of personal care appliances	0.20	0.21	105
READING	**$163.58**	**$195.42**	**119**
Newspaper subscriptions	51.70	83.73	162
Newspaper, nonsubscriptions	17.18	20.53	119
Magazine subscriptions	22.62	28.77	127
Magazines, nonsubscriptions	11.55	6.73	58
Books purchased through book clubs	10.18	13.39	132
Books not purchased through book clubs	49.50	40.58	82
Encyclopedia and other reference book sets	0.85	1.68	198
EDUCATION	**$570.70**	**$227.43**	**40**
College tuition	326.09	136.53	42
Elementary/high school tuition	90.14	43.80	49
Other school tuition	19.26	4.54	24
Other school expenses including rentals	27.44	5.32	19
Books, supplies for college	47.87	12.46	26
Books, supplies for elementary, high school	12.22	1.06	9
Books, supplies for day care, nursery school	3.13	0.35	11
Miscellaneous school expenses and supplies	44.55	23.39	53

(continued)

(continued from previous page)

	average spending of total consumer units	consumer units headed by 65-to-74-year-olds	
		average spending	indexed spending*
TOBACCO PRODUCTS AND SMOKING SUPPLIES	**$263.69**	**$212.51**	**81** '
Cigarettes	232.31	181.97	78
Other tobacco products	28.78	27.29	95
Smoking accessories	2.60	3.26	125
FINANCIAL PRODUCTS AND SERVICES	**$847.31**	**$745.30**	**88**
Miscellaneous fees, gambling losses	53.32	72.26	136
Legal fees	135.79	128.12	94
Funeral expenses	63.05	139.94	222
Safe deposit box rental	6.69	11.88	178
Checking accounts, other bank service charges	24.51	10.99	45
Cemetery lots, vaults, and maintenance fees	19.65	55.08	280
Accounting fees	48.99	58.49	119
Miscellaneous personal services	39.17	14.80	38
Finance charges, except mortgage and vehicles	249.40	126.40	51
Occupational expenses	102.65	21.54	21
Expenses for other properties	99.61	102.50	103
Interest paid, home equity line of credit (other property)	0.49	–	–
Credit card memberships	3.98	3.32	83
CASH CONTRIBUTIONS	**$1,000.90**	**$1,196.13**	**120**
Cash contributions to nonhousehold members, including students, alimony, child support	253.98	76.11	30
Gifts of cash, stocks, bonds to nonhousehold members	225.03	521.93	232
Contributions to charities	101.95	121.11	119
Contributions to religious organizations	390.25	447.26	115
Contributions to educational organizations	16.88	16.18	96
Political contributions	6.20	8.27	133
Other contributions	6.61	5.26	80
PERSONAL INSURANCE AND PENSIONS	**$3,223.06**	**$1,362.04**	**42**
Life and other personal insurance	**378.63**	**406.19**	**107**
Life, endowment, annuity, other personal insurance	369.48	393.30	106
Other nonhealth insurance	9.15	12.88	141

(continued)

(continued from previous page)

	average spending of total consumer units	consumer units headed by 65-to-74-year-olds	
		average spending	indexed spending*
Pensions and Social Security	**$2,844.43**	**$955.85**	**34**
Deductions for government retirement	81.02	26.17	32
Deductions for railroad retirement	2.26	–	–
Deductions for private pensions	339.22	80.48	24
Nonpayroll deposit to retirement plans	376.65	214.26	57
Deductions for Social Security	2,045.27	634.93	31
PERSONAL TAXES	**$3,241.49**	**$1,706.48**	**53**
Federal income tax	2,467.90	1,257.40	51
State and local income tax	644.81	245.19	38
Other taxes	128.78	203.89	158
GIFTS*	**$1,059.44**	**$1,082.64**	**102**
FOOD	**67.73**	**46.93**	**69**
Cakes and cupcakes	2.73	1.38	51
Cheese	3.16	2.29	72
Fresh fruits	6.23	2.26	36
Candy and chewing gum	11.56	10.41	90
Board (including at school)	23.79	10.00	42
HOUSING	**273.22**	**214.95**	**79**
Housekeeping supplies	**36.73**	**41.26**	**112**
Miscellaneous household products	6.62	3.67	55
Lawn and garden supplies	2.04	2.38	117
Stationery, stationery supplies, giftwrap	20.71	21.67	105
Postage	4.08	10.40	255
Household textiles	**8.35**	**11.46**	**137**
Bedroom linens	4.18	5.69	136
Appliances and miscellaneous housewares	**27.34**	**24.70**	**90**
Major appliances	6.41	7.76	121
Small appliances and miscellaneous housewares	20.93	16.94	81
China and other dinnerware	2.46	0.76	31
Glassware	3.97	4.81	121
Nonelectric cookware	3.57	2.02	57
Tableware, nonelectric kitchenware	3.76	0.79	21
Small electric kitchen appliances	3.51	5.31	151

(continued)

(continued from previous page)

	average spending of total consumer units	consumer units headed by 65-to-74-year-olds	
		average spending	indexed spending*
Miscellaneous household equipment	**$66.08**	**$57.69**	**87**
Infants' equipment	2.43	0.79	33
Other household decorative items	24.94	20.78	83
Telephones and accessories	3.14	–	–
Indoor plants, fresh flowers	16.63	17.08	103
Computers and hardware, nonbusiness use	7.19	6.55	91
Other housing	**134.72**	**79.84**	**59**
Repair or maintenance services	5.04	2.83	56
Housing while attending school	36.57	13.65	37
Natural gas (renter)	3.26	3.06	94
Electricity (renter)	13.58	13.68	101
Telephone services in home city, excluding mobile car phone	16.34	8.72	53
Water, sewerage maintenance (renter)	2.61	3.59	138
Baby-sitting and child care, someone else's home	3.73	–	–
Day care centers, nurseries, and preschools	19.65	0.24	1
Housekeeping services	4.07	0.61	15
Gardening, lawn care service	4.24	4.15	98
Moving, storage, freight express	2.59	8.21	317
Infants' furniture	2.07	2.90	140
APPAREL AND SERVICES	**252.24**	**259.55**	**103**
Men and boys, aged 2 or older	**61.29**	**73.16**	**119**
Men's coats and jackets	2.99	2.37	79
Men's accessories	4.73	5.12	108
Men's sweaters and vests	3.45	4.02	117
Men's active sportswear	3.31	10.38	314
Men's shirts	12.60	8.63	68
Men's pants	7.88	2.05	26
Boys' shirts	4.76	7.71	162
Boys' pants	3.25	4.86	150
Women and girls, aged 2 or older	**81.19**	**99.18**	**122**
Women's coats and jackets	3.17	3.61	114
Women's dresses	7.83	11.45	146
Women's vests and sweaters	6.06	7.24	119
Women's shirts, tops, blouses	12.70	16.71	132
Women's pants	6.09	8.95	147

(continued)

	average spending of total consumer units	consumer units headed by 65-to-74-year-olds	
		average spending	indexed spending*
Women's shorts and shorts sets	$2.22	$0.49	22
Women's active sportswear	4.13	3.39	82
Women's nightwear	6.03	2.84	47
Women's hosiery	2.19	3.57	163
Women's suits	2.25	4.52	201
Women's accessories	5.86	11.53	197
Girls' dresses and suits	4.80	4.79	100
Girls' shirts, blouses, sweaters	5.38	1.35	25
Girls' skirts and pants	2.72	5.39	198
Children under age 2	**32.52**	**23.24**	**71**
Infant dresses, outerwear	7.54	4.65	62
Infant underwear	15.64	9.98	64
Infant nightwear, loungewear	2.94	2.81	96
Infant accessories	4.41	3.99	90
Other apparel products and services	**77.24**	**63.96**	**83**
Watches	7.41	6.89	93
Jewelry	41.18	38.00	92
Men's footwear	7.81	3.37	43
Boys' footwear	3.24	2.04	63
Women's footwear	11.83	10.58	89
Girls' footwear	3.81	2.92	77
TRANSPORTATION	**56.74**	**119.41**	**210**
New cars	7.05	24.95	354
New trucks	4.52	39.37	871
Used cars	9.67	17.81	184
Gasoline on out-of-town trips	13.52	13.61	101
Miscellaneous auto repair, servicing	2.94	1.15	39
Airline fares	6.89	8.81	128
Local transportation on out-of-town trips	2.25	2.68	119
Ship fares	3.09	2.39	77
HEALTH CARE	**30.35**	**27.23**	**90**
Physician services	2.23	4.37	196
Dental services	4.76	5.02	105
Hospital service other than room	2.79	0.71	25
Care in convalescent or nursing home	8.05	2.15	27
Prescription drugs	2.17	4.53	209

(continued)

(continued from previous page)

	average spending of total consumer units	consumer units headed by 65-to-74-year-olds	
		average spending	indexed spending*
ENTERTAINMENT	**$98.92**	**$114.07**	**115**
Toys, games, hobbies, tricycles	40.95	39.68	97
Movie, other admissions, out-of-town trips	7.77	5.74	74
Admission to sports events, out-of-town trips	2.59	1.91	74
Fees for recreational lessons	3.33	1.25	38
Community antenna or cable TV	3.96	3.79	96
Color TV, portable/table model	2.88	1.35	47
VCRs and video disc players	2.84	2.19	77
Video game hardware and software	2.17	2.56	118
Tape recorders and players	2.93	12.22	417
Sound components and component systems	2.09	0.99	47
Musical instruments and accessories	2.13	12.96	608
Veterinary services	2.18	3.49	160
Athletic gear, game tables, exercise equipment	5.97	0.70	12
EDUCATION	**155.44**	**162.99**	**105**
College tuition	119.23	120.07	101
Elementary, high school tuition	10.29	27.17	264
Other school expenses, including rentals	4.33	2.23	52
College books, supplies	9.80	5.31	54
Miscellaneous school supplies	8.35	7.05	84
ALL OTHER GIFTS	**124.80**	**137.51**	**110**
Out-of-town trip expenses	46.85	53.78	115

*The index compares the spending of consumer units headed by 65-to-74-year-olds with the spending of the average consumer unit by dividing the spending of 65-to-74-year-olds by average spending in each category and multiplying by 100. An index of 100 means the spending of 65-to-74-year-olds in the category equals average spending. An index of 132 means the spending of 65-to-74-year-olds is 32 percent above average, while an index of 75 means the spending of 65-to-74-year-olds is 25 percent below average.

** This figure does not include the amount paid for mortgage principle, which is considered an asset.

*** Expenditures on gifts are also included in the preceding product and service categories. Food spending, for example, includes the amount spent on food gifts. Only gift categories with spending of $2.00 or more by the average consumer unit are shown.

Note: The Bureau of Labor Statistics uses consumer units rather than households as the sampling unit in the Consumer Expenditure Survey. For the definition of consumer unit, see the Glossary. (–) means the sample is too small to make a reliable estimate.

Source: Bureau of Labor Statistics, unpublished data from the 1997 Consumer Expenditure Survey; calculations by New Strategist

Householders Aged 75 or Older
Are More Willing to Spend

The spending of householders aged 75 or older is rising to meet the average.

In 1990, householders aged 75 or older spent just 54 percent as much as the average household. By 1997, their spending had grown to 58 percent of the average, $20,279 versus $34,819. The spending of householders aged 75 or older is below average in part because their households are small, averaging only 1.5 persons compared to 2.5 persons in the average household.

Despite their small size, households headed by people aged 75 or older spend close to or more than average on a variety of items. They spend almost an average amount on fresh fruits and 25 percent more than the average household on whiskey (reflecting the fact that older Americans prefer whiskey to wine or beer). They spend twice as much as the average household on both home security and gardening services. They spend 13 percent more on gardening supplies and 16 percent more on postage (reflecting the preferences of older Americans for letter writing rather than e-mailing).

Naturally, this age group spends much more than the average household on out-of-pocket health care costs, including 70 percent more for health insurance and 45 percent more for eye care services. Householders aged 75 or older spend nearly as much as the average household on newspaper subscriptions and 7 percent more for magazine subscriptions. They spend more than three times the average amount on gifts of cash, stocks, or bonds to nonhousehold members.

◆ The generation now aged 75 or older lived through the Depression, the memories of which influence spending. As younger generations with no memory of those harsh economic times enter the age group, the spending of householders aged 75 or older will continue to rise to meet the average.

Average and Indexed Spending of Householders Aged 75 or Older, 1997

(average annual spending of total consumer units and average annual and indexed spending of consumer units headed by people aged 75 or older, 1997)

	average spending of total consumer units	consumer units headed by people aged 75 or older	
		average spending	indexed spending*
Number of consumer units (in 000s)	105,576	9,827	–
Average before-tax income	$39,926.00	$19,425.00	49
Average annual spending	34,819.38	20,278.71	58
FOOD	**$4,801.35**	**$2,786.29**	**58**
FOOD AT HOME	2,880.00	1,923.50	67
Cereals and bakery products	453.00	309.44	68
Cereals and cereal products	161.39	102.88	64
Flour	8.79	8.12	92
Prepared flour mixes	15.04	10.73	71
Ready-to-eat and cooked cereals	91.15	58.44	64
Rice	18.37	9.66	53
Pasta, cornmeal, and other cereal products	28.03	15.93	57
Bakery products	291.60	206.56	71
Bread	83.43	63.11	76
White bread	40.89	26.13	64
Bread, other than white	42.55	36.97	87
Crackers and cookies	68.27	49.31	72
Cookies	45.01	30.29	67
Crackers	23.26	19.02	82
Frozen and refrigerated bakery products	23.35	16.72	72
Other bakery products	116.56	77.42	66
Biscuits and rolls	40.96	28.93	71
Cakes and cupcakes	34.51	15.75	46
Bread and cracker products	4.45	2.58	58
Sweetrolls, coffee cakes, doughnuts	23.13	18.81	81
Pies, tarts, turnovers	13.50	11.35	84
Meats, poultry, fish, and eggs	**743.12**	**465.36**	**63**
Beef	223.55	128.49	57
Ground beef	82.77	48.96	59

(continued)

	average spending of total consumer units	consumer units headed by people aged 75 or older	
		average spending	indexed spending*
Roast	$40.48	$23.29	58
Chuck roast	13.02	7.56	58
Round roast	12.85	7.76	60
Other roast	14.61	7.97	55
Steak	87.48	44.51	51
Round steak	16.70	11.68	70
Sirloin steak	23.01	9.95	43
Other steak	47.76	22.88	48
Other beef	12.81	11.72	91
Pork	157.13	115.02	73
Bacon	25.42	21.70	85
Pork chops	39.23	23.48	60
Ham	37.28	25.78	69
Ham, not canned	35.12	24.03	68
Canned ham	2.16	1.74	81
Sausage	24.12	15.92	66
Other pork	31.07	28.15	91
Other meats	96.03	60.16	63
Frankfurters	22.83	11.44	50
Lunch meats (cold cuts)	65.55	42.31	65
Bologna, liverwurst, salami	23.82	15.09	63
Other lunch meats	41.73	27.22	65
Lamb, organ meats, and others	7.92	6.41	81
Lamb and organ meats	7.34	6.31	86
Mutton, goat, and game	0.58	0.10	17
Poultry	145.01	81.01	56
Fresh and frozen chickens	113.38	68.31	60
Fresh and frozen whole chickens	29.77	22.58	76
Fresh and frozen chicken parts	83.61	45.73	55
Other poultry	31.63	12.69	40
Fish and seafood	88.54	53.74	61
Canned fish and seafood	14.18	11.72	83
Fresh fish and shellfish	50.95	32.27	63
Frozen fish and shellfish	23.41	9.74	42
Eggs	32.59	26.93	83

(continued)

(continued from previous page)

	average spending of total consumer units	consumer units headed by people aged 75 or older	
		average spending	indexed spending*
Dairy products	**$313.68**	**$212.22**	**68**
Fresh milk and cream	128.12	91.05	71
Fresh milk, all types	118.78	83.44	70
Cream	9.34	7.62	82
Other dairy products	185.56	121.16	65
Butter	14.63	10.46	71
Cheese	94.33	57.93	61
Ice cream and related products	52.91	38.82	73
Miscellaneous dairy products	23.69	13.95	59
Fruits and vegetables	**475.62**	**386.35**	**81**
Fresh fruits	150.47	142.95	95
Apples	28.47	20.50	72
Bananas	31.44	29.99	95
Oranges	17.62	14.90	85
Citrus fruits, excluding oranges	13.42	17.69	132
Other fresh fruits	59.52	59.87	101
Fresh vegetables	142.75	108.95	76
Potatoes	26.15	19.59	75
Lettuce	19.27	12.47	65
Tomatoes	23.87	16.45	69
Other fresh vegetables	73.46	60.44	82
Processed fruits	102.28	82.36	81
Frozen fruits and fruit juices	15.02	10.25	68
Frozen orange juice	8.44	5.85	69
Frozen fruits	2.02	1.88	93
Frozen fruit juices, excluding orange juice	4.57	2.53	55
Canned fruits	13.97	15.45	111
Dried fruits	6.03	7.53	125
Fresh fruit juice	19.82	14.02	71
Canned and bottled fruit juice	47.43	35.10	74
Processed vegetables	80.13	52.08	65
Frozen vegetables	26.57	14.98	56
Canned and dried vegetables and juices	53.56	37.11	69
Canned beans	11.79	7.18	61
Canned corn	7.26	4.87	67
Canned miscellaneous vegetables	16.80	13.41	80
Dried peas	0.23	0.26	113

(continued)

(continued from previous page)

	average spending of total consumer units	consumer units headed by people aged 75 or older	
		average spending	indexed spending*
Dried beans	$2.58	$1.38	53
Dried miscellaneous vegetables	7.18	4.41	61
Dried processed vegetables	0.22	0.06	27
Frozen vegetable juices	0.28	0.20	71
Fresh and canned vegetable juices	7.22	5.35	74
Other food at home	**894.58**	**550.13**	**61**
Sugar and other sweets	114.30	78.58	69
Candy and chewing gum	69.26	44.90	65
Sugar	18.93	14.57	77
Artificial sweeteners	3.48	4.51	130
Jams, preserves, other sweets	22.63	14.61	65
Fats and oils	81.05	68.13	84
Margarine	11.74	12.91	110
Fats and oils	24.50	22.71	93
Salad dressings	24.68	15.55	63
Nondairy cream and imitation milk	8.50	7.63	90
Peanut butter	11.63	9.32	80
Miscellaneous foods	403.06	252.35	63
Frozen prepared foods	77.61	55.11	71
Frozen meals	20.73	24.17	117
Other frozen prepared foods	56.88	30.93	54
Canned and packaged soups	32.87	29.56	90
Potato chips, nuts, and other snacks	84.53	42.85	51
Potato chips and other snacks	66.83	28.03	42
Nuts	17.70	14.82	84
Condiments and seasonings	86.12	56.94	66
Salt, spices, and other seasonings	19.07	13.02	68
Olives, pickles, relishes	10.54	9.53	90
Sauces and gravies	39.86	17.32	43
Baking needs and miscellaneous products	16.65	17.07	103
Other canned/packaged prepared foods	121.94	67.90	56
Prepared salads	15.05	10.50	70
Prepared desserts	9.95	9.12	92
Baby food	27.86	3.08	11
Miscellaneous prepared foods	68.44	43.77	64
Vitamin supplements	0.64	1.44	225

(continued)

(continued from previous page)

	average spending of total consumer units	consumer units headed by people aged 75 or older	
		average spending	indexed spending*
Nonalcoholic beverages	$244.51	$129.76	53
Cola	90.51	34.16	38
Other carbonated drinks	42.94	20.24	47
Coffee	48.80	39.04	80
Roasted coffee	32.65	22.95	70
Instant and freeze-dried coffee	16.15	16.09	100
Noncarbonated fruit flavored drinks, including nonfrozen lemonade	19.22	5.06	26
Tea	14.76	11.11	75
Nonalcoholic beer	0.34	0.57	168
Other nonalcoholic beverages and ice	27.93	19.58	70
Food prepared by household on out-of-town trips	51.65	21.32	41
FOOD AWAY FROM HOME	**1,921.35**	**862.79**	**45**
Meals at restaurants, carry-outs, other	**1,477.51**	**720.99**	**49**
Lunch	501.92	278.25	55
Dinner	740.70	357.11	48
Snacks and nonalcoholic beverages	119.38	22.85	19
Breakfast and brunch	115.51	62.78	54
Board (including at school)	**51.88**	**20.99**	**40**
Catered affairs	**83.52**	**4.39**	**5**
Food on out-of-town trips	**223.90**	**112.90**	**50**
School lunches	**54.03**	**1.09**	**2**
Meals as pay	**30.51**	**2.44**	**8**
ALCOHOLIC BEVERAGES	**$309.22**	**$110.73**	**36**
At home	**180.13**	**74.97**	**42**
Beer and ale	90.92	19.29	21
Whiskey	13.40	16.69	125
Wine	55.32	18.71	34
Other alcoholic beverages	20.50	20.28	99
Away from home	**129.09**	**35.76**	**28**
Beer and ale	39.50	7.59	19
Wine	24.30	7.48	31
Other alcoholic beverages	32.81	9.40	29
Alcoholic beverages purchased on trips	32.48	11.29	35

(continued)

(continued from previous page)

	average spending of total consumer units	consumer units headed by people aged 75 or older	
		average spending	indexed spending*
HOUSING	**$11,272.04**	**$7,107.16**	**63**
SHELTER	**6,343.87**	**3,557.22**	**56**
Owned dwellings**	**3,934.87**	**2,108.65**	**54**
Mortgage interest and charges	2,225.26	260.38	12
Mortgage interest	2,109.06	229.03	11
Interest paid, home equity loan	57.21	19.08	33
Interest paid, home equity line of credit	58.84	12.12	21
Prepayment penalty charges	0.16	0.15	94
Property taxes	971.15	890.99	92
Maintenance, repairs, insurance, other expenses	738.46	957.29	130
Homeowner's and related insurance	230.91	274.59	119
Fire and extended coverage	8.02	10.09	126
Homeowner's insurance	222.88	264.49	119
Ground rent	37.16	66.24	178
Maintenance and repair services	365.61	535.78	147
Painting and papering	45.31	61.26	135
Plumbing and water heating	36.61	70.13	192
Heat, air conditioning, electrical work	63.28	87.13	138
Roofing and gutters	72.99	138.10	189
Other repair and maintenance services	124.47	165.28	133
Repair/replacement of hard surface flooring	21.17	12.77	60
Repair of built–in appliances	1.79	1.12	63
Maintenance and repair materials	83.91	38.07	45
Paints, wallpaper, and supplies	18.33	6.39	35
Tools/equipment for painting, wallpapering	1.97	0.69	35
Plumbing supplies and equipment	6.87	5.86	85
Electrical supplies, heating/cooling equipment	4.55	1.80	40
Hard surface flooring, repair and replacement	7.13	1.78	25
Roofing and gutters	7.77	10.40	134
Plaster, paneling, siding, windows, doors, screens, awnings	14.97	2.27	15
Patio, walk, fence, driveway, masonry, brick, and stucco work	0.92	0.16	17
Landscape maintenance	5.19	1.27	24
Miscellaneous supplies and equipment	16.21	7.47	46
Insulation, other maintenance/repair	9.22	7.33	80

(continued)

(continued from previous page)

	average spending of total consumer units	consumer units headed by people aged 75 or older	
		average spending	indexed spending*
Finish basement, remodel rooms, build patios, walks, etc.	$6.99	$0.14	2
Property management and security	19.58	38.63	197
Property management	16.49	32.28	196
Management and upkeep services for security	3.09	6.35	206
Parking	1.30	3.98	306
Rented dwellings	**1,983.18**	**1,222.50**	**62**
Rent	1,876.81	1,183.83	63
Rent as pay	72.36	20.46	28
Maintenance, insurance, and other expenses	34.02	18.21	54
Tenant's insurance	9.76	10.13	104
Maintenance and repair services	16.62	7.08	43
Repair or maintenance services	15.42	7.08	46
Repair and replacement of hard surface flooring	1.17	–	–
Repair of built-in appliances	0.03	–	–
Maintenance and repair materials	7.63	1.00	13
Paint, wallpaper, and supplies	1.57	0.12	8
Painting and wallpapering	0.17	0.01	6
Plastering, paneling, roofing, gutters, etc.	1.22	0.83	68
Patio, walk, fence, driveway, masonry, brick, and stucco work	0.02	–	–
Plumbing supplies and equipment	0.36	–	–
Electrical supplies, heating and cooling equipment	0.08	–	–
Miscellaneous supplies and equipment	2.94	0.03	1
Insulation, other maintenance and repair	1.04	0.03	3
Materials for additions, finishing basements, remodeling rooms	1.65	–	–
Construction materials for jobs not started	0.25	–	–
Hard surface flooring	0.74	–	–
Landscape maintenance	0.53	–	–
Other lodging	**425.82**	**226.07**	**53**
Owned vacation homes	133.69	86.23	64
Mortgage interest and charges	58.02	29.32	51
Mortgage interest	56.46	29.32	52
Interest paid, home equity loan	0.66	–	–
Interest paid, home equity line of credit	0.89	–	–

(continued)

(continued from previous page)

	average spending of total consumer units	consumer units headed by people aged 75 or older	
		average spending	indexed spending*
Property taxes	$54.83	$34.89	64
Maintenance, insurance, and other expenses	20.84	22.02	106
Homeowner's and related insurance	5.03	3.23	64
Homeowner's insurance	4.67	2.98	64
Fire and extended coverage	0.36	0.25	69
Ground rent	1.63	9.01	553
Maintenance and repair services	9.66	5.17	54
Maintenance and repair materials	0.81	0.17	21
Property management and security	3.41	3.72	109
Property management	2.96	2.62	89
Management and upkeep services for security	0.45	1.10	244
Parking	0.29	0.72	248
Housing while attending school	66.35	–	–
Lodging on out-of-town trips	225.77	139.84	62
UTILITIES, FUELS & PUBLIC SERVICES	**2,412.30**	**1,953.79**	**81**
Natural gas	**300.96**	**334.48**	**111**
Natural gas (renter)	60.81	23.80	39
Natural gas (owner)	238.55	308.71	129
Natural gas (vacation)	1.60	1.96	123
Electricity	**908.67**	**751.39**	**83**
Electricity (renter)	212.54	86.84	41
Electricity (owner)	687.53	658.00	96
Electricity (vacation)	8.60	6.55	76
Fuel oil and other fuels	**107.72**	**126.52**	**117**
Fuel oil	55.18	74.25	135
Fuel oil (renter)	4.92	3.32	67
Fuel oil (owner)	49.77	70.47	142
Fuel oil (vacation)	0.49	0.47	96
Coal	0.99	–	–
Coal (renter)	0.02	–	–
Coal (owner)	0.97	–	–
Bottled/tank gas	43.84	47.14	108
Gas (renter)	4.66	3.35	72
Gas (owner)	36.37	42.07	116
Gas (vacation)	2.81	1.72	61

(continued)

(continued from previous page)

	average spending of total consumer units	consumer units headed by people aged 75 or older	
		average spending	indexed spending*
Wood and other fuels	$7.72	$5.13	66
Wood and other fuels (renter)	1.53	0.98	64
Wood and other fuels (owner)	5.80	4.15	72
Wood and other fuels (vacation)	0.39	–	–
Telephone services	**809.05**	**457.96**	**57**
Telephone services in home city, excluding mobile car phones	756.44	452.06	60
Telephone services for mobile car phones	52.61	5.89	11
Water and other public services	**285.90**	**283.45**	**99**
Water and sewerage maintenance	207.28	196.56	95
Water and sewerage maintenance (renter)	28.28	10.70	38
Water and sewerage maintenance (owner)	176.95	184.39	104
Water and sewerage maintenance (vacation)	2.06	1.47	71
Trash and garbage collection	76.00	85.33	112
Trash and garbage collection (renter)	8.78	3.34	38
Trash and garbage collection (owner)	65.66	79.97	122
Trash and garbage collection (vacation)	1.56	2.01	129
Septic tank cleaning	2.62	1.55	59
Septic tank cleaning (renter)	0.19	–	–
Septic tank cleaning (owner)	2.41	1.56	65
HOUSEHOLD OPERATIONS	**548.50**	**525.81**	**96**
Personal services	**263.10**	**149.19**	**57**
Baby-sitting and child care in your own home	34.39	0.02	0
Baby-sitting and child care in someone else's home	37.37	1.12	3
Care for elderly, invalids, handicapped, etc.	26.95	138.23	513
Adult day care centers	3.79	0.12	3
Day care centers, nurseries, and preschools	160.60	9.69	6
Other household expenses	**285.40**	**376.62**	**132**
Housekeeping services	75.34	128.59	171
Gardening, lawn care services	72.44	151.07	209
Water softening services	4.51	4.53	100
Nonclothing laundry and dry cleaning, sent out	10.20	4.30	42
Nonclothing laundry and dry cleaning, coin-operated	4.91	2.36	48
Termite/pest control services	11.55	13.90	120
Other home services	15.94	29.89	188
Termite/pest control products	0.12	0.01	8

(continued)

(continued from previous page)

	average spending of total consumer units	consumer units headed by people aged 75 or older	
		average spending	indexed spending*
Moving, storage, and freight express	$34.75	$7.52	22
Appliance repair, including service center	13.50	16.40	121
Reupholstering and furniture repair	10.87	4.75	44
Repairs/rentals of lawn/garden equipment, hand/power tools, etc.	5.13	8.66	169
Appliance rental	1.05	–	–
Rental of office equipment for nonbusiness use	0.43	0.08	19
Repair of miscellaneous household equipment and furnishings	1.53	0.20	13
Repair of computer systems for nonbusiness use	2.47	2.64	107
Computer information services	20.65	1.71	8
HOUSEKEEPING SUPPLIES	**454.93**	**367.52**	**81**
Laundry and cleaning supplies	**115.85**	**72.98**	**63**
Soaps and detergents	65.05	36.15	56
Other laundry cleaning products	50.80	36.83	73
Other household products	**210.07**	**170.22**	**81**
Cleansing and toilet tissue, paper towels, and napkins	64.42	49.29	77
Miscellaneous household products	89.90	58.03	65
Lawn and garden supplies	55.74	62.91	113
Postage and stationery	**129.01**	**124.32**	**96**
Stationery, stationery supplies, giftwrap	62.61	48.67	78
Postage	62.53	72.73	116
Delivery services	3.88	2.93	76
HOUSEHOLD FURNISHINGS & EQUIPMENT	**1,512.44**	**702.82**	**46**
Household textiles	**79.12**	**32.82**	**41**
Bathroom linens	11.13	3.96	36
Bedroom linens	34.28	13.40	39
Kitchen and dining room linens	2.40	0.81	34
Curtains and draperies	16.73	7.58	45
Slipcovers and decorative pillows	2.10	0.73	35
Sewing materials for household items	11.20	5.91	53
Other linens	1.28	0.43	34
Furniture	**387.34**	**94.70**	**24**
Mattresses and springs	46.56	12.36	27
Other bedroom furniture	63.99	4.18	7

(continued)

(continued from previous page)

	average spending of total consumer units	consumer units headed by people aged 75 or older	
		average spending	indexed spending*
Sofas	$93.81	$22.50	24
Living room chairs	47.42	32.89	69
Living room tables	20.60	3.00	15
Kitchen and dining room furniture	48.69	5.11	10
Infants' furniture	9.87	0.90	9
Outdoor furniture	13.61	2.95	22
Wall units, cabinets, and other furniture	42.81	10.82	25
Floor coverings	**77.74**	**101.51**	**131**
Wall-to-wall carpeting	38.82	14.95	39
Wall-to-wall carpeting (renter)	1.94	0.19	10
Wall-to-wall carpeting, installed	1.37	–	–
Wall-to-wall carpeting, not installed carpet squares	0.56	0.19	34
Wall-to-wall carpeting, replacement (owner)	36.88	14.76	40
Wall-to-wall carpeting, not installed carpet squares	2.68	1.21	45
Wall-to-wall carpeting, installed	34.20	13.55	40
Room-size rugs and other floor covering, nonpermanent	38.93	86.56	222
Major appliances	**169.18**	**108.90**	**64**
Dishwashers (built-in), garbage disposals, range hoods (renter)	0.82	0.55	67
Dishwashers (built-in), garbage disposals, range hoods (owner)	11.65	14.41	124
Refrigerators and freezers (renter)	9.52	5.03	53
Refrigerators and freezers (owner)	48.08	28.85	60
Washing machines (renter)	5.46	–	–
Washing machines (owner)	17.56	8.00	46
Clothes dryers (renter)	4.40	0.83	19
Clothes dryers (owner)	11.82	7.19	61
Cooking stoves, ovens (renter)	2.83	1.00	35
Cooking stoves, ovens (owner)	19.23	18.17	94
Microwave ovens (renter)	2.96	1.38	47
Microwave ovens (owner)	6.63	5.42	82
Portable dishwashers (renter)	0.41	–	–
Portable dishwashers (owner)	0.26	–	–
Window air conditioners (renter)	1.69	0.73	43
Window air conditioners (owner)	3.24	2.08	64

(continued)

(continued from previous page)

	average spending of total consumer units	consumer units headed by people aged 75 or older	
		average spending	indexed spending*
Electric floor cleaning equipment	$15.68	$11.26	72
Sewing machines	3.55	1.23	35
Miscellaneous household appliances	**3.39**	**2.80**	**83**
Small appliances and miscellaneous housewares	91.91	48.52	53
Housewares	66.12	25.76	39
Plastic dinnerware	1.75	0.45	26
China and other dinnerware	8.86	4.26	48
Flatware	4.68	1.62	35
Glassware	8.25	2.07	25
Silver serving pieces	2.31	0.49	21
Other serving pieces	1.74	0.35	20
Nonelectric cookware	15.05	8.34	55
Tableware, nonelectric kitchenware	23.48	8.17	35
Small appliances	25.79	22.75	88
Small electric kitchen appliances	16.67	9.04	54
Portable heating and cooling equipment	9.12	13.72	150
Miscellaneous household equipment	**707.15**	**316.37**	**45**
Window coverings	13.71	4.07	30
Infants' equipment	7.05	0.20	3
Laundry and cleaning equipment	13.70	15.18	111
Outdoor equipment	18.42	6.07	33
Clocks	4.51	2.33	52
Lamps and lighting fixtures	12.53	2.76	22
Other household decorative items	134.12	63.89	48
Telephones and accessories	96.54	39.45	41
Lawn and garden equipment	39.37	28.50	72
Power tools	16.31	1.83	11
Office furniture for home use	10.61	0.51	5
Hand tools	9.29	2.39	26
Indoor plants and fresh flowers	52.33	30.14	58
Closet and storage items	8.94	3.70	41
Rental of furniture	3.41	0.44	13
Luggage	9.72	4.92	51
Computers and computer hardware, nonbusiness use	162.66	23.90	15
Computer software and accessories, nonbusiness use	24.72	2.88	12
Telephone answering devices	3.31	1.19	36

(continued)

(continued from previous page)

	average spending of total consumer units	consumer units headed by people aged 75 or older	
		average spending	indexed spending*
Calculators	$1.92	$0.16	8
Business equipment for home use	2.33	1.01	43
Other hardware	23.27	50.28	216
Smoke alarms (owner)	0.86	0.59	69
Smoke alarms (renter)	0.19	0.06	32
Other household appliances (owner)	8.78	3.41	39
Other household appliances (renter)	1.47	0.67	46
Miscellaneous household equipment and parts	27.10	25.84	95
APPAREL AND SERVICES	**$1,729.06**	**$734.93**	**43**
Men's apparel	**322.98**	**119.57**	**37**
Suits	35.18	9.63	27
Sportcoats and tailored jackets	15.19	3.11	20
Coats and jackets	29.80	13.94	47
Underwear	12.52	4.15	33
Hosiery	9.91	6.02	61
Nightwear	2.93	1.47	50
Accessories	30.27	7.36	24
Sweaters and vests	15.84	5.74	36
Active sportswear	12.24	9.03	74
Shirts	75.81	21.52	28
Pants	64.52	31.88	49
Shorts and shorts sets	13.76	4.42	32
Uniforms	2.25	–	–
Costumes	2.79	1.29	46
Boys' (aged 2 to 15) apparel	**83.88**	**8.36**	**10**
Coats and jackets	8.33	1.65	20
Sweaters	2.81	0.45	16
Shirts	18.34	0.84	5
Underwear	3.08	0.15	5
Nightwear	1.94	0.28	14
Hosiery	3.66	0.12	3
Accessories	3.94	0.71	18
Suits, sportcoats, and vests	2.89	0.67	23
Pants	21.85	2.43	11
Shorts and shorts sets	8.66	0.45	5
Uniforms	4.41	0.40	9

(continued)

(continued from previous page)

	average spending of total consumer units	consumer units headed by people aged 75 or older	
		average spending	indexed spending*
Active sportswear	$2.65	$0.11	4
Costumes	1.33	0.10	8
Women's apparel	**574.26**	**381.05**	**66**
Coats and jackets	44.33	35.08	79
Dresses	84.25	42.77	51
Sportcoats and tailored jackets	2.77	7.39	267
Sweaters and vests	40.39	33.03	82
Shirts, blouses, and tops	93.73	68.68	73
Skirts	18.35	8.76	48
Pants	70.48	36.55	52
Shorts and shorts sets	22.34	5.11	23
Active sportswear	29.74	26.86	90
Nightwear	24.73	12.48	50
Undergarments	29.71	19.87	67
Hosiery	22.88	17.20	75
Suits	38.30	32.39	85
Accessories	45.42	31.51	69
Uniforms	3.20	–	–
Costumes	3.64	3.38	93
Girls' (aged 2 to 15) apparel	**106.01**	**11.90**	**11**
Coats and jackets	6.50	0.71	11
Dresses and suits	13.42	3.62	27
Shirts, blouses, and sweaters	25.74	1.82	7
Skirts and pants	19.49	1.29	7
Shorts and shorts sets	9.67	0.95	10
Active sportswear	6.86	1.42	21
Underwear and nightwear	6.75	0.90	13
Hosiery	5.29	0.48	9
Accessories	5.64	0.46	8
Uniforms	3.17	0.09	3
Costumes	3.48	0.15	4
Children under age 2	**77.05**	**18.02**	**23**
Coats, jackets, and snowsuits	3.28	0.97	30
Outerwear including dresses	15.01	2.43	16
Underwear	43.93	12.13	28
Nightwear and loungewear	4.38	0.91	21
Accessories	10.45	1.57	15

(continued)

(continued from previous page)

	average spending of total consumer units	consumer units headed by people aged 75 or older	
		average spending	indexed spending*
Footwear	**$314.52**	**$137.60**	**44**
Men's	100.43	19.39	19
Boys'	27.90	–	–
Women's	157.11	112.93	72
Girls'	29.08	5.29	18
Other apparel products and services	**250.35**	**58.42**	**23**
Material for making clothes	4.07	1.33	33
Sewing patterns and notions	4.82	1.96	41
Watches	29.70	2.98	10
Jewelry	142.02	27.23	19
Shoe repair and other shoe services	2.38	1.98	83
Coin-operated apparel laundry and dry cleaning	20.79	6.59	32
Apparel alteration, repair, and tailoring services	6.10	3.65	60
Clothing rental	3.85	0.18	5
Watch and jewelry repair	5.08	3.04	60
Professional laundry, dry cleaning	31.24	9.14	29
Clothing storage	0.30	0.34	113
TRANSPORTATION	**$6,456.86**	**$2,785.28**	**43**
VEHICLE PURCHASES	**2,735.76**	**1,058.97**	**39**
Cars and trucks, new	**1,228.89**	**574.09**	**47**
New cars	700.22	489.12	70
New trucks	528.67	84.98	16
Cars and trucks, used	**1,463.52**	**484.88**	**33**
Used cars	895.31	387.84	43
Used trucks	568.22	97.04	17
Other vehicles	**43.35**	**–**	**–**
New motorcycles	26.39	–	–
Used motorcycles	15.32	–	–
GASOLINE AND MOTOR OIL	**1,097.52**	**460.72**	**42**
Gasoline	985.31	417.50	42
Diesel fuel	10.10	5.38	53
Gasoline on out-of-town trips	89.11	34.63	39
Motor oil	12.10	2.88	24
Motor oil on out-of-town trips	0.90	0.35	39

(continued)

(continued from previous page)

	average spending of total consumer units	consumer units headed by people aged 75 or older	
		average spending	indexed spending*
OTHER VEHICLE EXPENSES	$2,230.41	$1,049.91	47
Vehicle finance charges	292.81	43.33	15
Automobile finance charges	161.70	31.48	19
Truck finance charges	116.10	9.33	8
Motorcycle and plane finance charges	1.52	–	–
Other vehicle finance charges	13.49	2.52	19
Maintenance and repairs	681.62	393.31	58
Coolant, additives, brake, transmission fluids	5.70	1.51	26
Tires	87.94	43.85	50
Parts, equipment, and accessories	51.31	14.48	28
Vehicle audio equipment	2.00	–	–
Vehicle products	6.95	0.17	2
Miscellaneous auto repair, servicing	51.74	34.59	67
Body work and painting	32.29	19.37	60
Clutch, transmission repair	47.92	24.33	51
Drive shaft and rear-end repair	5.73	1.53	27
Brake work	55.82	28.21	51
Repair to steering or front-end	17.41	12.75	73
Repair to engine cooling system	19.98	13.45	67
Motor tune-up	45.05	20.64	46
Lube, oil change, and oil filters	54.29	34.83	64
Front-end alignment, wheel balance, rotation	12.13	6.92	57
Shock absorber replacement	4.98	3.02	61
Gas tank repair, replacement	1.20	0.97	81
Tire repair and other repair work	29.63	15.03	51
Vehicle air conditioning repair	19.07	22.36	117
Exhaust system repair	18.52	19.97	108
Electrical system repair	29.34	21.59	74
Motor repair, replacement	75.45	44.85	59
Auto repair service policy	7.16	8.89	124
Vehicle insurance	754.99	410.90	54
Vehicle rental, leases, licenses, other charges	500.99	202.37	40
Leased and rented vehicles	331.25	117.27	35
Rented vehicles	41.03	17.66	43
Auto rental	7.73	1.99	26
Auto rental, out-of-town trips	26.78	14.40	54

(continued)

(continued from previous page)

	average spending of total consumer units	consumer units headed by people aged 75 or older	
		average spending	indexed spending*
Truck rental	$1.85	$0.36	19
Truck rental, out-of-town trips	4.29	–	–
Leased vehicles	290.22	99.61	34
Car lease payments	162.28	46.80	29
Cash downpayment (car lease)	16.16	49.79	308
Termination fee (car lease)	1.81	0.03	2
Truck lease payments	98.37	3.00	3
Cash downpayment (truck lease)	10.63	–	–
Termination fee (truck lease)	0.97	–	–
State and local registration	94.62	53.00	56
Driver's license	7.42	3.73	50
Vehicle inspection	8.74	5.12	59
Parking fees	28.20	9.76	35
Parking fees in home city, excluding residence	24.37	9.22	38
Parking fees, out-of-town trips	3.83	0.54	14
Tolls	13.19	2.21	17
Tolls on out-of-town trips	4.32	1.63	38
Towing charges	5.04	1.60	32
Automobile service clubs	8.19	8.05	98
PUBLIC TRANSPORTATION	**393.16**	**215.68**	**55**
Airline fares	248.82	131.85	53
Intercity bus fares	10.51	7.13	68
Intracity mass transit fares	55.77	14.84	27
Local transportation on out-of-town trips	12.61	11.94	95
Taxi fares and limousine service on trips	7.40	7.01	95
Taxi fares and limousine service	9.51	6.85	72
Intercity train fares	21.19	12.75	60
Ship fares	26.40	22.81	86
School bus	0.95	0.48	51
HEALTH CARE	**$1,840.71**	**$2,799.04**	**152**
HEALTH INSURANCE	**881.28**	**1,494.20**	**170**
Commercial health insurance	**203.37**	**101.11**	**50**
Traditional fee-for-service health plan (not BCBS)	100.09	81.08	81
Preferred provider health plan (not BCBS)	103.29	20.03	19
Blue Cross, Blue Shield	**192.51**	**309.37**	**161**
Traditional fee-for-service health plan	62.93	81.98	130

(continued)

	average spending of total consumer units	consumer units headed by people aged 75 or older	
		average spending	indexed spending*
Preferred provider health plan	$46.45	$22.93	49
Health maintenance organization	47.39	25.57	54
Commercial Medicare supplement	31.92	173.60	544
Other BCBS health insurance	3.82	5.30	139
Health maintenance plans (HMOs)	**229.07**	**57.52**	**25**
Medicare payments	**160.92**	**668.48**	**415**
Commercial Medicare supplements/			
other health insurance	**95.40**	**357.72**	**375**
Commercial Medicare supplement (not BCBS)	60.66	302.93	499
Other health insurance (not BCBS)	34.74	54.78	158
MEDICAL SERVICES	**531.04**	**475.29**	**90**
Physician's services	133.59	94.67	71
Dental services	203.56	186.07	91
Eye care services	27.14	39.42	145
Service by professionals other than physicians	37.03	26.51	72
Lab tests, X-rays	22.93	12.80	56
Hospital room	35.07	17.35	49
Hospital services other than room	52.37	8.81	17
Care in convalescent or nursing home	13.09	77.43	592
Repair of medical equipment	0.62	4.12	665
Other medical services	5.64	8.11	144
DRUGS	**320.44**	**691.26**	**216**
Nonprescription drugs	75.43	97.63	129
Nonprescription vitamins	28.43	29.09	102
Prescription drugs	216.58	564.54	261
MEDICAL SUPPLIES	**107.95**	**138.30**	**128**
Eyeglasses and contact lenses	59.73	50.89	85
Hearing aids	11.42	46.11	404
Topicals and dressings	29.47	23.82	81
Medical equipment for general use	2.43	3.07	126
Supportive/convalescent medical equipment	2.62	6.41	245
Rental of medical equipment	0.60	1.61	268
Rental of supportive, convalescent medical equipment	1.67	6.38	382
ENTERTAINMENT	**$1,813.28**	**$860.88**	**47**
FEES AND ADMISSIONS	**470.74**	**179.67**	**38**

(continued)

(continued from previous page)

	average spending of total consumer units	consumer units headed by people aged 75 or older	
		average spending	indexed spending*
Recreation expenses, out-of-town trips	$24.70	$9.74	39
Social, recreation, civic club membership	75.12	38.39	51
Fees for participant sports	72.62	44.39	61
Participant sports, out-of-town trips	30.30	8.16	27
Movie, theater, opera, ballet	86.71	39.17	45
Movie, other admissions, out-of-town trips	41.93	14.59	35
Admission to sports events	33.51	4.77	14
Admission to sports events, out-of-town trips	13.98	4.86	35
Fees for recreational lessons	67.17	5.86	9
Other entertainment services, out-of-town trips	24.70	9.74	39
TELEVISION, RADIO, SOUND EQUIPMENT	**577.33**	**313.78**	**54**
Television	**403.51**	**277.11**	**69**
Community antenna or cable TV	262.34	208.69	80
Black and white TV sets	0.67	0.40	60
Color TV, console	25.17	11.05	44
Color TV, portable/table model	39.96	32.59	82
VCRs and video disc players	26.58	11.78	44
Video cassettes, tapes, and discs	22.15	5.41	24
Video game hardware and software	19.74	1.56	8
Repair of TV, radio, and sound equipment	6.65	5.54	83
Rental of television sets	0.24	0.11	46
Radios and sound equipment	**173.81**	**36.67**	**21**
Radios	11.76	–	–
Tape recorders and players	6.57	–	–
Sound components and component systems	29.86	2.59	9
Miscellaneous sound equipment	0.63	3.94	625
Sound equipment accessories	5.23	3.96	76
Satellite dishes	3.41	1.52	45
Compact disc, tape, record, video mail order clubs	10.59	3.68	35
Records, CDs, audio tapes, needles	39.41	6.09	15
Rental of VCR, radio, sound equipment	0.45	–	0
Musical instruments and accessories	23.96	9.93	41
Rental and repair of musical instruments	1.64	0.29	18
Rental of video cassettes, tapes, discs, films	40.30	4.67	12
PETS, TOYS, PLAYGROUND EQUIPMENT	**326.53**	**128.44**	**39**
Pets	**198.03**	**72.77**	**37**

(continued)

(continued from previous page)

	average spending of total consumer units	consumer units headed by people aged 75 or older	
		average spending	indexed spending*
Pet food	$87.23	$42.68	49
Pet purchase, supplies, and medicines	40.15	9.85	25
Pet services	17.17	4.54	26
Veterinary services	53.49	15.70	29
Toys, games, hobbies, and tricycles	**127.68**	**55.67**	**44**
Playground equipment	**0.82**	**–**	**–**
OTHER ENTERTAINMENT SUPPLIES, EQUIPMENT, SERVICES	**438.68**	**238.99**	**54**
Unmotored recreational vehicles	**37.97**	**146.77**	**387**
Boats without motor and boat trailers	8.48	–	–
Trailers and other attachable campers	29.49	146.77	498
Motorized recreational vehicles	**145.96**	**10.46**	**7**
Motorized campers	26.17	7.59	29
Other vehicles	10.62	1.29	12
Motor boats	109.17	1.58	1
Rental of recreational vehicles	**3.35**	**0.55**	**16**
Outboard motors	**3.27**	**–**	**–**
Docking and landing fees	**9.52**	**2.06**	**22**
Sports, recreation, exercise equipment	**128.96**	**22.82**	**18**
Athletic gear, game tables, exercise equipment	60.02	19.25	32
Bicycles	15.27	0.90	6
Camping equipment	9.34	–	–
Hunting and fishing equipment	16.11	0.70	4
Winter sports equipment	5.50	0.13	2
Water sports equipment	4.52	0.26	6
Other sports equipment	16.29	0.87	5
Rental and repair of miscellaneous sports equipment	1.91	0.71	37
Photographic equipment and supplies	**89.92**	**43.23**	**48**
Film	21.36	5.89	28
Other photographic supplies	1.07	0.16	15
Film processing	29.36	7.31	25
Repair and rental of photographic equipment	0.49	–	–
Photographic equipment	14.19	1.17	8
Photographer fees	23.45	28.70	122
Fireworks	**3.98**	**12.30**	**309**

(continued)

(continued from previous page)

	average spending of total consumer units	consumer units headed by people aged 75 or older	
		average spending	indexed spending*
Souvenirs	$0.74	–	–
Visual goods	3.15	$0.79	25
Pinball, electronic video games	11.85	–	–
PERSONAL CARE PRODUCTS AND SERVICES	**$527.62**	**$376.37**	**71**
Personal care products	**241.86**	**138.96**	**57**
Hair care products	51.00	26.17	51
Hair accessories	6.89	2.86	42
Wigs and hairpieces	1.22	0.42	34
Oral hygiene products	26.96	20.08	74
Shaving products	11.45	4.67	41
Cosmetics, perfume, and bath products	109.99	63.38	58
Deodorants, feminine hygiene, miscellaneous products	29.80	19.16	64
Electric personal care appliances	4.56	2.22	49
Personal care services	**285.76**	**237.41**	**83**
Personal care services (female)	188.30	188.78	100
Personal care services (male)	97.25	48.41	50
Repair of personal care appliances	0.20	0.22	110
READING	**$163.58**	**$147.86**	**90**
Newspaper subscriptions	51.70	86.75	168
Newspaper, nonsubscriptions	17.18	7.63	44
Magazine subscriptions	22.62	24.13	107
Magazines, nonsubscriptions	11.55	2.87	25
Books purchased through book clubs	10.18	9.07	89
Books not purchased through book clubs	49.50	17.26	35
Encyclopedia and other reference book sets	0.85	0.15	18
EDUCATION	**$570.70**	**$61.06**	**11**
College tuition	326.09	44.48	14
Elementary/high school tuition	90.14	–	–
Other school tuition	19.26	2.85	15
Other school expenses including rentals	27.44	0.84	3
Books, supplies for college	47.87	3.07	6
Books, supplies for elementary, high school	12.22	0.46	4
Books, supplies for day care, nursery school	3.13	0.26	8
Miscellaneous school expenses and supplies	44.55	9.10	20

(continued)

	average spending of total consumer units	consumer units headed by people aged 75 or older	
		average spending	indexed spending*
TOBACCO PRODUCTS AND SMOKING SUPPLIES	**$263.69**	**$87.12**	**33**
Cigarettes	232.31	75.73	33
Other tobacco products	28.78	10.49	36
Smoking accessories	2.60	0.91	35
FINANCIAL PRODUCTS AND SERVICES	**$847.31**	**$463.30**	**55**
Miscellaneous fees, gambling losses	53.32	78.56	147
Legal fees	135.79	30.45	22
Funeral expenses	63.05	87.21	138
Safe deposit box rental	6.69	11.85	177
Checking accounts, other bank service charges	24.51	6.26	26
Cemetery lots, vaults, and maintenance fees	19.65	53.81	274
Accounting fees	48.99	48.79	100
Miscellaneous personal services	39.17	7.57	19
Finance charges, except mortgage and vehicles	249.40	55.65	22
Occupational expenses	102.65	6.50	6
Expenses for other properties	99.61	74.77	75
Interest paid, home equity line of credit (other property)	0.49	–	–
Credit card memberships	3.98	1.87	47
CASH CONTRIBUTIONS	**$1,000.90**	**$1,485.34**	**148**
Cash contributions to nonhousehold members, including students, alimony, child support	253.98	40.85	16
Gifts of cash, stocks, bonds to nonhousehold members	225.03	816.02	363
Contributions to charities	101.95	190.42	187
Contributions to religious organizations	390.25	392.93	101
Contributions to educational organizations	16.88	23.81	141
Political contributions	6.20	7.47	120
Other contributions	6.61	13.84	209
PERSONAL INSURANCE AND PENSIONS	**3,223.06**	**473.36**	**15**
Life and other personal insurance	**378.63**	**244.48**	**65**
Life, endowment, annuity, other personal insurance	369.48	238.43	65
Other nonhealth insurance	9.15	6.05	66

(continued)

(continued from previous page)

	average spending of total consumer units	consumer units headed by people aged 75 or older	
		average spending	indexed spending*
Pensions and Social Security	**$2,844.43**	**$228.88**	**8**
Deductions for government retirement	81.02	0.19	0
Deductions for railroad retirement	2.26	–	–
Deductions for private pensions	339.22	9.24	3
Nonpayroll deposit to retirement plans	376.65	71.60	19
Deductions for Social Security	2,045.27	147.85	7
PERSONAL TAXES	**$3,241.49**	**$834.71**	**26**
Federal income tax	2,467.90	616.71	25
State and local income tax	644.81	79.39	12
Other taxes	128.78	138.61	108
GIFTS*	**$1,059.44**	**$652.35**	**62**
FOOD	**67.73**	**35.53**	**52**
Cakes and cupcakes	2.73	0.17	6
Cheese	3.16	0.50	16
Fresh fruits	6.23	13.43	216
Candy and chewing gum	11.56	3.95	34
Board (including at school)	23.79	10.91	46
HOUSING	**273.22**	**165.63**	**61**
Housekeeping supplies	**36.73**	**23.90**	**65**
Miscellaneous household products	6.62	3.06	46
Lawn and garden supplies	2.04	2.04	100
Stationery, stationery supplies, giftwrap	20.71	11.07	53
Postage	4.08	5.32	130
Household textiles	**8.35**	**6.62**	**79**
Bedroom linens	4.18	4.21	101
Appliances and miscellaneous housewares	**27.34**	**12.08**	**44**
Major appliances	6.41	1.69	26
Small appliances and miscellaneous housewares	20.93	10.39	50
China and other dinnerware	2.46	3.28	133
Glassware	3.97	0.83	21
Nonelectric cookware	3.57	2.05	57
Tableware, nonelectric kitchenware	3.76	0.21	6
Small electric kitchen appliances	3.51	2.53	72

(continued)

(continued from previous page)

	average spending of total consumer units	consumer units headed by people aged 75 or older	
		average spending	indexed spending*
Miscellaneous household equipment	**$66.08**	**$28.56**	**43**
Infants' equipment	2.43	0.20	8
Other household decorative items	24.94	11.27	45
Telephones and accessories	3.14	0.60	19
Indoor plants, fresh flowers	16.63	13.18	79
Computers and hardware, nonbusiness use	7.19	0.27	4
Other housing	**134.72**	**94.47**	**70**
Repair or maintenance services	5.04	5.93	118
Housing while attending school	36.57	–	–
Natural gas (renter)	3.26	6.78	208
Electricity (renter)	13.58	18.37	135
Telephone services in home city, excluding mobile car phone	16.34	8.27	51
Water, sewerage maintenance (renter)	2.61	3.68	141
Baby-sitting and child care, someone else's home	3.73	0.22	6
Day care centers, nurseries, and preschools	19.65	3.23	16
Housekeeping services	4.07	12.96	318
Gardening, lawn care service	4.24	17.84	421
Moving, storage, freight express	2.59	0.13	5
Infants' furniture	2.07	0.90	43
APPAREL AND SERVICES	**252.24**	**132.30**	**52**
Men and boys, aged 2 or older	**61.29**	**45.61**	**74**
Men's coats and jackets	2.99	1.85	62
Men's accessories	4.73	2.48	52
Men's sweaters and vests	3.45	3.74	108
Men's active sportswear	3.31	6.96	210
Men's shirts	12.60	7.22	57
Men's pants	7.88	8.80	112
Boys' shirts	4.76	0.84	18
Boys' pants	3.25	2.02	62
Women and girls, aged 2 or older	**81.19**	**48.04**	**59**
Women's coats and jackets	3.17	3.20	101
Women's dresses	7.83	1.78	23
Women's vests and sweaters	6.06	6.71	111
Women's shirts, tops, blouses	12.70	6.27	49
Women's pants	6.09	1.37	22

(continued)

(continued from previous page)

	average spending of total consumer units	consumer units headed by people aged 75 or older	
		average spending	indexed spending*
Women's shorts and shorts sets	$2.22	$0.24	11
Women's active sportswear	4.13	2.74	66
Women's nightwear	6.03	5.25	87
Women's hosiery	2.19	3.47	158
Women's suits	2.25	0.79	35
Women's accessories	5.86	0.88	15
Girls' dresses and suits	4.80	3.62	75
Girls' shirts, blouses, sweaters	5.38	1.82	34
Girls' skirts and pants	2.72	0.94	35
Children under age 2	**32.52**	**16.55**	**51**
Infant dresses, outerwear	7.54	1.94	26
Infant underwear	15.64	11.40	73
Infant nightwear, loungewear	2.94	0.91	31
Infant accessories	4.41	1.32	30
Other apparel products and services	**77.24**	**22.10**	**29**
Watches	7.41	0.66	9
Jewelry	41.18	9.40	23
Men's footwear	7.81	0.08	1
Boys' footwear	3.24	–	–
Women's footwear	11.83	6.29	53
Girls' footwear	3.81	5.29	139
TRANSPORTATION	**56.74**	**78.30**	**138**
New cars	7.05	44.96	638
New trucks	4.52	–	–
Used cars	9.67	12.11	125
Gasoline on out-of-town trips	13.52	8.22	61
Miscellaneous auto repair, servicing	2.94	0.46	16
Airline fares	6.89	3.29	48
Local transportation on out-of-town trips	2.25	3.35	149
Ship fares	3.09	0.74	24
HEALTH CARE	**30.35**	**52.97**	**175**
Physician services	2.23	0.28	13
Dental services	4.76	6.78	142
Hospital service other than room	2.79	(0.16)	–6
Care in convalescent or nursing home	8.05	34.72	431
Prescription drugs	2.17	3.20	147

(continued)

(continued from previous page)

	average spending of total consumer units	consumer units headed by people aged 75 or older	
		average spending	indexed spending*
ENTERTAINMENT	**$98.92**	**$48.94**	**49**
Toys, games, hobbies, tricycles	40.95	30.78	75
Movie, other admissions, out-of-town trips	7.77	3.03	39
Admission to sports events, out-of-town trips	2.59	1.01	39
Fees for recreational lessons	3.33	0.44	13
Community antenna or cable TV	3.96	4.33	109
Color TV, portable/table model	2.88	0.83	29
VCRs and video disc players	2.84	0.69	24
Video game hardware and software	2.17	0.72	33
Tape recorders and players	2.93	–	–
Sound components and component systems	2.09	–	–
Musical instruments and accessories	2.13	0.23	11
Veterinary services	2.18	0.80	37
Athletic gear, game tables, exercise equipment	5.97	0.14	2
EDUCATION	**155.44**	**50.37**	**32**
College tuition	119.23	40.85	34
Elementary, high school tuition	10.29	–	–
Other school expenses, including rentals	4.33	0.21	5
College books, supplies	9.80	1.77	18
Miscellaneous school supplies	8.35	4.78	57
ALL OTHER GIFTS	**124.80**	**88.32**	**71**
Out-of-town trip expenses	46.85	39.96	85

* The index compares the spending of consumer units headed by people aged 75 or older with the spending of the average consumer unit by dividing the spending of people aged 75 or older by average spending in each category and multiplying by 100. An index of 100 means the spending of people aged 75 or older in the category equals average spending. An index of 132 means the spending of people aged 75 or older is 32 percent above average, while an index of 75 means the spending of people aged 75 or older is 25 percent below average.
** This figure does not include the amount paid for mortgage principle, which is considered an asset.
*** Expenditures on gifts are also included in the preceding product and service categories. Food spending, for example, includes the amount spent on food gifts. Only gift categories with spending of $2.00 or more by the average consumer unit are shown.
Note: The Bureau of Labor Statistics uses consumer units rather than households as the sampling unit in the Consumer Expenditure survey. For the definition of consumer unit, see the Glossary. (–) means the sample is too small to make a reliable estimate.
Source: Bureau of Labor Statistics, unpublished data from the 1997 Consumer Expenditure Survey; calculations by New Strategist

9

Wealth

◆ Median net worth peaks in the 55-to-64 age group at $110,800, then falls slowly with age.

◆ Older Americans have few financial assets. Even those aged 55 to 64, who are approaching retirement, have a median of just $32,300 saved for a rainy day.

◆ The most important nonfinancial asset among Americans of all ages, including those aged 55 or older, is a home.

◆ Americans aged 65 or older are less likely to be in debt than the average householder. Among those aged 75 or older, a 30 percent minority have any debt.

◆ The homeownership rate is at a record high. Those most likely to own their home are householders aged 65 to 74, with an ownership rate of 82 percent in 1998.

Net Worth Rises with Age

Net worth peaks in the 55-to-64 age group.

The median net worth of American households stood at $56,400 in 1995 (the latest data available). Net worth, which is one of the most important measures of wealth, is what remains after a household's debts are subtracted from its assets.

Net worth rises with age to a peak in the 55-to-64 age group. The youngest householders, under age 35, had a median net worth of just $11,400 in 1995. People in this age group are buying homes, starting careers, and having children. Most take on debt to achieve these goals—educational loans, mortgages, and credit card charges. Net worth rises in middle age as people pay off their debts, peaking in the 55-to-64 age group—at $110,800 in 1995. At this age, many people own their homes free and clear. They can afford to buy cars and other necessities without taking on debt. They have accumulated substantial retirement savings as well.

Net worth slowly declines after age 65 as people spend their wealth in retirement. Nevertheless, the net worth of householders aged 65 or older is greater than that of householders under age 55—primarily because many older householders no longer have mortgage debt reducing their net worth.

♦ For most households, the value of their home is the single largest component of net worth. As older Americans pay down their mortgages, net worth steadily rises.

Householders aged 55 to 64 have the most wealth

(median net worth of households by age of householder, 1995)

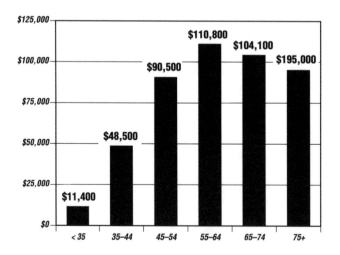

Net Worth of Households by Age of Householder, 1995

(median net worth of households by age of householder, 1995)

	median net worth
Total households	**$56,400**
Under age 35	11,400
Aged 35 to 44	48,500
Aged 45 to 54	90,500
Aged 55 to 64	110,800
Aged 65 to 74	104,100
Aged 75 or older	95,000

Source: Federal Reserve Board, Family Finances in the U.S.: Recent Evidence from the Survey of Consumer Finances, *Federal Reserve Bulletin, January 1997*

Older Americans Have Not Saved Much for a Rainy Day

Financial assets peak in the 55-to-64 age group.

The median value of the financial assets held by householders aged 55 to 64 was $32,300 in 1995 (the latest data available). While substantially greater than the median of $13,000 held by the average household, this paltry figure would not last long if it had to support someone in retirement. Householders aged 65 or older have even less in financial assets—$19,100 for those aged 65 to 74, and $20,900 for those aged 75 or older. Older Americans have amassed few financial assets because they knew they could depend on Social Security and employer-provided pensions to support them in retirement.

The only financial asset owned by the majority of older Americans is transaction accounts (checking and savings accounts). At least 88 percent of householders aged 55 or older own such accounts, but their median value ranges from just $3,000 to $5,000. Forty-seven percent of householders aged 55 to 64 have retirement accounts, but their value stood at a median of just $32,800 in 1995 for those with such accounts. Only 15 percent of householders in the 55-to-64 age group own stocks or mutual funds. Stock ownership is greater among those aged 65 or older, but never rises above 21 percent.

After transactions accounts, life insurance is the most common financial asset owned by householders aged 65 or older. More than one-third own life insurance, but the median value of this asset is just $5,000.

♦ While older Americans have a reputation for being savers, in fact they have saved little because the federal government and employers guaranteed them a comfortable retirement. Boomers and younger generations are not so fortunate. As they save for retirement and age into their fifties and sixties, the financial assets of older Americans are likely to grow.

Financial Assets of Householders Aged 55 or Older, 1995

(percent of total households and householders aged 55 or older owning financial assets, and median value of asset for owners, by type of asset, 1995)

	total	55 to 64	65 to 74	75 or older
Percent owning asset				
Any financial asset	**90.8%**	**90.5%**	**92.0%**	**93.8%**
Transaction accounts	87.1	88.2	91.1	93.0
Certificates of deposit	14.1	16.2	23.9	34.1
Savings bonds	22.9	19.6	17.0	15.3
Bonds	3.0	2.9	5.1	7.0
Stocks	15.3	14.9	18.0	21.3
Mutual funds	12.0	15.2	13.7	10.4
Retirement accounts	43.0	47.2	35.0	16.5
Life insurance	31.4	37.5	37.0	35.1
Other managed assets	3.8	7.1	5.6	5.7
Other financial assets	11.0	9.0	10.4	5.3
Median value of asset for owners				
Any financial asset	**$13,000**	**$32,300**	**$19,100**	**$20,900**
Transaction accounts	2,100	3,000	3,000	5,000
Certificates of deposit	10,000	14,000	17,000	11,000
Savings bonds	1,000	1,100	1,500	4,000
Bonds	26,200	10,000	58,000	40,000
Stocks	8,000	17,000	15,000	25,000
Mutual funds	19,000	55,000	50,000	50,000
Retirement accounts	15,600	32,800	28,500	17,500
Life insurance	5,000	6,000	5,000	5,000
Other managed assets	30,000	42,000	26,000	100,000
Other financial assets	3,000	9,000	9,000	35,000

Source: Federal Reserve Board, Family Finances in the U.S.: Recent Evidence from the Survey of Consumer Finances, *Federal Reserve Bulletin, January 1997*

Value of Nonfinancial Assets Falls in Old Age

Smaller homes may account for the decline.

For the average American household, the median value of nonfinancial assets amounted to $83,000 in 1995 (the latest data available). While householders aged 55 to 74 have more nonfinancial assets than the average household, those aged 75 or older have less.

Among all householders, the most commonly owned nonfinancial asset is a vehicle (owned by 84 percent). Vehicles are also the most commonly owned nonfinancial asset among householders aged 55 to 74. Among householders aged 75 or older, a slightly larger proportion own a home than a car (73.0 percent versus 72.8 percent). The vehicles owned by householders aged 65 or older are worth less than those owned by the average household. Behind this difference may be the fact that older householders own fewer vehicles.

The homes owned by householders aged 55 or older are not worth as much as the average home. The median value of homes owned by 55-to-64-year-olds stood at $85,000 in 1995, while the value of homes owned by people aged 65 or older was an even lower $80,000. This compares with a median value of $90,000 for the average home. The difference in housing value is probably due to the fact that older householders have smaller-than-average homes.

♦ Although the homes of people aged 55 or older are not worth as much as the average home, older Americans have more wealth than the average householder because they have little debt.

Nonfinancial Assets of Householders Aged 55 or Older, 1995

(percent of total households and householders aged 55 or older owning nonfinancial assets, and median value of asset for owners, by type of asset, 1995)

	total	*55 to 64*	*65 to 74*	*75 or older*
Percent owning asset				
Any nonfinancial asset	**91.1%**	**94.0%**	**92.5%**	**90.2%**
Vehicles	84.2	88.7	82.0	72.8
Primary residence	64.7	82.1	79.0	73.0
Investment real estate	17.5	26.9	26.5	16.6
Business	11.0	11.7	7.9	3.8
Other nonfinancial asset	9.0	9.8	8.9	5.4
Median value of asset for asset owners				
Any nonfinancial asset	**$83,000**	**$107,000**	**$93,500**	**$79,000**
Vehicles	10,000	11,900	8,000	5,300
Primary residence	90,000	85,000	80,000	80,000
Investment real estate	50,000	82,500	55,000	20,000
Business	41,000	75,000	100,000	30,000
Other nonfinancial asset	10,000	10,000	16,000	15,000

Source: Federal Reserve Board, Family Finances in the U.S.: Recent Evidence from the Survey of Consumer Finances, *Federal Reserve Bulletin, January 1997*

Debt Falls in Old Age

Most householders aged 75 or older are debt free.

Only 30 percent of households headed by people aged 75 or older have any debt. Among those with debt, the median amount owed was just $2,000 in 1995 (the latest data available).

Among all households, 75 percent have debts, owing a median of $22,500 in 1995. Credit card debt is most common, held by 48 percent of households. Older householders are less likely to have credit card debt than the average household, with the proportion ranging from 43 percent among householders aged 55 to 64 to just 18 percent of householders aged 75 or older.

Installment loans (primarily for vehicles) are the second most common type of debt, held by 47 percent of households. Again, older householders are less likely to hold this type of debt than the average household, with the figure ranging from 36 percent for 55-to-64-year-olds to just 10 percent of people aged 75 or older.

Mortgage debt is held by 41 percent of all households, and by a slightly higher 46 percent of householders aged 55 to 64. Only 25 percent of householders aged 65 to 74 still have mortgages, however, as do an even smaller 7 percent of those aged 75 or older.

♦ If boomers refinance their homes to pay for their children's college education, as many claim they will do, then the proportion of older householders with mortgage debt will climb.

Declining debt

(percent of householders aged 55 or older with debt, 1995)

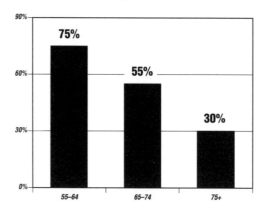

Debt of Householders Aged 55 or Older, 1995

(percent of total households and householders aged 55 or older with debt and median value of debt for those with debt, by type of debt, 1995)

	total	55 to 64	65 to 74	75 or older
Percent with debt				
Any debt	**75.2%**	**75.2%**	**54.5%**	**30.1%**
Mortgage and home equity	41.1	45.8	24.8	7.1
Installment	46.5	36.0	16.7	9.6
Other lines of credit	1.9	1.4	1.3	0.0
Credit card	47.8	43.4	31.3	18.3
Investment real estate	6.3	12.5	5.0	1.5
Other debt	9.0	7.5	5.5	3.6
Median value of debt for debtor households				
Any debt	**$22,500**	**$25,800**	**$7,700**	**$2,000**
Mortgage and home equity	51,000	36,000	19,000	15,900
Installment	6,100	5,900	4,900	3,900
Other lines of credit	3,500	3,500	3,800	–
Credit card	1,500	1,300	800	400
Investment real estate	28,000	26,000	36,000	8,000
Other debt	2,000	4,000	2,000	3,000

Note: (–) means sample is too small to make a reliable estimate.
Source: Federal Reserve Board, Family Finances in the U.S.: Recent Evidence from the Survey of Consumer Finances, *Federal Reserve Bulletin, January 1997*

Homeownership Peaks in 65-to-74 Age Group

More than 82 percent of householders aged 65 to 74 own a home.

The homeownership rate has reached a record high in the U.S. In 1998, 66.2 percent of households owned their home. Behind this record is the lofty homeownership rate of older Americans.

People aged 55 or older are more likely to own a home than younger people. In 1998, 79.5 percent of householders aged 55 or older owned their home. The rate of homeownership among older Americans stands at 78.7 percent among householders aged 55 to 59, rises to a peak of 82.3 percent among those aged 65 to 74, then falls to 66.1 percent among the oldest householders, aged 85 or older. Behind the lower ownership rate of the oldest householders is the fact that many of them are elderly widows who can no longer maintain a home by themselves. Some move into nursing homes or residential care communities while others move into apartments closer to their children.

◆ As the affluence of older Americans has grown, so has their rate of homeownership. Today, home equity accounts for most of the wealth of older Americans.

Most older Americans own homes

(percent of householders aged 55 or older who own their home, 1998)

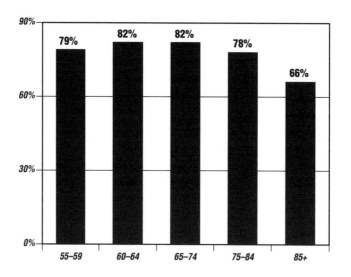

Homeownership of Householders Aged 55 or Older, 1998

(number and percent of total householders and householders aged 55 or older who own their home, 1998; numbers in thousands)

	number	owners	
	number	number	percent
Total households	**102,528**	**67,873**	**66.2%**
Total aged 55 or older	**34,569**	**27,492**	**79.5**
Aged 65 or older	21,497	16,999	79.1
Aged 75 or older	10,225	7,725	75.6
Aged 85 or older	2,135	1,411	66.1
Aged 55 to 59	6,974	5,490	78.7
Aged 60 to 64	6,098	5,003	82.0
Aged 65 to 74	11,272	9,274	82.3
Aged 75 to 84	8,090	6,314	78.0
Aged 85 or older	2,135	1,411	66.1

Source: Bureau of the Census, detailed tables from Household and Family Characteristics: March 1998, *Current Population Reports, P20-515, 1998; calculations by New Strategist*

For More Information

The federal government is a rich source of accurate and reliable data about almost every aspect of American life. Below are the web site addresses of the federal agencies collecting the data analyzed in this book, as well as the web site addresses of other organizations whose data appear here. Also listed are the phone numbers of organizations mentioned in this book, as well as government subject specialists, arranged alphabetically by topic. A list of State Data Centers and Small Business Development Centers appears here as well. Researchers can contact these centers for help in tracking down demographic and economic information.

Web Site Addresses

Bureau of the Census .... http://www.census.gov
Bureau of Labor Statistics .... http://www.bls.gov
Current Population Survey home page .... http://www.bls.census.gov/cps
Consumer Expenditure Survey home page .... http://www.bls.gov/csxhome.htm
Employee Benefit Research Institute .... http://www.ebri.org
National Center For Education Statistics .... http://nces.ed.gov
National Center For Health Statistics .... http://www.cdc.gov/nchswww
National Endowment for the Arts .... http://arts.endow.gov
National Opinion Research Center .... http://www.norc.uchicago.edu

Telephone Numbers of Subject Specialists and Organizations

Absences from work, Staff 202-606-6378
Aging population, Staff 301-457-2422
Ancestry, Staff 301-457-2403
Apportionment, Ed Byerly 301-457-2381
Census, 1990 tabulations, Staff 301-457-2422
Census, 2000 plans, Arthur Cresce/John Stuart 301-457-3947/3949
Census Bureau Customer Services 301-457-4100
Child care, Martin O'Connell/Lynne Casper 301-457-2416
Children, Staff 301-457-2465
Citizenship, Staff 301-457-2403
College graduate job outlook, Mark Mittelhauser 202-606-5707
Commuting, Phil Salopek/Celia Boertlein 301-457-2454
Consumer Expenditure Survey, Staff 202-606-6900
Contingent workers, Sharon Cohany 202-606-6378
County population, Staff 301-457-2422
Crime, Kathleen Creighton 301-457-3925
Current employment analysis, Philip Rones 202-606-6378
Current Population Survey (general information), Staff 301-457-4100
Demographic surveys (general information), Staff 301-457-3773
Disability, Jack McNeil/Bob Bennefield 301-763-8300/8213
Discouraged workers, Staff 202-606-6378

Displaced workers, Steve Hipple 202-606-6378
Economic Census, 1997
- Accommodations, Fay Dorsett 301-457-2687
- Census promotions, Herb Gerardi 301-457-2989
- Communications industry, Jack Moody 301-457-2689
- Construction, Pat Horning 301-457-4680
- Financial and insurance, Laurie Torene 301-457-2824
- Food services, Fay Dorsett 301-457-2687
- General information, Robert Marske 301-457-2547
- Internet dissemination, Paul Zeisset 301-457-4151
- Manufacturing, durable goods, Kenneth Hansen 301-457-4755
- Manufacturing, nondurable goods, Michael Zampogna 301-457-4810
- Mining, Pat Horning 301-457-4680
- Minority/women-owned businesses, Valerie Strang 301-457-3316
- North American Industry Class. Sys., Bruce Goldhirsch 301-457-2589
- Puerto Rico, outlying areas, territories, Eddie Salyers 301-457-3318
- Real estate and rental/leasing, Steve Roman 301-457-2824
- Retail trade and accomodations, Fay Dorsett 301-457-2687
- Services, Jack Moody 301-457-2689
- Transportation and utilities, establishments, Jim Poyer 301-457-2786
- Vehicle Inventory and Use Survey, Kim Moore 301-457-2797
- Wholesale trade, John Trimble 301-457-2725
Education, training statistics, Alan Eck 202-606-5705
Education surveys, Steve Tourkin 301-457-3791
Educational attainment, Staff 301-457-2464
Emigration/illegal immigrants, Staff 301-457-2403
Employee Benefit Research Institute, Staff 202-659-0670
Employee benefits, Staff 202-606-6222
Employee tenure, Jennifer Martel 202-606-6378
Employment and unemployment , Staff 301-457-3242
Employment and Earnings periodical, Gloria P. Green 202-606-6373 x255
Employment and unemployment trends, Staff 202-606-6378
Employment Situation News Release, Staff 202-606-6378
Equal employment opportunity data, Staff 301-457-3242
Fertility, Amara Bachu 301-457-2449
Flexitime and shift work, Thomas Beers 202-606-6378
Foreign born, Staff 301-457-2403
General Social Survey, National Opinion Research Center 773-753-7500
Group quarters population, Denise Smith 301-457-2378
HealthFocus, Linda C. Gilbert 515-274-1307
Health surveys, Adrienne Quasney 301-457-3879
Hispanic statistics, Staff 301-457-2403
Home-based work, Staff 202-606-6378
Homeless, Annetta Clark Smith 301-457-2378

Census Regional Offices

Atlanta, GA .... 404-730-3833 / 3964

Boston, MA .... 617-424-0510 / 0565

Charlotte, NC .... 704-344-6144 / 6548

Chicago, IL .... 708-562-1740 / 1791

Dallas, TX .... 214-640-4470 / 4434

Denver, CO .... 303-969-7750 / 6769

Detroit, MI .... 313-259-1875 / 5169

Kansas City, KS .... 913-551-6711 / 5839

Los Angeles, CA .... 818-904-6339 / 6249

New York, NY .... 212-264-4730 / 3863

Philadelphia, PA .... 215-656-7578 / 7550

Seattle, WA .... 206-553-5835 / 5859

State Data Centers And Business/Industry Data Centers

Below are listed the State Data Center and Business/Industry Data Center (BIDC) lead agency contacts only. Lead data centers are usually state government agencies, universities, or libraries that head up a network of affiliate centers. Every state has a State Data Center. The asterisks (*) identify states that also have Business/Industry Data Centers. In some states, one agency serves as the lead for both the State Data Centers and the Business/Industry Data Centers. The Business/Industry Data Center is listed separately if there is a separate agency serving as the lead.

Alabama, Annette Watters, University of Alabama 205-348-6191

Alaska, Kathryn Lizik, Department of Labor 907-465-2437

*Arizona, Betty Jeffries, Department of Security 602-542-5984

Arkansas, Sarah Breshears, University of Arkansas at Little Rock 501-569-8530

California, Linda Gage, Department of Finance 916-323-4086

Colorado, Rebecca Picaso, Department of Local Affairs 303-866-2156

Connecticut, Bill Kraynak, Office of Policy & Management 860-418-6230

*Delaware, Mike Mahaffie, Development Office 302-739-4271

District of Columbia, Herb Bixhorn, Mayor's Office of Planning 202-727-6533

*Florida, Pam Schenker, Dept. of Labor & Employment Security 850-488-1048

Georgia, Robert Giacomini, Georgia Institute of Technology 404-894-9416

Guam, Rose Deaver, Department of Commerce .... 011-671-475-0325 / 6

Hawaii, Jan Nakamoto, Dept. of Business, Econ. Dev., & Tourism 808-586-2493

Idaho, Alan Porter, Department of Commerce 208-334-2470

Illinois, Suzanne Ebetsch, Bureau of the Budget 217-782-1381

*Indiana, Sylvia Andrews, State Library 317-232-3733

Indiana BIDC, Carol Rogers, Business Research Center 317-274-2205

Iowa, Beth Henning, State Library 515-281-4350

Kansas, Marc Galbraith, State Library 913-296-3296

*Kentucky, Ron Crouch, University of Louisville 502-852-7990

Louisiana, Karen Paterson, Office of Planning & Budget 504-342-7410

*Maine .... [Currently being reorganized]

*Maryland, Jane Traynham, Office of Planning 410-767-4450

*Massachusetts, John Gaviglio, Mass. Inst. for Social and Econ. Res 413-545-3460

Michigan, Carolyn Lauer, Dept. of Management & Budget 517-373-7910

*Minnesota, David Birkholz, State Demographer's Office 612-296-2557

Minnesota BIDC, David Rademacher, State Dem. Office 612-297-3255

*Mississippi, Rachael McNeely, University of Mississippi 601-232-7288

Mississippi BIDC, Deloise Tate, Dept. of Econ. & Comm. Dev 601-359-3593

*Missouri, Debra Pitts, State Library 573-526-7648

Missouri BIDC, Steve Garrotto, Small Business Dev. Centers 573-882-0344

*Montana, Patricia Roberts, Department of Commerce 406-444-2896

Nebraska, Jerome Deichert, University of Nebraska-Omaha 402-595-2311

Nevada, Linda Nary, State Library & Archives 702-687-8326

New Hampshire, Thomas Duffy, Office of State Planning 603-271-2155

*New Jersey, David Joye, Department of Labor 609-984-2595

*New Mexico, Kevin Kargacin, University of New Mexico 505-277-6626

*New York, Staff, Department of Economic Development 518-474-1141

*North Carolina, Staff, State Library 919-733-6418

North Dakota, Richard Rathge, State University 701-231-8621

Northern Mariana Islands, Juan Borja, Dept. of Commerce 011-670-664-3034

*Ohio, Barry Bennett, Department of Development 614-466-2115

*Oklahoma, Jeff Wallace, Department of Commerce 405-815-5184

Oregon, George Hough, Portland State Univ. .... 503-725-5159 / 1-800-547-8887x5159

*Pennsylvania, Diane Shoop, Penns. State Univ. at Harrisburg 717-948-6336

Puerto Rico, Lillian Torres Aguirre, Planning Bd. .... 787-728-4430 / 723-6200x2502

Rhode Island, Paul Egan, Department of Administration 401-277-6493

South Carolina, Mike MacFarlane, Budget & Control Board 803-734-3780

South Dakota, Theresa Bendert, Univ. of South Dakota 605-677-5287

Tennessee, Don Walli, State Planning Office 615-741-1676

Texas, Steve Murdock, Texas A&M University .... 409-845-5115 / 5332

*Utah, David Abel, Office of Planning & Budget 801-538-1036

Vermont, Sybil McShane, Department of Libraries 802-828-3261

*Virginia, Don Lillywhite, Virginia Employment Commission 804-786-8026

Virgin Islands, Frank Mills, Univ. of the Virgin Islands 340-693-1027

*Washington, Yi Zhao, Office of Financial Management 360-902-0599

*West Virginia, Delphine Coffey, Office of Comm. & Industrial Dev. 304-558-4010

West Virginia BIDC, Randy Childs, Center for Econ. Research 304-293-7832

*Wisconsin, Robert Naylor, Department of Administration 608-266-1927

Wisconsin BIDC, David Mohn, Univ. of Wisconsin-Madison 608-262-3097

Wyoming, Wenlin Liu, Dept. of Administration & Fiscal Control 307-777-7504

Glossary

adjusted for inflation Incomes and changes in income have been adjusted for the rise in the cost of living, or the consumer price index (CPI-U-XI). In this book, any year-to-year changes in income or spending are shown in inflation-adjusted dollars.

Asian In this book, the term "Asian" includes both Asians and Pacific Islanders.

baby boom Americans born between 1946 and 1964.

baby bust Americans born between 1965 and 1976; also known as Generation X.

central city The largest city in a metropolitan area is called the central city. The balance of the metropolitan area outside the central city is regarded as the "suburbs."

consumer unit (on spending tables only) For convenience, the terms consumer unit and household are used interchangeably in the spending section of this book, although consumer units are somewhat different from the Census Bureau's households. A consumer unit comprises all related members of a household or a financially independent member of a household. A household may consist of more than one consumer unit.

dual-earner couple A married couple in which both the householder and the householder's spouse are in the labor force.

earnings One type of income. *See also* Income.

employed All civilians who did any work as paid employees or farmers/self-employed workers, or who worked 15 hours or more as unpaid farm workers or in a family-owned business, during the reference period. All those who have jobs but are temporarily absent from their jobs due to illness, bad weather, vacation, labor management dispute, or personal reasons are considered employed.

expenditure The transaction cost including excise and sales taxes of goods and services acquired during the survey period. The full cost of each purchase is recorded even though full payment may not have been made at the date of purchase. Average expenditure figures may be artificially low for infrequently purchased items such as cars because figures are calculated using all consumer units within a demographic segment rather than just purchasers. Expenditure estimates include money spent on gifts for others.

family A group of two or more people (one of whom is the householder) related by birth, marriage, or adoption and living in the same household.

family household A household maintained by a householder who lives with one or more people related to him or her by blood, marriage, or adoption.

female/male householder A woman/man who maintains a household without a spouse present. May head family or nonfamily household.

full-time employment Full-time employment is 35 or more hours of work per week during a majority of the weeks worked.

full-time, year-round Indicates 50 or more weeks of full-time employment during the previous calendar year.

geographic regions The four major regions and nine census divisions of the United States are the state groupings as shown below:

Northeast:
—New England: Connecticut, Maine, Massachusetts, New Hampshire, Rhode Island, and Vermont
—Middle Atlantic: New Jersey, New York, and Pennsylvania

Midwest:
—East North Central: Illinois, Indiana, Michigan, Ohio, and Wisconsin
—West North Central: Iowa, Kansas, Minnesota, Missouri, Nebraska, North Dakota, and South Dakota

South:
—South Atlantic: Delaware, District of Columbia, Florida, Georgia, Maryland, North Carolina, South Carolina, Virginia, and West Virginia
—East South Central: Alabama, Kentucky, Mississippi, and Tennessee
—West South Central: Arkansas, Louisiana, Oklahoma, and Texas

West:
—Mountain: Arizona, Colorado, Idaho, Montana, Nevada, New Mexico, Utah, and Wyoming
—Pacific: Alaska, California, Hawaii, Oregon, and Washington

Generation X Americans born between 1965 and 1976; also known as the baby-bust generation.

Hispanic Persons who identify their origin as Mexican, Puerto Rican, Central or South American, or some other Hispanic origin. Persons of Hispanic origin may be of any race. In other words, there are black Hispanics, white Hispanics, Asian Hispanics, and Native American Hispanics.

household All the persons who occupy a housing unit. A household includes the related family members and all the unrelated persons, if any, such as lodgers, foster children, wards, or employees who share the housing unit. A person living alone is counted as a household. A group of unrelated people who share a housing unit as roommates or unmarried partners is also counted as a household. Households do not include group quarters such as college dormitories, prisons, or nursing homes.

household, race/ethnicity of Households are categorized according to the race or ethnicity of the householder only.

householder The householder is the person (or one of the persons) in whose name the housing unit is owned or rented or, if there is no such person, any adult member. With married couples, the householder may be either the husband or the wife. The householder is the reference person for the household.

householder, age of The age of the householder is used to categorize households into age groups. Married couples, for example, are classified according to the age of either the husband or the wife, depending on which one identified him- or herself as the householder.

income Money received in the preceding calendar year by a person aged 15 or older from any of the following sources: (1) earnings from longest job (or self-employment); (2) earnings from jobs other than longest job; (3) unemployment compensation; (4) workers' compensation; (5) Social Security; (6) Supplemental Security income; (7) public assistance; (8) veterans' payments; (9) survivor benefits; (10) disability benefits; (11) retirement pensions; (12) interest; (13) dividends; (14) rents and royalties or estates and trusts; (15) educational assistance; (16) alimony; (17) child support; (18) financial assistance from outside the household, and other periodic income. Income is reported in several ways in this book. Household income is the combined income of all household members. Income of a person is all income accruing to the person from all sources. Earnings is the amount of money a person receives from his or her job.

job tenure The length of time a person has been employed continuously by the same employer.

labor force The labor force tables in this book are for the civilian labor force, which includes both the employed and the unemployed—people who are looking for work.

labor force participation rate The percentage of the civilian noninstitutional population that is in the civilian labor force, which includes both the employed and the unemployed.

married couples with/without children under age 18 Refers to married couples with/without own children under age 18 living in the same household. Couples without children under age 18 may be parents of grown children who live elsewhere, or they could be childless couples.

median The median is the value that divides the population or households into two equal portions: one below and one above the median. Medians can be calculated for income, age, and many other characteristics.

median income The amount that divides the income distribution into two equal groups, one-half having incomes above the median, one-half having incomes below the median. The median for households or families is based on all households or families. The median for persons is based on all persons aged 15 or older with income.

metropolitan area An area qualifies for recognition as a metropolitan area if it includes a city of at least 50,000 population, or it includes a Census Bureau–defined urbanized area of at least 50,000 with a total

metropolitan population of at least 100,000 (75,000 in New England). In addition to the county containing the main city or urbanized area, a metropolitan area may include other counties having strong commuting ties to the central county.

Millennial generation Americans born between 1997 and 1994.

nonfamily household A household maintained by a householder who lives alone or with people to whom he or she is not related.

nonfamily householder A householder who lives alone or with nonrelatives.

non-Hispanic People who did not identify themselves as Hispanic on the Current Population Survey or the 1990 Census are classified as non-Hispanic. Non-Hispanics may be of any race.

nonmetropolitan area Counties that are not classified as metropolitan areas.

occupation Occupational classification is based on the kind of work a person did at his or her job during the previous calendar year. If a person changed jobs during the year, the data refer to the occupation of the job held the longest during that year.

outside central city The portion of a metropolitan county or counties that falls outside of the central city or cities; generally regarded as the suburbs.

own children Own children in a family are sons and daughters, including stepchildren and adopted children, of the householder. The totals include never-married children living away from home in college dormitories.

owner occupied A housing unit is owner occupied if the owner lives in the unit, even if it is mortgaged or not fully paid for. A cooperative or condominium unit is owner occupied only if the owner lives in it. All other occupied units are classified as renter occupied.

part-time employment Part-time employment is less than 35 hours of work per week in a majority of the weeks worked during the year.

percent change The change (either positive or negative) in a measure expressed as a proportion of the starting measure. When median income changes from $20,000 to $25,000, for example, this is a 25 percent increase.

percentage point change The change (either positive or negative) in a value which is already expressed as a percentage. When the labor force participation rate changes from 70 percent to 75 percent, for example, this is a 5 percentage point increase.

poverty level The official income threshold below which families and persons are classified as living in poverty. The threshold rises each year with inflation and varies depending on family size and age of householder. In 1997, the poverty threshold for a family of four was $16,400.

proportion or share The value of a part expressed as a percentage of the whole. If there are 4 million people aged 25 and 3 million of them are white, then the white proportion is 75 percent.

race Race is self-reported and appears in four categories in this book: white, black, Native American, and Asian. A household is assigned the race of the householder.

rounding Percentages are rounded to the nearest one-tenth of a percent; therefore, the percentages in a distribution do not always add to exactly 100.0 percent, although totals are always shown as 100.0. Moreover, individual figures are rounded

to the nearest 1,000 without being adjusted to group totals, which are independently rounded; percentages are based on the unrounded numbers.

self-employment A person is categorized as self-employed if he or she was self-employed in the job held longest during the reference period. People who report self-employment from a second job are excluded, but those who report wage-and-salary income from a second job are included. Unpaid workers in family businesses are excluded. Self-employment statistics include only nonagricultural workers and exclude people who work for themselves in incorporated businesses.

sex ratio The number of men per 100 women.

suburbs *See* Outside central city.

unemployed Unemployed people are those who, during the survey period, had no employment but were available and looking for work. Those who were laid off from their jobs and were waiting to be recalled are also classified as unemployed.

Bibliography

Bureau of the Census

Internet web site, http://www.census.gov

——1998 Current Population Survey, unpublished data

——*Educational Attainment in the United States: March 1998*, detailed tables from Current Population Reports, P20-513, 1998

——*Fertility of American Men*, Population Division Working Paper No. 14, 1996

——*Geographic Mobility: March 1996 to March 1997*, Current Population Reports, P20-510, 1998

——*Household and Family Characteristics: March 1998*, detailed tables from Current Population Reports, P20-515, 1998

——*Marital Status and Living Arrangements: March 1998*, Current Population Reports, P20-514, 1998

——*Money Income in the United States: 1997*, Current Population Reports, P60-200, 1998

——*Population Projections of the United States by Age, Sex, Race, and Hispanic Origin: 1995 to 2050*, Current Population Reports, P25-1130, 1996

——*Poverty in the United States: 1997*, Current Population Reports, P60-201, 1998

——*Projections of the Total Population of States: 1995 to 2025*; PPL-47, 1996

——*School Enrollment—Social and Economic Characteristics of Students: October 1996*, Current Population Reports, P20-500, 1998

——*Statistical Abstract of the United States: 1998* (118th edition) Washington, DC 1998

——*U.S. Population Estimates, by Age, Sex, Race, and Hispanic Origin: 1980 to 1991*, Current Population Reports, P25-1095, 1993

——*Voting and Registration in the Election of November 1996*, Current Population Reports, P20-504, 1998

Bureau of Labor Statistics

Internet web site, http://www.bls.gov

——1997 Consumer Expenditure Survey, unpublished data

——*Contingent and Alternative Employment Arrangements*, February 1997

——*Employment and Earnings*, January 1991

——*Employment and Earnings*, January 1999

——*Handbook of Labor Statistics*, Bulletin 2340, 1989

——*Monthly Labor Review*, November 1997

——*Work at Home in 1997*, USDL 98-93

Federal Reserve Board

——*Family Finances in the U.S.: Recent Evidence from the Survey of Consumer Finances*, Federal Reserve Bulletin, January 1997

HealthFocus

> P. O. Box 7174, Des Moines, IA 50309-7174, 515-274-1307
>
> ——*1997 HealthFocus Trend Report*

National Alliance for Caregiving and The American Association of Retired Persons

> ——*Family Caregiving in the U.S.—Findings from a National Survey*, Final Report, 1997

National Center for Health Statistics

> Internet web site, http://www.cdc.gov/nchswww
>
> ——*An Overview of Home Health and Hospice Care Patients: 1996 National Home and Hospice Care Survey*, Advance Data, No. 297, 1998
>
> ——*Births and Deaths: Preliminary Data for 1997*, National Vital Statistics Report, Vol. 47, No. 4, 1998
>
> ——*Births and Deaths: United States, 1996*, Monthly Vital Statistics Report, Vol. 46, No. 1 (S)2, 1997
>
> ——*Characteristics of Elderly Nursing Home Residents: Data from the 1995 National Nursing Home Survey*, Advance Data, No. 289, 1997
>
> ——*Current Estimates from the National Health Interview Survey, 1995*, Series 10, No. 199, 1998
>
> ——*Deaths: Final Data for 1996*, National Vital Statistics Report, Vol. 47, No. 9, 1998
>
> ——*Health, United States, 1996-97*
>
> ——*Health, United States, 1998*
>
> ——*National Ambulatory Medical Care Survey: 1996 Summary*, Advance Data, No. 295, 1997

National Endowment for the Arts

> Internet web site, http://arts.endow.gov
>
> ——*1997 Survey of Public Participation in the Arts, Summary Report*, 1998

National Opinion Research Center

> Internet web site, http://www.norc.uchicago.edu
>
> ——1976 General Social Survey, unpublished data
>
> ——1994 General Social Survey, unpublished data
>
> ——1996 General Social Survey, unpublished data

U.S. Department of Agriculture

> Internet web site http://www.barc.usda.gov
>
> ——1994–95 National Survey on Recreation and the Environment, Forest Service
>
> ——ARS Food Surveys Research Group, *1994 and 1995 Continuing Survey of Food Intakes by Individuals*
>
> ——ARS Food Surveys Research Group, *1994 and 1995 Diet and Health Knowledge Survey*

Index

marital status, 230, 234;
poverty rate, 180–81
White Americans:
   by Hispanic origin, 240–44, 271–88;
   employment status, 188–90;
   household types, 214, 217;
   households with children, 220, 224;
   income, 129, 134–35;
   labor force, 188–90;
   life expectancy by age and sex, 121–22;
   marital status by sex, 230, 234;
   population, 240–44, 271–88;
   poverty rate, 180–82
White, non-Hispanic Americans:
   income, 123, 147, 156–57, 167–68;
   population, 240–42;
women:
   alternative work arrangements, by type, 205–06;
   children ever born, 77–78;
   earnings by educational attainment, 169, 174–77;
   eating away from home, 73–74;
   educational attainment, 51–53, 56–58, 60;
   employment status, 186–88, 190;
   food consumption, 71–72;
   frequency of exercise by, 79–80;
   full-time workers, 199–200;
   home health care recipients, 105–06;
   income, 123, 144, 146, 158–68;
   job tenure of, 201–02;
   labor force participation, 183–88, 190–92, 199–210;
   life expectancy, by race and age, 120–22;
   living alone, 211–17, 225, 227, 229;
   living alone, by income, 136–43;
   living arrangements, 225, 227;
   marital status, 230–34;
   nursing home residents, 105, 107;
   part-time workers, 183, 199–200;
   population, 236–37, 252–61, 245–48;
   poverty rate, by race and Hispanic origin, 180–81;
   projections of labor force participation, 209–10;

school enrollment, 61–64;
self-employed, 203–04;
smoking behavior, by age, 67, 84, 86
work arrangements, alternative, 205–06
workers:
   at home, 207–08;
   by occupation, 193–98;
   contract, 205–06;
   full-time, by sex, 199–200;
   on call, 205–06;
   part-time, by sex, 183, 199–200;
   temporary, 205–06;